# From Logic to Logic Programming

## Foundations of Computing

Michael Garey and Albert Meyer, editors

# From Logic to Logic Programming

Kees Doets

The MIT Press
Cambridge, Massachusetts
London, England

This book was set in Computer Modern by the author and was printed and bound in the United States of America.

Library of Congress Cataloging-in-Publication Data

Doets, Kees.
From logic to logic programming / Kees Doets.
    p.    cm. — (Foundations of computing)
   Includes bibliographical references and index.
   ISBN 0-262-04142-1
   1. Logic programming.  I. Title.  II. Series.
QA76.63.D64   1994
005.1—dc20

93-6196
CIP

# Contents

# Series Foreword

Theoretical computer science has now undergone several decades of development. The "classical" topics of automata theory, formal languages, and computational complexity have become firmly established, and their importance to other theoretical work and to practice is widely recognized. Stimulated by technological advances, theoreticians have been rapidly expanding the areas under study, and the time delay between theoretical progress and its practical impact has been decreasing dramatically. Much publicity has been given recently to breakthroughs in cryptography and linear programming, and steady progress is being made on programming language semantics, computational geometry, and efficient data structures. Newer, more speculative, areas of study include relational databases, VLSI theory, and parallel and distributed computation. As this list of topics continues expanding, it is becoming more and more difficult to stay abreast of the progress that is being made and increasingly important that the most significant work be distilled and communicated in a manner that will facilitate further research and application of this work. By publishing comprehensive books and specialized monographs on the theoretical aspects of computer science, the series on Foundations of Computing provides a forum in which important research topics can be presented in their entirety and placed in perspective for researchers, students, and practitioners alike.

Michael R. Garey
Albert R. Meyer

# Preface

Resolution is a single-rule refutability technique for logical formulas that, at least in principle, is suitable for use on the computer. This book discusses resolution in the versions for three logical formalisms: propositional logic, first-order logic, and the so-called Horn-fragment of first-order logic, in the context of which it is called (definite) *logic programming*. Resolution in propositional logic forms the basis for the first-order version. Though the version for the Horn-fragment appears to be just a special case of the one for full first-order logic, it nevertheless is the most important of the three since it can be given a computational component also. As a recent logic programming symposium announcement puts it, *initial interest in logic programming derived from the discoveries that a simple fragment of logic, Horn clauses, could be given a computational interpretation and that a programming language, Prolog, could be designed from that simple fragment.* In fact, since resolution forms the main logical ingredient of Prolog, logic programming can be looked at as providing a theoretical basis for this programming language.

Chapter 1 of this book contains preliminaries on mathematical induction, trees, multisets and ordinals. Propositional resolution — also called the *cut* rule, which permits one to derive $\Delta \vee \Gamma$ from $\Delta \vee A$ and $\Gamma \vee \neg A$ — is dealt with in Chapter 2, which also contains all necessary preliminary details on propositional calculus. Chapter 3 is about general first-order logic. After a speedy, but essentially complete, introduction to the syntax and semantics of this formalism, resolution is defined as that particular case of *unrestricted* resolution producing most general resolvents, unrestricted resolution being the extension of the propositional resolution rule that allows preliminary instantiation of the premisses. This approach yields completeness rather smoothly. Chapter 4 introduces (positive) programs, their least Herbrand models, and program-definability. Chapter 5 follows an approach to logic programming similar to the one of Chapter 3: resolution again is defined as that particular case of *unrestricted* resolution that, in a precise sense, produces most general results. Compared with the traditional, ad-hoc way of defining resolvents, the slightly more abstract approach advocated here has several advantages. For instance, invariance with respect to renamings is immediate. Our approach also makes evident that maximal generality of *derivations* (resolution iterated) has two sources: the particular way in which resolvents are defined, and the non-confusion of variables. This clarifies an important issue on which the existing literature (with a multitude of competing approaches on "standardization-apart") does not seem to have a clear-cut answer. The resulting form of the Lifting Theorem generalizes known results. Chapter 6 generalizes resolution over the Herbrand algebra to resolution over non-standard algebras and contains general information on infinite derivations. Chapter 7 contains a crash course on recursive function theory, shows that all recursive functions are program-computable, and ends with a self-contained presentation of results of Blair and Kunen, showing that greatest fixed points may be very complex. Finally, Chapter 8 contains what is probably the first completely adequate description of the notion of SLDNF-tree, discusses Fitting's 3-valued interpretation, and presents Stärk's completeness theorem.

A reader with some logical background who is primarily interested in logic programming can skip Chapters 2 and 3 (with the exception of the discussion of unification in Section 3.8). The core of logic programming theory is in Chapters 4 and 5. Except for minor things (e.g., Chapter 8 uses the material on lifting ground steps from Chapter 6), Chapters 6, 7 and 8 can be read independently from one another.

The material of this book lends itself easily to exercises with algorithmic solutions. Though we certainly do not want to underestimate the value of exercises of this type (to carry out at least *some* of them will be necessary to get a feeling of what is going on), it is not the purpose of this book to teach people to behave like computers. Thus, if readers wish to find conjunctive, prenex, clausal, and Skolem forms, unify sequences of terms and refute formulas or compute functions using (SLD) (SLDNF) resolution, they can easily think of the necessary exercises themselves, or find them in one of the references listed at the end.

With [Apt 90] as a starting point, the actual writing of this book began in the summer of 1991 as a joint enterprise of Krzysztof Apt and myself, beginning with Krzysztof teaching me the basics of Unix, Emacs and LaTeX. One year later, I more or less finished my part of the undertaking, leaving to my co-author matters dealing with applications and Prolog, mainly centering around termination and occur check. Due to circumstances partly unforeseen, Krzysztof unfortunately had to leave the project, and I decided to publish the material in its present form. However, the contents still bear the marks of our (quite fruitful) cooperation, and the debts I owe to my former co-author cannot be overestimated. In particular, the definition of SLDNF tree in Chapter 8 is a result of joint efforts.

Finally, many thanks are due to my colleague Maarten de Rijke for his patience and ingenuity in solving a number of problems relating to the incorporation of sty files supplied by the publisher, and to the people of MIT Press, in particular to Beth LaFortune Gies and Bob Prior, for a fine cooperation.

# From Logic to Logic Programming

# 1 Preliminaries

The notations from set theory and logic that we use are standard. Explanations can be found at the beginning of the list of notations at the end of this book.

## 1.1 Mathematical Induction

The set $\{0, 1, 2, \ldots\}$ of *natural numbers* 0, 1, 2,... is designated by $\mathbb{N}$. Note that 0 is considered to be a natural number (the first one).

**Principle 1.1 (Induction)** *If $E$ is a property of natural numbers such that*
*(i) $E(0)$ — i.e., $E$ holds of 0 — and*
*(ii) for every natural number $n$: if $E(n)$, then $E(n+1)$*
*then $E$ holds of every natural number.* ∎

Though this principle sounds pretty much obvious, it is nevertheless the main tool for proving universal statements of the form $\forall n \in \mathbb{N} : E(n)$. A *proof by induction* of such a statement thus consists of proving two things:

(i) $E(0)$.

This is called the *basis* of the induction.

(ii) $\forall n \in \mathbb{N}\, [E(n) \Rightarrow E(n+1)]$.

This is called the *induction step*.

To carry out the induction step, you clearly must *assume* that an unspecified natural number $n$ satisfies $E$ — this assumption is called the *induction hypothesis* — and you have to show, presumably making use of this assumption, that $n+1$ satisfies $E$, as well. The nice thing about a proof with induction is that the induction hypothesis comes free. For a first example of a proof by induction, see Theorem 1.2.

Induction sometimes is formulated and used with *sets* of numbers instead of properties:

If $X$ is a set of natural numbers such that

(i) $0 \in X$, and

(ii) for all $n \in \mathbb{N}$, if $n \in X$, then $n+1 \in X$;

then $X = \mathbb{N}$.

This form is equivalent with the previous one, as with any property $E$ of natural numbers is associated the set $X := \{n \in \mathbb{N} \mid E(n)\}$ of numbers satisfying $E$, and, conversely, a subset $X \subset \mathbb{N}$ of $\mathbb{N}$ determines the property $E(n) :\equiv n \in X$ of being an element of $X$.[1]

A variant of induction is the following principle of *strong induction*. Again, we give the version with properties.

---

[1] We use := and :≡ for: *is by definition equal to*, resp.: *is by definition equivalent with*.

**Theorem 1.2 (Strong Induction)** *If $E$ is a property of natural numbers such that*

$$\forall n \left[ (\forall m < n : E(m)) \Rightarrow E(n) \right],$$

*then every natural number satisfies $E$.*

Note that, for $n = 0$, the condition $\forall m < n : E(m)$ is trivially satisfied (there are no natural numbers $< 0$), and therefore the implication $(\forall m < 0 : E(m)) \Rightarrow E(0)$ amounts to $E(0)$. This explains the "disappearance" of the basis of the induction compared with 1.1.

Strong induction is called *strong* because the induction hypothesis that the induction step is allowed to use here is stronger than the one of 1.1: in order to show that $E(n)$, you may suppose that *for all* $m < n$, $E(m)$ instead of only for $m = n - 1$. Nevertheless, strong induction is *provable* from simple induction, via a trick.

**Proof.** Define a second property $E'$ by

$$E'(n) :\equiv \forall m < n : E(m).$$

The hypothesis of the theorem exactly says that $E'(n) \Rightarrow E(n)$. Therefore, to prove the conclusion of the theorem, it suffices to show that

$$\forall n \in \mathbb{N} \, E'(n).$$

This we do, using ordinary induction "with respect to $n$".
*Basis.*
     That $E'(0)$ holds is evident, as 0 is the least natural number; and so the statement $\forall m < 0 \, E(m)$ holds vacuously.
*Induction step.*
     *Induction hypothesis:* Assume that $E'(n)$, where $n$ is an arbitrary number.
     We have to show that $E'(n + 1)$ holds. This amounts to: $\forall m < n + 1 : E(m)$. Now since we have the equivalence $m < n + 1 \Leftrightarrow m < n \vee m = n$, this again amounts to: $[\forall m < n : E(m)] \wedge E(n)$. However, the first conjunct simply coincides with the induction hypothesis, and it implies the second conjunct by assumption. ∎

In the future, numbers usually occur in a concealed way only. For instance, we shall often deal with formal expressions. Expressions are finite sequences of symbols; hence, their *length* is a natural number. It follows that statements of the form 'for every expression $A$, we have that ... $A$...' are open to proof by induction with respect to the length of the expressions involved. Still other forms of induction shall be dealt with when the need arises.

**Exercises**

**1.1** (*Least number principle*) Prove that every non-empty set of natural numbers has a *least* element. Thus, descending infinite sequences $n_0 > n_1 > n_2 > \cdots$ of natural numbers do not exist.

*Hint.* Assume that $\emptyset \neq X \subset \mathbb{N}$. Apply strong induction to the property $E(n) :\equiv n \in \mathbb{N} - X$.

**1.2** Show: if the property $E$ of natural numbers and $p \in \mathbb{N}$ are such that (i) $E(p)$; (ii) $\forall n \in \mathbb{N} [E(n) \Rightarrow E(n+1)]$, then $\forall n \geq p \, E(n)$.

**1.3** Assume that $E(0)$, $E(1)$ and $E(n) \Rightarrow E(n+2)$. Show that $\forall n \in \mathbb{N} \, E(n)$.

**1.4** Assume that the function $f : \mathbb{N} \rightarrow \mathbb{N}$ is such that $\forall n \in \mathbb{N} \, (f(n+1) \leq f(n))$. 1. Show that for some $m \in \mathbb{N}$: $f(m+1) = f(m)$. 2. Show that for some $m \in \mathbb{N}$: $\forall n \, f(m+n) = f(m)$.

**1.5** Assume that $f : \mathbb{N} \rightarrow \mathbb{N}$ is such that $\forall n, m \in \mathbb{N} \, (n < m \Rightarrow f(n) < f(m))$. Show: $\forall n \in \mathbb{N} \, (n \leq f(n))$.

## 1.2 Trees

The remaining sections of this chapter may be omitted until needed. They discuss trees and König's Lemma (the present section), multisets, multiset ordering and well-foundedness (Section 1.3) and ordinals (Section 1.4).

Let $X$ and $Y$ be sets. The set of all ordered pairs $(x, y)$ with $x \in X$ and $y \in Y$ is denoted by $X \times Y$. For $X = Y$, $X^2 := X \times X$. A (binary) *relation* on a set $X$ is a mapping $R$ that assigns to every pair of elements $(x, y) \in X^2$ a statement $xRy$ that is either *true* or *false*. For instance, the familiar ordering $<$ of the set of natural numbers $\mathbb{N}$ assigns to the ordered pair $(2, 5)$ the true statement that $3 < 5$, whereas it assigns to $(3, 3)$ the false one that $3 < 3$. The standard set-theoretic viewpoint identifies a relation $R$ on $X$ with the subset $\{(x, y) \mid xRy\}$ of $X^2$ of pairs $(x, y)$ for which $xRy$ is true, and this is what we usually shall do. Thus, $<$ is identified with the set $\{(n, m) \mid n < m\}$, which contains $(2, 5)$ but does not contain $(3, 3)$.

In this chapter, all relations are *binary*. However, the notion of $n$-ary relation ($n \in \mathbb{N}$, $n \neq 2$), which occurs from Chapter 3 onwards, is obtained entirely similarly, this time assigning statements to $n$-tuples from $X^n$ of elements from the relevant domain $X$. An 1-ary relation also is called *unary*. A unary relation is identified with the set of things satisfying it.

**Definition 1.3** A *directed graph* is a structure $(T, R)$ where $T$ is a non-empty set and $R$ is a binary relation on $T$. Let $(T, R)$ be a directed graph. A (backward $R$-) *path* from

$s \in T$ to $t \in T$ is a finite sequence $s_0 = s, \ldots, s_n = t$ $(n \geq 1)$ such that for all $i < n$, $s_{i+1} R s_i$.

A structure $\mathcal{T} = (T, R, u)$, where $(T, R)$ is a directed graph and $u \in T$, is a *tree* if for all $s \in T$ there is a unique path from $u$ to $s$.

The elements of $T$ are called the *nodes* of $\mathcal{T}$, and $u$ is the *root* of $\mathcal{T}$. The pairs $(s, t) \in R$ are called *edges* of $\mathcal{T}$.

If $sRt$, then $s$ is called a *child* of $t$ and $t$ the *parent* of $s$. A childless node is a *leaf*. If there is a path from $t$ to $s$, then $s$ is a *descendant* of $t$.

$\mathcal{T}$ is *finitely branching* if every node has at most finitely many children.

The notion of path is extended to infinite sequences as follows. An infinite sequence $t_0, t_1, t_2, \ldots$ will be called a path if every finite initial sequence $t_0, \ldots, t_n$ is a path in the aforementioned sense. A *branch* through $\mathcal{T}$ is a maximal path; that is, a path that starts from the root and either ends in a leaf or is infinite.                                      ∎

Note our convention that paths and branches run backwards in the relation $R$: our trees "grow against" the direction given by $R$.

If we picture a tree with its relation $R$ directed downwards, it looks more or less like a tree found in nature, growing upward from the root towards its leaves (if any). This is the picture of the proof trees in Chapters 2 and 3.

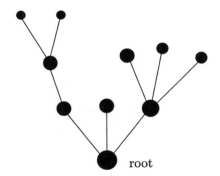

However, the resolution trees occurring from Chapter 5 onwards usually will be pictured growing downward.

**Remark 1.4**

(i) If $\mathcal{T} = (T, R, u)$ is a tree, then from the unicity condition in the definition it follows that $R$ has no *loops*. That is, there is no path from a node to that same node. In practice, however, we frequently employ trees that do appear to have loops. To get a tree properly satisfying the defining condition, we may imagine that one node has several different *occurrences* in the tree. For instance, the one-element "tree" $(\{u\}, \{(u, u)\}, u)$ must be thought of as infinite, its root $u$ having infinitely many occurrences forming an infinite branch $u_0, u_1, u_2, \ldots$.

(ii) Note that a tree $\mathcal{T}$ is completely described by specifying

- its root,
- for every node, what its children are. ∎

The following is the one simple but useful result on finitely branching trees.

**Lemma 1.5 (König)** *Every infinite, finitely branching tree has an infinite branch.*

**Proof.** Let $\mathcal{T} = (T, R, u)$ be an infinite, finitely branching tree. We use the *pigeon-hole principle*: if an infinite set is partitioned in finitely many pieces, then (since a finite union of finite sets must be finite) at least one of the pieces must be infinite.

Construct the required branch $u_0 = u, u_1, u_2, \ldots$ through $\mathcal{T}$ such that for every $i$, $u_i$ has infinitely many descendants.

To begin with, $u_0 = u$ has infinitely many descendants, since $T$ is infinite. Suppose the path $u_0 = u, \ldots, u_n$ is found such that $u_n$ has infinitely many descendants. Every descendant of $u_n$ either is a child of $u_n$ or a descendant of one of the finitely many children of $u_n$. By the pigeon-hole principle, $u_n$ has a child $u_{n+1}$ with infinitely many descendants. This completes the construction of our branch. ∎

## 1.3  Multisets

In (the presentation of) a set, order and multiplicity do not count. In a multiset, order still does not count, but multiplicity does. To motivate the formal definition, consider the case of the *characteristic function* of a subset $A \subset X$ of a given set $X$. This is the function $\chi_A : X \rightarrow \{0, 1\}$ defined by

$$\chi_A(x) = \begin{cases} 1 & \text{if } x \in A \\ 0 & \text{if } x \notin A. \end{cases}$$

Note that $A$ can be recovered from its characteristic function, since we have that $A = \{x \in X \mid \chi_A(x) = 1\}$. Now, a characteristic function is just a special type of multiset.

**Definition 1.6** Let $X$ be a set. A *multiset* over $X$ is a function $f : X \rightarrow \mathbb{N}$.
The elements of $D(f) := \{x \in X \mid f(x) \neq 0\}$ are called *elements* of $f$.
For $x \in D(f)$, the number $f(x)$ is called the *multiplicity* of $x$ in $f$.
$f$ is called *finite* if $D(f)$ is finite. In that case, $|f| := \sum_{x \in D(f)} f(x)$ is called the *number of elements* of $f$. ∎

**Notation 1.7** If $f$ is a finite multiset over $X$, $D(f) = \{x_1, \ldots, x_n\}$, and $e : \{1, \ldots, |f|\} \rightarrow D(f)$ is such that, for $1 \leq i \leq n$, $\{j \in Dom(e) \mid e(j) = x_i\}$ has exactly $f(x_i)$ elements, then $f$ may be written as $\{\{e(1), \ldots, e(|f|)\}\}$.

In this notation, when $e(j) = x_i$, $e(j)$ is called an *occurrence* of $x_i$.                              ∎

**Example.** If $D(f) = \{0, 1, 2\}$, $f(0) = 2$, $f(1) = 1$ and $f(2) = 3$, then $|f| = 6$ and $f$ can be written as, e.g., $\{\{0, 0, 1, 2, 2, 2\}\}$, $\{\{2, 0, 1, 0, 2, 2\}\}$ and $\{\{1, 2, 0, 2, 0, 2\}\}$. This notation of multisets allows for the use of the set-theoretic operations of union, intersection and subtraction. E.g., $\{\{3, 3, 4, 4, 7, 9\}\} = (\{\{3, 7, 7, 9\}\} - \{\{7\}\}) \cup \{\{3, 4, 4\}\}$.                              ∎

A relation $R$ on $X$ is *transitive* if for all $x, y, z \in X$, if both $xRy$ and $yRz$, then $xRz$. For instance, the ordering $<$ on $\mathbb{N}$ is transitive.

The following lemma says that every relation — conceived of as a set of pairs — is contained in a transitive one, and among those, there is a least one.

**Lemma 1.8** *Let $R$ be a binary relation on the set $X$. There is a least transitive relation $S$ on $X$ such that $R \subset S$.*

**Proof.** Define $S$ by: $xSy$ iff there is a backward $R$-path from $y$ to $x$.                              ∎

**Definition 1.9** The least transitive relation containing $R$ is called the *transitive closure* of $R$; we denote it by $R^{tr}$.                              ∎

**Examples.** If $R$ is the successor relation on $\mathbb{N}$ defined by: $nRm :\equiv n + 1 = m$, then $R^{tr}$ is the familiar ordering $<$ of $\mathbb{N}$. If $R$ is the child-parent relation in some tree, then $R^{tr}$ is the descendant relation. If $R$ is the relation of parenthood between humans, then $R^{tr}$ is the one of ancestorship.                              ∎

The next definition introduces the multiset ordering.

A *(partial) ordering* of $X$ is a relation $<$ on $X$ that is *irreflexive* (for no $x \in X$, $x < x$) and transitive. For instance, since trees do not have loops, the descendant relation on a tree is a partial ordering.

A partial ordering $<$ of $X$ is *linear* if for every two different $x, y \in X$ either $x < y$ or $y < x$. For instance, the ordering $<$ of $\mathbb{N}$ is linear, but the descendant relation of a tree usually is not.

To avoid unnecessary abstractness, the reader may as well digest what follows with $X = \mathbb{N}$ and $<$ the usual ordering of $\mathbb{N}$ in mind.

**Definition 1.10** Let $<$ be a partial ordering of the set $X$. The *multiset ordering* over $(X, <)$ is the transitive closure of the relation of *immediate precedence* on the collection of *finite* multisets over $X$, where $g$ *immediately precedes* $f$ iff for some $x \in D(f)$, we have (i) $g(x) = f(x) - 1$, (ii) $\forall y < x[g(y) \geq f(y)]$ and (iii) $\forall y \not< x[g(y) = f(y)]$.                              ∎

Thus, $g$ precedes $f$ if it can be obtained from $f$ by replacing one occurrence of an element $x$ of $f$ by some occurrences of elements $y < x$.

**Example.** For $X = \mathbb{N}$, we have

$$\{\{3, 3, 4, 4, 7, 9\}\} \text{ immediately precedes } \{\{3, 7, 7, 9\}\},$$

since $\{\{3, 3, 4, 4, 7, 9\}\} = (\{\{3, 7, 7, 9\}\} - \{\{7\}\}) \cup \{\{3, 4, 4\}\}$: to obtain $\{\{3, 3, 4, 4, 7, 9\}\}$ from $\{\{3, 7, 7, 9\}\}$, one (occurrence of the) element 7 of $\{\{3, 7, 7, 9\}\}$ is replaced by the finite multiset $\{\{3, 4, 4\}\}$ of elements all smaller than 7. ∎

**Definition 1.11** A binary relation on a set is *well-founded* if it has no infinite path. A well-founded linear ordering is called a *well-ordering*. ∎

Along a well-founded relation there may be arbitrarily long infinite increasing sequences (see Section 1.4), but every decreasing sequence must come to a stop at some minimal element after finitely many steps.

All finite linear orderings and $(\mathbb{N}, <)$ are well-orderings (Exercise 1.1). $(\mathbb{N}, >)$ is a linear ordering that is not a well-ordering.

Note that a tree is well-founded iff it has no infinite branch. So, König's Lemma may be stated as follows: every well-founded, finitely branching tree is finite.

The purpose of the rest of this section is to show that (Theorem 1.13) the multiset ordering over a well-founded partial ordering is well-founded.

**Lemma 1.12** *The transitive closure of a well-founded relation is well-founded.*

**Proof.** See Exercise 1.9. ∎

**Theorem 1.13** *The multiset ordering over a well-founded ordering is well-founded.*

**Proof.** By Lemma 1.12, it suffices to show that the immediate precedence relation, whose transitive closure is the multiset ordering, is well-founded. We argue by contradiction. Assume that $f_0, f_1, f_2, \ldots$ is an infinite sequence of multisets over the well-founded partial ordering $(X, <)$ such that for all $i$: $f_{i+1}$ immediately precedes $f_i$. For each $i$ then, $f_{i+1}$ is obtained from $f_i$ by replacing one occurrence of some $x \in D(f_i)$ by occurrences of elements $y < x$. Let us denote the occurrence of $x$ that has been replaced in $f_i$ by $x_i$. Let $\mathcal{T}$ be the tree of these occurrences $x_i$, where we stipulate that $x_j$ is a *child* of $x_i$ iff $x_j$ is one of the occurrences replacing $x_i$ to obtain $f_{i+1}$ from $f_i$. Thus, if $x_j$ is a child of $x_i$, then $j \geq i + 1$. In general, $j \neq i + 1$, since $x_j$ might get replaced at a much later stage of the sequence. (The "roots" of $\mathcal{T}$ are the occurrences of elements of $f_0$ eventually replaced, so $\mathcal{T}$ really might be a finite union of trees. This defect can be remedied by adding one new root, joining these trees.)

Note that, since we only consider *finite* multisets, $\mathcal{T}$ is a *finitely branching* tree. By König's Lemma 1.5, $\mathcal{T}$ must have an infinite branch. However, the occurrences along such a branch are descending in the well-founded ordering $<$, a contradiction. ∎

A nice feature of Theorem 1.13 is that it can be iterated. For instance, the *multiset ordering of the multiset ordering of* $(\mathbb{N}, <)$ again is well-founded, etc.

We close with a couple of characterizations of the notion of well-foundedness of which 1.14(iii) is the most elegant (compare Theorem 1.2). In (ii), $y \in Y$ is $\prec$-*minimal* if for no $x \in Y$, $x \prec y$.

**Lemma 1.14** *Let $\prec$ be a relation on $T$. The following conditions are equivalent:*

*(i) $\prec$ is well-founded on $T$,*

*(ii) every non-empty set $Y \subset T$ has a $\prec$-minimal element,*

*(iii) (strong) $\prec$-induction holds:*

*if $X \subset T$ is such that $\forall t \in T \, [\forall s \prec t (s \in X) \Rightarrow t \in X]$, then $X = T$,*

**Proof.** See Exercise 1.8. ∎

**Exercises**

**1.6** Complete the proof of Lemma 1.8.

**1.7** Let $R$ be a relation on the set $X$.
Show: for all $x, z \in X$, $x R^{tr} z \Leftrightarrow x R z \vee \exists y (x R^{tr} y \wedge y R z)$. Show: if $R$ is well-founded, then there is exactly one relation $S$ satisfying the condition $x S z \Leftrightarrow x R z \vee \exists y (x S y \wedge y R z)$.

**1.8** Prove Lemma 1.14.

**1.9** Prove Lemma 1.12.
*Hint.* Use the form of Lemma 1.14(iii) and copy the proof of Theorem 1.2 using Exercise 1.7; or, simpler, but less elegantly, just use the definition of well-foundedness.

**1.10** In *Smullyan's Ball Game*, you, the only player of the game, are given a box with (finitely many) balls, each of them carrying a natural number. A *move* in the game consists in replacing one ball (the choice is free) with as many balls as you wish (but no more than finitely many), each carrying a number less than the number of the one it replaces. Show that, no matter how you choose your moves, you'll end up with an *empty* box eventually. (Alas! your last move probably will be to remove a ball carrying the number zero . . . )

**1.11** Generalize Smullyan's Ball Game (and the accompanying theorem), replacing the balls by boxes containing finitely many boxes, containing finitely many boxes, . . . containing numbered balls.

**1.12** Suppose that $<$ is a linear ordering of the set $X$ such that both $<$ and its converse $>$ are well-orderings. Show that $X$ is finite.

*Hint.* Assume that $<$ is a well-ordering of the infinite set $X$. Construct an infinite increasing sequence $x_0 < x_1 < x_2 < \cdots$ by repeatedly using Lemma 1.14(ii).

## 1.4    Ordinals and Cardinals

Ordinals are used here and there in Chapters 4, 7 and 8 (to index fixed point hierarchies) and in 6 (to measure heights of well-founded trees). These objects arise as a generalization of the notion of natural numbers as follows. Natural numbers have a *cardinal*, as well as an *ordinal*, character. In their cardinal guise, they are used to measure the number of elements of *finite* sets. For instance, the set of planets of the solar system has *cardinal number* 9. Ordinally, natural numbers are used to pinpoint positions in finite linear orderings: Earth is the 3rd planet of the solar system. Ordinally also, they measure lengths of finite linear orderings: Pluto is the 9th and last of the row of planets. However, cardinal and ordinal aspects of natural numbers collapse to the same thing since the final outcome of the counting process of a finite set is independent of the way of counting. Putting this more abstractly:

**Proposition 1.15** *All linear orderings of the same finite set are isomorphic.*

**Proof.** Induction with respect to the number of elements of the set.                        ∎

By the way:

**Definition 1.16** An *isomorphism* between the relational systems (linear orderings, well-orderings, trees, ... ) $(X, R)$ and $(Y, S)$ is a bijection $h : X \rightarrow Y$ such that for all $a, b \in X$: $xRy \Leftrightarrow h(a)Sh(b)$.

$(X, R)$ and $(Y, S)$ are *isomorphic* in case there exists an isomorphism between them.     ∎

Proposition 1.15 does not hold any longer if the restriction to finite sets is removed, even when restricted to linear orderings that are well-orderings. For instance, consider $\mathbb{N}$. The familiar ordering $<$ of $\mathbb{N}$ orders the naturals according to the following listing: $0, 1, 2, 3, \ldots$ Exchanging 2 and 5 results in the following list: $0, 1, 5, 3, 4, 2, 6, 7, \ldots$ Here, the corresponding well-ordering still is isomorphic with $(\mathbb{N}, <)$. A non-isomorphic one is obtained by removing 0 as the first element and adding it as the last one: $1, 2, 3, \ldots, 0$. This procedure can be iterated, producing infinitely many non-isomorphic well-orderings of $\mathbb{N}$. Still another one is obtained by putting the odd numbers after the even ones: $0, 2, 4, \ldots, 1, 3, 5, \ldots$ etc.

Natural numbers simultaneously serve as cardinal numbers of finite sets and as *order types* of finite linear (well-) orderings. Order types are thought of as associated to (linear) orderings in such a way that orderings are isomorphic iff they obtain the same type. Now:

**Definition 1.17** An *ordinal* is the order type of a well-ordered set.                    ∎

(Notations for) the first few ordinals are:

$0, 1, 2, \ldots$ (the natural numbers are also used as the order types of finite orderings)

$\omega$ (the order type of $(\mathbb{N}, <)$)

$\omega + 1, \omega + 2, \ldots, \omega + \omega = \omega \cdot 2,$

$\omega \cdot 2 + 1, \omega \cdot 2 + 2, \ldots, \omega \cdot 3, \ldots, \omega \cdot 4, \ldots$

$\omega \cdot \omega = \omega^2, \omega^2 + 1, \ldots, \omega^2 + \omega, \ldots, \omega^2 + \omega \cdot 2, \ldots, \omega^3, \ldots$

$\omega^\omega, \ldots, \omega^\omega + \omega^3 \cdot 5 + \omega + 1, \ldots$

$\omega^{\omega^\omega}, \ldots$

It will be more or less clear what the notations of addition, multiplication and exponentiation here stand for. $\omega + 1$ is the ordinal of the ordering of natural numbers according to the listing $1, 2, 3, \ldots, 0$; $\omega + 2$ is the ordinal of $2, 3, 4, \ldots, 0, 1$ and $\omega \cdot 2$ is the ordinal of $0, 2, 4, \ldots, 1, 3, 5, \ldots$.

From the way in which the ordinals are generated it is seen that they are well-ordered themselves. However, there is no ordinal corresponding to this well-ordering since the ordinals do not form a *set*. (This is the way set theory escapes the *Burali-Forti paradox*.)

The ordinals displayed in the previous list are all *countable*, that is, they are types of well-orderings of (subsets of) $\mathbb{N}$. (In fact, they are types of *recursive* well-orderings, cf. Chapter 7.) Set theory also provides for uncountable ordinals, but we will not encounter these.

**Definition 1.18** Let $\prec$ be a well-ordering of the set $X$. The *height $ht(x)$* of an element $x \in X$ is the order type of $\{y \in X \mid y \prec x\}$. The *height $ht(X)$* of $(X, \prec)$ is the order type of $(X, \prec)$.

If $R$ is only well-founded on $X$, for instance, $(X, R, u)$ might be a well-founded tree, *height* is defined by recursion along $R$ by $ht(x) = sup\{ht(y) + 1 \mid yRx\}$. (If $A$ is a set of ordinals, then $supA$ is the least ordinal that is $\geq$ all ordinals in $A$.) *Height* of $(X, R)$ itself then is defined by $ht(X) := sup\{ht(x) + 1 \mid x \in X\}$.                    ∎

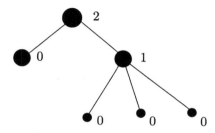

tree of height 3

Note that the height of a tree is measured from the leaves down to the root. In a tree, leaves have height 0. So if a tree consists of a root only, this root obtains height 0, and the tree itself has height 1.

For basic facts on cardinals (which we shall seldom use), see any introduction in set theory. A set is *countable* if it can be rendered as $\{a_i \mid i \in \mathbb{N}\}$. That is, it is either finite or of the same power as $\mathbb{N}$.

### Exercises

**1.13** Describe a well-ordering of $\mathbb{N}$ in type $\omega \cdot \omega$.

A concrete well-ordering of type $\omega^\omega$ is much harder to come by, but see Exercise 1.16.

**1.14** Suppose that $<$ is a relation on $X$, that $\prec$ is a well-founded relation on $Y$ and that $h : X \to Y$ is such that for all $a, b \in X$: $a < b \Rightarrow h(a) \prec h(b)$. Show that $<$ is well-founded.

**1.15** Let $\mathcal{T}$ be a well-founded tree. Show: if $\mathcal{T}$ is finitely branching, then it has finite height.

**\*1.16** [2] With a multiset $f$ over $(\mathbb{N}, <)$, associate the ordinal $\varphi(f) := \omega^{n_1} \cdot f(n_1) + \cdots + \omega^{n_k} \cdot f(n_k)$, where $n_1, \cdots, n_k$ are the elements of $D(f)$ in decreasing order. Now, use Exercise 1.14 to give an alternative proof of Theorem 1.13 for the case of multisets over $(\mathbb{N}, <)$. (It follows that the multiset ordering over $(\mathbb{N}, <)$ has order type $\omega^\omega$.)

## 1.5  Notes

Theorem 1.13 is from [Dershowitz/Manna 79].
Exercise 1.10 is from [Smullyan 79].

---

[2] A \* indicates that an exercise may be difficult or needs material not treated in this book.

# 2 Propositional Logic

Propositional logic is that part of logic which deals with the connectives $\neg$, $\wedge$, $\vee$, $\rightarrow$ and $\leftrightarrow$. The first few sections of this chapter consist of a speedy introduction to syntax, semantics and conjunctive normal forms. Though our treatment here is quite complete, previous contact with the material can be an advantage. In Section 2.4 the treatment is more elaborate.

In this chapter and the next one, satisfiability of formulas is the central issue. Resolution is a combinatorial, proof-theoretic approach to establishing (un)satisfiability that does not involve truth tables. Formulas are introduced in the next section; the satisfiability notion is in Definition 2.5. The method of resolution is dealt with in Section 2.4 of this chapter.

## 2.1 Syntax

The *language* of propositional logic consists of the following symbols.

   (i) infinitely many *variables* or *proposition letters*,

  (ii) the *connectives*: *negation* $\neg$, *conjunction* $\wedge$, *disjunction* $\vee$, *implication* $\rightarrow$, *equivalence* $\leftrightarrow$,

 (iii) parentheses.

We can now form finite sequences of these symbols. Our interest concerns a special type of sequence, the *formulas* of propositional logic:

**Definition 2.1** The collection of *formulas* is the smallest one satisfying:

   (i) all variables (sequences of length 1) are formulas,
  (ii) if the sequences $\varphi$ and $\psi$ are formulas, then so are

   - the *negation* of $\varphi$, $\neg\varphi$,

   - the *implication* of $\varphi$ and $\psi$, $(\varphi\rightarrow\psi)$ and

   - the *equivalence* of $\varphi$ and $\psi$, $(\varphi\leftrightarrow\psi)$,

 (iii) if $\varphi_0,\ldots,\varphi_{n-1}$ are formulas, then so are

   - the *conjunction* of $\varphi_0,\ldots,\varphi_{n-1}$, $(\varphi_0 \wedge \cdots \wedge \varphi_{n-1})$ and

   - the *disjunction* of $\varphi_0,\ldots,\varphi_{n-1}$, $(\varphi_0 \vee \cdots \vee \varphi_{n-1})$. ∎

For instance, the sequence $((A \wedge B)\rightarrow C)$ (where $A$, $B$ and $C$ are variables) is a formula: $A$, $B$ and $C$ are formulas (by 2.1(i)), hence, $(A \wedge B)$ is one (by 2.1(iii)), therefore, $((A \wedge B)\rightarrow C)$ is a formula (2.1(ii)).

For the conjunction of a sequence of formulas $\varphi_0, \ldots, \varphi_{n-1}$ we also use the notation $\bigwedge_{i<n} \varphi_i$. If $\Phi$ is the set of formulas $\{\varphi_i \mid i < n\}$, this conjunction can also be denoted simply by $\bigwedge \Phi$. Similarly, disjunctions can be written as $\bigvee_{i<n} \varphi_i$ or $\bigvee \Phi$.

The formulas you encounter when constructing a formula using the instructions of the definition are its *subformulas*. Thus, the subformulas of $((A \wedge B) \to C)$ are $A$, $B$, $C$, $(A \wedge B)$ and the formula $((A \wedge B) \to C)$ itself.

Putting this differently:

**Definition 2.2** A *subformula* of a formula $\varphi$ is an uninterrupted subsequence of $\varphi$ that itself is a formula.                                                                                    ∎

Though $(A \to C)$ is a subsequence of $((A \wedge B) \to C)$ that is a formula, it is not an uninterrupted one and so it is not a subformula. The same goes for $(B \to C)$ and $((B) \to C)$. The sequence $B) \to C$ *is* an uninterrupted subsequence, but it is not a formula (for instance, cf. Exercise 2.1).

Formulas $(\varphi_0 \wedge \cdots \wedge \varphi_{n-1})$ and $(\varphi_0 \vee \cdots \vee \varphi_{n-1})$ are called *conjunctions* resp. *disjunctions* and $\varphi_0, \ldots, \varphi_{n-1}$ are called their *conjuncts* resp. *disjuncts*.

In most presentations of the subject, $\wedge$ and $\vee$ are *binary* connectives. That is: 2.1(iii) usually is restricted to the case where $n = 2$, so that every conjunction has two conjuncts, and every disjunction has two disjuncts. Our choice to have $\wedge$ and $\vee$ of indefinite arity is dictated by the desire to have a simpler presentation of resolution later on.

Part (iii) of Definition 2.1 even has two "degenerate" cases. First, we allow that $n = 1$ and have formally indistinguishable conjunctions and disjunctions $(\varphi)$ of length 1, which, except for the outer parentheses, are indistinguishable from their sole conjunct/disjunct $\varphi$ itself. We even admit $n = 0$. In that case, we *do* distinguish and let the empty *con*junction be denoted by $\top$ (*verum*) and the empty *dis*junction by $\bot$ (*falsum*).

**On not writing parentheses.** If confusion is unlikely, we may drop parentheses in our notation of formulas. We shall always leave out outermost parentheses. (And so the distinction between a formula $\varphi$ and the length-1 conjunction and disjunction $(\varphi)$ vanishes completely.) Also, we shall assume that $\wedge$ and $\vee$ bind stronger than $\to$ and $\leftrightarrow$. Thus, e.g., with $A \wedge B \to C$ we mean the formula $((A \wedge B) \to C)$.                  ∎

Since formulas, considered as sequences of symbols, have finite length, it is possible to use induction with respect to length when proving universal statements about them. Somewhat more elegant is the use of strong induction on the number of (occurrences of) connectives. *Formula induction* is a slight variant of this, and parallels the formulation of Definition 2.1. Formally, it makes precise the requirement in Definition 2.1 that the class of formulas is the *smallest* one satisfying the closure principles stated.

**Lemma 2.3 (Formula Induction)** *Suppose that $E$ is a property of formulas such that*

(i) *every variable satisfies E,*
(ii) *if $\varphi$ and $\psi$ satisfy E, then so do $\neg\varphi$, $(\varphi\rightarrow\psi)$ and $(\varphi\leftrightarrow\psi)$,*
(iii) *if $\varphi_0, \ldots, \varphi_{n-1}$ satisfy E, then so do $(\varphi_0 \wedge \cdots \wedge \varphi_{n-1})$ and $(\varphi_0 \vee \cdots \vee \varphi_{n-1})$.*
*Then every formula has E.*                                                                            ∎

## Exercises

By way of example:

**2.1** Show that every formula has an even number of parentheses.
*Hint.* Formula induction.

**2.2** A *construction tree* for $\varphi$ is a finite tree of formulas, with root $\varphi$. Its leaves are propositional variables, and for every node $\psi$,

- if $\psi = \neg\xi$, then $\xi$ is the only child of $\psi$,
- if $\psi = (\psi_1\rightarrow\psi_2)$ or $\psi = (\psi_1\leftrightarrow\psi_2)$, then the children of $\psi$ are exactly $\psi_1$ and $\psi_2$,
- if $\psi = \bigwedge \Phi$ or $\psi = \bigvee \Phi$, then the children of $\psi$ are exactly the elements of $\Phi$.

Show that every formula has a (unique) construction tree.
Note that the subformulas of $\varphi$ are precisely the formulas in the construction tree for $\varphi$.

## 2.2  Semantics

Intuitively, the formulas of propositional logic stand for *statements*. Statements can be either *true* or *false*. The symbols **t** and **f** stand for the *truth values* TRUE resp. FALSE. (Instead of these letters, the numbers 1 and 0 are also in use.)

Every connective has a *truth table* that explains how the truth value of a compound formula using it is calculated from the truth values of its components. Hence, the truth table in a sense represents the *meaning* of the connective. Here follow the truth tables:

| $\varphi$ | $\psi$ | $\neg\varphi$ | $\varphi \wedge \psi$ | $\varphi \vee \psi$ | $\varphi\rightarrow\psi$ | $\varphi\leftrightarrow\psi$ |
|---|---|---|---|---|---|---|
| t | t | f | t | t | t | t |
| t | f |   | f | t | f | f |
| f | t | t | f | t | t | f |
| f | f |   | f | f | t | t |

For conjunctions and disjunctions of arbitrarily many formulas, we stipulate that $\varphi_0 \wedge \cdots \wedge \varphi_{n-1}$ obtains **t** iff *every* $\varphi_i$ $(i < n)$ has value **t**, and $\varphi_0 \vee \cdots \vee \varphi_{n-1}$ obtains **t** iff *at least one* $\varphi_i$ $(i < n)$ has value **t**. It follows that the empty conjunction $\top$ has the value **t**, since trivially, all its conjuncts have this value. (Also trivially true, but irrelevant, is that all conjuncts of $\top$ have value **f**.) Similarly, $\bot$ has the value **f** since there is no disjunct in $\bot$ that has value **t**. By this stipulation, the length-1 conjunction and disjunction $(\varphi)$ obviously have the same value as $\varphi$, and so there is not much harm in confusing them.

Associating a truth value with a formula starts with associating truth values to its variables:

**Definition 2.4** A *truth assignment* is a function mapping variables to truth values.  ∎

If $\gamma$ is a truth assignment for the variables in the formula $\varphi$, then we can calculate the *truth value* of $\varphi$ *under* $\gamma$ using the truth tables. For instance, if the $\gamma$ assigns **t** to the variables $A$ and $B$ and **f** to $C$, then, following truth tables, $A \wedge B$ obtains **t** and $A \wedge B \rightarrow C$ obtains **f**. A more elaborate example is in the proof of Lemma 2.7.

**Definition 2.5** We say that $\gamma$ *satisfies* $\varphi$, notation: $\gamma \models \varphi$, if $\varphi$ obtains the truth value **t** under $\gamma$.

A formula is *satisfiable* if it is satisfied by some truth assignment for its variables.  ∎

The symbol $\models$ occurs in a couple of different contexts, which should not be confused.

**Definition 2.6**

(i) $\gamma$ *satisfies* the set $\Gamma$ of formulas, notation: $\gamma \models \Gamma$, if it satisfies every formula in $\Gamma$;

(ii) $\varphi$ is *logically valid*, notation: $\models \varphi$, if $\varphi$ is satisfied by *every* assignment;

(iii) $\varphi$ is a *logical consequence of*, or *follows logically from* the set of formulas $\Gamma$, notation: $\Gamma \models \varphi$, if every assignment satisfying $\Gamma$ satisfies $\varphi$, as well;

(iv) $\varphi$ and $\psi$ are called *equivalent*, notation: $\varphi \sim \psi$, if they are satisfied by the same assignments.  ∎

For instance, $\top$, $\neg\bot$ and $A \rightarrow A$ are logically valid, $\neg A$ follows logically from $\{\neg(B \rightarrow A)\}$, and $A \rightarrow \neg B$ and $B \rightarrow \neg A$ are equivalent.

The next section uses the equivalences of the following lemma.

**Lemma 2.7**

(i) $\neg\neg\varphi \sim \varphi$; $(\varphi \rightarrow \psi) \sim (\neg\varphi \vee \psi)$; $(\varphi \leftrightarrow \psi) \sim (\neg\varphi \vee \psi) \wedge (\varphi \vee \neg\psi)$,

(ii) $\neg(\varphi_1 \wedge \cdots \wedge \varphi_k) \sim \neg\varphi_1 \vee \cdots \vee \neg\varphi_k$;
$\neg(\varphi_1 \vee \cdots \vee \varphi_k) \sim \neg\varphi_1 \wedge \cdots \wedge \neg\varphi_k$ *(DeMorgan laws)*,

(iii) $\varphi_1 \wedge (\varphi_2 \wedge \cdots \wedge \varphi_k) \sim \varphi_1 \wedge \cdots \wedge \varphi_k$; $\varphi_1 \vee (\varphi_2 \vee \cdots \vee \varphi_k) \sim \varphi_1 \vee \cdots \vee \varphi_k$,

(iv) $\varphi \vee (\psi_1 \wedge \cdots \wedge \psi_k) \sim (\varphi \vee \psi_1) \wedge \cdots \wedge (\varphi \vee \psi_k)$;
$\varphi \wedge (\psi_1 \vee \cdots \vee \psi_k) \sim (\varphi \wedge \psi_1) \vee \cdots \vee (\varphi \wedge \psi_k)$ *(left distributive laws)*.

**Proof.** See Exercise 2.5. To give just one example, here follows the calculation for the first DeMorgan law for the case $k = 2$. Note that the presence of $k$ variables needs the checking of $2^k$ possible distributions of truth values among these variables. In the following table, each row calculates the values of $\neg(\varphi_1 \wedge \varphi_2)$ and $\neg\varphi_1 \vee \neg\varphi_2$ for one of the four possible distributions of truth values over the constituents $\varphi_1$ and $\varphi_2$ indicated on the left.

| $\varphi_1$ | $\varphi_2$ | $\neg$ | ($\varphi_1$ | $\wedge$ | $\varphi_2$) | $\neg$ | $\varphi_1$ | $\vee$ | $\neg$ | $\varphi_2$ |
|---|---|---|---|---|---|---|---|---|---|---|
| t | t | f | t | t | t | f | t | f | f | t |
| t | f | t | t | f | f | f | t | t | t | f |
| f | t | t | f | f | t | t | f | t | f | t |
| f | f | t | f | f | f | t | f | t | t | f |

In this table, the intermediate results of the calculations corresponding to subformulas are written beneath the main connective of the subformula. We see that both formulas obtain the same value under every possible distribution of truth values. ∎

**Exercises**

**2.3** Show that $\varphi \sim \psi$ iff $\models(\varphi \leftrightarrow \psi)$.

The next exercise shows (un)satisfiability and validity to be closely related.

**2.4** Show that $\varphi$ is unsatisfiable iff $\models \neg\varphi$.

**2.5** Prove Lemma 2.7.

## 2.3 Conjunctive Normal Form

The propositional variant of resolution handles only formulas of a special type, the so-called *conjunctive normal forms*. The Conjunctive Normal Form Theorem 2.9 states that every formula has an equivalent of that type, and the proof of this result shows how to find such an equivalent. Therefore, it is this theorem that makes resolution adequate to deal with all propositional formulas.

**Definition 2.8** Variables and negations of variables are called (*positive* resp. *negative*) *literals*.

A formula is called a *conjunctive normal form* (c.n.f.) if it is a conjunction of disjunctions of literals. ∎

Thus, the "general form" of a c.n.f. looks as follows:

$$(L_1^1 \vee \cdots \vee L_{n_1}^1) \wedge \cdots \wedge (L_1^m \vee \cdots \vee L_{n_m}^m)$$

where each $L^i_j$ is a literal. This c.n.f. has $m$ conjuncts; its $i$-th conjunct $(1 \leq i \leq m)$ is the disjunction of the $n_i$ literals $L^i_1, \ldots, L^i_{n_i}$.

There is a dual notion of *disjunctive normal form*: these are disjunctions of conjunctions of literals. They are of no importance for the theory of resolution.

**Example.** If $A$ and $B$ are variables, then $A$ (a length-1 conjunction of one length-1 disjunction), $\neg A$, $\neg A \vee B$ (a length-1 conjunction of one length-2 disjunction), $\neg A \wedge B$ (a length-2 conjunction of two length-1 disjunctions) and $(\neg A \vee B) \wedge (\neg A \vee \neg B)$ are examples of conjunctive normal forms.

$A \vee (\neg A \wedge B)$ is *not* a conjunctive normal form (but it is a *disjunctive* normal form). ∎

**Theorem 2.9 (Conjunctive Normal Form)** *Every formula has an equivalent in conjunctive normal form.*

**Proof.** The desired conjunctive normal form is produced in a number of steps, using the equivalences of Lemma 2.7.

  (i) Elimination of unwanted connectives.

   Replace subformulas $\varphi {\rightarrow} \psi$ and $\varphi {\leftrightarrow} \psi$ by their equivalents: $\neg \varphi \vee \psi$ resp. $(\neg \varphi \vee \psi) \wedge (\varphi \vee \neg \psi)$.

 (ii) Pushing negation signs inside.

   Replace subformulas $\neg(\varphi_1 \wedge \cdots \wedge \varphi_k)$ and $\neg(\varphi_1 \vee \cdots \vee \varphi_k)$ by their equivalents $\neg \varphi_1 \vee \cdots \vee \neg \varphi_k$ resp. $\neg \varphi_1 \wedge \cdots \wedge \neg \varphi_k$, erasing double negations whenever encountered; i.e., replacing subformulas $\neg\neg\varphi$ by $\varphi$.

(iii) Erasing parentheses in conjunctions and disjunctions.

 (iv) Applying distribution.

   Replace subformulas $\varphi \vee (\psi_1 \wedge \cdots \wedge \psi_k)$ and $(\psi_1 \wedge \cdots \wedge \psi_k) \vee \varphi$ by their equivalents: $(\varphi \vee \psi_1) \wedge \cdots \wedge (\varphi \vee \psi_k)$ resp. $(\psi_1 \vee \varphi) \wedge \cdots \wedge (\psi_k \vee \varphi)$.

Eventually, the required conjunctive normal form will show up.                ∎

**Example.** $\neg(A \wedge (B \wedge C {\rightarrow} D))$ is transformed successively in
  (step 1) $\neg(A \wedge (\neg(B \wedge C) \vee D))$,
  (step 2) $\neg A \vee \neg(\neg(B \wedge C) \vee D)$,
  (2 again) $\neg A \vee (\neg\neg(B \wedge C) \wedge \neg D)$,
  (2 once more) $\neg A \vee ((B \wedge C) \wedge \neg D)$,
  (step 3) $\neg A \vee (B \wedge C \wedge \neg D)$,
  (step 4) $(\neg A \vee B) \wedge (\neg A \vee C) \wedge (\neg A \vee \neg D)$.     ∎

**Exercises**

**2.6** In the proof of Theorem 2.9, implicit use is made of the fact that replacement, in a formula, of a subformula by an equivalent will result in an equivalent of that formula. Prove this.

*Solution:* Formula induction.

(a) The subformula of $\varphi$ to be replaced is $\varphi$ itself. In this case, the result is evident.

(b) The subformula to be replaced is a *proper* one. For instance, $\varphi$ is a conjunction $\psi \wedge \chi$, and the replacement concerns a subformula of $\psi$. Induction hypothesis: the result holds for $\psi$. Therefore, the result $\psi'$ of the replacement of the subformula in $\psi$ is an equivalent of $\psi$. It is now easy to check that $\varphi$ is equivalent with $\psi' \wedge \chi$. (Every formula $(\psi \leftrightarrow \psi') \rightarrow (\psi \wedge \chi \leftrightarrow \psi' \wedge \chi)$ is logically valid.)

The cases where $\varphi$ is a disjunction or a negation are similar.

**\* 2.7** The last line in the proof of Theorem 2.9 requires an argument. Show that the process of repeatedly applying steps 1–4 (i) terminates, and (ii) produces, in fact, a formula in conjunctive normal form.

**2.8** Prove that every formula has an equivalent in *disjunctive normal form* (d.n.f.).

*Hint.* Here are three different methods to produce a d.n.f.

1. Parallel the proof of Theorem 2.9.

2. $\varphi$ has $\neg\neg\varphi$ as an equivalent. Form a c.n.f.-equivalent of $\neg\varphi$ and push the remaining negation symbol inside.

3. Construct the truth table of $\varphi$. A d.n.f. for $\varphi$ can now be read off immediately. (To every row that has $\mathbf{t}$ in the final column corresponds a disjunct; if $\mathbf{t}$ (resp., $\mathbf{f}$) occurs in the row under the variable $A$, then $A$ (resp., $\neg A$) is a conjunct of this disjunct.)

**2.9** Assume that $\neg$, $\wedge$ and $\vee$ are the only connectives in the formula $\varphi$. $\varphi^d$ is the formula obtained from $\varphi$ by exchanging $\wedge$ and $\vee$. Show: $\varphi$ is logically valid iff $\neg\varphi^d$ is logically valid.

**2.10** $A, B, C, D$ and $E$ are variables. Give equivalents in conjunctive normal form for

  (i) $(A \wedge B) \leftrightarrow (C \vee D)$,

  (ii) $(((\neg A \vee B) \wedge \neg C) \vee D) \wedge \neg E$.

**2.11** Give d.n.f.'s for

  (i) $(\neg A \vee B) \wedge (C \vee \neg D)$,

  (ii) $\neg((A \vee B) \rightarrow C)$.

It is in the nature of our subject that we shall discuss algorithmic decidability now and then. For an intuitive definition of this concept and related ones, see Definition 7.1 in Chapter 7.

**2.12** Produce a simple (in fact, trivial) decision method for satisfiability for formulas in disjunctive normal form.

**2.13** Show that the following procedure outputs, for a given propositional formula $\varphi$, a c.n.f. $\psi$ (in general, *not* an equivalent of $\varphi$) that is satisfiable iff $\varphi$ is satisfiable.
Enumerate all subformulas $\varphi_0, \ldots, \varphi_m = \varphi$ of $\varphi$. Fix a sequence of variables $p_0, \ldots, p_m$ corresponding to these formulas. $\psi$ is the conjunction of $p_m$ (which corresponds to $\varphi$) and formulas in the variables $p_0, \ldots, p_m$ obtained as follows. For all $i \leq m$ such that $\varphi_i$ is not a variable: if $\varphi_i$ is $\neg\varphi_j$, then a c.n.f. of $p_i \leftrightarrow \neg p_j$ is one of the conjuncts of $\psi$; if $\varphi_i$ is $\varphi_j \to \varphi_k$, then a c.n.f. of $p_i \leftrightarrow (p_j \to p_k)$ is one of them, etc.

## 2.4   Resolution

Resolution for propositional logic is a method with which one can test conjunctive normal forms for (un)satisfiability. To obtain a somewhat simplified exposition, it is useful to present the conjunctive normal form to be tested in its so-called *clausal form*.

**Definition 2.10** A *clause* is a finite set of literals.
A *clausal form* is a set of clauses.
The *clausal form* of the c.n.f.

$$(L_1^1 \vee \cdots \vee L_{n_1}^1) \wedge \cdots \wedge (L_1^m \vee \cdots \vee L_{n_m}^m)$$

is the set of clauses $\{\{L_1^1, \ldots, L_{n_1}^1\}, \ldots, \{L_1^m, \ldots, L_{n_m}^m\}\}$.                         ∎

Two (syntactically) different conjunctive normal forms can have the same clausal form. For instance, $(A \vee A) \wedge (A \vee B)$ and $(A) \wedge (B \vee A)$ both have the clausal form $\{\{A\}, \{A, B\}\}$: since $\{A, A\} = \{A\}$ and $\{A, B\} = \{B, A\}$, we have that $\{\{A, A\}, \{A, B\}\} = \{\{A\}, \{A, B\}\} = \{\{A\}, \{B, A\}\}$.

**Lemma 2.11** *If two conjunctive normal forms have the same clausal form, then they are logically equivalent.*

**Proof.** See Exercise 2.14.                                                                         ∎

Logically interpreted, a clause stands for the *disjunction* of its elements. Thus: if $\gamma$ is a truth assignment for the variables in the clause $C$, then $\gamma$ satisfies $C$ iff $\gamma$ satisfies at least one literal in $C$.

Again, there are two degenerate cases. The *singleton* clause $\{L\}$ stands for the "disjunction" $(L)$. The *empty* clause stands for the empty disjunction $\bot$; as a clause, it has its own notation:

**Notation 2.12** The notation for the empty clause is □.                                        ∎

Next comes the simple definition of propositional resolution.

**Definition 2.13** Assume that $C$ and $D$ are clauses and $A$ a variable such that $A \in C$ and $\neg A \in D$. The clause $(C - \{A\}) \cup (D - \{\neg A\})$ is called a (*propositional*) *resolvent* of $C$ and $D$ with respect to $A$.                                                                                  ∎

Thus, clauses $C$ and $D$ have a resolvent in case a variable $A$ exists such that $A \in C$ and $\neg A \in D$ (or conversely). The resolvent with respect to this variable is obtained by removing $A$ resp. $\neg A$ from $C$ resp. $D$ and joining their remains.

For instance, $\{A, \neg B, C\}$ and $\{\neg A, B, C\}$ have the resolvents $\{\neg B, B, C\}$ (with respect to $A$) and $\{A, \neg A, C\}$ (with respect to $B$). They do not have a resolvent with respect to $C$.

**Definition 2.14** (*Propositional*) *resolution* is forming (propositional) resolvents repeatedly.

More precisely: a *propositional derivation* of a clause $E$ from a set $\Sigma$ of clauses is a finite tree $\mathcal{T}$ such that

   (i) $E$ is the root of $\mathcal{T}$,

   (ii) every leaf of $\mathcal{T}$ belongs to $\Sigma$,

   (iii) every non-leaf $D$ of $\mathcal{T}$ has children $D_1$ and $D_2$ of which it is a propositional resolvent. (It is allowed that $D_1 = D_2$, but see Exercise 2.18.)

The number of non-leaf nodes of a derivation is its number of *steps*.

The notation: $\Sigma \vdash_p E$ is used when $E$ is so derivable from $\Sigma$.

A propositional derivation of $\square$ from $\Sigma$ is called a *refutation* of $\Sigma$. $\Sigma$ is *refutable* if it has a refutation.                                                                                     ∎

For instance: here is a two-step refutation of the set $\{\{\neg A\}, \{A, B\}, \{\neg B\}\}$:

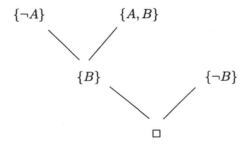

The next two results establish that every derivable clause follows logically from the set from which it is derived.

**Lemma 2.15** *If $E$ is a resolvent of $C$ and $D$, then $\{C, D\} \models E$.*

**Proof.** We have to show that every truth assignment $\gamma$ for the variables involved that satisfies both $C$ and $D$ also satisfies $E$. Assume that $E = (C - \{A\}) \cup (D - \{\neg A\})$ and $\gamma \models \{C, D\}$.

(i) $\gamma \not\models A$. Since we have $\gamma \models C$, $\gamma$ must satisfy some literal in $C - \{A\}$. However, this literal also occurs in $E$, and so we have that $\gamma \models E$.

(ii) $\gamma \models A$. Thus, $\gamma \not\models \neg A$. Since we have $\gamma \models D$, $\gamma$ must satisfy some literal in $D - \{\neg A\}$ which also is in $E$: again we have that $\gamma \models E$.                            ∎

The next result expresses that the derivability notion is *sound* with respect to the one involving truth tables: every derived clause follows logically.

**Corollary 2.16 (Soundness)** *If $\Sigma \vdash_p C$, then $\Sigma \models C$.*

**Proof.** Let $\mathcal{T}$ be a derivation of $C$ from $\Sigma$. We apply strong induction with respect to the number of steps of the derivation and use Lemma 2.15. If $\mathcal{T}$ has no steps, then its only element is $C$, $C \in \Sigma$, and the result is immediate. Otherwise, $C$ is a resolvent of its children clauses $C_1$ and $C_2$ in $\mathcal{T}$. The subderivations of $\mathcal{T}$ that derive $C_1$ and $C_2$ from $\Sigma$ have at least one step less than $\mathcal{T}$. By induction hypothesis, $\Sigma \models C_i$ ($i = 1, 2$). Since by Lemma 2.15, $\{C_1, C_2\} \models C$, it follows that $\Sigma \models C$.                            ∎

By definition, $\Sigma \models \square$ means: every assignment that satisfies $\Sigma$, satisfies $\square$. However, $\square$ is unsatisfiable. Thus, $\Sigma \models \square$ is just another way of expressing that $\Sigma$ is unsatisfiable. Therefore, the following is just a special case of the Soundness Corollary 2.16:

**Corollary 2.17** *If $\Sigma \vdash_p \square$, then $\Sigma$ is unsatisfiable.*                            ∎

The next converse expresses that refutability is *complete* with respect to the truth table notion of unsatisfiability: resolution is capable of establishing refutability of any unsatisfiable clause set.

**Theorem 2.18 (Completeness)** *If $\Sigma$ is unsatisfiable, then $\Sigma \vdash_p \square$.*

For the proof of Theorem 2.18 we need a combinatorial result: Lemma 2.21, and a few notions.

**Definition 2.19** Suppose that $P$ is a collection of sets. A set $J$ is called

(i) *meet* of $P$ if $\forall C \in P : J \cap C \neq \emptyset$, that is: $J$ intersects every set in $P$,
(ii) *minimal meet* of $P$ if $J$ is a meet of $P$ but it has no proper subset that still is a meet of $P$.                            ∎

If $P$ is a collection of non-empty sets, then a meet of $P$ always exists; e.g., the union $\bigcup P$ of all sets in $P$ will be an obvious example of such a meet. However, to find *minimal* meets can be more difficult, and sometimes they simply do not exist.

**Examples.**

(i) Every element of $P := \{\{1, 2\}, \{2, 3\}, \{1, 3\}\}$ is a minimal meet of $P$.

(ii) Define $C_n := \{n, n + 1, n + 2, \ldots\}$. The collection $\{C_n \mid n \in \mathbb{N}\}$ has no minimal meet. ∎

**Lemma 2.20** *Assume that $J$ is a meet of $P$. The following conditions are equivalent:*

*(i) $J$ is a minimal meet of $P$;*

*(ii) $\forall a \in J \, \exists C \in P : J \cap C = \{a\}$.*

**Proof.** (ii) ⇒ (i) If $a \in J$, then $J - \{a\}$ is not a meet: by (ii), take $C \in P$ such that $J \cap C = \{a\}$. $J - \{a\}$ does not intersect $C$.

(i) ⇒ (ii) If (ii) does not hold, then $a \in J$ exists such that for every $C$ in $P$: if $a \in J \cap C$, then $J \cap C$ has yet another element $\neq a$. Thus, the proper subset $J - \{a\}$ of $J$ also is a meet of $P$. ∎

**Lemma 2.21** *Every collection of finite, non-empty sets has a minimal meet.*

**Proof.** Suppose that $P$ is a collection of finite, non-empty sets. To simplify the argument, we assume that an enumeration $x_0, x_1, x_2, \ldots$ of all elements occurring in the sets of $P$ can be given. (That is, we assume that $\bigcup P$ is *countable*. This condition will be satisfied in every situation where we apply the lemma.) Put $J_0 := \{x_0, x_1, x_2, \ldots\}$. Note that $J_0$ is a meet of $P$. Define the sequence $J_1, J_2, J_3, \ldots$ as follows. If $J_0 - \{x_0\}$ is a meet as well, put $J_1 := J_0 - \{x_0\}$. If not, put $J_1 := J_0$. In other words: throw away $x_0$ if its dismissal does not result in a set that no longer is a meet of $P$. $J_2$ is defined similarly: this is $J_1 - \{x_1\}$ in case this set still is a meet of $P$; and otherwise we put $J_2 := J_1$, etc.

All sets $J_n$ produced are meets for $P$. We now let $J$ be the set of objects $x$ that are members of *every* $J_n$, that is: $J$ consists of the objects *not* thrown away.

Since every $A \in P$ is finite, we cannot have thrown away all of its elements: if $x_k$ is the element with the largest index in $A$, then $J_{k+1}$ would have no element in $A$; and hence it would not be a meet of $P$, contrary to construction. Therefore, $J$ is a meet of $P$. But now, $J$ also is a *minimal* meet: if $x_k \in J$ could be left out, then we would have thrown it away when forming $J_{k+1}$. ∎

**Proof** of the Completeness Theorem 2.18.

Assume that $\square$ is not derivable from the set of clauses $\Sigma$. The following argument produces a truth assignment that satisfies every clause in it.

Let $\Delta$ be the set of *all* clauses derivable from $\Sigma$. Let $P$ consist of the clauses in $\Delta$ the literals of which are all *positive*, i.e., variables. Note that $P$ is a collection of finite, *non-empty* sets (as, by assumption, $\square$ is not an element of $\Delta$). Apply Lemma 2.21: let $J$ be a minimal meet for $P$. Identify $J$ with the truth assignment that assigns **t** to every variable in $J$ and **f** to every other variable. Then, since $J$ is a meet of $P$, we have that

$J \models P$.

*Claim.* $J \models \Delta$.

Hence, since $\Sigma \subset \Delta$: $J \models \Sigma$.

*Proof of claim.* Pick $C \in \Delta$. We prove that $J \models C$ using induction with respect to the number of *negative* literals in $C$.

*Basis.* If this number is 0, then we have $C \in P$, and hence $J \models C$, as noted previously.

*Induction step.* Choose a negative literal $\neg A$ in $C$. If $A \notin J$, then $J \models C$. So, assume that $A \in J$. By Lemma 2.20, $D \in P$ exists such that $J \cap D = \{A\}$. Note that $(C - \{\neg A\}) \cup (D - \{A\})$ is a resolvent of $C$ and $D$ — and hence, an element of $\Delta$ — that has one negative literal less than $C$. By induction hypothesis, this resolvent is satisfied by $J$. Therefore, $J$ satisfies at least one of the constituents $C - \{\neg A\}$ and $D - \{A\}$ of the resolvent. However, it does not satisfy the second one by choice of $D$. Therefore, $J \models C - \{\neg A\}$. A fortiori, $J \models C$.                                                                      ∎

## Exercises

**2.14** Prove Lemma 2.11. What about its converse?

**2.15** Bring first in conjunctive normal form (if necessary) and rewrite in clausal form ($A, B, C$ are variables):

  (i) $\neg A$,
  (ii) $A \wedge \neg B$,
  (iii) $\neg A \vee B$,
  (iv) $\neg(\neg A \wedge B \wedge \neg C)$,
  (v) $(\neg A \wedge \neg B \wedge C) \vee (A \wedge \neg B \wedge \neg C)$,
  (vi) $A \leftrightarrow (\neg B \wedge C)$.

**2.16** Form all possible resolvents of the following pairs of clauses:

  (i) $\{A, B\}$ ; $\{\neg A, \neg B\}$ (cf. Exercise 2.21),
  (ii) $\{\neg A, \neg B, \neg C\}$ ; $\{\neg B, C\}$,
  (iii) $\{A, \neg A\}$ ; $\{A, \neg A\}$ (cf. Exercise 2.18).

**2.17** Produce all possible resolvents of two clauses in the following sets:

  (i) $\{\{\neg A, \neg B\}, \{\neg A, B\}, \{A\}\}$,
  (ii) $\{\{A, B, C\}, \{\neg B, \neg C\}, \{\neg A, \neg C\}\}$,
  (iii) $\{\{\neg A, \neg B\}, \{B, C\}, \{\neg C, A\}\}$,
  (iv) $\{\{\neg A\}, \{A, B, \neg C\}, \{C, \neg A\}\}$.

**2.18** Show: if $E$ is a resolvent of $C$ and $D$, and $C = D$, then $E = C = D$.

**2.19** Show: if $E$ is a resolvent of $C$ and $\{A, \neg A\}$, then $E = C$.

**2.20** Show:

(i) $\varphi \in \Sigma \Rightarrow \Sigma \vdash_p \varphi$;

(ii) if $\Sigma \vdash_p \varphi$ and $\forall \psi \in \Sigma \, (\Pi \vdash_p \psi)$, then $\Pi \vdash_p \varphi$.

**2.21** Is $\square$ resolvent of $\{A, B\}$ and $\{\neg A, \neg B\}$?

*Hint.* Find out whether $\{\{A, B\}, \{\neg A, \neg B\}\}$ is satisfiable.

**2.22** Show that every collection with a finite meet has a minimal meet.

**2.23** Prove that every *finite* collection of non-empty sets has a minimal meet.

**2.24**   (i) What is the minimal meet for the collection $P := \{\{n, n+1\} \mid n \in \mathbb{N}\}$ produced by the proof of Lemma 2.21?

(ii) Give the first 14 elements of the minimal meet for $\{\{n, 2n\} \mid n \in \mathbb{N}\}$, produced by this proof.

(iii) Idem, for $\{\{n, n+1, \ldots, 2n\} \mid n \in \mathbb{N}\}$, but now only the first 6 elements.

If a finite set $S$ of clauses is unsatisfiable, this can be demonstrated by deriving $\square$ from $S$ using resolution. However, what if $S$ happens to be satisfiable? The following exercise shows that, if $S$ is *finite*, then the set of all clauses derivable from $S$ is finite as well; and hence a systematic search eventually shows $\square$ to be underivable. Thus, resolution can be used also to ascertain *satisfiability* of finite sets of clauses. This contrasts strongly with the case of resolution in first-order logic, dealt with in the next chapter.

**2.25** Let $V$ be a set of $n$ propositional variables.

(i) There are $2n$ literals using variables from $V$. How many clauses are there?

(ii) Give an upper bound on the number of derivations of height $k$ in which the clauses use only variables from $V$.

(iii) Let $S$ be a set of clauses using the variables from $V$. $\mathcal{R}^m(S)$ is the set of clauses derivable from $S$ by a derivation of height $\leq m$. Show that for some $m$, $\mathcal{R}^m(S)$ contains every clause that is derivable from $S$.

(iv) Describe a decision method (cf. Definition 7.1) for satisfiability of finite sets of clauses based on resolution.

**2.26** $A$, $B$ and $C$ are propositional variables. Is $\square$ derivable from the following sets of clauses? If so, give a derivation. If not, give an argument showing that such a derivation does not exist.

(i) $\{\{A, B\}, \{B, C\}, \{A, C\}, \{\neg A, \neg B\}, \{\neg B, \neg C\}, \{\neg A, \neg C\}\}$,

(ii) $\{\{A, B\}, \{B, C\}, \{\neg A, \neg B\}, \{\neg B, \neg C\}, \{\neg A, \neg C\}\}$.

**2.27** Use conjunctive normal forms and resolution to show that the following formulas are unsatisfiable.

(i) $(A{\leftrightarrow}(B{\rightarrow}C)) \wedge (A{\leftrightarrow}B) \wedge (A{\rightarrow}\neg C)$,

(ii) $\neg(((A{\rightarrow}B){\rightarrow}\neg B){\rightarrow}\neg B)$,

(iii) $((A \wedge B) \vee (A \wedge C) \vee (B \wedge C)) \wedge ((\neg A \wedge \neg B) \vee (\neg A \wedge \neg C) \vee (\neg B \wedge \neg C))$.

**2.28** Give a simple example showing that the implication $\Sigma{\models}C \Rightarrow \Sigma \vdash_p C$ can be false when $C \neq \square$.

**2.29** Let $X$ be a set and $P := \{\{a,b\} \mid a,b \in X \wedge a \neq b\}$. Show: if $X$ has at least 2 elements (i.e., if $P \neq \emptyset$), then: $Y$ is a minimal meet for $P$ iff, for some $a \in X$, we have $Y = X - \{a\}$.

**2.30** Assume that $\Phi$ is a collection of non-empty pairwise disjoint sets, and $P := \{\{a,b\} \mid \exists X \in \Phi (a, b \in X)\}$. Let $Y$ be a minimal meet for $P$. Show: if $X \in \Phi$, then $X - Y$ contains exactly one element.

**2.31** $A \subset \mathbb{N}$ is *co-finite* if $\mathbb{N} - A$ is finite. Show that a collection $U \subset \mathbb{N}$ exists, containing all co-finite sets and such that 1. $A \in U \wedge A \subset B \subset \mathbb{N} \Rightarrow B \in U$; 2. $A, B \in U \Rightarrow A \cap B \in U$; 3. $A \subset \mathbb{N} \Rightarrow (A \in U \Leftrightarrow \mathbb{N} - A \notin U)$. (A collection with these properties is called an *ultrafilter* over $\mathbb{N}$.)

*Hint.* Apply Lemma 2.21 to the collection $\{K \subset \mathcal{P}(\mathbb{N}) \mid K$ is finite and $\bigcup K$ is co-finite$\}$.

**2.32** Give a different proof of the Completeness Theorem 2.18, along the following lines. Assume that $\square$ is not derivable from the set of clauses $\Sigma$. Again, let $\Delta$ be the set of all clauses derivable from clauses in $\Sigma$ using resolution. Thus, $\square \notin \Delta$. The aim is to construct a satisfying assignment $\gamma$ for $\Delta$. Fix an enumeration $p_0$, $p_1$, $p_2, \dots$ of all propositional variables. For $C \in \Delta$, let $i(C)$ be the largest index of a variable occurring in $C$ (n.b.: $C \neq \emptyset$!). Recursively define the value $\gamma(p_j)$ by the following stipulation: $\gamma(p_j) := \mathbf{t}$, *unless* there exists $D \in \Delta$, such that $i(D) = j$, which is not satisfied by this choice of $\gamma(p_j)$; in which case we of course put $\gamma(p_j) := \mathbf{f}$. Show that $C \in \Delta \Rightarrow \gamma{\models}C$, using strong induction with respect to $i(C)$.

*Hint.* Assume that $C \in \Delta$ and $\gamma \not\models C$. Let $j := i(C)$. Show: 1. $\gamma(p_j) = \mathbf{f}$; 2. $\neg p_j \notin C$, $p_j \in C$; 3. Modify $\gamma$ to $\gamma'$ by changing the value in $p_j$ to $\mathbf{t}$. Then $D \in \Delta$ exists such that $i(D) = j$ and $\gamma' \not\models D$; 4. $p_j \notin D$, $\neg p_j \in D$; 5. $B := (C - \{p_j\}) \cup (D - \{\neg p_j\})$ is a resolvent of $C$ and $D$ in $\Delta$; 6. $i(B) < j$; 7. $\gamma{\models}B$; 8. $\gamma \not\models (C - \{p_j\})$; 9. $\gamma \not\models (D - \{\neg p_j\})$; 10. $\gamma \not\models B$.

The following is a fundamental result of propositional logic.

**Theorem 2.22 (Compactness of Propositional Logic)** *If every finite subset of an infinite set $\Sigma$ of formulas is satisfiable, then $\Sigma$ is satisfiable as well.*

**\*2.33** Prove Theorem 2.22.

*Hint.* A refutation can only involve finitely many clauses.

**\*2.34** Complete the following sketch of a proof of König's Lemma 1.5, using the Compactness Theorem.

Let $\mathcal{T} = (T, R, u)$ be an infinite, finite branching tree. Choose a propositional variable $A_t$ for every element $t \in T$. $\Sigma$ is the set of all formulas of one of the following forms:

(i)   $A_t \rightarrow \neg A_s$, if $A_t$ is not a descendant of $A_s$ and $A_s$ is not a descendant of $A_t$;

(ii)  $A_{t_1} \vee \cdots \vee A_{t_m}$, if every branch passes through one of $A_{t_1}, \ldots, A_{t_m}$;

(iii) $\neg A_t$, whenever $t$ is a leaf of $T$.

Show that every finite subset of $\Sigma$ is satisfiable.

Now, assume that $\gamma \models \Sigma$. Show that $\{t \in T \mid \gamma(A_t) = \mathbf{t}\}$ is a branch through $\mathcal{T}$. (A slightly simpler proof is possible if $\mathcal{T}$ has no leaves. We can take care of this, restricting the argument to the subtree of nodes which have infinitely many descendants.)

**\*2.35** Prove the general case of Lemma 2.21, *without* the countability assumption. *Hint.* Use a well-ordering of $\bigcup P$, or apply *Zorn's Lemma*.

## 2.5   Notes

The satisfiability problem for propositional formulas is one of the prominent examples of NP-completeness. If you have solved Exercise 2.12 correctly, it is obvious that the satisfiability problem for d.n.f.'s is much simpler than the problem for general formulas. It follows that (if P$\neq$NP) it cannot be that simple to produce disjunctive normal forms. This is quite remarkable in view of Exercise 2.13.

The proof of the Completeness Theorem 2.18 given here, via Lemma 2.21, is from [Bezem 90], which also contains a number of variations and refinements.

Exercise 2.30 (which positively —and unexpectedly— answers the problem whether Lemma 2.21 is an equivalent of the Axiom of Choice) is due to Hurkens; see the note [Bezem/Hurkens 92].

Exercise 2.31 shows Lemma 2.21 to be closely related to the boolean prime ideal theorem.

The Compactness Theorem 2.22 expresses that the space of truth assignments is compact in the product topology corresponding to the discrete space $\{\mathbf{t}, \mathbf{f}\}$. Note that it does not refer to resolution, though the proof suggested in Exercise 2.33 uses this concept.

# 3 First-order Logic

## 3.1 Introduction

The contents of the previous chapter can be described as follows. Resolution in propositional logic is a decision method for satisfiability of conjunctive normal forms (more precisely, of clausal forms). Thanks to the Conjunctive Normal Form Theorem 2.9, resolution can be used also to test an arbitrary formula for unsatisfiability: the only extra thing needed is to put it in conjunctive normal form first.

The purpose of this chapter is to extend the resolution technique to first-order logic where, next to the connectives, we also have the quantifiers ∀ and ∃. We shall see that the first-order variant of resolution is a decision method for unsatisfiability of *universal* sentences with a *matrix* in conjunctive normal form (see the following details). However, here the method produces a result that is weaker than the one for propositional logic: in case the initial sentence is *unsatisfiable* the method will yield a proof witnessing this fact, but it cannot always witness *satisfiability*. This is called *positive decidability* of first-order unsatisfiability (Definition 7.1). The Theorem of Church (Theorem 7.19) explains that this shortcoming is unavoidable.

Not every first-order sentence has a universal equivalent. However, for every sentence a universal sentence (its *Skolem Form*) can be produced that is satisfiable iff the original one is, and this, of course, suffices. This reduction to universal form is described in Section 3.6, which may be skipped by readers primarily interested in resolution.

The basics of first-order logic are explained in Sections 3.2 and 3.3 (some previous contact with this material is an advantage); subsequently we establish positive decidability of first-order unsatisfiability in Sections 3.4–3.6. Finally, resolution is dealt with in Sections 3.7–3.9.

## 3.2 Syntax

In propositional logic, there are three categories of symbols: variables, connectives and parentheses. In first-order logic (more precisely, in *a* first-order logical language), there are seven.

(i) infinitely many (*individual*) *variables*,

(ii) symbols for the logical operations; next to the connectives ¬, ∧ , ∨ , →, ↔ we now also have the *universal quantifier* ∀ and the *existential quantifier* ∃,

(iii) symbols indicating grouping: parentheses, and now also the *comma*,

(iv) much later, the *identity symbol* $\approx$ will be used,

 (v) *relation symbols*,

(vi) *function symbols*,

(vii) *constant symbols*, or (*individual*) *constants*.

Categories (i)–(iv) are fixed for every first-order language; but categories (v)–(vii), the so-called *non-logical* symbols, may vary. A (first-order) *language* is determined by the choice of (v)–(vii); therefore, a language will be identified with its set of non-logical symbols. We always suppose that categories (i)–(vii) are pairwise disjoint and that to every relation and function symbol a positive natural number (its *arity* has been associated.

In the following passages, some such language is always thought to be fixed.

In propositional logic, there is only one type of expression of any importance: the formula. Here, there are two: *terms* (which are intended to be descriptions of objects) and *formulas* (intended to describe statements). The definitions of these classes take the same form as that of the formulas in propositional logic.

**Definition 3.1** *Terms*:

  (i) all variables and constant symbols,

 (ii) all sequences $\mathbf{f}(t_1, \ldots, t_n)$ in which $\mathbf{f}$ is an $n$-ary function symbol and $t_1, \ldots, t_n$ are terms (formed previously).                                                                    ∎

Thus, if $\mathbf{f}$ and $\mathbf{s}$ are (2- resp. 1-ary) function symbols, $\mathbf{c}$ is a constant symbol and $y$ is a variable, then $\mathbf{f}(\mathbf{s}(y), \mathbf{f}(\mathbf{s}(\mathbf{c}), y))$ is a term.

Recall the principle of *formula induction* corresponding to the notion of propositional formula; similarly, there is a principle of *term induction* corresponding to the present notion of term:

**Lemma 3.2 (Term Induction)** *Suppose that $E$ is a property of terms such that*

  *(i) every variable and constant symbol satisfies $E$, and*

 *(ii) if $t_1, \ldots, t_n$ satisfy $E$ and $\mathbf{f}$ is an $n$-ary function symbol, then $\mathbf{f}(t_1, \ldots, t_n)$ satisfies $E$.*

*Then every term satisfies $E$.*                                                                             ∎

**Definition 3.3** $Var(t)$ denotes the set of all variables occurring in the term $t$.
A variable-free term (i.e., a term $t$ for which $Var(t) = \emptyset$) is called *ground*.                ∎

**Definition 3.4** *Formulas*:

  (i) all sequences $\mathbf{r}(t_1, \ldots, t_n)$ in which $\mathbf{r}$ is an $n$-ary relation symbol and $t_1, \ldots, t_n$ are terms: the *atomic* formulas or *atoms*,

(ii) sequences $s \approx t$ ($s$ and $t$ terms) — at least, when $\approx$ is present: the *identities*,

(iii) combinations $\neg\varphi$, $(\varphi_0 \wedge \cdots \wedge \varphi_{n-1})$, $(\varphi_0 \vee \cdots \vee \varphi_{n-1})$, $(\varphi\rightarrow\psi)$, $(\varphi\leftrightarrow\psi)$, $\forall x\varphi$ and $\exists x\varphi$ in which $\varphi$, $\varphi_0, \ldots, \varphi_{n-1}$, $\psi$ are formulas and $x$ is a variable. ∎

For the principle of *formula induction* corresponding to the present notion of formula, cf. Exercise 3.1.

**Definition 3.5** The quantifier combinations $\forall x$ and $\exists x$ that begin the quantifications $\forall x\varphi$ resp., $\exists x\varphi$ have $\varphi$ as their *scope*.

Quantifiers $\forall x$, $\exists x$ *bind* every occurrence of $x$ in their scope — at least, if such an occurrence is not already in a smaller scope of such a quantifier occurring inside the scope of the first one.

Occurrences of variables that are not bound are called *free*.

A *sentence* is a formula without free variables.

$Var(\varphi)$ denotes the set of variables that have a *free* (!) occurrence in the formula $\varphi$.

An expression without variables or quantifiers is called *ground*. ∎

Thus, only the first occurrence of $x$ in $(\mathbf{r}(x)\rightarrow\exists x\mathbf{q}(x,y))$ is free in this formula. Adding one universal quantifier $\forall x$, $\forall x(\mathbf{r}(x)\rightarrow\exists x\mathbf{q}(x,y))$ has no free occurrences of $x$. The quantifier $\forall x$ only binds the occurrence of $x$ in $\mathbf{r}(x)$; it does not bind the one in the $\mathbf{q}$-atom (bound already by $\exists x$).

**On not writing parentheses**, continued. We go on using the conventions on not writing parentheses from the previous chapter and add a couple of new ones.

In terms, we often omit parentheses around arguments of a unary function symbol: '$\mathbf{fffc}$' stands for the term $\mathbf{f}(\mathbf{f}(\mathbf{f}(\mathbf{c})))$.

Also, we sometimes omit parentheses around arguments of relation symbols and the comma between them. Thus: '$\mathbf{r}xy$' stands for the atom $\mathbf{r}(x,y)$. ∎

**Exercise**

**3.1** Formulate a principle of *formula induction* parallelling Definition 3.4.

## 3.3  Semantics

Formulas in propositional logic are interpreted using truth assignments. In first-order logic, the appropriate concept is that of a *model*.

**Definition 3.6** Suppose that the language $\mathcal{L} = \mathcal{R} \cup \mathcal{F} \cup \mathcal{C}$ consists of relation symbols from the set $\mathcal{R}$, function symbols from $\mathcal{F}$ and constant symbols from $\mathcal{C}$. Then an $\mathcal{L}$-*model* is a complex

$$\mathbf{A} = (A, \ldots, r, \ldots, f, \ldots, c, \ldots)_{\mathbf{r}\in\mathcal{R},\mathbf{f}\in\mathcal{F},\mathbf{c}\in\mathcal{C}}$$

in which $A$ is a non-empty set, the *universe* of **A**, and **A** has

   (i) an $n$-ary relation $r \subset A^n$ over $A$ corresponding to each $n$-ary relation symbol $\mathbf{r} \in \mathcal{R}$,

  (ii) an $n$-ary function $f : A^n \rightarrow A$ for each $n$-ary function symbol $\mathbf{f} \in \mathcal{F}$,

 (iii) an element (*constant*) $c \in A$ for each constant symbol $\mathbf{c} \in \mathcal{C}$.        ∎

For instance, if $\mathcal{L}$ consists of a (binary) function symbol $\mathbf{f}$, a (binary) relation symbol $\mathbf{r}$ and a constant symbol $\mathbf{c}$, then $(\mathbb{N}, +, <, 0)$ is an example of an $\mathcal{L}$-model.

The object $\sigma$ is called the *interpretation* or the *meaning* of the non-logical symbol $\sigma$ in the model **A**. Usually, we assume that $r$ shall be the interpretation of $\mathbf{r}$, $f$ the interpretation of $\mathbf{f}$, etc. Usually also, we assume that $A$ is the universe of the model **A**, $B$ the one of the model **B**, etc.

In the context of a model **A**, terms are intended to stand for (descriptions of) certain elements of $A$, and formulas are meant to stand for certain statements about **A**, *at least*, as long as no (free) variables are around. If they are around, we first have to specify which elements of the universe they stand for. There are *two* standard solutions for this predicament, which are essentially equivalent.

The first solution consists in the use of *assignments*, mappings from variables to elements of the universe (cf. Definition 3.10), to keep track of which variables stand for which elements. The second solution expands the language with constant symbols for *all* elements of the universe and (temporarily) replaces variables by these constants. The second solution sounds more complicated but leads to a slightly simpler notation, and so we opt for this one.

**Definition 3.7** Let **A** be a model for a language $\mathcal{L}$.

The *A-language* $\mathcal{L}_A$ is obtained from $\mathcal{L}$ by the addition of *all* elements of $A$ as new constant symbols. The model **A** is adjusted to this expanded language by the stipulation that every new "constant symbol" $a \in A$ shall have itself as interpretation.

*A-terms*, *A-formulas* and *A-sentences* are terms, formulas and sentences in the expanded language $\mathcal{L}_A$.        ∎

**Remarks.** In forming $\mathcal{L}_A$ we usually do not care whether an element $a \in A$ already is interpretation of an $\mathcal{L}$-constant symbol or not; we add it as a new constant symbol anyway.

If the readers do not like terms and formulas (usually thought of as sequences of concrete symbols) containing elements of some abstract universe $A$ that need not be symbols at all, let them add a constant symbol **a** for every element $a \in A$ with the stipulation that it shall be interpreted as $a$.        ∎

The next definition of the notion of value follows the way in which terms are built.

In it, we suppress the mentioning of the underlying language; from now on, some such language $\mathcal{L}$ is thought to be fixed as a parameter throughout the discussion.

**Definition 3.8** If $\mathbf{A}$ is a model and $t$ a ground $A$-term, the following rules determine an element $t^{\mathbf{A}}$ of $A$: the *value* of $t$ *in* $\mathbf{A}$.

(i) If $t = \mathbf{c}$ is a constant symbol of the original language, the value $t^{\mathbf{A}} = c$ is given by the model $\mathbf{A}$.

(ii) If $t = a \in A$ is a new constant symbol, then $t^{\mathbf{A}} = a$, in agreement with Definition 3.7.

(iii) Finally, if $t = \mathbf{f}(t_1, \ldots, t_n)$ is a complex term formed by the $n$-ary function symbol $\mathbf{f}$ and the ground $A$-terms $t_1, \ldots, t_n$ (where the values $t_i^{\mathbf{A}}$ are thought of as determined already), then $t^{\mathbf{A}} = f(t_1^{\mathbf{A}}, \ldots, t_n^{\mathbf{A}})$ ($f$ being the interpretation of $\mathbf{f}$ given by $\mathbf{A}$). ∎

As a particular case, by leaving out part (ii), Definition 3.8 determines the values of ground terms of the original language, before the addition of elements of $A$ as constant symbols has taken place.

By the way, this definition only serves theoretical purposes, and the rules given are used in proofs for general results only. In *concrete* (simple) cases it will always be pretty clear what the value of a certain ground term will be. Much the same goes for the next, even more cumbersome, definition: the *truth definition* for $A$-sentences, which similarly follows the corresponding generating process.

**Definition 3.9** If $\mathbf{A}$ is a model and $\varphi$ is an $A$-sentence, *truth* of $\varphi$ in $\mathbf{A}$ is denoted by: $\mathbf{A} \models \varphi$. This relation is determined by the following rules, which distinguish the form of $\varphi$:

$$\mathbf{A} \models \mathbf{r}(t_1, \ldots, t_n) \iff r(t_1^{\mathbf{A}}, \ldots, t_n^{\mathbf{A}}) \ (r \text{ the } \mathbf{A}\text{-interpretation of } \mathbf{r})$$

$$\mathbf{A} \models s \approx t \iff s^{\mathbf{A}} = t^{\mathbf{A}}$$

$$\mathbf{A} \models \neg\varphi \iff \mathbf{A} \not\models \varphi$$

$$\mathbf{A} \models (\varphi_0 \wedge \cdots \wedge \varphi_{n-1}) \iff \text{for all } i < n, \ \mathbf{A} \models \varphi_i \ (\text{and similarly for } \vee, \rightarrow, \text{ and } \leftrightarrow)$$

$$\mathbf{A} \models \exists x \varphi \iff \text{for some } a \in A, \ \mathbf{A} \models \varphi\{x/a\}$$

$$\mathbf{A} \models \forall x \varphi \iff \text{for every } a \in A, \ \mathbf{A} \models \varphi\{x/a\}.$$

Here, the $A$-*sentence* $\varphi\{x/a\}$ is obtained from the $A$-*formula* $\varphi$ by replacing every *free* occurrence of the variable $x$ by the new constant symbol $a \in A$. ∎

Again, Definition 3.9 determines, as a particular case, the notion of truth-in-a-model for sentences of the old language. But this time, we cannot simply drop some equivalences in order to obtain this particular case. For instance, truth-in-$\mathbf{A}$ of an $\mathcal{L}$-sentence $\forall x \varphi$ is defined in terms of truth-in-$\mathbf{A}$ of all $\mathcal{L}_A$-sentences $\varphi\{x/a\}$ ($a \in A$).

Note that the equivalences pertaining to the connectives precisely say that $\models$ respects the truth tables for $\neg, \wedge, \vee, \ldots$.

The next definition introduces $A$-assignments, which map variables to elements in $A$ and can be used to transform formulas into $\mathcal{L}_A$-sentences.

**Definition 3.10**

   (i) An $A$-*assignment for* a term $t$ resp. a formula $\varphi$ is a function $\alpha$ from variables to elements of $A$, such that $Var(t) \subset Dom(\alpha)$, resp. $Var(\varphi) \subset Dom(\alpha)$.
  (ii) If $\alpha$ is an $A$-assignment and $t$ is a term, then $t\alpha$ is the $A$-term obtained from $t$ by replacing every variable in $Dom(\alpha) \cap Var(t)$ by its $\alpha$-image.
 (iii) If $\alpha$ is an $A$-assignment and $\varphi$ is a formula, then the $A$-formula $\varphi\alpha$ is obtained from $\varphi$ by replacing every *free* occurrence of a variable in $Dom(\alpha) \cap Var(\varphi)$ by its $\alpha$-image. ∎

Thus, if $\alpha(x) = a$ and $\alpha(y) = b$, $a, b \in A$, then $(\mathbf{r}(x){\to}\exists x\mathbf{q}(x,y))\alpha$ is the $A$-sentence $\mathbf{r}(a){\to}\exists x\mathbf{q}(x,b)$. In this context, the following notations (expanding the one used in Definition 3.9) sometimes are useful.

**Notation 3.11** If $x$ is a variable and $a \in A$, then $x/a$ denotes the ordered pair $(x, a)$. Thus, in agreement with the set-theoretic concept of a function as set of pairs, if $x_1, \ldots, x_n$ are different variables and $a_1, \ldots, a_n \in A$, then $\{x_1/a_1, \ldots, x_n/a_n\}$ is the $A$-assignment $\alpha$ with $Dom(\alpha) = \{x_1, \ldots, x_n\}$ such that, for $1 \leq i \leq n$: $\alpha(x_i) = a_i$.
If $Var(t) = \{x_1, \ldots, x_n\}$, then $t$ can be written as $t = t(x_1, \ldots, x_n)$ and $t(a_1, \ldots, a_n)$ then is used to denote $t\{x_1/a_1, \ldots, x_n/a_n\}$. Similarly, if $Var(\varphi) = \{x_1, \ldots, x_n\}$, then $\varphi$ can be written as $\varphi(x_1, \ldots, x_n)$ and $\varphi(a_1, \ldots, a_n)$ is short for $\varphi\{x_1/a_1, \cdots, x_n/a_n\}$. ∎

Satisfiability of $\mathcal{L}$-formulas can now be defined via truth-in-**A** of $\mathcal{L}_A$-sentences.

**Definition 3.12** The $A$-assignment $\alpha$ for the $(A$-$)$ formula $\varphi$ *satisfies* $\varphi$ in the model **A** if $\mathbf{A}{\models}\varphi\alpha$.
A formula is *satisfiable* if it is satisfied in some model by some assignment. ∎

In particular, a sentence is satisfiable if it is true in some model. (A sentence has no free variables to assign values to.) The purpose of much of this chapter consists in explaining a version of resolution adequate with respect to this notion of satisfiability.

Other uses of $\models$ (similar to the situation in propositional logic and not to be confused with each other) are given next.

**Definition 3.13** Let $\varphi$ be a formula, $\Gamma$ a set of formulas, and **A** a model.

   (i) $\varphi$ is *valid* or *true* in **A**, or **A** is a *model of* $\varphi$, notation: $\mathbf{A}{\models}\varphi$, if it is satisfied by every $A$-assignment in **A**,
  (ii) **A** is a model of $\Gamma$, notation: $\mathbf{A}{\models}\Gamma$, if it is a model of every formula in $\Gamma$,
 (iii) $\models\varphi$, $\varphi$ is (logically) *valid*, if $\varphi$ is valid in every model,

(iv) $\Gamma \models \varphi$, $\varphi$ *is a logical consequence of* or *follows logically from* $\Gamma$, if $\varphi$ is valid in every model of $\Gamma$,

(v) $\varphi \sim \psi$, $\varphi$ is *(logically) equivalent with* $\psi$, if $\models (\varphi \leftrightarrow \psi)$.    ∎

The following lemma collects some examples of logical validities and equivalences involving quantifiers.

**Lemma 3.14** *If $\varphi$, $\psi$ and $\varphi_i$ $(i < n)$ are formulas, then:*

(i) $\forall x \forall y \varphi \sim \forall y \forall x \varphi$ ; $\exists x \exists y \varphi \sim \exists y \exists x \varphi$,

(ii) $\models (\exists x \forall y \varphi \rightarrow \forall y \exists x \varphi)$ *(but $\forall y \exists x \varphi \rightarrow \exists x \forall y \varphi$ is not valid)*,

(iii) $\neg \forall x \varphi \sim \exists x \neg \varphi$ ; $\neg \exists x \varphi \sim \forall x \neg \varphi$,

(iv) *if $x$ is not free in $\varphi$, then $\forall x \varphi \sim \exists x \varphi \sim \varphi$,*

(v) $\forall x(\varphi_0 \wedge \cdots \wedge \varphi_{n-1}) \sim (\forall x \varphi_0 \wedge \cdots \wedge \forall x \varphi_{n-1})$ ;
$\exists x(\varphi_0 \vee \cdots \vee \varphi_{n-1}) \sim (\exists x \varphi_0 \vee \cdots \vee \exists x \varphi_{n-1})$,

(vi) $\models [\forall x(\varphi \rightarrow \psi) \rightarrow (\forall x \varphi \rightarrow \forall x \psi)]$ ; $\models [\forall x(\varphi \rightarrow \psi) \rightarrow (\exists x \varphi \rightarrow \exists x \psi)]$,

(vii) $\models [\forall x(\varphi \leftrightarrow \psi) \rightarrow (\forall x \varphi \leftrightarrow \forall x \psi)]$ ; $\models [\forall x(\varphi \leftrightarrow \psi) \rightarrow (\exists x \varphi \leftrightarrow \exists x \psi)]$.

**Proof.** See Exercise 3.2.    ∎

**Exercises**

**3.2** Give a proof of Lemma 3.14 based on Definition 3.9. (If you find this convenient, assume that $\varphi$, $\psi$ and $\varphi_i$ are atomic.)

**3.3** Prove: if $\varphi$ is a *sentence* and **A** a model, then we have: $\mathbf{A} \models \neg \varphi$ iff $\mathbf{A} \not\models \varphi$.
Give a simple example of a formula for which this equivalence fails.

**3.4** (Compare Exercise 2.4.) Show: a formula is unsatisfiable iff its negation is logically valid.

**3.5** Determine which of the following sentences are logically valid and which are unsatisfiable. Note that a sentence may be either valid, unsatisfiable, or neither.

(i) $\forall x \forall y(\mathbf{p}x \vee \mathbf{q}y) \vee \exists x \exists y(\neg \mathbf{p}x \wedge \neg \mathbf{q}y)$,

(ii) $\neg \exists x \exists y \mathbf{p}xy \vee \exists x \mathbf{p}xx$,

(iii) $\exists x \exists y \mathbf{p}xy \vee \neg \exists x \mathbf{p}xx$,

(iv) $\forall x \forall y(\mathbf{p}xy \vee \neg \mathbf{p}yx)$,

(v) $\forall x \mathbf{p}xx \rightarrow \exists x \forall y(\mathbf{p}xy \rightarrow \mathbf{p}yx)$,

(vi) $\forall x \mathbf{p}xx \rightarrow \forall y \exists x(\mathbf{p}xy \rightarrow \mathbf{p}yx)$,

(vii) $\exists x \forall y(\mathbf{p}xy \leftrightarrow \neg \mathbf{p}yy)$ (compare the Russell paradox),

(viii) $\exists x \forall y(\mathbf{r}xy \leftrightarrow \neg \exists z(\mathbf{r}yz \wedge \mathbf{r}zy))$ (cf. Example 3.40).

For the case of partial orderings, the notion of isomorphism was introduced by Definition 1.16. Here follows the notion for models generally.

**Definition 3.15** A bijection $h : A \to B$ is an *isomorphism* between the $\mathcal{L}$-models **A** and **B** if

(i) for every $\mathcal{L}$-relation symbol **r** and $a_1, \ldots, a_n \in A$:
$\mathbf{r^A}(a_1, \ldots, a_n) \Leftrightarrow \mathbf{r^B}(h(a_1), \ldots, h(a_n))$
($\mathbf{r^A}$ and $\mathbf{r^B}$ the interpretations of **r** in **A** resp. **B**),

(ii) for every $\mathcal{L}$-function symbol **f** and $a_1, \ldots, a_n \in A$:
$h(\mathbf{f^A}(a_1, \ldots, a_n)) = \mathbf{f^B}(h(a_1), \ldots, h(a_n))$
($\mathbf{f^A}$ and $\mathbf{f^B}$ the interpretations of **f** in **A** resp. **B**),

(iii) for every $\mathcal{L}$-constant symbol **c**: $h(\mathbf{c^A}) = \mathbf{c^B}$
($\mathbf{c^A}$ and $\mathbf{c^B}$ the interpretations of **c** in **A** resp. **B**).

Models **A** and **B** are *isomorphic*, notation: $\mathbf{A} \cong \mathbf{B}$, if there is an isomomorphism between them.                                                                                                    ∎

The following exercise shows that isomorphic models are first-order indistinguishable.

**3.6** Suppose that $h$ is an isomorphism between **A** and **B**. Show that for every term $t = t(x_1, \ldots, x_n)$, for every formula $\varphi = \varphi(x_1, \ldots, x_n)$, all $a_1, \ldots, a_n \in A$ and every sentence $\psi$:

(i) $h(t^{\mathbf{A}}[a_1, \ldots, a_n]) = t^{\mathbf{B}}[h(a_1), \ldots, h(a_n)]$,

(ii) $\mathbf{A} \models \varphi[a_1, \ldots, a_n] \Leftrightarrow \mathbf{B} \models \varphi[h(a_1), \ldots, h(a_n)]$,

(iii) $\mathbf{A} \models \psi \Leftrightarrow \mathbf{B} \models \psi$.

*Hint.* For (i), use term induction, for (ii) formula induction. (iii) is a special case of (ii).

## 3.4   Quantifier-free Sentences

As usual, let a language $\mathcal{L}$, that is, a collection of non-logical symbols, be fixed. Recall (Definitions 3.3 and 3.5) that a *ground term* has no variables and a *ground sentence* has neither variables nor quantifiers. We can view first-order logic as an applied propositional logic by letting the ground atoms of $\mathcal{L}$ play the role of propositional variables. In order that at least some ground atom is present, we have to make the assumption that $\mathcal{L}$ contains at least one relation symbol and at least one constant symbol.

Now, under the identification:

$$\text{propositional variables} = \text{ground atoms}$$

the *propositional formulas* clearly coincide with the *ground sentences*.

From this point of view, every ground sentence can be interpreted in *two* ways:

(i) as a sentence in first-order logic, in a *model*,

(ii) as a formula in propositional logic, using a *truth assignment* for its ground atoms.

Lemma 3.16 makes evident that the difference between these two interpretations is negligable. The proof of this lemma is not difficult, though it may be surprising when seen for the first time. It introduces the notion of a *Herbrand model*. This is a (simple) type of model that will be quite prominent in what follows, and therefore the proof deserves thorough attention.

**Lemma 3.16** *Let $\mathcal{L}$ be a language containing at least one constant symbol. Assume that $\Sigma$ is a set of ground sentences. The following are equivalent.*

*(i) $\Sigma$ is satisfiable in the sense of first-order logic (i.e., by a model),*

*(ii) $\Sigma$ is satisfiable in the sense of propositional logic (i.e., by a truth assignment).*

**Proof.** (i)$\Rightarrow$(ii) Assume that $\mathbf{A}$ is a model in which all sentences of $\Sigma$ are valid. Define the truth assignment $\gamma$ on ground atoms $\varphi$ by: $\gamma(\varphi) = \mathbf{t}$ iff $\mathbf{A}\models\varphi$. Using formula induction (Exercise 3.1), we show that for every ground sentence $\varphi$: $\gamma\models\varphi \Leftrightarrow \mathbf{A}\models\varphi$.

0. $\varphi$ is a ground atom. Then the conditions $\gamma\models\varphi$ and $\gamma(\varphi) = \mathbf{t}$ are synonymous, and the equivalence holds by definition of $\gamma$.

1. $\varphi$ is $\neg\psi$. Then by induction hypothesis we have that $\gamma\models\psi \Leftrightarrow \mathbf{A}\models\psi$. But then: $\gamma\models\varphi$

      iff: $\gamma \models \neg\psi$ (since $\varphi = \neg\psi$)

      iff: $\gamma \not\models \psi$ (by truth tables)

      iff: $\mathbf{A} \not\models \psi$ (by induction hypothesis)

      iff: $\mathbf{A}\models\neg\psi$ (by Definition 3.9)

      iff: $\mathbf{A}\models\varphi$ (again since $\varphi = \neg\psi$).

2. $\varphi$ is $(\varphi_0 \wedge \cdots \wedge \varphi_{k-1})$. Then by induction hypothesis the equivalence holds for all $\varphi_i$ and the result again follows by truth tables and Definition 3.9.

3. Other connectives: similarly.

(ii)$\Rightarrow$(i) Now assume that we have a truth assignment $\gamma$ for ground atoms satisfying all sentences in $\Sigma$. We produce a model $\mathbf{A}$ as follows. The universe $A$ of $\mathbf{A}$ consists of all ground terms. Note that $A \neq \emptyset$, since the language contains constant symbols by assumption, and constant symbols are examples of ground terms. We next define interpretations $\sigma$ for the non-logical symbols $\boldsymbol{\sigma}$ occurring in the sentences in $\Sigma$. For constant and function symbols, we use the *canonical* interpretation, explained now under 1 and 2.

1. CONSTANT SYMBOLS

For a constant symbol $\mathbf{c}$ we put $c := \mathbf{c}$; the interpretation of $\mathbf{c}$ is the symbol $\mathbf{c}$ itself.

2. FUNCTION SYMBOLS

For an $n$-ary function symbol $\mathbf{f}$ we define the $n$-ary function $f$ over $A$ by $f(t_1, \ldots, t_n) := \mathbf{f}(t_1, \ldots, t_n)$.

**Note.** At the *left-hand side* of this defining equation, the *function* $f$ is applied to the arguments $t_1, \ldots, t_n$ from $A$; at the *right-hand side* of the equation the ground term $\mathbf{f}(t_1, \ldots, t_n)$ is formed out of the function symbol $\mathbf{f}$ and these terms.

We still have to give interpretations for the relation symbols involved. However, we already can calculate the values of ground terms in our model. The following lemma says that the answer is rather simple: the value of a ground term is the term itself.

**Lemma 3.17** *For ground terms $t$ we have: $t^{\mathbf{A}} = t$.*

**Proof.** Term induction 3.2.
$t$ is a constant symbol $\mathbf{c}$. But then $\mathbf{c}^{\mathbf{A}} = \mathbf{c}$ by definition.
$t = \mathbf{f}(t_1, \ldots, t_n)$, where $\mathbf{f}$ is a $n$-ary function symbol and $t_1, \ldots, t_n$ are ground terms. By induction hypothesis, for $1 \leq i \leq n$ we have: $t_i^{\mathbf{A}} = t_i$. But then
$t^{\mathbf{A}} = (\mathbf{f}(t_1, \ldots, t_n))^{\mathbf{A}} = f(t_1^{\mathbf{A}}, \ldots, t_n^{\mathbf{A}})$   by Definition 3.8
$\quad = f(t_1, \ldots, t_n)$   by induction hypothesis
$\quad = \mathbf{f}(t_1, \ldots, t_n) = t$   by definition of the function $f$. ∎

**Definition 3.18** The *Herbrand universe* (relative to a given language) is the set of all ground terms. Notation: $HU$.
A *Herbrand model* is a model that has $HU$ as its universe, whereas the interpretation of constant and function symbols is canonical. (But the interpretation of relation symbols can be just anything.) ∎

So apparently we are involved in the construction of a Herbrand model, since $A = HU$. We complete the definition of $\mathbf{A}$ by giving interpretations for the relation symbols. This is the place where we use the truth assignment $\gamma$.

3. RELATION SYMBOLS
If $\mathbf{r}$ is an $n$-ary relation symbol, then its interpretation, the $n$-ary relation $r$, is defined by:
$$r(t_1, \ldots, t_n) :\equiv \gamma(\mathbf{r}(t_1, \ldots, t_n)) = \mathbf{t}.$$
In other words, we let $r(t_1, \ldots, t_n)$ be true just in case $\gamma$ assigns $\mathbf{t}$ to the atom $\mathbf{r}(t_1, \ldots, t_n)$.

The definition of the model $\mathbf{A}$ is complete.
In order that $\mathbf{A} \models \Sigma$, it again suffices to establish the following equivalence for all ground formulas $\varphi$:
$$\mathbf{A} \models \varphi \Leftrightarrow \gamma \models \varphi,$$
since $\gamma \models \Sigma$ by hypothesis. Again, this is done using formula induction.

For atoms $\mathbf{r}(t_1, \ldots, t_n)$ this is seen as follows:

$$
\begin{aligned}
\mathbf{A} \models \mathbf{r}(t_1, \ldots, t_n) &\iff r(t_1^{\mathbf{A}}, \ldots, t_n^{\mathbf{A}}) && \text{by Definition 3.9} \\
&\iff r(t_1, \ldots, t_n) && \text{by Lemma 3.17} \\
&\iff \gamma(\mathbf{r}(t_1, \ldots, t_n)) = \mathbf{t} && \text{by definition of } r \\
&\iff \gamma \models \mathbf{r}(t_1, \ldots, t_n) && \text{synonymous with the previous.}
\end{aligned}
$$

The induction steps for the connectives are trivial as before.

This finally ends the proof of Lemma 3.16. ∎

**Example.** $\Sigma = \{\mathbf{r}(\mathbf{c}) \wedge (\mathbf{r}(\mathbf{d}) \rightarrow \mathbf{r}(\mathbf{c}))\}$ is satisfied by the truth assignment that maps $\mathbf{r}(\mathbf{c})$ to $\mathbf{t}$ and $\mathbf{r}(\mathbf{d})$ to $\mathbf{f}$. The corresponding Herbrand model has universe $\{\mathbf{c}, \mathbf{d}\}$, and the interpretation of the unary relation symbol $\mathbf{r}$ is the set $r = \{\mathbf{c}\}$. ∎

We close this section with some elaborations on the notion of a Herbrand model.

**Definition 3.19** A language is *algebraic* if it does not contain relation symbols. A model for an algebraic language is called an *algebra*.

The *algebraic part* of a language is its subset of function and constant symbols.

The *Herbrand algebra $HA$* (relative to the language given) is the part common to all Herbrand models: it is the model for the algebraic part of the language whose universe is $HU$ and that only interprets the function and constant symbols of the language in the canonical way previously explained. ∎

If the language does not contain function symbols, then the Herbrand universe $HU$ coincides with the set of constant symbols. In the simplest non-trivial case, $HU$ is generated from just one individual constant, say $\mathbf{o}$, by means of just one unary function symbol, say $\mathbf{s}$.

**Notation 3.20** In this situation, we identify the ground term

$$
\underbrace{\mathbf{s}(\ldots \mathbf{s}(\mathbf{o}) \ldots)}_{n}
$$

that has $n$ occurrences of $\mathbf{s}$ with the number $n \in \mathbb{N}$. By this identification, $HU = \mathbb{N}$. Thus, the constant symbol $\mathbf{o}$ is interpreted as the number 0, and $\mathbf{s}$ is interpreted as the successor function $S$, which sends a number $n \in \mathbb{N}$ to its immediate successor $S(n) := n + 1$. ∎

Though Herbrand models are quite special, it is in the nature of our subject that we shall be dealing with them most of the time, and only now and then with more general types of models. There are *two* ways in which Herbrand models deviate from arbitrary ones. Consider the $\mathbf{o}, \mathbf{s}$-case. Here, every Herbrand model is infinite, since it has $\mathbb{N}$ as its universe. However, an arbitrary model for this language may very well be finite. For instance, consider the algebra $Mod(3)$ over the set $\{0, 1, 2\}$, interpreting **o** again as 0, but interpreting **s** by the function $s$ defined by $s(0) = 1$, $s(1) = 2$, and $s(2) = 0$. So, one difference between a Herbrand model and an arbitrary one is that, in Herbrand models, different ground terms are always evaluated differently.

There are also models for this language that *extend* the Herbrand interpretation. For instance, the algebra $\mathbb{N} + Mod(3)$, with universe $\mathbb{N} \cup \{0', 1', 2'\}$, the constant **o** still interpreted as the number 0, whereas **s** is interpreted as successor on $\mathbb{N}$ and acts on $\{0', 1', 2'\}$ as it does on $Mod(3)$. Another possibility is the set $\mathbb{Z}$ of all integers, **o** still interpreted as 0 and **s** as successor. Still another one is the algebra with universe the set $TM$ of *all* terms (variables allowed), which interprets function and constant symbols canonically. And of course, there are endless variations and combinations. Thus, a second difference between a Herbrand model and an arbitrary one is that its universe exactly consists of the (interpretations of) ground terms.

**Remark 3.21** A more abstract but essentially equivalent notion of a Herbrand model **A** is obtained by requiring that the term-evaluation mapping $t \mapsto t^{\mathbf{A}}$ from $HU$ to $A$ is a bijection: injective (different ground terms evaluated differently) and surjective (every element value of a ground term). ∎

Obviously, we can add another one to the equivalents of Lemma 3.16:

**Lemma 3.22** *Assume that $\Sigma$ is a set of ground sentences. The following are equivalent:*

*(i) $\Sigma$ has a model,*

*(ii) $\Sigma$ has a Herbrand model,*

*(iii) $\Sigma$ is satisfiable in the sense of propositional logic.*

**Proof.** The implication (i) $\Rightarrow$ (iii) is given by Lemma 3.16, and (iii) $\Rightarrow$ (ii) was in fact established by the proof of that lemma. That (ii) $\Rightarrow$ (i) is evident. ∎

### Exercises

**3.7** The Herbrand algebra for $\{\mathbf{o}, \mathbf{s}\}$ satisfies the following *free equality axioms*:

(i) $\mathbf{s}x \approx \mathbf{s}y \rightarrow x \approx y$

(ii) $\mathbf{o} \not\approx \mathbf{s}x$

(iii) $x \not\approx \mathbf{s}x$, $x \not\approx \mathbf{s}\mathbf{s}x$, $x \not\approx \mathbf{s}\mathbf{s}\mathbf{s}x$, ...

(iv) $x \approx \mathbf{o} \vee \exists y (x \approx \mathbf{s}y)$.

Check which of these axioms are true in the algebras previously described ($Mod(3)$, $\mathbb{N} + Mod(3)$, the integers $\mathbb{Z}$, the algebra $\mathbb{N} + \mathbb{Z}$ (see Example 6.4) consisting of $\mathbb{N}$ plus a disjoint copy of the integers, the canonical algebra based on the set of all terms $TM$). Produce an algebra in which (ii) and (iii) hold but (i) and (iv) don't.

**3.8** Let $\varphi$ be a ground sentence. Show that the following are equivalent.

  (i) $\varphi$ is logically valid in the sense of first-order logic,
 (ii) $\varphi$ is true in every Herbrand model,
(iii) $\varphi$ is logically valid in the sense of propositional logic.

*Hint.* Use Exercise 3.4.

**3.9** Note that, under the identification: propositional variables = atomic formulas, the propositional formulas coincide with the quantifier-free formulas. Now, assume that $\Sigma$ is a set of quantifier-free formulas (free variables are allowed). Show that the following are equivalent: 1. $\Sigma$ is satisfiable in the sense of first-order logic (i.e., for some model $\mathbf{A}$ and some $A$-assignment $\alpha$, we have $\mathbf{A} \models \varphi\alpha$ for all $\varphi \in \Sigma$); 2. $\Sigma$ is satisfiable in the sense of propositional logic (i.e., by a truth assignment for *atomic formulas*).

*Hint.* Modify the proof of Lemma 3.16. For $2 \Rightarrow 1$, consider the canonical algebra over the set of all terms $TM$ and let $\alpha$ be the identity assignment.

## 3.5   Universal Sentences

The result of the previous section can be pushed a little further. For this, we must know something about *substitutions* and their effect on values of terms and satisfaction of formulas first. Compare Definition 3.10 and Notation 3.11: a substitution in fact is an assignment into the set of all terms.

**Definition 3.23** A *substitution* is a function $\theta$ from all variables to terms, such that its *domain* $Dom(\theta) := \{x \mid x \neq \theta(x)\}$ is *finite*.

In the context of substitutions, it is common to use a *postfix*-notation: $x\theta := \theta(x)$.

If $x$ is a variable and $t$ a term, then $x/t$ (a *binding* of $x$) denotes the ordered pair $(x,t)$. Thus, $\{x_1/t_1, \ldots, x_n/t_n\}$, where $x_1, \ldots, x_n$ are pairwise different variables, is the substitution that has $\{x_1, \ldots, x_n\}$ (more precisely: $\{x_i \mid x_i \neq t_i\}$) as its domain and, for $1 \leq i \leq n$, assigns the term $t_i$ to the variable $x_i$.

If $t$ is a term and $\theta$ is a substitution, then $t\theta$ (the *$\theta$-instance* of $t$) is the term obtained from $t$ by replacing every occurrence of a variable $x \in Var(t)$ by its $\theta$-image $x\theta$. And if $\varphi$ is a formula, then the formula $\varphi\theta$ (the *$\theta$-instance* of $\varphi$) is obtained from $\varphi$ by replacing every *free* occurrence of a variable $x \in Var(\varphi)$ by its $\theta$-image.

$\theta$ is called *ground for* the expression $E$ if $x\theta$ is ground for every $x \in Var(E)$. $\theta$ is *ground* if $x\theta$ is a ground term for every $x \in Dom(\theta)$. ∎

For the moment, this definition suffices. Later on, in Section 3.8, more will come.

**Notation.** Compare Notation 3.11. If $E = E(x_1, \ldots, x_n)$ is a term or a formula and $\theta = \{x_1/t_1, \ldots, x_n/t_n\}$, then we write $E(t_1, \ldots, t_n)$ as short for $E\theta$. ∎

We need some technical (though rather evident) results about the relationship between the interpretation of an expression and its instances.

**Lemma 3.24** *Assume that $\theta$ is a ground substitution, that $\mathbf{A}$ is a model and $\alpha$ is the $\mathbf{A}$-assignment defined on $Dom(\theta)$ by: $\alpha(x) = (x\theta)^{\mathbf{A}}$. Then*

*(i) if $\theta$ is ground for the term $t$, then: $(t\theta)^{\mathbf{A}} = (t\alpha)^{\mathbf{A}}$,*

*(ii) if $\theta$ is ground for the quantifier-free formula $\varphi$, then: $\mathbf{A} \models \varphi\theta \iff \mathbf{A} \models \varphi\alpha$.*

To appreciate this lemma, note the difference between $t\theta$ and $\varphi\theta$ on the one hand, and $t\alpha$ and $\varphi\alpha$ on the other: e.g., $t\theta$ can be very complicated compared to $t$, since application of $\theta$ may substitute complicated terms for variables in $t$; however, $t\alpha$ has the "same degree" of complexity as $t$ since now only (new) constant symbols are being substituted. Of course, since $\alpha(x) = (x\theta)^{\mathbf{A}}$, the constant substituted by $\alpha$ for $x$ has the same value as the term substituted by $\theta$, and this intuitively explains why the lemma is true. The calculations of the values of $t\theta$ and $t\alpha$, according to the rules of Definition 3.8, parallel each other until terms $x\theta$ resp. $x\alpha$ are reached, which have the same value anyway. Something similar can be said about ascertaining truth of $\varphi\theta$ and $\varphi\alpha$ in $\mathbf{A}$ using the rules of Definition 3.9.

**Proof.** (i) Induction on $t$.

1. $t$ is the variable $x$. Then $(x\theta)^{\mathbf{A}} = \alpha(x) = (x\alpha)^{\mathbf{A}}$.

2. $t$ is the constant symbol $\mathbf{c}$. Then $(\mathbf{c}\theta)^{\mathbf{A}} = \mathbf{c}^{\mathbf{A}} = (\mathbf{c}\alpha)^{\mathbf{A}}$.

3. $t = \mathbf{f}(t_1, \ldots, t_n)$. By inductive hypothesis, for $1 \leq i \leq n$ we have $(t_1\theta)^{\mathbf{A}} = (t_1\alpha)^{\mathbf{A}}$. Now: $(t\theta)^{\mathbf{A}} = (\mathbf{f}(t_1\theta, \ldots, t_n\theta))^{\mathbf{A}} = f((t_1\theta)^{\mathbf{A}}, \ldots, (t_n\theta)^{\mathbf{A}}) = f((t_1\alpha)^{\mathbf{A}}, \ldots, (t_n\alpha)^{\mathbf{A}}) = \mathbf{f}(t_1\alpha, \ldots, t_n\alpha)^{\mathbf{A}} = (\mathbf{f}(t_1, \ldots, t_n)\alpha)^{\mathbf{A}} = (t\alpha)^{\mathbf{A}}$.

(ii) Induction on $\varphi$. For $\varphi$ an atom $\mathbf{r}(t_1, \ldots, t_n)$ we have, using (i):

$$
\begin{aligned}
\mathbf{A} \models \mathbf{r}(t_1, \ldots, t_n)\theta \quad &\Leftrightarrow \quad \mathbf{A} \models \mathbf{r}(t_1\theta, \ldots, t_n\theta) \\
&\Leftrightarrow \quad r((t_1\theta)^{\mathbf{A}}, \ldots, (t_n\theta)^{\mathbf{A}}) \\
&\Leftrightarrow \quad r((t_1\alpha)^{\mathbf{A}}, \ldots, (t_n\alpha)^{\mathbf{A}}) \\
&\Leftrightarrow \quad \mathbf{A} \models \mathbf{r}(t_1\alpha, \ldots, t_n\alpha) \\
&\Leftrightarrow \quad \mathbf{A} \models \mathbf{r}(t_1, \ldots, t_n)\alpha.
\end{aligned}
$$

The induction steps corresponding to the connectives are all straightforward. ∎

**Remark.** Assume that the model $\mathbf{A}$ considered in Lemma 3.24(ii) is Herbrand. By Lemma 3.17 we then have, for $x \in Dom(\theta)$, $\alpha(x) = (x\theta)^{\mathbf{A}} = x\theta = \theta(x)$; i.e.: $\alpha = \theta$. The equality $(t\theta)^{\mathbf{A}} = (t\alpha)^{\mathbf{A}}$ and the equivalence $\mathbf{A} \models \varphi\theta \Leftrightarrow \mathbf{A} \models \varphi\alpha$ apparently reduce to trivialities. However, as just remarked, the terms and formulas here must be conceived of differently. That, in a Herbrand model, one simple constant symbol $\alpha(x)$ can actually be a composite must be considered a coincidence connected with the particular way in which the notion of Herbrand model is defined. The confusion would disappear when using Herbrand models as suggested by Remark 3.21.                                     ∎

The following definition introduces the objects of interest of this section.

**Definition 3.25** If $\varphi$ is a formula with $Var(\varphi) = \{x_1, \ldots, x_n\}$, then $\forall\varphi$ denotes the *(universal) closure* $\forall x_1 \cdots \forall x_n \varphi$ of $\varphi$ and $\exists\varphi$ the *existential closure* $\exists x_1 \cdots \exists x_n \varphi$, $\forall$ here being short for the sequence $\forall x_1 \cdots \forall x_n$ and $\exists$ as short for $\exists x_1 \cdots \exists x_n$.
A sentence $\forall x_1 \cdots \forall x_n \varphi$ (resp., $\exists x_1 \cdots \exists x_n \varphi$) is called *universal* (resp. *existential*) if $\varphi$ is quantifier-free. In that case, $\forall x_1 \cdots \forall x_n$ (resp. $\exists x_1 \cdots \exists x_n$) is called the *prefix* and $\varphi$ the *matrix* of $\forall\varphi$ ($\exists\varphi$).                                                             ∎

**Remark 3.26** A universal sentence will often be confused with its matrix. The justification for this is that they both have the same models. For, the universal closure $\forall\varphi$ is true in a model **A** iff (by Definition 3.9) for all $A$-assignments $\alpha$ for $\varphi$ we have $\mathbf{A}\models\varphi\alpha$ iff (by Definition 3.13(i)) $\varphi$ is true in **A**.                                               ∎

Part (i) of the next result forms the logical explanation of arguments like: if everyone is mortal, then so is Socrates. As to part (ii), witnessing Socrates die, we are entitled to the conclusion that someone is mortal.

**Corollary 3.27** *Suppose that $\varphi$ is a quantifier-free formula and $\theta$ a substitution that is ground for $\varphi$. Then*

*(i) $\forall\varphi\models\varphi\theta$,*
*(ii) $\varphi\theta\models\exists\varphi$.*

**Proof.** (i) Suppose that $\mathbf{A}\models\forall\varphi$. That is, by Remark 3.26: for every $A$-assignment $\alpha$ for $\varphi$ we have $\mathbf{A}\models\varphi\alpha$. In particular, this must be true for the assignment $\alpha$ defined by $\alpha(x) := (x\theta)^{\mathbf{A}}$. Apply Lemma 3.24. (ii) Similarly.                                  ∎

In a later section, we shall need to generalize these results slightly.

**Definition 3.28** If $\varphi$ is a quantifier-free formula, then both $ground(\varphi)$ and $ground(\forall\varphi)$ denote the set of all ground instances of $\varphi$ (all *sentences* of the form $\varphi\theta$). ($ground(\varphi)$ also is called the *Skolem expansion* of $\varphi$.)
If $P$ is a set of quantifier-free formulas and/or universal sentences, then $ground(P)$ denotes the union of all sets $ground(\varphi)$ for $\varphi \in P$.                                        ∎

The following is a satisfiability criterion for sets of universal sentences.

**Theorem 3.29 (Herbrand)** *Suppose that $P$ is a set of universal sentences. The following are equivalent.*

    *(i) $P$ has a model,*

    *(ii) $P$ has a Herbrand model,*

    *(iii) $ground(P)$ is satisfiable.*

**Note.** By Lemma 3.16 or Lemma 3.22, it makes no difference whether we interpret *satisfiability* in (iii) either in propositional or in first-order logic.

**Proof.** (ii) $\Rightarrow$ (i). This is evident.

(i) $\Rightarrow$ (iii). By Corollary 3.27, every sentence in $ground(P)$ follows logically from $P$. That is, every model of $P$ is a model of $ground(P)$ as well.

(iii) $\Rightarrow$ (ii). Assume that $ground(P)$ is satisfiable. By Lemma 3.22, there exists a Herbrand model **A** for $ground(P)$.

*Claim:* **A** also is a model for $P$!

This is an immediate consequence of the fact that, in a Herbrand model, *every element is the value of a ground term* (by Lemma 3.17, an element $t \in HU$ is the value of $t$ itself) and half of the following Lemma 3.30.    ∎

**Lemma 3.30** *Suppose that* **A** *is a model with the property that*

    *every element $a \in A$ is the value of a ground term: $A = \{t^{\mathbf{A}} \mid t \in HU\}$.*

*If $\varphi$ is a quantifier-free formula, then* $\mathbf{A} \models \forall \varphi$ *iff* **A** *is a model of $ground(\varphi)$.*

**Proof.** Corollary 3.27 is responsible for the trivial half. Now, assume that $\mathbf{A} \models ground(\varphi)$, where $Var(\varphi) = \{x_1, \ldots, x_n\}$. By Remark 3.26, we have to show that $\mathbf{A} \models \varphi \alpha$ for an arbitrary $A$-assignment $\alpha = \{x_1/a_1, \ldots x_n/a_n\}$ for $\varphi$. For $1 \leq i \leq n$, choose a ground term $t_i$ such that $t_i^{\mathbf{A}} = a_i$. Let $\theta$ be the substitution $\theta = \{x_1/t_1, \ldots x_n/t_n\}$. $\theta$ is ground for $\varphi$. By hypothesis, $\mathbf{A} \models \varphi \theta$. By Lemma 3.24, $\mathbf{A} \models \varphi \alpha$.    ∎

**Example.** Consider the universal sentence $\forall x [\mathbf{r}(\mathbf{so}) \wedge (\mathbf{r}(x) \rightarrow \mathbf{r}(\mathbf{ss}x))]$. The elements $0 = \mathbf{o}$, $1 = \mathbf{so}$, $2 = \mathbf{sso}$, $3 = \mathbf{ssso}$, ... form the universe $\mathbb{N}$ of the Herbrand model. Taking the set $r := \{1, 3, 5, \ldots\}$ as interpretation of the relation symbol $\mathbf{r}$ over this universe, the result is a Herband model for it. Another one is obtained by letting $r$ be $\mathbb{N}^+$. Try to find two more Herbrand models for this sentence.    ∎

**Example.** Suppose that $\mathbf{c}$ is a constant symbol and $\mathbf{r}$ a 1-ary relation symbol. Every Herbrand model for this language has but one element: $\mathbf{c}$. A model of the (satisfiable) sentence $\mathbf{r}(\mathbf{c}) \wedge \exists x \neg \mathbf{r}(x)$ must have at least two elements; and so there is no Herbrand model for this sentence (suited to its own language). This sentence is not universal. Thus, it is not true that every satisfiable sentence has a Herbrand model corresponding to *its own* language.    ∎

By the Conjunctive Normal Form Theorem 2.9 (which of course holds in the extended context of first-order logic for quantifier-free formulas), we always can transform the matrix $\varphi$ of a universal sentence into conjunctive normal form. Satisfiability of $ground(\varphi)$ (and hence, by Theorem 3.29, of $\forall\varphi$) can then be tested using the concept of resolution from the previous chapter. Letting ground atoms take over the role of propositional variables, we consider clauses made up of ground atoms and their negations and try to derive the empty clause $\square$.

**Example 3.31** Look at the following universal sentence. $\mathbf{r}$ is a binary relation symbol, $\mathbf{c}$ is a constant symbol and $\mathbf{f}$ is a 1-ary function symbol.

$$\forall y \forall w \, [(\neg\mathbf{r}(\mathbf{c},y) \vee \neg\mathbf{r}(y,w) \vee \neg\mathbf{r}(w.y)) \wedge (\mathbf{r}(\mathbf{c},y) \vee \mathbf{r}(y,\mathbf{f}y)) \wedge (\mathbf{r}(\mathbf{c},y) \vee \mathbf{r}(\mathbf{f}y,y))].$$

Using the ground substitution $\{y/\mathbf{c}, w/\mathbf{c}\}$ the first conjunct of the matrix produces the clause $\{\neg\mathbf{r}(\mathbf{c},\mathbf{c})\}$ (the three disjuncts all produce the same instance), the second conjunct is responsible for $\{\mathbf{r}(\mathbf{c},\mathbf{c}), \mathbf{r}(\mathbf{c},\mathbf{fc}))\}$, and the third one makes $\{\mathbf{r}(\mathbf{c},\mathbf{c}), \mathbf{r}(\mathbf{fc},\mathbf{c})\}$. The first two have a resolvent $\{\mathbf{r}(\mathbf{c},\mathbf{fc})\}$, the first and third produce $\{\mathbf{r}(\mathbf{fc},\mathbf{c})\}$. Next we use the ground substitution $\{y/\mathbf{fc}, w/\mathbf{c}\}$; under it, the first conjunct produces the clause $\{\neg\mathbf{r}(\mathbf{c},\mathbf{fc}), \neg\mathbf{r}(\mathbf{fc},\mathbf{c})\}$ (first and third disjunct producing the same instance). Together with the clauses derived previously, we reach the empty clause $\square$ in two more propositional resolution steps. ∎

**Discussion.**
Suppose that a matrix (a quantifier-free formula) $\varphi$ in conjunctive normal form is given. If $ground(\varphi)$ is not satisfiable, then $\square$ can be derived using propositional resolution from the set of clauses that are, in fact, nothing else but conjuncts of sentences in $ground(\varphi)$. Such a refutation consists of finitely many clauses, and so it can use only finitely many clauses corresponding to conjuncts of sentences in $ground(\varphi)$. These finitely many clauses, in turn, can have used only finitely many ground terms as replacements of occurring variables.

In Example 3.31, we used only *two* ground terms in the derivation of $\square$: $\mathbf{c}$ en $\mathbf{fc}$.

If the matrix $\varphi$ has no function symbols, then constant symbols are the only ground terms, and of these, only finitely many can occur in the matrix. Then $ground(\varphi)$ is finite; the number of clauses that resolution is able to produce is finite too. In such a case, resolution is a test for satisfiability as well; just produce all resolvents possible, there is an end to this (and it is clear when that stage has been reached). If $\square$ is one of the clauses produced, then the original sentence is unsatisfiable, and if not, it is satisfiable. The situation is completely similar to the one of propositional resolution, cf. Exercise 2.25.

However, if the matrix contains but one function symbol, then infinitely many ground terms are generated, infinitely many ground substitutions are possible, and a problem arises: which do you need to derive □?

In case the original universal sentence happens to be unsatisfiable, and the search has been systematic, not skipping any ground substitution, then □ *has to* be derived at some time or other. But in the case of a satisfiable sentence, the search will go on for ever. You may try more and more complex ground substitutions without □ ever being derived. Still worse, you may not even notice that your search is in vain.

So, resolution here usually only produces *half* of what we would like: it will always signalize unsatisfiability, but often, satisfiability is not signalized. This is called *positive decidability* of unsatisfiability of universal formulas. According to the Theorem of Church 7.19 (and the existence of Skolem transforms, Theorem 3.34), this cannot be remedied. Nevertheless, in a sense there is an answer to the problem of which instances are needed to derive □. This is given by the notion of resolution for first-order logic, dealt with in the last section of this chapter.

**Exercises**

**3.10** The universal sentence

$$\forall x[\mathbf{r}(\mathbf{c}) \wedge \neg\mathbf{r}(\mathbf{fc}) \wedge \mathbf{r}(\mathbf{fffc}) \wedge (\mathbf{r}(x) \vee \neg\mathbf{r}(\mathbf{fff}x)) \wedge (\neg\mathbf{r}(x) \vee \mathbf{r}(\mathbf{ff}x))]$$

is unsatisfiable. Give a set of ground clauses, instances of conjuncts of the matrix, from which □ may be derived.

**\*3.11** Let $\varphi$ be a quantifier-free formula. Show that the following are equivalent.

  (i)  $\models \exists \varphi$,
  (ii) there are finitely many substitutions $\theta_0, \ldots, \theta_{k-1}$ ground for $\varphi$ such that
      $\models \varphi\theta_0 \vee \cdots \vee \varphi\theta_{k-1}$.

Give an example which shows that in (ii) we can not always have $k = 1$.
*Hint.* Use Theorem 3.29 and the Compactness Theorem 2.22 of propositional logic.

## 3.6   Prenex and Skolem Forms

The previous section established positive decidability of unsatisfiability for universal sentences with matrix in conjunctive normal form. This section discusses two transformations with which this result extends to arbitrary first-order sentences. The reader primarily interested in resolution can skip to Section 3.7.

**Definition 3.32** A formula is called *prenex* if it has the form

$$Q_1 x_1 \cdots Q_n x_n \varphi,$$

where $\varphi$ is quantifier-free, $x_1, \ldots, x_n$ are pairwise different variables, and for $1 \le i \le n$, either $Q_i = \forall$ or $Q_i = \exists$.

$Q_1 x_1 \cdots Q_n x_n$ is called the *prefix* of the formula and $\varphi$ is called its *matrix*. ∎

Compare Definition 3.25; note that a universal sentence is a prenex sentence, the prefix of which consists of universal quantifiers only.

**Theorem 3.33 (Prenex Normal Form)** *Every formula has a logical equivalent in prenex form with the same free variables.*

**Theorem 3.34 (Skolem Form)** *To every prenex sentence there exists a universal sentence (in general containing new constant and function symbols) that is satisfiable iff the original one is.*

The universal sentence of the last theorem is called the *Skolem form* or *transform* of the prenex sentence.

The constructions of prenex and Skolem forms are effective processes (see the proofs of Theorems 3.33 and 3.34 in subsections 3.6.1 resp. 3.6.2).

**Corollary 3.35** *Logical validity and unsatisfiability in first-order logic are positively decidable.*

**Proof.** Note that a sentence is logically valid iff its negation is unsatisfiable; so if we can positively decide on unsatisfiability, then so can we on logical validity. To decide whether a sentence $\varphi$ is unsatisfiable, produce an equivalent prenex form and a subsequential Skolem form $\forall\psi$, where $\psi$ is in conjunctive normal form. By Theorem 3.29, $\varphi$ is unsatisfiable iff $ground(\psi)$ is. To test whether $ground(\psi)$ is unsatisfiable, systematically generate its elements one by one (using more and more complex ground terms) and start producing propositional resolvents. If indeed $ground(\psi)$ is unsatisfiable, $\square$ will turn up eventually. ∎

The proofs of Theorems 3.33 and 3.34 need a strengthened form of Lemma 3.24 and a nasty notion. Since intuitively the construction of prenex and Skolem forms is quite straightforward, readers troubled by the next few technical results should skip proofs here.

**Definition 3.36**

(i) The term $t$ is *substitutable* for the variable $x$ *in* the formula $\varphi$ if $\varphi$ does not contain a free occurrence of $x$ in the scope (Definition 3.5) of a quantifier binding a variable from $Var(t)$.

(ii) The substitution $\theta$ is called *admissible* for $\varphi$ if for every variable $x \in Var(\varphi)$: $x\theta$ is substitutable for $x$ in $\varphi$. ∎

Thus, $t$ is not substitutable for $x$ in $\varphi$ if, applying the substitution $\{x/t\}$ to $\varphi$, some variable in $t$ becomes bound in the resulting expression.

Clearly, ground terms are always substitutable and ground substitutions are always admissible; for a quantifier-free formula, every term is substitutable and every substitution is admissible.

**Example.**
The variable $y$ is not substitutable for $x$ in $\exists y \mathbf{r}(x, y)$.
$\forall x \exists y \mathbf{r}(x, y) \rightarrow (\exists y \mathbf{r}(x, y))\{x/y\}$, that is: $\forall x \exists y \mathbf{r}(x, y) \rightarrow \exists y \mathbf{r}(y, y)$, is not logically valid (just consider the model $(\mathbb{N}, <)$). ∎

Thus it is not always the case (contrary to what might be expected on the basis of Corollary 3.27) that truth of $\forall x \varphi$ implies truth of $\varphi\{x/t\}$. For this, $t$ needs to be substitutable for $x$ in $\varphi$. This illustrates necessity of the admissibility condition in Corollary 3.38(i).

The next lemma extends Lemma 3.24(i) in allowing $\theta$ to be non-ground for $t$ and it extends 3.24(ii) in allowing $\theta$ to be non-ground for $\varphi$ and $\varphi$ to contain quantifiers.

**Lemma 3.37** *Suppose that $\mathbf{A}$ is a model, $\theta$ a substitution and $\beta$ an A-assignment. Let the A-assignment $\alpha$ be defined by $\alpha(x) = (x\theta\beta)^{\mathbf{A}}$. Then*
(i) *if $t$ is a term, then $(t\alpha)^{\mathbf{A}} = (t\theta\beta)^{\mathbf{A}}$;*
(ii) *if $\varphi$ is a formula and $\theta$ is admissible for $\varphi$, then: $\mathbf{A}\models\varphi\alpha$ iff $\mathbf{A}\models\varphi\theta\beta$.*
**Proof.** (i) This only slightly extends the proof of the corresponding part of Lemma 3.24 and is left to the reader.
(ii) Induction with respect to $\varphi$. Basis and induction steps for the connectives are straightforward. Here follows the induction step for the $\forall$-case. We may as well assume that $Dom(\theta) \subset Dom(\alpha) = Var(\varphi) - \{x\}$ and $x \in Var(\varphi)$. Then:
$\mathbf{A}\models(\forall x \varphi)\alpha$
        iff for all $a \in A$: $\mathbf{A}\models\varphi(\alpha \cup \{x/a\})$ (by Definition 3.9)
        iff for all $a \in A$: $\mathbf{A}\models\varphi\theta(\beta \cup \{x/a\})$ (by inductive hypothesis for $\varphi$, applied to $\alpha \cup \{x/a\}$ and $\beta \cup \{x/a\}$, since $\theta$ a fortiori is admissible for $\varphi$ and does not affect $x$)
        iff $\mathbf{A}\models(\forall x(\varphi\theta))\beta$ (by Definition 3.9)
        iff $\mathbf{A}\models(\forall x \varphi)\theta\beta$ (since $x \notin Dom(\theta)$). ∎

**Corollary 3.38** *If $\theta$ is admissible for the formula $\varphi$, then*
(i) $\forall\varphi\models\varphi\theta$,
(ii) $\varphi\theta\models\exists\varphi$.
**Proof.** As Corollary 3.27, but this time using Lemma 3.37. ∎

### 3.6.1 Prenex Form

Here follows the proof of the Prenex Form Theorem 3.33.

Suppose that $\varphi$ is a formula for which we want to construct a prenex equivalent. We may as well suppose that $\neg$, $\wedge$ and $\vee$ are the only connectives occurring in $\varphi$. We now use the following equivalences (read from left to right; the first two are given by Lemma 3.14) to "pull quantifiers out" of a negation, a conjunction or a disjunction:

(i) $\neg \forall x \psi \sim \exists x \neg \psi$,

(ii) $\neg \exists x \psi \sim \forall x \neg \psi$,

(iii) $(\forall x \psi \wedge \chi) \sim \forall y (\psi\{x/y\} \wedge \chi)$,

(iv) $(\exists x \psi \wedge \chi) \sim \exists y (\psi\{x/y\} \wedge \chi)$,

(v) $(\forall x \psi \vee \chi) \sim \forall y (\psi\{x/y\} \vee \chi)$,

(vi) $(\exists x \psi \vee \chi) \sim \exists y (\psi\{x/y\} \vee \chi)$;

and similarly if the quantifier to be pulled does not occur in the *first* con- or disjunct. For the variable $y$ we have the choice between $x$ (but only in case $x$ does not occur free in $\chi$) and some arbitrary variable not occurring in $\psi$ or $\chi$. The fact that the formulas displayed are equivalences indeed needs Corollary 3.38. The reason to change the bound variable $x$ to $y$ if it is free in $\chi$ is clear; otherwise, the quantifier, after pulling it out, suddenly would bind the occurrences of $x$ in $\chi$ and equivalence would be lost.

Note that we have to apply these equivalences *inside* a given formula. This needs the result from the following exercise. ∎

### Exercise

**3.12** Show: replacement, in a formula, of a subformula by an equivalent, results in an equivalent of the original formula.

### 3.6.2 Skolem Form

Here follows the proof of the Skolem Form Theorem 3.34.

Suppose that $\forall x_1 \cdots \forall x_n \exists y \varphi$ is a prenex sentence. By Definition 3.32, no two different occurrences of quantifiers in the prefix bind the same variable. Note that $\varphi$ is allowed here to contain quantifiers as well. We have exhibited the prefix $\forall x_1 \cdots \forall x_n \exists y$ only up to and including the first *existential* quantifier. However, possible quantifiers in $\varphi$ will not bind $x_1, \ldots, x_n$ (or $y$). Since $\varphi$ does not contain quantifiers binding $x_1, \ldots, x_n$, $y$ cannot occur free in $\varphi$ in the scope of such a quantifier.

Now assume that $\mathbf{f}$ is an $n$-ary function symbol not occurring in $\varphi$. If $n = 0$, i.e., if no universal quantifiers precede the first existential one, this means that $\mathbf{f}$ is a *constant* symbol instead of a *function* symbol. It follows that the term $\mathbf{f}(x_1, \ldots, x_n)$ is substitutable for $y$ in $\varphi$; hence, the substitution $\{y/\mathbf{f}(x_1, \ldots, x_n)\}$ is admissible for $\varphi$.

In the context of the following lemma, $\mathbf{f}$ is referred to as a *Skolem function symbol*.

**Lemma 3.39** $\forall x_1 \cdots \forall x_n \exists y \varphi$ *is satisfiable iff* $\forall x_1 \cdots \forall x_n \varphi\{y/\mathbf{f}(x_1, \ldots, x_n)\}$ *is satisfiable.*

**Proof.** For ease of notation, suppose that $n = 1$; i.e., we are dealing with the sentence $\forall x \exists y \varphi(x, y)$.

$\Leftarrow$ By Corollary 3.38, we have $\varphi\{y/\mathbf{f}(x)\} \models \exists y \varphi$. That is, every model of $\forall x \varphi\{y/\mathbf{f}(x)\}$ is a model of $\forall x \exists y \varphi$ as well.

$\Rightarrow$ Assume that $\mathbf{A}$ is a model appropriate to the language of $\varphi$ in which $\forall x \exists y \varphi(x, y)$ is true. That is, to every $a \in A$ there exists $b \in A$ such that $\mathbf{A} \models \varphi(a, b)$. Let $f(a)$ be one of those $b$'s. Then $f : A \to A$ and for all $a \in A$ we have $\mathbf{A} \models \varphi(a, f(a))$. Adjust $\mathbf{A}$ to the language expanded with $\mathbf{f}$ by taking $f$ as interpretation of this symbol. Let $\mathbf{A}'$ be the model so obtained. By Lemma 3.37 we have for all $a$: $\mathbf{A}' \models \varphi(a, \mathbf{f}(a))$, i.e., $\mathbf{A}' \models \forall x \varphi(x, \mathbf{f}(x))$. ∎

By repeated application of Lemma 3.39, all existential quantifiers from the prefix of our prenex sentence are eliminated in favor of new function symbols. Eventually, the required Skolem form appears. ∎

**On strategy.** In the construction of the prenex form we often have a choice as to which quantifier is pulled out first. It is profitable to follow a strategy by which Skolem function symbols will get the least number of arguments, since this may simplify the ensuing resolution process. This usually will mean pulling out existential quantifiers first.

**Example 3.40** Consider the sentence

$$\exists x \forall y \, [\mathbf{r}xy \leftrightarrow \neg \exists z (\mathbf{r}yz \wedge \mathbf{r}zy)]. \tag{3.6.1}$$

This sentence is unsatisfiable. Assume that $(A, R)$ is a model for it. Then an element $a \in A$ exists such that

$$\forall y \in A \, [Ray \leftrightarrow \neg \exists z \in A(Ryz \wedge Rzy)]. \tag{3.6.2}$$

In particular, for $y := a$,

$$Raa \leftrightarrow \neg \exists z \in A(Raz \wedge Rza). \tag{3.6.3}$$

Evidently we also have

$$Raa \to \exists z \in A(Raz \wedge Rza)$$

(take $z := a$).

As a consequence, $Raa$ cannot hold. Therefore, by (3.6.3), we have $\exists z \in A(Raz \wedge Rza)$. For instance, assume that $b \in A$ is such that $Rab \wedge Rba$. From (3.6.2) it now follows, taking $y := b$, that

$$Rab \leftrightarrow \neg \exists z \in A(Rbz \wedge Rzb).$$

But of course we also have, by choice of $b$, that

$$Rab \rightarrow \exists z \in A(Rbz \wedge Rzb)$$

(take $z := a$). Therefore we have $\neg Rab$, a contradiction.

In order to establish unsatisfiability using propositional resolution, we first produce a prenex equivalent for (3.6.1). Eliminate $\leftrightarrow$:

$$\exists x \forall y \, [[\neg \mathbf{r}xy \vee \neg \exists z(\mathbf{r}yz \wedge \mathbf{r}zy)] \wedge [\mathbf{r}xy \vee \exists z(\mathbf{r}yz \wedge \mathbf{r}zy)]].$$

Pulling the second $z$-quantifier out in two steps, we obtain

$$\exists x \forall y \exists z \, [[\neg \mathbf{r}xy \vee \neg \exists z(\mathbf{r}yz \wedge \mathbf{r}zy)] \wedge [\mathbf{r}xy \vee (\mathbf{r}yz \wedge \mathbf{r}zy)]].$$

Pulling out the other $z$-quantifier one step, we obtain first

$$\exists x \forall y \exists z \, [[\neg \mathbf{r}xy \vee \forall z \neg(\mathbf{r}yz \wedge \mathbf{r}zy)] \wedge [\mathbf{r}xy \vee (\mathbf{r}yz \wedge \mathbf{r}zy)]].$$

But now we have to change $z$ to some new variable $w$ before we can move it over the free $z$ in the right conjunct; the required prenex form finally is (after applying DeMorgan in left conjunct and distribution in the right one)

$$\exists x \forall y \exists z \forall w \, [(\neg \mathbf{r}xy \vee \neg \mathbf{r}yw \vee \neg \mathbf{r}wy) \wedge (\mathbf{r}xy \vee \mathbf{r}yz) \wedge (\mathbf{r}xy \vee \mathbf{r}zy)].$$

The Skolem transformation (Lemma 3.39) introduces a constant symbol $\mathbf{c}$ (for the first existential quantifier $\exists x$) and a 1-ary function symbol $\mathbf{f}$ (for the second one $\exists z$), and we obtain finally

$$\forall y \forall w \, [(\neg \mathbf{r}(\mathbf{c}, y) \vee \neg \mathbf{r}(y, w) \vee \neg \mathbf{r}(w, y)) \wedge (\mathbf{r}(\mathbf{c}, y) \vee \mathbf{r}(y, \mathbf{f}(y))) \wedge (\mathbf{r}(\mathbf{c}, y) \vee \mathbf{r}(\mathbf{f}(y), y))].$$

This is the universal sentence of Example 3.31.                                                          ▮

### Exercises

**3.13** Construct prenex and Skolem forms for the following sentences:

   (i) $\exists x(\forall y \exists z \mathbf{p}(x, y, z) \wedge \exists z \forall y \neg \mathbf{p}(x, y, z))$,

   (ii) $\forall x(\exists y \mathbf{q}(x, y) \vee \forall y \exists z \mathbf{r}(x, y, z))$,

(iii) $\forall x(\neg\exists x\mathbf{p}(x,y)\rightarrow\exists x\mathbf{q}(x,x))$.

**3.14** Produce Skolem forms for the following sentences and unsatisfiable finite subsets of Herbrand expansions:

(i) $\exists x\forall y\mathbf{r}(x,y)\wedge\forall y\exists x\neg\mathbf{r}(y,x)$,

(ii) $\neg(\forall x\mathbf{p}x\vee\exists y\neg\mathbf{q}y)\wedge(\forall z\mathbf{p}z\vee\exists w\neg\mathbf{q}w)$.

**3.15** Show, via Skolem form and propositional resolution, unsatisfiability of the following sentences:

(i) $\exists x\forall y(\mathbf{r}(x,y)\leftrightarrow\neg\mathbf{r}(y,y))$,

(ii) $\exists x\forall y[\mathbf{r}(x,y)\leftrightarrow\neg\exists z\exists u(\mathbf{r}(y,z)\wedge\mathbf{r}(z,u)\wedge\mathbf{r}(u,y))]$.

**3.16** $\varphi$, $\psi$ and $\chi$ are three different quantifier-free formulas such that $Var(\varphi)=Var(\psi)=\{x,y\}$ and $Var(\chi)=\{u,v\}$ Consider the sentence $\exists x\neg(\exists y\varphi\vee\forall y\psi)\vee\forall u\exists v\chi$.

(i) In how many ways can you pull out quantifiers to obtain a prenex normal form for this sentence?

(ii) Which of these forms would be your choice if you had to produce a Skolem form next, in order to apply resolution?

(iii) Describe the Skolem form of the prenex form of your choice.

**3.17** Prove that the relation of logical consequence: $\varphi\models\psi$ (where $\varphi$ and $\psi$ are first-order sentences) is positively decidable.

### 3.6.3  Compactness

The following result is the *Compactness Theorem* of first-order logic. Compare Theorem 2.22.

**Theorem 3.41 (Compactness)** *If every finite subset of an infinite set of first-order sentences is satisfiable, then so is the set itself.*

**Proof.** Exercise 3.18.                                                                            ∎

The following model-theoretic material is used only in Chapters 6 and 8 but, since it rests on the Compactness Theorem, is best put here. It will not be needed until much later and can safely be skipped until then.

**Definition 3.42** Suppose that the models $\mathbf{A}$ and $\mathbf{B}$ have the same language $\mathcal{L}$. $\mathbf{A}$ is a *submodel* of $\mathbf{B}$, and $\mathbf{B}$ an *extension* of $\mathbf{A}$, notation: $\mathbf{A}\subset\mathbf{B}$, if $A\subset B$, and:

(i) if $\mathbf{r}$ is an $n$-ary relation or function symbol, then the interpretation $\mathbf{r}^{\mathbf{A}}$ of $\mathbf{r}$ in $\mathbf{A}$ is the *restriction* to $A$ of the interpretation $\mathbf{r}^{\mathbf{B}}$ of $\mathbf{r}$ in $\mathbf{B}$, that is, $\mathbf{r}^{\mathbf{A}}$ coincides with $\mathbf{r}^{\mathbf{B}}$ on $A^n$,

(ii) if $\mathbf{c}$ is a constant symbol, then its interpretations in $\mathbf{A}$ and $\mathbf{B}$ are the same.

**A** is an *elementary submodel* of **B** and **B** an *elementary extension* of **A**, notation: **A** ≺ **B**, if

(i) **A** ⊂ **B**, and

(ii) *A*-assignments satisfy the same formulas in **A** as in **B**; equivalently, **A** and **B** satisfy the same *A*-sentences. ∎

For instance, $(\mathbb{N}, <) \subset (\mathbb{Z}, <)$, but $(\mathbb{N}, <) \not\prec (\mathbb{Z}, <)$, since 0 has a predecessor in $\mathbb{Z}$ but not in $\mathbb{N}$. Natural examples of elementary submodels are harder to come by, though it is the content of Lemma 3.43 that they exist in abundance. However, without proof we mention the facts that the algebra $\mathbb{N} + \mathbb{Z}$ (cf. Exercise 3.7) elementarily extends the Herbrand algebra $\mathbb{N}$ corresponding to the language $\{\mathbf{o}, \mathbf{s}\}$, and the ordering of the reals elementarily extends the ordering of the rationals.

The Compactness Theorem is responsible for the fact that elementary extensions abound.

**Lemma 3.43** *Every infinite model has a proper elementary extension.*

**Proof.** Suppose that **A** is an infinite model. Let $\Sigma$ be the set of all *A*-sentences true in **A**. Add one new constant symbol **c** to the language and consider the set $\Gamma := \Sigma \cup \{\neg \mathbf{c} \approx a \mid a \in A\}$. Every finite subset of $\Gamma$ is satisfiable (use **A** with a suitable interpretation of **c**). By compactness, $\Gamma$ has a model that we may take to be an elementary extension of **A**. The sentences $\neg \mathbf{c} \approx a$ take care that the interpretation of **c** is different from each $a \in A$ and so the extension is proper. ∎

**Exercises**

**3.18** Prove Theorem 3.41.

*Hint.* Use Skolem forms; note that a derivation of □ from ground instances of conjuncts can use only finitely many of such ground instances.

The following is the *Downward Löwenheim-Skolem Theorem* for countable sets of sentences.

**Theorem 3.44 (Löwenheim-Skolem)** *Every countable satisfiable set of sentences has a countable model.*

**3.19** Prove Theorem 3.44.

*Hint.* Use the solution to Exercise 3.18.

**3.20** Show: if **A** ⊂ **B**, then **A** and **B** satisfy the same quantifier-free *A*-sentences.

*Hint.* Induction on the sentence involved.

**3.21** Let **A** be a model and suppose that $\Phi = (\varphi^i \mid i \in \mathbb{N})$ is an infinite sequence of formulas $\varphi^i$ with only $x$ free. Suppose that for every $N \in \mathbb{N}$: $\mathbf{A} \models \exists x \bigwedge_{i<N} \varphi^i$. Show: some elementary extension **B** of **A** has an element $b$ such that for all $i \in \mathbb{N}$: $\mathbf{B} \models \varphi^i \{x/b\}$.

**3.22** Assume that the models $\mathbf{A}_i$ form a *chain*: $\mathbf{A}_0 \subset \mathbf{A}_1 \subset \mathbf{A}_2 \subset \cdots$. Show that there is a unique model $\mathbf{A}$ such that $A = \bigcup_n A_n$ and such that for all $n$: $\mathbf{A}_n \subset \mathbf{A}$.

Show: if, in fact, the models form an *elementary* chain: $\mathbf{A}_0 \prec \mathbf{A}_1 \prec \mathbf{A}_2 \prec \cdots$, then (*Elementary Chain Lemma*) for all $n$: $\mathbf{A}_n \prec \mathbf{A}$.

*Hint.* For the second part: induction on sentences, keeping $n$ variable. Part of the argument is the following. Suppose that $\mathbf{A} \models \exists x \varphi$, $\exists x \varphi$ an $A_n$-sentence. Say, $\mathbf{A} \models \varphi\{x/a\}$, $a \in A$. Now $A = \bigcup_i A_i$; for instance, $a \in A_m$, where we may assume that $n < m$. Then $\mathbf{A}_m \models \exists x \varphi$, and hence $\mathbf{A}_n \models \exists x \varphi$, as, by assumption, $\mathbf{A}_n \prec \mathbf{A}_m$.

## 3.7 Resolution: The Unrestricted Version

The basic idea of resolution in first-order logic is that propositional resolution steps (involving clauses corresponding to ground instances of conjuncts of the matrix of a Skolem transform) that are "similar" can be done all at the same time, before the instantiating process has taken place, thus saving steps. More importantly, the method solves the problem of *which* ground instances are needed to derive $\square$.

We begin with *unrestricted* resolution, of which the proper resolution notion is just a special case.

Since we are in first-order logic, atoms — variables allowed now! — again take over the role of propositional variables. Thus, a *literal* (cf. Definition 2.8) is an atom (a *positive literal*) or the negation of an atom (a *negative* literal). A *clause* is a finite set of literals (cf. Definition 2.10). Since clauses originate from conjuncts of a universal Skolem form, variables should be thought of as *quantified universally*; that is, a clause $C$ represents the universal closure $\forall \bigvee C$ of the disjunction $\bigvee C$ of the elements of $C$.

In the rest of this chapter, the notation $C\alpha$ is used for the set of $\alpha$-instances of literals in $C$: $C\alpha := \{L\alpha \mid L \in C\}$.

Recall that (Definition 2.13) in the propositional case, the clause $(C - \{A\}) \cup (D - \{\neg A\})$ is a *resolvent* of $C$ and $D$ when $A \in C$ and $\neg A \in D$. In the present context, in which propositional variables are identified with ground atoms (see Section 3.4), we must require $C$ and $D$ to be ground here. Compare Example 3.31 and the discussion given there. From now on we drop this requirement, and allow variables in clauses when forming resolvents. When applied to clauses containing variables, a transition of the type described is still referred to as a *propositional resolution step*. The derivability relation it defines is written, as before, as $\vdash_p$.

We now relax this notion of resolution by admitting preliminary instantiations.

**Definition 3.45** An *unrestricted resolvent* of two clauses is a propositional resolvent of instances of those clauses. ∎

To explain this definition in somewhat more detail: suppose that $P$, $C$, $N$ and $D$ are clauses such that $P \cap C = N \cap D = \emptyset$ and $\alpha$ and $\beta$ are substitutions. Then $C\alpha \cup D\beta$ is an unrestricted resolvent of the clauses $P \cup C$ and $N \cup D$ in case an atom $A$ exists such that $P\alpha = \{A\}$ and $N\beta = \{\neg A\}$ (or vice versa). In this situation, we will say that $C\alpha \cup D\beta$ is an unrestricted resolvent of the clauses $P \cup C$ and $N \cup D$ *with respect to* the subclauses $P$ and $N$.

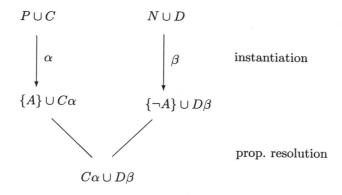

The clauses $P$ and/or $N$ may have been singletons (one-element sets) already, but this is not required by the definition. However, $\alpha$ and $\beta$ *must* collapse $P$ resp. $N$ to singletons $P\alpha$ and $N\beta$ of opposite literals. (In the next section we shall say that $\alpha$ and $\beta$ *unify* $P$ resp. $N$.)

**Example.** Let $C = \{\neg \mathbf{r}(x, \mathbf{f}y), \mathbf{s}(x, \mathbf{f}z)\}$ and $D = \{\mathbf{r}(z, \mathbf{f}z), \mathbf{r}(\mathbf{f}y, u)\}$. Then application of $\alpha := \{x/\mathbf{f}y, y/\mathbf{f}y, z/y\}$ transforms $C$ into $\{\neg \mathbf{r}(\mathbf{f}y, \mathbf{ff}y), \mathbf{s}(\mathbf{f}y, \mathbf{f}y)\}$; application of $\beta := \{z/\mathbf{f}y, u/\mathbf{ff}y\}$ transforms $D$ into the singleton $\{\mathbf{r}(\mathbf{f}y, \mathbf{ff}y)\}$. A propositional resolvent of the instances $C\alpha$ and $D\beta$ is $\{\mathbf{s}(\mathbf{f}y, \mathbf{f}y)\}$, which thus is an unrestricted resolvent of $C$ and $D$ with respect to the subclauses $\{\neg \mathbf{r}(x, \mathbf{f}y)\}$ and $D$ itself.  ∎

Compare Definition 2.14 with the following one.

**Definition 3.46** *Unrestricted resolution* is forming unrestricted resolvents repeatedly. More precisely: an *unrestricted derivation* of a clause $E$ from a set $\Sigma$ of clauses is a finite tree $\mathcal{T}$ such that

(i) $E$ is the root of $\mathcal{T}$,
(ii) every leaf of $\mathcal{T}$ belongs to $\Sigma$,
(iii) every non-leaf $D$ of $\mathcal{T}$ has children $D_1$ and $D_2$ of which it is an unrestricted resolvent. (Again, it is allowed that $D_1 = D_2$, see Exercise 3.25.)

The number of non-leaf nodes of a derivation is its number of *steps*.

The notation: $\Sigma \vdash_u E$ is used when there exists an unrestricted derivation of $E$ from $\Sigma$. An unrestricted derivation of $\square$ from $\Sigma$ is called an unrestricted *refutation* of $\Sigma$. $\Sigma$ is unrestrictedly *refutable* if it has an unrestricted refutation.  ∎

**Example.** To see that unrestricted resolution can economize on steps compared with propositional resolution, consider the following clauses $\{r(c)\}$, $\{r(fc)\}$, $\{\neg r(x), s(x)\}$, $\{\neg s(x), q(x)\}$, and $\{\neg q(c), \neg q(fc), \neg r(c)\}$.

Using the instances $\{\neg r(c), s(c)\}$, $\{\neg r(fc), s(fc)\}$ of the third clause and $\{\neg s(c), q(c)\}$, $\{\neg s(fc), q(fc)\}$ of the fourth, we successively derive $\{s(c)\}$, $\{s(fc)\}$, $\{q(c)\}$, $\{q(fc)\}$, $\{\neg q(fc), \neg r(c)\}$, $\{\neg r(c)\}$, $\square$ in 7 steps using proposional resolution.

Applying unrestricted resolution to the original clauses, we derive $\{\neg r(x), q(x)\}$, $\{q(c)\}$, $\{q(fc)\}$, $\{\neg q(fc), \neg r(c)\}$, $\{\neg r(c)\}$, $\square$ in 6 steps.

The gain is not impressive, but the principle is clear.  ∎

We recall a couple of notions from Definition 3.13, but now in the context of clauses and clausal forms.

**Definition 3.47**

   (i) **A** is a *model of* the clause $C$, notation: $\mathbf{A}\models C$, if $\mathbf{A}\models\forall\bigvee C$; that is, every $A$-assignment satisfies at least one literal of $C$,

   (ii) **A** is a *model of* a set of clauses if it is a model of every clause in the set,

   (iii) the clause $C$ *follows logically from* the set of clauses $S$, notation: $S\models C$, if every model of $S$ is a model of $C$, as well.  ∎

**Lemma 3.48** *If $E$ is an unrestricted resolvent of $C$ and $D$, then $\{C, D\} \models E$.*

**Proof.** Immediate from the corresponding fact for propositional resolution (Lemma 2.15) and Corollary 3.27.  ∎

The following *soundness* result asserts that, from a set of clauses, we can only derive logical consequences.

**Corollary 3.49 (Soundness)** *If $\Sigma \vdash_u E$, then $\Sigma\models E$.*

**Proof.** See Exercise 3.23.  ∎

**Corollary 3.50** *If $\Sigma$ is unrestrictedly refutable, then $\Sigma$ is unsatisfiable.*

**Proof.** Immediate from 3.49, since $\square$ is not satisfiable.  ∎

The following result is not of much interest in itself. However, by "lifting" (to be explained later) it produces the completeness result we're aiming for (Theorem 3.80 of Section 3.9).

**Theorem 3.51 (Unrestricted Completeness)** *Every unsatisfiable set of clauses is unrestrictedly refutable.*

**Proof.** If $\Sigma$ is unsatisfiable, then, by Theorem 3.29, so is $ground(\Sigma)$. Hence by completeness of propositional resolution (which applies here, by Lemma 3.22), Theorem 2.18, $ground(\Sigma) \vdash_p \square$.

Let $\mathcal{T}$ be a derivation of $\square$ from $ground(\Sigma)$ using propositional resolution. In $\mathcal{T}$, every leaf is ground instance of a clause from $\Sigma$. Replace every leaf by the clause from $\Sigma$ from which it is an instance. The resulting tree clearly is an unrestricted derivation of $\square$ from $\Sigma$. ∎

**Exercises**

**3.23** Prove Corollary 3.49.
*Hint.* Strong induction with respect to the height of the derivation given. The induction step uses Lemma 3.48. Compare the proof of Corollary 2.16.

**3.24** Note that Theorem 3.51 claims the implication: $\Sigma \models C \Rightarrow \Sigma \vdash_u C$, *only* for $C = \square$. Show (by giving a simple example) that this may be false for $C \neq \square$. (Compare Exercise 2.28.)

**3.25** In propositional resolution, it is not useful to form a resolvent of identical clauses. (Cf. Exercise 2.18.) Discuss this case here.
*Hint.* Consider $\{\neg \mathbf{r}x, \mathbf{r}\mathbf{f}x\}$.

**3.26** Derive $\square$, using unrestricted resolution from, or give a Herbrand model for the following:

  (i) $\{\{\mathbf{r}(x,y), \mathbf{r}(y,x)\}, \{\neg \mathbf{r}(x, \mathbf{f}x)\}\}$,
  (ii) $\{\{\mathbf{r}(x,y), \mathbf{r}(y,z)\}, \{\neg \mathbf{r}(x, \mathbf{f}x)\}\}$,
  (iii) $\{\{\neg \mathbf{p}x, \mathbf{p}\mathbf{f}\mathbf{f}x\}, \{\neg \mathbf{q}x, \mathbf{q}\mathbf{f}\mathbf{f}x\}, \{\mathbf{p}x, \mathbf{q}x\}, \{\neg \mathbf{p}x, \neg \mathbf{q}x\}\}$.

**3.27** Assume that $\Sigma \vdash_p D$ and that $\alpha$ is a substitution. Show that for some $E \subset D\alpha$ we have that $\{C\alpha \mid C \in \Sigma\} \vdash_p E$.
(The example $\Sigma := \{\{\mathbf{r}(\mathbf{a}), \mathbf{r}(\mathbf{b}), \mathbf{r}(x)\}, \{\neg \mathbf{r}(\mathbf{a}), \mathbf{r}(\mathbf{c})\}\}$, $D := \{\mathbf{r}(\mathbf{b}), \mathbf{r}(x), \mathbf{r}(\mathbf{c})\}$ and $\alpha := \{x/\mathbf{a}\}$ shows we cannot require $E = D\alpha$.)

## 3.8  Unification

Before going on to the proper notion of resolution, we need to discuss the syntactical notion of unification.

Recall (Definition 3.23) that a *substitution* is a function $\theta$ mapping the variables to terms such that $Dom(\theta) = \{x \mid x \neq x\theta\}$ is finite ($x\theta$ denotes the value of $\theta$ at the variable $x$). The notation $\{x_1/x_1\theta, \ldots, x_n/x_n\theta\}$ for $\theta$ is used in case $Dom(\theta) = \{x_1, \ldots, x_n\}$.

For a quantifier-free expression $E$, the expression $E\theta$ is obtained from $E$ replacing every variable by its $\theta$-image. Thus:

**Lemma 3.52** $x \in Var(E\theta)$ *iff for some* $y \in Var(E)$, *we have that* $x \in Var(y\theta)$. ∎

**Definition 3.53** By $\epsilon$ we denote the identity substitution (which has an empty domain). If $V$ is a set of variables, then $\theta|V := \{x/\theta \mid x \in V \cap Dom(\theta)\}$ is the *restriction* of $\theta$ to $V$. ∎

**Definition 3.54** If $\theta$ and $\lambda$ are substitutions, then the substitution $\theta\lambda$, the *composition* of $\theta$ and $\lambda$, is defined by: $x(\theta\lambda) = (x\theta)\lambda$. ∎

In this defining equation for $\theta\lambda$, the right-hand side denotes the expression obtained from the term $x\theta$ by replacing variables by their $\lambda$-image.

Note that composition does not commute. E.g., $\{x/y\}\{y/z\} = \{x/z, y/z\}$, whereas $\{y/z\}\{x/y\} = \{x/y, y/z\}$.

**Lemma 3.55** *If* $t$ *is a term and* $\theta$, $\lambda$ *are substitutions, then* $(t\theta)\lambda = t(\theta\lambda)$.

**Proof.** Induction with respect to $t$.
For $t$ a constant symbol: $(t\theta)\lambda = t = t(\theta\lambda)$.
For $t$ a variable, this is immediate from Definition 3.54.
Finally, assume $t = \mathbf{f}(s_1, \ldots, s_n)$, and (induction hypothesis) $(s_1\theta)\lambda = s_1(\theta\lambda), \ldots, (s_n\theta)\lambda = s_n(\theta\lambda)$. Then: $(t\theta)\lambda = (\mathbf{f}(s_1, \ldots, s_n)\theta)\lambda = \mathbf{f}(s_1\theta, \ldots, s_n\theta)\lambda = \mathbf{f}((s_1\theta)\lambda, \ldots, (s_n\theta)\lambda) = \mathbf{f}(s_1(\theta\lambda), \ldots, s_n(\theta\lambda)) = \mathbf{f}(s_1, \ldots, s_n)(\theta\lambda) = t(\theta\lambda)$. ∎

**Remark.** Substitutions $\alpha$ and $\beta$ are considered to be equal iff $Dom(\alpha) = Dom(\beta)$ and for every $x \in Dom(\alpha)$: $x\alpha = x\beta$; equivalently, if they are equal as functions in the usual set-theoretic sense, that is, for *every* variable $x$: $x\alpha = x\beta$. ∎

**Lemma 3.56** *If* $\theta$, $\lambda$ *and* $\sigma$ *are substitutions, then* $(\theta\lambda)\sigma = \theta(\lambda\sigma)$.

**Proof.** $x[(\theta\lambda)\sigma] = [x(\theta\lambda)]\sigma = [(x\theta)\lambda]\sigma = (x\theta)(\lambda\sigma) = x[\theta(\lambda\sigma)]$. (The third equality uses 3.55.) ∎

As a consequence of this lemma, we can save on parentheses, indiscriminately writing $(\theta\lambda)\sigma = \theta(\lambda\sigma) = \theta\lambda\sigma$.

**Definition 3.57** $\alpha$ is called a *renaming* for the term or atom $E$ if $\alpha$ is injective on $Var(E)$ and maps variables to *variables*. In that case, $E\alpha$ is called a *variant* of $E$. ∎

**Example.** $\mathbf{f}(x, \mathbf{g}y)$ is a variant of $\mathbf{f}(y, \mathbf{g}x)$, but not of $\mathbf{f}(x, \mathbf{g}x)$. ∎

The following lemma says that the relation *variant of* is symmetric:

**Lemma 3.58** *If* $\alpha$ *is a renaming for* $E$, *then there exists a renaming* $\beta$ *for* $E\alpha$ *such that* $E\alpha\beta = E$. ∎

**Lemma 3.59** *If $E\alpha\beta = E$, then $\alpha$ is a renaming for $E$.*

**Proof.** Assume that $E\alpha\beta = E$. If $x \in Var(E)$ and $x\alpha$ is no variable, then $x\alpha\beta$ can be no variable either. And if $x, y \in Var(E)$ are different but $x\alpha = y\alpha$, then we have $x\alpha\beta = y\alpha\beta$ as well. ∎

**Lemma 3.60** *For terms or atoms $A$ and $B$, the following are equivalent:*
  *(i) $A$ and $B$ are instances of each other,*
  *(ii) $A$ and $B$ are variants of each other.*

**Proof.** (ii) ⇒ (i) This is clear.
(i) ⇒ (ii) Assume $B = A\theta$, $A = B\lambda$. Then $A = B\lambda = A\theta\lambda$. Now, use Lemma 3.59. ∎

Next, we introduce a crucial, at first sight perhaps obvious, but tricky notion. (See Exercise 3.28.)

**Definition 3.61** The substitution $\theta$ is *more general than* the substitution $\lambda$ if, for some $\sigma$, we have that $\lambda = \theta\sigma$. ∎

The notion of unification applies equally to *expressions* (terms or atoms), *sequences* of expressions and *sets* of expressions.

**Definition 3.62** The substitution $\theta$ *unifies* or is a *unifier* of
  (i) the expressions $A$ and $B$ if $A\theta = B\theta$,
  (ii) the sequences of expressions $(A_1, \ldots, A_n)$ and $(B_1, \ldots, B_n)$ if, for $1 \le i \le n$, $\theta$ unifies $A_i$ and $B_i$.
  (iii) the set of expressions $K$ if $K\theta := \{L\theta \mid L \in K\}$ has exactly one element.
A unifier $\theta$ for certain expressions (resp. sequences of expressions or a set of expressions) is called *most general*, or a *most general unifier* (*mgu* for short) if it is more general than every other unifier of these expressions (resp., sequences or set) in the sense of Definition 3.61. ∎

Unification of *sets* of *atoms* is the relevant notion for resolution in first-order logic, but it can be defined (see Lemma 3.66) via the one for *sequences* of *terms*, which is dealt with now. Usually (in particular in the later chapters on logic programming), we need to unify atoms only. Note that atoms involving different relation symbols do not unify, and $\mathbf{r}(s_1, \ldots, s_n)$ and $\mathbf{r}(t_1, \ldots, t_n)$ unify just in case the sequences of terms $(s_1, \ldots, s_n)$ and $(t_1, \ldots, t_n)$ do. Thus, atom unification is reduced to unification of sequences of terms as well.

**Theorem 3.63 (Unification)** *There is an algorithm that, when applied to a pair of sequences of terms, produces an mgu for those sequences in case a unifier exists, and ends with failure otherwise.*
*In particular, if a unifier exists, then an mgu exists as well.*

**Proof.** Suppose that we are given a pair of sequences of terms $(s_1, \ldots, s_n)$ and $(t_1, \ldots, t_n)$. As a first step, this pair is transformed into the set $\{s_1 \approx t_1, \ldots, s_n \approx t_n\}$ of identities (the use of the identity symbol '$\approx$' here is only a suggestive notational convenience). In connection with such sets, we employ the following:

**Terminology.**

- $\alpha$ *unifies* the set $\{s_1 \approx t_1, \ldots, s_n \approx t_n\}$, of course, if it unifies the related sequences $(s_1, \ldots, s_n)$ and $(t_1, \ldots, t_n)$,

- sets of identities are called *equivalent* if they have the same unifiers,

- a set $\{v_1 \approx u_1, \ldots, v_m \approx u_m\}$ is called *solved*, in case

   (i) the $v_i$ are pairwise different *variables*

   (ii) no $v_i$ occurs in a term $u_j$ $(1 \leq i, j \leq m)$.

By (i), a solved set $V := \{v_1 \approx u_1, \ldots, v_m \approx u_m\}$ determines a substitution $\theta := \{v_1/u_1, \ldots, v_m/u_m\}$.

Condition (ii) makes $\theta$ *unify* $V$: $v_i\theta = u_i = u_i\theta$.

Finally, note that $\theta$ even is a *mgu* of $V$: if $\lambda$ is a substitution such that, for $1 \leq i \leq m$, $v_i\lambda = u_i\lambda$, then $v_i\lambda = u_i\lambda = v_i\theta\lambda$, and of course, $x\lambda = x\theta\lambda$ for variables different from the $v_i$; hence: $\lambda = \theta\lambda$.

*Claim:*

the Unification Algorithm described next either transforms a set of identities into a solved equivalent, or it terminates with failure if unification is impossible.

**The Unification Algorithm.**

Repeat the following procedure. Choose an identity from your set that allows one of the following 6 actions (if such a choice is impossible, the algorthm terminates). The action depends on the form of the identity.

1. $\mathbf{f}(s_1, \ldots, s_n) \approx \mathbf{f}(t_1, \ldots, t_n)$:

   replace this by the identities $s_1 \approx t_1, \ldots, s_n \approx t_n$.

   (If $\mathbf{f}$ is a constant symbol, $\mathbf{f} \approx \mathbf{f}$ is erased.)

2. $\mathbf{f}(s_1, \ldots, s_n) \approx \mathbf{g}(t_1, \ldots, t_m)$ $(\mathbf{f} \neq \mathbf{g})$:

   terminate with failure.

   ($\mathbf{f}$ and/or $\mathbf{g}$ can be constant symbols here)

3. $x \approx x$ ($x$ a variable):

   erase the identity.

4. $t \approx x$ ($t$ not a variable):

   replace the identity by $x \approx t$.

5. $x \approx t$ ($t$ different from $x$, $x$ occurring in $t$):

   terminate with failure.

6. $x \approx t$ ($t$ different from $x$, $x$ does not occur in $t$ and $x$ occurs in at least one of the other identities):

   maintain this identity and apply the substitution $\{x/t\}$ to the others.

**Proof** of Claim:

(i) Every action 1, 3, 4, 6 transforms a set into an equivalent one. For 1, 3 and 4 this is clear.

For 6: note first that if $x\theta = t\theta$, then $\theta = \{x/t\}\theta$.

Now suppose that one action 6 transforms $V := \{x \approx t\} \cup W$ into $V' := \{x \approx t\} \cup W\{x/t\}$. Then:

$\theta$ unifies $V$

$\qquad$ iff: $x\theta = t\theta$ and $\theta$ unifies $W$

$\qquad$ iff: $x\theta = t\theta$ and $\{x/t\}\theta$ unifies $W$ (as $x\theta = t\theta$ implies that $\theta = \{x/t\}\theta$)

$\qquad$ iff: $x\theta = t\theta$ and $\theta$ unifies $W\{x/t\}$

$\qquad$ iff: $\theta$ unifies $V'$.

(ii) The algorithm terminates. Otherwise, it produces an infinite sequence of sets.

Then in particular, the algorithm does not terminate with failure, and situations described under 2 and 5 of the algorithm never occur.

For a given variable $x$, item 6 can be used only once (it eliminates $x$ from every other identity, and 1, 4 and 6 cannot re-introduce $x$ again). Thus, 6 is only applied finitely many times and, from a certain stage onwards, will not be applied any more.

Finally, 1 and 4 decrease the number of function symbols on the left of $\approx$. Thus the number of their applications must be finite, as well. Hence, from a certain stage onwards, only action 3 is used, an impossibility.

(iii) A *successful* termination clearly can happen only at a *solved* set.

(iv) Since the algorithmic actions respect equivalence, a solved set that is the outcome of a successful termination has the same unifiers as the initial set; in particular, it has the same mgu's. Therefore, the mgu associated with the solved set also is an mgu of the initial one.

(v) Termination with failure clearly happens only at a set for which a unifier does not exist; and then the initial set has no unifier either. ∎

Mgu's obtained by the algorithm satisfy some additional properties.

**Definition 3.64** An mgu $\theta$ for $(s_1, \ldots, s_n)$ and $(t_1, \ldots, t_n)$ is *idempotent* if $\theta\theta = \theta$, it is *relevant* if every variable in its domain occurs in some of the terms $s_i$ or $t_i$ $(1 \leq i \leq n)$ and, for $x \in Dom(\theta)$, every variable in $x\theta$ also occurs in some of these terms. $\blacksquare$

**Lemma 3.65** *Mgu's obtained by the unification algorithm are both idempotent and relevant.*

**Proof.** Idempotent: since mgu's are constructed from solved sets of identities (cf. condition (ii) of *solved* and Exercise 3.37). Relevant: the algorithm clearly does not introduce new variables (also, cf. Exercise 3.38). $\blacksquare$

Unification of sets of atoms can be reduced to unifying two sequences of terms by the following recipe.

**Lemma 3.66** *A substitution unifies the set of atoms* $\{\mathbf{r}(t_1^1, \ldots, t_n^1), \ldots, \mathbf{r}(t_1^k, \ldots, t_n^k)\}$ *($k \geq 2$) just in case it unifies the sequences* $(t_1^1, \ldots, t_n^1, \ldots, t_1^{k-1}, \ldots, t_n^{k-1})$ *and* $(t_1^2, \ldots, t_n^2, \ldots, t_1^k, \ldots, t_n^k)$. $\blacksquare$

We end this section with an axiomatic characterisation of the notion of equivalence between sets of equalities, which is not needed for the rest of this chapter.

For $\alpha$ a substitution, let $E_\alpha := \{x \approx x\alpha \mid x \in Dom(\alpha)\}$ be the associated set of identities.

**Lemma 3.67** *Suppose that $\alpha$ and $\sigma$ are substitutions. Then the following are equivalent:*

*(i) $\sigma$ unifies $E_\alpha$,*

*(ii) $\sigma = \alpha\sigma$.*

*Moreover, if $\alpha$ is idempotent, these conditions amount to*

*(iii) for some $\xi$, $\sigma = \alpha\xi$.*

**Proof.** The equivalence of (i) and (ii) follows by inspection. That (ii) implies (iii) is trivial. Finally, if $\sigma = \alpha\xi$ and $\alpha$ is idempotent, then $\sigma = \alpha\xi = \alpha\alpha\xi = \alpha\sigma$. $\blacksquare$

The following definition introduces *Clark's Equality Theory* CET. It is closely related to the unification algorithm, as the following results will show.

**Definition 3.68** The formulas of the following three types are called the *Free Equality Axioms*; they determine *Clark's Equality Theory*, for short: CET.

(i) $\mathbf{f}(x_1, \ldots, x_n) \approx \mathbf{f}(y_1, \ldots, y_n) \rightarrow (x_1 \approx y_1 \wedge \cdots \wedge x_n \approx y_n)$,

(ii) $\mathbf{f}(x_1, \ldots, x_n) \not\approx \mathbf{g}(y_1, \ldots, y_m)$ ($\mathbf{f}$, $\mathbf{g}$ *different*),

(iii) $x \not\approx t$ (if the variable $x$ is a proper subterm of $t$). $\blacksquare$

Here, we conceive of individual constants as 0-argument function symbols; therefore, (ii) includes formulas like $\mathbf{c} \not\approx \mathbf{g}(y_1, \ldots, y_m)$ and $\mathbf{c} \not\approx \mathbf{d}$ ($\mathbf{c}$ and $\mathbf{d}$ different constant symbols). (iii) is usually called the *occur check* axiom. Its name will become clear after we've established the connection between CET and unification.

For the case of one constant symbol and one unary function symbol, these axioms were spelled out previously in Exercise 3.7. One model of CET is the Herbrand algebra $HA$ of closed terms (Definition 3.19); another is the canonical algebra $TM$ of *all* terms. Note that a substitution is nothing but an assignment into this model, and a substitution *unifies* two terms $s$ and $t$ iff it *satisfies* the identity $s \approx t$ in $TM$.

**Lemma 3.69** *Suppose that the algebra $I$ satisfies $CET$ and that $E$ is a set of identities satisfied by the $I$-assignment $\sigma$. Then $E$ has an (idempotent) mgu $\alpha$ such that $\sigma = \alpha\sigma$.*

**Proof.** Feed $E$ to the unification algorithm. By induction it is verified that, for every set $F$ of identities the algorithm produces, we have that $I \models F\sigma$. In particular, the algorithm cannot terminate with failure, and we have $I \models E_\alpha\sigma$, where $\alpha$ is the (idempotent) mgu eventually produced by the algorithm. Thus (compare Lemma 3.67), $\sigma = \alpha\sigma$. ∎

**Lemma 3.70** *Suppose that $E$ is a (finite) set of identities and $s$ and $t$ are terms. The following are equivalent:*

*(i) $CET \models \bigwedge E \rightarrow s \approx t$,*
*(ii) $s$ and $t$ are unified by every unifier of $E$,*
*(iii) $s$ and $t$ are unified by every mgu of $E$.*

**Proof.**
(i) $\Rightarrow$ (ii). Suppose that $\alpha$ unifies $E$, i.e., that $\alpha$ satisfies $E$ in $TM$. By (i), $\alpha$ satisfies $s = t$ in $TM$, i.e.: it unifies $s$ and $t$.
(ii) $\Rightarrow$ (iii). Trivial.
(iii) $\Rightarrow$ (i). Suppose that $I \models CET$, and $\sigma$ satisfies $E$ in $I$. By Lemma 3.69, there exists an (idempotent) mgu $\alpha$ of $E$ such that $\sigma = \alpha\sigma$. By (iii), $s\alpha = t\alpha$. But then, $s \approx t$ trivially is satisfied by $\sigma$ in $I$. ∎

Recall that sets of equations $E$ and $F$ are called *equivalent* if they have the same unifiers. Given a set of equations, every operation from the unification algorithm (items 1, 3, 4 and 6) produces an equivalent one. The following corollary enables us to more easily establish equivalences of sets of identities.

**Corollary 3.71** *For sets of identities $E$ and $F$, the following are equivalent:*

*(i) $CET \models (\bigwedge E \leftrightarrow \bigwedge F)$,*
*(ii) $E$ and $F$ are equivalent,*
*(iii) $E$ and $F$ have the same mgu's.* ∎

## Exercises

**3.28** Is $\{x/y\}$ more general than $\{x/\mathbf{c}\}$?
*Hint.* Compute $\{x/y\}\{y/\mathbf{c}\}$.

**3.29** Prove Lemma 3.55 for the case that $t$ is an arbitrary expression.

**3.30** Apply the unification algorithm to the following sets:
  (i) $\{\mathbf{p}(x,y),\mathbf{p}(y,\mathbf{f}z)\}$ (i.e., try to unify the sequences $(x,y)$ and $(y,\mathbf{f}z)$),
  (ii) $\{\mathbf{p}(\mathbf{c},y,\mathbf{f}y),\mathbf{p}(z,z,u)\}$,
  (iii) $\{\mathbf{p}(x,\mathbf{g}x),\mathbf{p}(y,y)\}$,
  (iv) $\{\mathbf{p}(x,\mathbf{g}x,y),\mathbf{p}(z,u,\mathbf{g}u)\}$,
  (v) $\{\mathbf{p}(\mathbf{g}x,y),\mathbf{p}(y,y),\mathbf{p}(u,\mathbf{f}w)\}$ (use the recipe from Lemma 3.66),
  (vi) $\{\mathbf{p}(x,\mathbf{f}y,z),\mathbf{p}(\mathbf{g}w,u,\mathbf{g}w),\mathbf{p}(v,v,\mathbf{g}w)\}$.

**3.31** You may have derived $\square$ in Exercise 3.26(i) in two steps. Can it be done in one?

**Definition 3.72** An expression $C$ is a *common instance* (c.i.) of $A$ and $B$ if for some substitutions $\alpha$ and $\beta$, $C = A\alpha = B\beta$. It is a *most general common instance* (m.g.c.i.) if it is a c.i. of which every other c.i. is an instance.  ∎

**3.32** Suppose that the expressions $A$ and $B$ have a c.i. $A\alpha = B\beta$. Show that they have an m.g.c.i. as well. (A proof can be extracted from the next section.)
Is there always an m.g.c.i. $C$ such that $Var(C) \subset Var(A) \cup Var(B)$?
*Hint.* Consider $A = \mathbf{f}(\mathbf{f}(x,y),z)$ and $B = \mathbf{f}(x,\mathbf{f}(y,z))$.

**3.33** The solution of Exercise 3.32 transforms the mgu-producing unification algorithm into one that produces m.g.c.i.'s. Show how to transform any m.g.c.i.-producing algorithm into one that produces mgu's.
*Hint.* Instead of unifying $s$ and $t$, find an m.g.c.i. of $\mathbf{f}(x,x)$ and $\mathbf{f}(s,t)$.

**3.34** Let $\alpha$ be an idempotent mgu of the set of identities $E$. Show:
  (i) $E\alpha \sim E$,
  (ii) $E \cup F \sim E \cup F\alpha$.

**3.35** Suppose that $E$ and $F$ are sets of equations, and $\alpha$ and $\beta$ are substitutions such that $\alpha$ is an mgu of $E$ and $\beta$ is an mgu of $F\alpha$. Show that $\alpha\beta$ is an mgu of $E \cup F$.

**3.36** Suppose that $Var(\alpha) \cap Dom(\beta) = \emptyset$. Show that $\alpha\beta = \alpha \cup \beta$.

**3.37** Show: $\theta$ is idempotent (i.e., $\theta\theta = \theta$) iff $Dom(\theta) \cap Ran(\theta) = \emptyset$.

**\*3.38** Show: every idempotent is relevant. (This *sounds* remarkable; relevance refers to the expressions to be unified, while idempotency does not. But note for instance that $\{x/u,y/v\}$ is a — both idempotent and relevant — mgu of $\mathbf{f}(x,y)$ and $\mathbf{f}(u,v)$ but not of $\mathbf{g}(x)$ and $\mathbf{g}(u)$: $\{x/u\}$ is a unifier and there is no $\alpha$ such that $\{x/u\} = \{x/u,y/v\}\alpha$.)

## 3.9   Resolution

If we seek to establish unsatisfiability of a (finite) set of clauses involving variables using propositional resolution, and at least one function symbol is present, then the problem arises which ground instances of the clauses should be tried. And if we use unrestricted resolution, there is the problem of which substitutions to apply to clauses. Resolution completely eliminates this problem (at least, up to renaming: Corollary 3.75).

**Definition 3.73** An element in a set $K$ of expressions is called *most general* if it has every element of $K$ as an instance.                                                                   ∎

By Lemma 3.60, most general elements (if they exist) are unique, up to renaming.

**Definition 3.74** A clause is a *resolvent* of clauses $C$ and $D$ *with respect to* the subclauses $P \subset C$ and $N \subset D$, if it is most general in the class of all unrestricted resolvents of $C$ and $D$ with respect to $P$ and $N$.                                                          ∎

**Corollary 3.75** *Up to renaming, a resolvent of clauses with respect to given subclauses is unique.*                                                                                            ∎

**Example.** Suppose that $C$ is $\{\mathbf{r}(x), \mathbf{q}(x, y)\}$ and $D$ is $\{\neg\mathbf{r}(\mathbf{s}x), \mathbf{q}(x, y)\}$. An unrestricted resolvent of these clauses (w.r.t. $\{\mathbf{r}(x)\}$ and $\{\neg\mathbf{r}(\mathbf{s}x)\}$) is $\{\mathbf{q}(\mathbf{s}x, y), \mathbf{q}(x, y)\}$ (take the $\{x/\mathbf{s}x\}$-instance of $C$); however, this is not a resolvent. An example of a resolvent is $\{\mathbf{q}(\mathbf{s}x, y), \mathbf{q}(x, z)\}$ (take the $\{x/\mathbf{s}x\}$-instance of $C$ and the $\{y/z\}$-instance of $D$).                  ∎

The main fact on resolution is contained in the following lemma.

**Lemma 3.76** *If two clauses have an unrestricted resolvent with respect to certain subclauses, then they also have a resolvent with respect to these subclauses.*

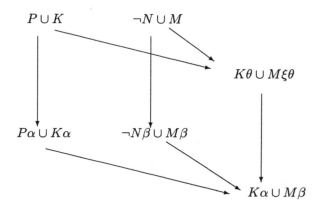

**Proof.** We need Theorem 3.63 on most general unification. Assume that $C = P \cup K$, $D = \neg N \cup M$ ($N$ a set of atoms; $\neg N := \{\neg A \mid A \in N\}$), that $P\alpha = N\beta$ is a singleton and $K\alpha \cup M\beta$ is the unrestricted resolvent of $C$ and $D$ with respect to $P$ and $\neg N$.

First, *separate variables*. That is, choose a renaming $\xi$ for $D$ such that $C$ and $D\xi$ have no variables in common.

*Claim: $P \cup N\xi$ is unifiable.*

*Proof:* Choose a substitution that *undoes* the effect $\xi$ has on $D$, i.e., such that $D\xi\delta = D$; cf. Lemma 3.58. Now, let $\gamma := \alpha|Var(C) \cup (\delta\beta)|Var(D\xi)$. (Note that $Var(C) \cap Var(D\xi) = \emptyset$ by choice of $\xi$.) We have $P\gamma = P\alpha = N\beta = N\xi\delta\beta = N\xi\gamma$ is a singleton, i.e, $\gamma$ unifies $P \cup N\xi$.

By Theorem 3.63, $P \cup N\xi$ has an mgu $\theta$. Since $P\theta = N\xi\theta$ is a singleton, $K\theta \cup M\xi\theta$ also is an unrestricted resolvent of $C$ and $D$ with respect to $P$ and $\neg N$.

*Claim: in fact, this is a resolvent of $C$ and $D$.*

For instance (comparing with the unrestricted resolvent $K\alpha \cup M\beta$), since $\theta$ most generally unifies $P$ an $N\xi$, there exists some $\sigma$ such that $\theta\sigma = \gamma$; hence, $(K\theta \cup M\xi\theta)\sigma = K\gamma \cup M\xi\gamma = K\alpha \cup M\beta$.

Obviously, the same argument works for every other unrestricted resolvent with respect to $P$ and $\neg N$. ∎

**Recipe.** The previous proof contains the following recipe for finding a resolvent (if there is one) of two clauses $P \cup K$ and $\neg N \cup M$ with respect to the subclauses $P$ and $\neg N$. First, apply a renaming $\xi$ to one of the clauses — say, $\neg N \cup M$ — such that the transformed clause $(\neg N \cup M)\xi$ has no variables in common with the other one, $P \cup K$. Next, find an mgu $\theta$ for $P \cup N\xi$ (for this, you can use the unification algorithm). The resolvent is $(K \cup M\xi)\theta$. ∎

**Definition 3.77** Define the derivability relation $\vdash$ like $\vdash_u$ (see Definition 3.46), but this time using *resolvents* instead of unrestricted resolvents.

A *refutation* is a derivation of □. ∎

Of course, we have the following Soundness Theorem.

**Theorem 3.78 (Soundness)** *If $\Sigma \vdash E$, then $\Sigma \models E$.*

**Proof.** Immediate from Theorem 3.49, since $\Sigma \vdash E$ implies $\Sigma \vdash_u E$. ∎

The main property of resolution is given by the following *Lifting Theorem*, which simply iterates Lemma 3.76.

**Theorem 3.79 (Lifting)** *If $\Sigma \vdash_u C$, then $C$ is an instance of a clause $D$ such that $\Sigma \vdash D$.*

**Proof.** Strong induction on the height of the unrestricted derivation, using the basic existence result, Lemma 3.76.

Assume that $\mathcal{T}$ is an unrestricted derivation of $C$ from $\Sigma$. We show that $C$ is an instance of a clause that has a derivation $\mathcal{T}'$ from $\Sigma$.

(i) $\mathcal{T}$ has height 1.

Take $\mathcal{T}' = \mathcal{T}$ and $D = C$.

(ii) $C$ is an unrestricted resolvent of its children $C_1$ and $C_2$ in $\mathcal{T}$.

The subtrees of $\mathcal{T}$ that derive $C_1$ and $C_2$ have heights less than $\mathcal{T}$. By induction hypothesis, there exist clauses $D_1$ and $D_2$ that are derivable from $\Sigma$ and of which $C_1$ and $C_2$ are instances. Obviously, $C$ is an unrestricted resolvent of $D_1$ and $D_2$. By 3.76, $D_1$ and $D_2$ have a resolvent $D$ that is derivable from $\Sigma$. By maximality of resolvents, $C$ is an instance of $D$. ∎

The following theorem expresses refutational completeness of the resolution method.

**Theorem 3.80 (Completeness)** *If $\Sigma$ is an unsatisfiable set of clauses, then $\Sigma$ is refutable: $\Sigma \vdash \square$.*

**Proof.** Suppose that $\Sigma$ is unsatisfiable. Then by Theorem 3.51: $\Sigma \vdash_u \square$. By the Lifting Theorem 3.79, $\square$ is instance of a clause $D$ such that $\Sigma \vdash D$. However, $\square$ *can be an instance of $\square$ only*, hence $D = \square$, and the result follows. ∎

**Corollary 3.81** *$\Sigma$ is an unsatisfiable set of clauses iff $\Sigma \vdash \square$.*

**Proof.** Immediate from Theorems 3.80 and 3.78. ∎

**Discussion.**

Suppose that $\forall \varphi$ is an unsatisfiable universal sentence with matrix $\varphi$ in conjunctive normal form. Let $S$ be the finite set of clauses corresponding to the conjuncts from $\varphi$. By Theorem 3.80, $S \vdash \square$. The virtues of resolution (compared with resolution applied to ground clauses) are that its derivations may be shorter and that it solves the problem of which elements of the possibly *infinite* set $ground(S)$ are actually needed to derive $\square$. Resolution finds these elements (and the ground terms involved) *automatically*. In the case that the finite $S$ is unsatisfiable, we can find a derivation of $\square$ in the following mechanical way (compare Exercise 2.25):

Define $\mathcal{R}(T) := T \cup \{C \mid C$ is resolvent of two clauses in $T\}$. Note that, if $T$ is finite, then so is $\mathcal{R}(T)$. Construct $\mathcal{R}^0(S), \mathcal{R}^1(S), \mathcal{R}^2(S), \ldots$ by: $\mathcal{R}^0(S) = S$, and $\mathcal{R}^{n+1}(S) = \mathcal{R}(\mathcal{R}^n(S))$. These sets are all finite, can be constructed effectively, and for some $n$ we must get $\square \in \mathcal{R}^n(S)$, obtaining our derivation.

However, contrasting to the case for propositional logic, the process may not stabilize, the sets $\mathcal{R}^n(S)$ may grow indefinitely, and we cannot tell beforehand how large an $n$

we must look for. Accordingly, the method gives *positive* decidability of unsatisfiability only, in agreement with Church's Theorem 7.19.

**Example.** $\mathcal{R}^0(S) = S = \{\{\neg\mathbf{r}(x), \mathbf{r}(\mathbf{f}x)\}\}$. $\mathcal{R}^1(S) = S \cup \{\{\neg\mathbf{r}(x), \mathbf{r}(\mathbf{ff}x)\}\}$, $\mathcal{R}^2(S) = \mathcal{R}^1(S) \cup \{\{\neg\mathbf{r}(x), \mathbf{r}(\mathbf{fff}x)\}\}$, etc. In *this* particular example, of course, we immediately see that □ is never encountered. But there are more complicated cases.                    ∎

**Exercises**

**3.39** Determine whether □ is derivable from the following sets of clauses. If so, give a derivation. If not, why?

(i) $\{\{\mathbf{r}(x,x)\}, \{\neg\mathbf{r}(x,\mathbf{f}x)\}, \{\mathbf{r}(x,\mathbf{f}x), \neg\mathbf{r}(\mathbf{f}x,y)\}, \{\mathbf{r}(x,y), \neg\mathbf{r}(x,z), \neg\mathbf{r}(y,z)\}\}$,

(ii) $\{\{\mathbf{r}(x,x)\}, \{\neg\mathbf{r}(x,\mathbf{f}x)\}, \{\mathbf{r}(x,\mathbf{f}x), \neg\mathbf{r}(\mathbf{f}x,y)\}, \{\neg\mathbf{r}(x,y), \mathbf{r}(x,z), \mathbf{r}(y,z)\}\}$.

**3.40** Show: $E$ is a resolvent of $C \cup \{A\}$ and $D \cup \{\neg B\}$ with respect to $\{A\}$ and $\{\neg B\}$ iff for some substitutions $\alpha$ and $\beta$: $Dom(\alpha) \subset Var(C, A)$, $Dom(\beta) \subset Var(D, B)$, $A\alpha = B\beta$ is a most general common instance of $A$ and $B$, $E = C\alpha \cup D\beta$, and $\alpha|[Var(C) - Var(A)]$ and $\beta|[Var(D) - Var(B)]$ injectively map variables to variables such that $\{x\alpha \mid x \in Var(C) - Var(A)\}$ and $\{x\beta \mid x \in Var(D) - Var(B)\}$ are disjoint.

## 3.10   Notes

The material in Subsection 3.6.3 on elementary extensions and chains forms the first few steps into first-order model theory. The "bible" for this subject is [Chang/Keisler 90]. A more recent reference is [Hodges 93].

Our Definition 3.23 of *substitution* has several alternatives in the literature. Also, there are many different notations for substitution. In the literature, one may also encounter the notations $\{t/x\}$, $[x/t]$ and $[t/x]$ for the substitution we have denoted by $\{x/t\}$, and both prefix $(\alpha E)$ and postfix notation $(E\alpha)$ are employed. The postfix notation we are using is slightly unfortunate (after all, a substitution is a function, and function application generally is denoted by prefixing), but quite common in the logic programming literature.

Corollary 3.35 also is a consequence of the *Completeness Theorem* of Gödel (1930). The methods used in the proof of Gödel's *Incompleteness Theorem* (1931) are essential for proving Church's Theorem 7.19, which says that Corollary 3.35 cannot be strengthened to *decidability* of first-order validity and unsatisfiability.

Exercise 3.27 is due to Daniel Mey.

The term *unrestricted resolution* is unfortunate since it seems to refer to a special type of resolution, whereas, on the contrary, resolution is a special type of the unrestricted version. However, in the context of linear resolution (Chapter 5) the term is generally accepted.

Theorem 3.63 is from [Robinson 65]. Since unification is the main computational component of resolution, it is desirable to have a fast unification algorithm. The one described by Robinson is not fast (it uses exponential time). Fast algorithms are due to [Martelli/Montanari 82] and [Paterson-Wegman 78]. The unification algorithm as presented here is due, at least in principle, to Herbrand (cf. [Herbrand 30], p. 124 in the French volume, p. 148 in the translated one) but was first explicitly described and proved adequate in [Martelli/Montanari 82]. The condition, in the last part of the algorithm (selected identity $x \approx t$), that the variable $x$ should not occur in the term $t$, is called the *occur check* condition. Remarkably, even though unification can be accomplished in linear time, this check usually is omitted in Prolog implementations for efficiency reasons. The effect of this omission has been studied, among others, by [Apt/Pellegrini 92]. The surprising outcome is that this usually does not lead to mistakes (although it affects soundness in principle). The problem whether the algorithm can lead to failure due to occur check for a given set of identities was recently shown to be NP-complete by van Emde Boas and Welling. For much more on unification, cf. [Lassez/Maher/Marriott 88].

Clark's equality axioms are from [Clark 78].

The traditional definition of resolution is rather ad-hoc. Here, the lifting property is used as the defining one. As a result, the proof of completeness becomes quite straight-forward.

# 4 Program-definability

## 4.1 Programs

The previous chapter introduced Herbrand models for universal sentences. The present one is devoted to Herbrand models for universal sentences of a special type: *rules*, and (finite) sets of those: *programs*.

Before describing and motivating the contents of this chapter, these notions are defined and some examples are given.

**Definition 4.1** A *rule* is a disjunction of literals containing exactly one positive literal called the *head* of the rule. The rest — the negative part — is called the *body* of the rule. ∎

A rule with head $A$ and negative literals $\neg B_1, \ldots, \neg B_m$ will be written thus:

$$A \leftarrow B_1, \ldots, B_m.$$

In first-order notation, this would be the implication (or its universal closure, cf. Remark 3.26)

$$B_1 \wedge \cdots \wedge B_m \rightarrow A;$$

thus, '$\leftarrow$' is just a reversed implication symbol, and the commas stand for conjunctions.

If $C$ is the sequence $C = (B_1, \ldots, B_m)$, then the rule displayed can be written as

$$A \leftarrow C.$$

A rule is allowed to have an *empty* body. It then has the form

$$A \leftarrow .$$

The first-order notation of this is the atom $A$ itself. Rules with empty body often are called *facts* or *unit clauses*.

**Definition 4.2** A *program* is a finite set of rules. ∎

**Example 4.3** The following two rules make up the program SUM (**sum** is a 3-ary relation symbol):

$$\mathbf{sum}(x, \mathbf{o}, x) \leftarrow$$
$$\mathbf{sum}(x, \mathbf{s}y, \mathbf{s}z) \leftarrow \mathbf{sum}(x, y, z).$$

Recall Definition 3.19 and the conventions of Notation 3.20 about representing $\mathbb{N}$ (with zero and successor function) as a Herbrand algebra generated from one constant symbol $\mathbf{o}$ (for zero) and one unary function symbol $\mathbf{s}$ (for successor).

Consider the Herbrand model over $HU = \mathbb{N}$ with the relation $sum := \{(n, m, n+m) \mid n, m \in \mathbb{N}\}$. This is a model of SUM. For, in the context of this model, the first rule expresses that $n + 0 = n$ for every number $n \in \mathbb{N}$; the second one expresses that if

$n + m = k$, then $n + Sm = Sk$; i.e., that $n + Sm = S(n + m)$.

(Note that the two equations $n + 0 = n$ and $n + Sm = S(n + m)$ enable us to evaluate every sum of natural numbers using the notation with 0 and $S$. E.g., $1 + 2 = S0 + SS0 = S(S0 + S0) = SS(S0 + 0) = SSS0 = 3$.) ∎

**Example 4.4** The following four rules involve a binary function symbol that is written as $[\,.\,|\,.\,]$ and two relation symbols **last** and **reverse** (modifying slightly Exercise 4.59):

$\text{\bf last}([x|[y|z]], [x|y], z) \leftarrow$

$\text{\bf last}([z|u], [z|v], y) \leftarrow \text{\bf last}(u, v, y)$

$\text{\bf reverse}([x|y], [y|x]) \leftarrow$

$\text{\bf reverse}(u, [y|w]) \leftarrow \text{\bf last}(u, v, y), \text{\bf reverse}(v, w).$

Let $HU$ be generated from **o**, **s** and $[\,.\,|\,.\,]$. A finite sequence $(t_1, \ldots, t_n)$ from $HU$ of length $n \geq 2$ is identified with the ground term $[t_1|[t_2|[t_3|\cdots t_n]]]$. A Herbrand model in which these rules are true is obtained by interpreting **last** as the relation that holds of $s$, $t = (t_1, \ldots, t_n)$ and $u$ iff $s = (t_1, \ldots, t_n, u)$ and **reverse** as the relation that holds of $s$ and $t$ iff they are the reverse of each other. ∎

The examples given explain programs by providing a *meaning* for them, in the form of a (Herbrand) model. This is a so-called *declarative* interpretation of programs. It is the subject of the present chapter to describe a special type of Herbrand model for programs. However, programs also have a computational, or *procedural*, content. Again, look at the previous examples. The second **sum**-rule may be interpreted as: in order to add $m + 1$ to $n$, first add $m$, and next take the successor of the result. The second **reverse**-rule may be interpreted as: to reverse a sequence $u$, split it up into last element $y$ and its remains $w$; now obtain $v$ by reversing $w$ and putting $y$ in front of the result. This clearly provides an algorithmic approach to reversing sequences.

Remarkably, it has turned out that even complicated algorithmic processes can be described by the simple type of first-order sentences that rules represent. This discovery is the main *raison d'être* for Prolog.

The procedural interpretation of programs by means of linear resolution and its relation to the declarative aspect is the subject of Chapter 5. For *positive* programs, as introduced here, the theory is quite unproblematic and well-established. Problems come up as soon as we admit negations, which is the subject of Chapter 8, with a mild introduction in Chapter 6.

The hurried reader can switch to linear resolution in Chapter 5 before finishing the present one. A first place from where such a switch can sensibly be made is after Corollary 4.8; a much better one is after Theorem 4.26. Section 4.6 serves as a source of examples that will be used in later chapters as well.

## 4.2   The Least Herbrand Model

By Theorem 3.29, a satisfiable set of universal sentences always has a Herbrand model. Since rules represent universal sentences of a special type (once again recall Remark 3.26; we confuse here a rule with the universal closure of the implication it represents), it turns out that programs have Herbrand models with a special character. This section looks further into the matter. However, before doing so, it is convenient to introduce a somewhat different way of viewing Herbrand models, namely as subsets of the *Herbrand base*.

**Definition 4.5** The *Herbrand base*, with respect to a given language, is the set of all ground atoms. The notation for the Herbrand base is $HB$.                                   ∎

Let $\mathbf{M}$ be a Herbrand model. $\mathbf{M}$ can be recovered from the subset $X := \{A \in HB \mid \mathbf{M}\models A\}$ of $HB$ of ground atoms true in $\mathbf{M}$. For, if $\mathbf{r}$ is any $n$-ary relation symbol, then its interpretation in $\mathbf{M}$ over $HU$ must be the relation $r$ given by

$$r(t_1, \ldots, t_n) \Leftrightarrow \mathbf{r}(t_1, \ldots, t_n) \in X.$$

*Proof:* By Lemma 3.17, $t_i^{\mathbf{M}} = t_i$ $(1 \le i \le n)$; thus:

$$
\begin{aligned}
r(t_1, \ldots, t_n) \quad &\Leftrightarrow \quad r(t_1^{\mathbf{M}}, \ldots, t_n^{\mathbf{M}}) \\
&\Leftrightarrow \quad \mathbf{M}\models\mathbf{r}(t_1, \ldots, t_n) \quad &&\text{(by Definition 3.9 of } \models) \\
&\Leftrightarrow \quad \mathbf{r}(t_1, \ldots, t_n) \in X \quad &&\text{(by definition of } X).
\end{aligned}
$$

Consequently, a Herbrand model henceforth will be identified with the associated set of ground atoms true in it. Conceived of this way, Herbrand models are subsets of $HB$.

The identification is succinctly put in the form of a lemma.

**Lemma 4.6** *If $A \in HB$ and $\mathbf{M}$ is a Herbrand model, then the following are equivalent:*

*(i)* $\mathbf{M}\models A$,

*(ii)* $A \in \mathbf{M}$.                                                                   ∎

As subsets of the Herbrand base, Herbrand models are partially ordered by set inclusion. Programs have the remarkable property that they have *least* Herbrand models. Obviously, every logical consequence $A \in HB$ of a program must belong to this least model. And it is precisely these atoms that form the least Herbrand model of the program.

**Definition 4.7** Let $P$ be a program. $M_P := \{A \in HB \mid P\models A\}$.                  ∎

Recall that (Definition 3.28) for $P$ a set of universal sentences and/or quantifier-free formulas, $ground(P)$ is the set of ground instances of the sentences or formulas in $P$. By Lemma 3.30, for such a set $P$ and a Herbrand model $\mathbf{M}$, that $\mathbf{M}\models P$ amounts to $\mathbf{M}\models ground(P)$.

The next theorem states that, indeed, (i) $M_P$ is a (Herbrand) model of $P$, and (ii) it is the least Herbrand model of $P$.

**Theorem 4.8**
   (i) $M_P\models P$,
   (ii) if $\mathbf{M}\subset HB$ is such that $\mathbf{M}\models P$, then $M_P\subset\mathbf{M}$.

**Proof.** (ii) Trivial: if $\mathbf{M}\models P$ and $A\in M_P$, then $P\models A$ and hence $\mathbf{M}\models A$.
(i) By Lemma 3.30, it suffices to establish that $M_P\models ground(P)$. Thus, consider a ground instance of a $P$-rule $A\leftarrow B_0,\ldots,B_{n-1}$ such that $M_P\models B_i$ $(i<n)$. That is, $P\models B_i$ $(i<n)$. Note that by Corollary 3.27, $P\models(B_0\wedge\cdots\wedge B_{n-1}\rightarrow A)$. Therefore, $P\models A$; i.e.: $M_P\models A$. ∎

We finish this subsection by presenting a characterization of $M_P$ in terms of implication trees that will be useful later on.

**Definition 4.9** An *implication tree* for an atom $B$ with respect to a program $P$ is a finite tree $\mathcal{T}$ of atoms with root $B$ such that for all $A\in\mathcal{T}$, there is an instance $A\leftarrow C$ of a $P$-rule such that the children of $A$ in $\mathcal{T}$ are exactly the atoms from $C$.

An implication tree is *ground* if all its nodes are. ∎

An implication tree for $A$ can be looked at as an extremely simple type of proof of $A$: see the following lemma; also, see Exercise 6.4.

**Lemma 4.10** *For a program $P$ and a ground atom $A$ the following are equivalent:*
   (i) $A\in M_P$,
   (ii) there is a ground implication tree for $A$.

**Proof.** (ii) $\Rightarrow$ (i) Strong induction with respect to the height of the implication tree $\mathcal{T}$ for $A$. Thus, suppose that $A\leftarrow C$ is ground instance of a $P$-rule and the children of $A$ in $\mathcal{T}$ are the atoms of $C$. Then every atom of $C$ has a ground implication tree that can be found as a subtree of $\mathcal{T}$. The heights of these subtrees are less than the one of $\mathcal{T}$. By induction hypothesis, the atoms of $C$ are (true) in $M_P$. It follows that $A\in M_P$.
(i) $\Rightarrow$ (ii) Let $\mathbf{M}$ be the Herbrand model consisting of those $A\in HB$ that have a ground implication tree. It suffices to show that $\mathbf{M}$ is a model of $P$ since then, by Theorem 4.8(ii), $M_P\subset\mathbf{M}$, and the implication follows. By Lemma 3.30, for $\mathbf{M}\models P$ it suffices to show that $\mathbf{M}\models ground(P)$. Thus, let $A\leftarrow C$ be a ground instance of a $P$-rule such that $\mathbf{M}\models\bigwedge C$. By definition of $\mathbf{M}$, every atom of $C$ has a ground implication tree. Then, however, a ground implication tree for $A$ can be formed from those trees, adding $A$ as a new root. ∎

## Exercises

**4.1** Show: the empty Herbrand model $\emptyset \subset HB$ is a model of the program $P$ iff every rule in $P$ has a non-empty body, that is, $P$ does not contain a fact.

Show: the largest Herbrand model $HB$ is a model of *every* program.

**4.2** Show that if $X$ and $Y$ are Herbrand models of the program $P$, then so is $X \cap Y$. What about $X \cup Y$? Give a proof that it is, or a simple counter-example showing that it need not be one.

**4.3** Give a Herbrand model for the program SUM (cf. Example 4.3) that is different from both $HB$ and $\{\mathbf{sum}(n, m, n + m) \mid n, m \in \mathbb{N}\}$.

**4.4** Let $C$ be a finite set of atomic formulas (variables allowed). Show: $P \models \exists \bigwedge C$ iff $M_P \models \exists \bigwedge C$.

**4.5** $\mathcal{L} = \{\mathbf{o}, \mathbf{s}, \mathbf{N}\}$. $P$ consists of the following two rules.

$\mathbf{N}(\mathbf{o}) \leftarrow$
$\mathbf{N}(\mathbf{s}x) \leftarrow \mathbf{N}(x).$

The universal sentence $\forall x \mathbf{N}(x)$ is true in $M_P$ (why?). Show: it does *not* logically follow from $P$.

(For an even simpler example, put $\mathcal{L} = \{\mathbf{o}, \mathbf{N}\}$ and $P = \{\mathbf{N}(\mathbf{o}) \leftarrow\}$.)

**4.6** Let $P$ be a program and $A$ and $B$ ground atoms. Show: if $P \models A \vee B$, then $P \models A$ or $P \models B$. Give an example of a set $P$ of universal sentences for which this implication fails.

**4.7** Let $P$ be a program and $\bigwedge C$ a conjunction of atoms. Show: if $P \models \exists \bigwedge C$, then some ground instance of $\bigwedge C$ logically follows from $P$. Give an example of a set $P$ of universal sentences for which this fails.

The following (trivial) remark can often be fruitfully applied whenever we have a concrete Herbrand model $\mathbf{M} \subset HB$ for which we want to verify that $\mathbf{M} = M_P$. It says that we only have to prove two things: (i) that $\mathbf{M}$ is a model of $P$, and (ii) that every atom in $\mathbf{M}$ follows logically from $P$.

**Remark 4.11** Let $P$ be a program, $HB$ the corresponding Herbrand base and $\mathbf{M} \subset HB$.

(i) if $\mathbf{M}$ is a model of $P$ (i.e.: $\mathbf{M} \models P$), then $M_P \subset \mathbf{M}$;
(ii) if every atom in $\mathbf{M}$ follows logically from $P$ (i.e.: $P \models \mathbf{M}$), then $\mathbf{M} \subset M_P$. ∎

In concrete cases, (i) usually follows by mere inspection, but (ii) may require an induction.

**4.8** Prove Remark 4.11. Which of the implications can be strengthened to an equivalence? Which one cannot? Why? Give an argument or a counter-example.

**4.9** $P$ consists of the following two rules:

  $\mathbf{r(o, y)} \leftarrow$
  $\mathbf{r(s}x, \mathbf{s}y) \leftarrow \mathbf{r}(x, y).$

Identify $M_P$.

*Hint.* Try $\{\mathbf{r}(n, m) | n \le m\}$. Use Remark 4.11. To prove that $n \le m \Rightarrow P \models \mathbf{r}(n, m)$, induct with respect to $n$.

**4.10** Again, suppose that $HU = \mathbb{N}$. Construct a simple program that has $\mathbf{M} :=$ $\{\mathbf{r}(n, m) \mid n > m\}$ as its least Herbrand model. Give a proof of this using Remark 4.11.

## 4.3   Fixed Points

This section puts the simple results of the previous section in the general perspective of inductive definability, using consequence operators.

    In the following definition, as in the sequel, we employ the following shorthand. If $C$ is a sequence from $HB$ and $X \subset HB$ a Herbrand model, then by $C \subset X$ we mean that every atom occurring in $C$ belongs to $X$; equivalently, that $\bigwedge C$ is true in $X$.

    The *powerset* $\mathcal{P}(K) := \{X \mid X \subset K\}$ is the collection of all subsets of the class $K$. Thus, the powerset $\mathcal{P}(HB)$ is the collection of all Herbrand models.

**Definition 4.12** Let $P$ be a program. The *immediate consequence operator* of $P$ is the function $T_P : \mathcal{P}(HB) \rightarrow \mathcal{P}(HB)$, which maps Herbrand models to Herbrand models and is defined by $T_P(X) := \{A \in HB \mid \text{for some } C \subset X : (A \leftarrow C) \in ground(P)\}$.     ■

**Example 4.13** Consider the program EVEN, made up of the following rules.

  $\mathbf{even(o)} \leftarrow$
  $\mathbf{even(ss}x) \leftarrow \mathbf{even}(x)$ .

Note that $M_{EVEN} = \{\mathbf{even}(2n) \mid n \in \mathbb{N}\}$. Let $T = T_{EVEN}$ be the associated immediate consequence operator. We have:

  $T(\emptyset) = \{\mathbf{even(o)}\},$
  $T(T(\emptyset)) = \{\mathbf{even(o)}, \mathbf{even(sso)}\}$, etc.;
  $T(HB) = T(\emptyset) \cup \{\mathbf{even}(n) \mid n \ge 2\},$
  $T(T(HB)) = T(T(\emptyset)) \cup \{\mathbf{even}(n) \mid n \ge 4\}$, etc.

Now, consider the program SUM of Example 4.3. Let $T = T_{SUM}$ be its immediate consequence operator. We have:

  $T(\emptyset) = \{\mathbf{sum}(n, 0, n) \mid n \in \mathbb{N}\},$
  $T(T(\emptyset)) = \{\mathbf{sum}(n, m, n + m) \mid m \le 1 \wedge n \in \mathbb{N}\},$
  $T(T(T(\emptyset))) = \{\mathbf{sum}(n, m, n + m) \mid m \le 2 \wedge n \in \mathbb{N}\}$, etc.;
  $T(HB) = T(\emptyset) \cup \{\mathbf{sum}(n, m, p) \mid n, m, p \in \mathbb{N}, m, p \ge 1\},$

$T(T(HB)) = T(T(\emptyset)) \cup \cup \{\mathbf{sum}(n, m, p) \mid n, m, p \in \mathbb{N}, m, p \geq 2\}$, etc.  ∎

For the following couple of definitions, the reader may think of the set $U$ as the Herbrand base and the function $T$ as an immediate consequence operator over it, but this is not necessary.

The primary interest concerns inductive pre-fixed points. Since co-inductive post-fixed points may appear somewhat mysterious and are not needed for much that is in this chapter and the next one, the reader may skip material referring to them and concentrate on parts (i), (ii) and (iv) of the following.

**Definition 4.14** Let $T : \mathcal{P}(U) \to \mathcal{P}(U)$ be an operator mapping subsets of $U$ to subsets of $U$. A set $X \subset U$ is called

  (i) *pre-fixed point* of $T$, or *$T$-closed*, if $T(X) \subset X$,
  (ii) *fixed point* of $T$ if $T(X) = X$,
  (iii) *post-fixed point* of $T$, or *$T$-supported*, if $X \subset T(X)$,
  (iv) *$T$-inductive* if it is included in every pre-fixed point of $T$,
  (v) *$T$-co-inductive* if it contains every post-fixed point of $T$.  ∎

**Remark.** The terminology of $T$-inductivity is justified as follows. Let $U := \mathbb{N}$ and $T(X) := \{0\} \cup \{n+1 \mid n \in X\}$. $\mathbb{N}$ is the only pre-fixed point of $T$, and it is $T$-inductive as well. Now $X$ is a pre-fixed point of $T$ iff $0 \in X \wedge \forall n \in X(n+1 \in X)$. Thus, inductivity of $\mathbb{N}$ here coincides with Principle 1.1 of mathematical induction.  ∎

**Example 4.15** $U = \mathbb{N}$, $T(X) := \{0\} \cup \{n+2 \mid n \in X\}$. This operator is closely related to the immediate consequence operator $T_{EVEN}$ of the program EVEN in Example 4.13.1. For $X \subset HB$, put $X' := \{n \mid \mathbf{even}(n) \in X\}$. Then $(T_{EVEN}(X))' = T(X')$.

  (i) Pre-fixed points: $\{2n \mid n \in \mathbb{N}\}$ and all sets of the form $\{2n \mid n \in \mathbb{N}\} \cup \{2n+1 \mid n \geq m\}$. In particular $(m = 0)$ $\mathbb{N}$ is a pre-fixed point.
  (ii) The only fixed point is $\{2n \mid n \in \mathbb{N}\}$.
  (iii) Post-fixed points: $\mathbb{N}$, and all sets $\{2n \mid n \leq m\}$.  ∎

Our interest in pre-fixed points is explained by the following lemma.

**Lemma 4.16** *Let $P$ be a program. For a Herbrand model $\mathbf{M}$, the following conditions are equivalent:*

  *(i) $\mathbf{M}$ is a pre-fixed point of $T_P$,*
  *(ii) $\mathbf{M} \models P$.*

**Proof.** (i)⇒(ii): Assume that (i) holds. Instead of $\mathbf{M}\models P$, we show that $\mathbf{M}\models ground(P)$, using Lemma 3.30. Thus, suppose that $(A \leftarrow C) \in ground(P)$. If $C \subset \mathbf{M}$, then $A \in T_P(\mathbf{M})$; therefore, by (i), $A \in \mathbf{M}$; and hence $A \leftarrow C$ is true in $\mathbf{M}$.

(ii)⇒(i): Conversely, assume that $\mathbf{M}$ satisfies $P$. Let $A$ be an atom in $T_P(\mathbf{M})$. Then for some ground instance $A \leftarrow C$ of a rule in $P$, we have $C \subset \mathbf{M}$. Then by (ii) $A \in \mathbf{M}$, proving (i). $\blacksquare$

**Example 4.17** From the facts given by Example 4.15 it follows that, one excepted, the Herbrand models of EVEN from Example 4.13 are of the form $\{\mathbf{even}(2n) \mid n \in \mathbb{N}\} \cup \{\mathbf{even}(2n+1) \mid n \geq m\}$. The exception is the least Herbrand model $\{\mathbf{even}(2n) \mid n \in \mathbb{N}\}$. $\blacksquare$

That programs have least Herbrand models can also be seen as a consequence of their operators being monotone.

**Definition 4.18** $T : \mathcal{P}(U) \rightarrow \mathcal{P}(U)$ is *monotone* if for all $X, Y \subset U$: if $X \subset Y$, then $T(X) \subset T(Y)$. $\blacksquare$

**Lemma 4.19** *Immediate consequence operators are monotone.* $\blacksquare$

**Lemma 4.20** *An operator has at most one inductive pre-fixed point and one co-inductive post-fixed point. The inductive pre-fixed point and the co-inductive post-fixed point of a monotone operator are fixed points.*

**Proof.** Suppose that $X$ and $Y$ both are inductive pre-fixed points. Since $X$ is a pre-fixed point and $Y$ is inductive, we have that $Y \subset X$. By symmetry, $X \subset Y$. The argument for co-inductive post-fixed points is similar. Now suppose that $X$ is an inductive pre-fixed point of $T$. That is, $T(X) \subset X$. By monotonicity, $T(T(X)) \subset T(X)$. Thus, $T(X)$ is a pre-fixed point. By inductivity of $X$, $X \subset T(X)$. Therefore, $X$ is a fixed point. $\blacksquare$

The lemma shows that inductive pre-fixed points are the same as inductive fixed points; similarly, co-inductive post-fixed points and co-inductive fixed points are the same. Since the inductive fixed point (if it exists) is contained in every (pre-) fixed point, it also is the *least* fixed point. Similarly, the co-inductive fixed point is the *greatest* one.

The following, completely general, result shows that these objects indeed exist (but of course, they may coincide).

**Theorem 4.21 (on Fixed Points)** *Every monotone operator has an inductive and a co-inductive fixed point.*

**Proof.** Suppose that $T : \mathcal{P}(U) \rightarrow \mathcal{P}(U)$ is monotone. For the inductive fixed point, let $K := \{X \subset U \mid T(X) \subset X\}$ be the collection of all pre-fixed points of $T$ and let

$M := \bigcap K = \bigcap_{X \in K} X$ be their intersection. Note that, since $U \in K$, we have $K \neq \emptyset$; therefore, $M$ is well-defined.

We show that $M$ is a pre-fixed point of $T$.

Let $X$ be an arbitrary pre-fixed point. Then $M \subset X$. Hence, by monotonicity, $T(M) \subset T(X)$; therefore, since $T(X) \subset X$, we have $T(M) \subset X$. Thus, $T(M)$ is included in *every* pre-fixed point. Therefore, $T(M)$ is included in the intersection $M$ of all pre-fixed points; that is, $M$ is a pre-fixed point itself.

From the definition of $M$, inductivity is immediate.

For co-inductive fixed points, see Exercise 4.11.                                           ∎

So, the existence of least Herbrand models once again follows from Lemma 4.19 and Theorem 4.21.

By the way, note that every program trivially has a *greatest* Herbrand model as well (not to be confused with the co-inductive fixed point of its operator), the Herbrand base $HB$ itself (Exercise 4.1).

**Notation 4.22** The least fixed point of a monotone operator $T : \mathcal{P}(U) \rightarrow \mathcal{P}(U)$ is denoted by $T\!\uparrow$; the greatest one by $T\!\downarrow$.

Thus for the immediate consequence operator of $P$, $T = T_P$, we have that $M_P = T_P\!\uparrow$. ∎

Readers who have never encountered least fixed points and who find the various definitions of $M_P$ rather too abstract may feel uneasy. They may be somewhat comforted by Theorem 4.26.

**Remark.** Examples of least fixed points occurring before are the sets of formulas and terms in propositional and first-order logic. Here, $U$ is the set of all finite sequences of symbols. Try to identify the monotone operators involved. For yet another example, see Exercise 4.15. In Chapter 8, two more examples of inductively defined sets occur. See Definitions 8.12 and 8.47. The formulation there is quite close to the ones for formulas and terms.                                                                                        ∎

**Exercises**

**4.11** Complete the proof of Theorem 4.21 for co-inductive fixed points.
*Hint.* The co-inductive fixed point is the *union* of all post-fixed points.

**\*4.12** If $S$ is a set of pairwise disjoint trees and $u$ is not a node of a tree in $S$, then $\mathcal{T} = \{u\} + \sum S$ is the tree the nodes of which are $u$ and those of the trees of $S$, with root $u$, such that the children of $u$ are the roots of the trees in $S$ and the children of a node in a tree $T \in S$ are the same as the children of this node in $T$.

Let **T** be the class of all trees. Define $\Gamma : \mathcal{P}\mathbf{T}) \rightarrow \mathcal{P}(\mathbf{T})$ by $\Gamma(X) := \{\{u\} + \sum S \mid S \subset X$ is a set of pairwise disjoint trees and $u$ is not in a tree of $S\}$.

Show: the elements of $\Gamma{\uparrow}$ are exactly the well-founded trees.

## 4.4   Hierarchies

Immediate consequence operators enjoy the property of being finitary, which is responsible for the fact that their least fixed points can be finitely approximated.

**Definition 4.23** An operator $T : \mathcal{P}(U){\to}\mathcal{P}(U)$ is called *finitary* if, for all $X \subset U$ and $A \in U$ such that $A \in T(X)$, there exists a *finite* $Y \subset X$ for which $A \in T(Y)$.  ∎

**Lemma 4.24** *Immediate consequence operators are finitary.*

**Proof.** Bodies of rules consist of finitely many atoms only.  ∎

Finite approximation of the least fixed point is established by the upward fixed point hierarchy.

**Definition 4.25** Let $T : \mathcal{P}(U) \to \mathcal{P}(U)$ be a monotone operator. The (finite) *stages of the upward hierarchy* of $T$ are the sets $T{\uparrow}n$ $(n \in \mathbb{N})$ recursively defined by

$$
\begin{aligned}
T{\uparrow}0 &= \emptyset, \\
T{\uparrow}(n+1) &= T(T{\uparrow}n).
\end{aligned}
$$

Finally, $T{\uparrow}\omega := \bigcup_{n\in\mathbb{N}} T{\uparrow}n$.  ∎

The next result says that the upward fixed point hierarchy corresponding to a monotone operator consists of an increasing sequence of sets inside the least fixed point; moreover, the least fixed point actually is given by the union of the hierarchy.

**Theorem 4.26** *Let $T : \mathcal{P}(U) \to \mathcal{P}(U)$ be monotone. Then:*

*(i) for all $n \in \mathbb{N}$: $T{\uparrow}n \subset T{\uparrow}(n+1)$,*
*(ii) for all $n \in \mathbb{N}$: $T{\uparrow}n \subset T{\uparrow}$,*
*(iii) $T{\uparrow}\omega \subset T{\uparrow}$,*
*(iv) if $T$ is finitary, then $T{\uparrow} = T{\uparrow}\omega$.*

**Proof.** (i) Induction with respect to $n$.
*Basis.* Trivially, $T{\uparrow}0 = \emptyset \subset T{\uparrow}1$.
*Induction step.* If $T{\uparrow}n \subset T{\uparrow}(n+1)$ (induction hypothesis), then, by monotonicity, $T{\uparrow}(n+1) = T(T{\uparrow}n) \subset T(T{\uparrow}(n+1)) = T{\uparrow}(n+2)$.
(ii) Again, induction with respect to $n$.
*Basis.* $T{\uparrow}0 = \emptyset \subset T{\uparrow}$.
*Induction step.* If $T{\uparrow}n \subset T{\uparrow}$ (induction hypothesis), then, by monotonicity and the fact that $T{\uparrow}$ is a fixed point of $T$, we have $T{\uparrow}(n+1) = T(T{\uparrow}n) \subset T(T{\uparrow}) = T{\uparrow}$.

(iii) This is immediate from (ii).

(iv) By (iii), it suffices to show that $T{\uparrow} \subset T{\uparrow}\omega$. By inductivity, $T{\uparrow} \subset T{\uparrow}\omega$ follows from the inclusion $T(T{\uparrow}\omega) \subset T{\uparrow}\omega$. For this, we use that $T$ is finitary. Assume that $A \in T(T{\uparrow}\omega)$. Then we have $A \in T(Y)$ for some finite subset $Y$ of $T{\uparrow}\omega$. Since $T{\uparrow}\omega = \bigcup_n T{\uparrow}n$, every $B \in Y$ is element of some $T{\uparrow}n$. Let $m$ be the *maximum* of these finitely many $n$. By part (i), $Y \subset T{\uparrow}m$. Hence, by monotonicity, $A \in T(Y) \subset T(T{\uparrow}m) = T{\uparrow}(m+1) \subset T{\uparrow}\omega$.  ∎

### Exercises

**4.13** Let $P$ be the program of Exercise 4.9. Compute $T_P{\uparrow}0$, $T_P{\uparrow}1$ and $T_P{\uparrow}2$. Describe $T_P{\uparrow}n$ generally.

**4.14** Show: $A \in T_P{\uparrow}n$ iff $A$ has a ground implication tree with respect to $P$ of height $\leq n$.

**4.15** Let $R$ be a binary relation on $X$. Define $\Gamma : \mathcal{P}(X^2) \to \mathcal{P}(X^2)$ by: $\Gamma(S) := R \cup \{(x,z) \mid \exists y((x,y) \in S \wedge yRz)\}$. Show that $R^{tr}$, the transitive closure of $R$ (Definition 1.9), is the least fixed point of $\Gamma$.

Give a monotone operator different from $\Gamma$ that also has $R^{tr}$ as its least fixed point.
*Hint.* See the proof of Lemma 1.8 and Exercise 1.7. Note that $\Gamma$ is finitary.

Thanks to immediate consequence operators being finitary, their least fixed points are reached at (or before) stage $\omega$ of the upward fixed point hierarchy. The next exercise describes the situation for arbitrary, not necessarily finitary, monotone operators.

**\*4.16** Let $T : \mathcal{P}(U) \to \mathcal{P}(U)$ be a monotone operator that is not necessarily finitary. The complete *upward hierarchy* of $T$ consists of the increasing series of sets $T{\uparrow}\alpha$ ($\alpha$ an ordinal) extending the ones of Definition 4.25 and recursively defined by

$$
\begin{aligned}
T{\uparrow}0 &= \emptyset, \\
T{\uparrow}(\alpha+1) &= T(T{\uparrow}\alpha), \\
T{\uparrow}\gamma &= \bigcup_{\xi < \gamma} T{\uparrow}\xi \quad (\gamma \text{ a limit}).
\end{aligned}
$$

Show that, for some ordinal $\alpha$ (of cardinality $\leq \mathcal{P}(U)$) we have that $T{\uparrow} = T{\uparrow}\alpha$. (The least such ordinal is called the *closure ordinal* of the upward hierarchy.)
*Hint.* Let $\alpha$ be the first ordinal for which $T{\uparrow}\alpha = T{\uparrow}(\alpha+1)$.

**4.17** (Compare Exercise 4.14.) Let $T : \mathcal{P}(U) \to \mathcal{P}(U)$ be monotone. Show: $a \in T{\uparrow}\alpha$ iff there is a tree of height $\leq \alpha$ with root $a$ such that for every node $b$, if $X$ is the set of children of $b$, then $b \in T(X)$.

The next definition of the downward hierarchy describes the situation for *greatest* fixed points, which are in some sense dual to least fixed points. (See Exercise 4.24.)

**Definition 4.27** Let $T : \mathcal{P}(U) \to \mathcal{P}(U)$ be a monotone operator. The *stages of the downward hierarchy* of $T$ are the sets $T{\downarrow}\alpha \subset U$ ($\alpha$ an *ordinal*), recursively defined by

$$
\begin{aligned}
T{\downarrow}0 &= U \\
T{\downarrow}(\alpha + 1) &= T(T{\downarrow}\alpha) \\
T{\downarrow}\gamma &= \bigcap_{\xi < \gamma} T{\downarrow}\xi
\end{aligned}
$$

where $\gamma$ is an arbitrary limit.                                                          ∎

The difference between upward and downward hierarchy is that the latter starts from $U$ instead of $\emptyset$ and uses intersections at limits.

**\*4.18** Let $T : \mathcal{P}(U) \to \mathcal{P}(U)$ be a monotone operator. Show that, for some ordinal $\alpha$ of cardinality $\leq \mathcal{P}(U)$, we have that $T{\downarrow} = T{\downarrow}\alpha$. (The least such ordinal is called the *closure ordinal* of the downward hierarchy.)
*Hint.* Compare Exercise 4.16 or deduce the result from 4.16 and Exercise 4.24.

**4.19** Identify $T_P{\downarrow}$ for the program $P$ of Exercise 4.9.

**4.20** $HU = \mathbb{N}$. $P$ has the following two rules:
$\mathbf{r}(\mathbf{s}x) \leftarrow \mathbf{r}(x)$
$\mathbf{q}(\mathbf{o}) \leftarrow \mathbf{r}(x)$.
Determine $T_P{\downarrow}\omega$, $T{\downarrow}(\omega + 1)$ and $T_P{\downarrow}$.

Exercise 4.20 illustrates that the closure ordinal of the downward hierarchy of a consequence operator can be $> \omega$, contrasting with the fact that the upward hierarchy always closes at or before $\omega$.

**4.21** Construct, for as many ordinals as you can, programs that downward close at that ordinal. (Details are given by Chapter 7, Section 7.3.)

The following exercise presents a useful sufficient condition for a consequence operator to have exactly one fixed point.

**4.22** Let $P$ be a program. Define the relation $\prec$ on the Herbrand base $HB$ of ground atoms by: $B \prec A$ iff for some rule $A \leftarrow L$ in $ground(P)$, $B$ occurs in $L$. Show: if $\prec$ is well-founded (Definition 1.11), then $T_P$ has *exactly one* fixed point. (Of course, there still may be lots of pre-fixed points.)
*Hint.* It suffices to verify the implication $A \in T_P{\downarrow} \Rightarrow A \in T_P{\uparrow}$. For this, use $\prec$-induction with respect to $A$ (that is: Lemma 1.14(iii)).

**4.23** Apply the criterion of Exercise 4.22 to the programs of Exercises 4.20 and 4.9.

**4.24** (The *dual* of a monotone operator) Let $T : \mathcal{P}(U) \to \mathcal{P}(U)$ be monotone. Define $T^d : \mathcal{P}(U) \to \mathcal{P}(U)$ by $T^d(X) := U - T(U - X)$. Show:

  (i) $T^d$ is monotone,
  (ii) for all ordinals $\alpha$, we have $T^d \uparrow \alpha = U - T \downarrow \alpha$ and $T^d \downarrow \alpha = U - T \uparrow \alpha$,
  (iii) $T^d(X) = X$ iff $T(U - X) = U - X$,
  (iv) $T^d \uparrow = U - T \downarrow; T^d \downarrow = U - T \uparrow$,
  (v) $T^{dd} = T$.

Give an example of a finitary operator with a non-finitary dual.

**4.25** Let $P$ be a program. We always have $\emptyset \subset M_P = T_P \uparrow \subset T_P \downarrow \subset T_P \downarrow \omega \subset HB$. Give four simple examples of programs, showing that the combinations

  1. $\emptyset \neq T_P \uparrow = T_P \downarrow = T_P \downarrow \omega \neq HB$,
  2. $\emptyset \neq T_P \uparrow = T_P \downarrow \neq T_P \downarrow \omega \neq HB$,
  3. $\emptyset \neq T_P \uparrow \neq T_P \downarrow = T_P \downarrow \omega \neq HB$ and
  4. $\emptyset \neq T_P \uparrow \neq T_P \downarrow \neq T_P \downarrow \omega \neq HB$

are all possible.

**4.26** Let $T : \mathcal{P}(U) \to \mathcal{P}(U)$ be a monotone operator over $U$ and suppose that $Z \subset U$. Show that $T$ has a least pre-fixed point containing $Z$.
*Hint.* Consider the least fixed point of the operation $T'$ defined by: $T'(X) := Z \cup T(X)$.

**Notation.** The least pre-fixed point of $T$ containing $Z$ is denoted by $T \uparrow (Z)$. ∎

**4.27** Let $T_1, T_2 : \mathcal{P}(U) \to \mathcal{P}(U)$ be monotone operators over $U$. Define the monotone operator $T : \mathcal{P}(U) \to \mathcal{P}(U)$ by: $T(X) := T_1(X) \cup T_2(X)$. Is it true that $T \uparrow = T_1 \uparrow \cup T_2 \uparrow$? Give a proof or a counter-example.
What if we change $\cup$ to $\cap$?

**4.28** Let $T : \mathcal{P}(U) \to \mathcal{P}(U)$ be a monotone operator over $U$. Let $T^+$ be defined by: $T^+(X) := X \cup T(X)$. Show that $T^+ \uparrow = T \uparrow$.

**4.29** Let $T : \mathcal{P}(U) \to \mathcal{P}(U)$ be a finitary monotone operator over $U$ and $Z \subset U$. Define the sets $T \uparrow n(Z)$ by recursion as follows.
  $T \uparrow 0(Z) = Z$ ;
  $T \uparrow (n + 1)(Z) = T^+(T \uparrow n(Z)) \ (= T \uparrow n(Z) \cup T(T \uparrow n(Z)))$.
Show that $T \uparrow (Z) = \bigcup_n T \uparrow n(Z)$.

Programs often are constructed in stages. The following lemma presents an alternative description for the least Herbrand model of such a program.

**Lemma 4.28 (Modularity Lemma)** *Suppose that $\mathcal{L}_1$ and $\mathcal{L}_2$ are languages such that $\mathcal{L}_1 \subset \mathcal{L}_2$; $HB_1$ is the Herbrand base of $\mathcal{L}_1$. Let $P_i$ be a program in $\mathcal{L}_i$ ($i = 1, 2$) such that:*

*no relation symbol in the head of a $P_2$-rule occurs in a $P_1$-rule.*

*Let $P := P_1 \cup P_2$ and let $T$, $T_1$ and $T_2$ be the operators of, resp., $P$, $P_1$ and $P_2$. Then*

(i) $T_1\!\uparrow = T\!\uparrow \cap HB_1$;

(ii) $HB_1 \cap T_2\!\uparrow(X) = HB_1 \cap X$;

(iii) $T\!\uparrow = T_2\!\uparrow(T_1\!\uparrow)$.

The third equation states that $T\!\uparrow$ may be obtained by first generating $T_1\!\uparrow$, and subsequently generating the least fixed point of $T_2$ containing $T_1\!\uparrow$.

**\*4.30** Prove Lemma 4.28.

The next exercise describes a stability property of programs with respect to the underlying language.

**4.31** Let $P$ be a program in the language $\mathcal{L}_1$. Suppose that $\mathcal{L}_1 \subset \mathcal{L}_2$. $HU_i$ is the Herbrand universe relative to $\mathcal{L}_i$ ($i = 1, 2$), $HB_i$ the Herbrand base. Let $M_i$ be the least Herbrand model $P$ generates over $HB_i$ ($i = 1, 2$). Show that $M_2 \cap HB_1 = M_1$.
What about the equality $M_2 = M_1$?
What is the situation for greatest fixed point models?

The following exercise describes a type of inductive definability that will be used in Chapter 8. But in fact, least Herbrand models of programs already furnish examples, see Exercise 4.33.

**\*4.32** (Simultaneous inductive definitions.) Assume that $T, S : \mathcal{P}(A) \times \mathcal{P}(A) \to \mathcal{P}(A)$ are monotone; that is, if $X_1 \subset X_2$ and $Y_1 \subset Y_2$, then $T(X_1, Y_1) \subset T(X_2, Y_2)$ (and similarly for $S$). Show: there are $I, J \subset A$ such that

(i) $T(I, J) \subset$ ; $S(I, J) \subset J$ (closure),

(ii) if $T(X, Y) \subset X$ and $S(X, Y) \subset Y$, then $I \subset X$ and $J \subset Y$ (induction).

**4.33** Suppose that $P$ is a program. Let $\mathcal{R} = \mathcal{R}_1 \cup \mathcal{R}_2$ be a partition of the set $\mathcal{R}$ of relation symbols of the language of $P$. Define $T(X) := \{A \in T_P(X) \mid A$ carries a relation symbol from $\mathcal{R}_1\}$ and $S(X) := \{A \in T_P(X) \mid A$ carries a relation symbol from $\mathcal{R}_2\}$. Let $I$ and $J$ be the sets the existence of which is claimed by Exercise 4.32. Show that $M_P = I \cup J$.

## 4.5 Definability

The next definition describes the objects defined by a program.

**Definition 4.29** Let $P$ be a program.

(i) *$P$ defines* the $n$-ary relation $r \subset HU^n$ *over $HU$ in* the $n$-ary relation symbol $\mathbf{r}$ if for all $t_1, \ldots, t_n \in HU$:

$$r(t_1, \ldots, t_n) \Longleftrightarrow P \models \mathbf{r}(t_1, \ldots, t_n).$$

(ii) *$P$ defines* the $n$-ary (partial) function $f : HU^n \to HU$ *over $HU$ in* the $(n+1)$-ary relation symbol $\mathbf{f}$ if for all $s, t_1, \ldots, t_n \in HU$:

$$f(t_1, \ldots, t_n) = s \Longleftrightarrow P \models \mathbf{f}(t_1, \ldots, t_n, s);$$

that is, if $P$ defines the *graph* $\{(t_1, \ldots, t_n, s) \mid f(t_1, \ldots, t_n) = s\}$ of $f$ in $\mathbf{f}$ in the sense of (i). ∎

Of course, by Definition 4.7, the right-hand side of the equivalence in 4.29(i) can be replaced by: $\mathbf{r}(t_1, \ldots, t_n) \in M_P$. Thus, program-definability is closely related to least Herbrand models. $P$ defines $r$ in $\mathbf{r}$ exactly in case $r$ is the interpretation of $\mathbf{r}$ in the least Herbrand model $M_P$ of $P$. The same goes for the function case.

In Chapter 7 (Theorem 7.17), we shall establish that a relation (resp., function) over $HU$ is program-definable in the sense defined iff it is positively decidable (resp., calculable). It follows that the results in Exercises 4.35 and 4.36 (closure of the class of program-definable relations under unions, intersections and existential quantifications) cannot be extended by closure under complementation and universal quantification.

### Exercises

**4.34** Let $P$ be a program that defines the relation $R$ in the binary relation symbol $\mathbf{r}$. Extend $P$ to $P^+$ by the following four rules involving $\mathbf{p}$ and $\mathbf{q}$:

$\mathbf{p}(x, y) \leftarrow \mathbf{r}(x, y)$
$\mathbf{p}(x, z) \leftarrow \mathbf{p}(x, y), \mathbf{p}(y, z)$
$\mathbf{q}(x, y) \leftarrow \mathbf{r}(x, y)$
$\mathbf{q}(x, z) \leftarrow \mathbf{q}(x, y), \mathbf{r}(y, z)$.

Show that $P^+$ defines the transitive closure $R^{tr}$ *both* in $\mathbf{p}$ and $\mathbf{q}$. Is the interpretation of $\mathbf{q}$ transitive in *every* Herbrand model of $P^+$?

**4.35** (Unions and intersections of program-definable relations are program-definable.) Suppose that $P_1$ and $P_2$ are two programs that do not have any relation symbol in common. Assume that $P_i$ defines the set $A_i \subset HU$ in the unary relation symbol $\alpha_i$ ($i = 1, 2$).

(i) Extend $P_1 \cup P_2$ to a program that defines $A_1 \cup A_2$ (in some relation symbol).

(ii) Extend $P_1 \cup P_2$ to a program that defines $A_1 \cap A_2$.

**4.36** (Existential quantification of a program-definable relation is program-definable.) Assume that $P$ defines the relation $r \subset HU^2$ in the binary relation symbol **r**. Define $s \subset HU$ by: $s(t) :\equiv \exists u \in HU\ r(t, u)$. Construct a program (an extension of $P$ with one rule) that defines $s$ in some unary relation symbol **s**.

The problem of which program-definable relations have a program-definable complement will be answered in Chapter 7. The next exercise shows that the equality relation, which is defined in **eq** by the rule $\mathbf{eq}(x, x) \leftarrow$, is one of them.

**\*4.37** (Also, see Exercise 4.52.) Recall Clark's equality axioms CET (Definition 3.68) relative to an algebraic language:

(i) $\mathbf{f}(x_1, \ldots, x_n) \approx \mathbf{f}(y_1, \ldots, y_n) \to (x_1 \approx y_1 \wedge \cdots \wedge x_n \approx y_n)$,

(ii) $\mathbf{f}(x_1, \ldots, x_n) \not\approx \mathbf{g}(y_1, \ldots, y_m)$ (**f**, **g** *different*),

(iii) $x \not\approx t$ (the variable $x$ a proper subterm of $t$).

The axioms of the first two types can be transformed into the following rules involving the binary relation symbol **noteq**:

(i) $\mathbf{noteq}(\mathbf{f}(x_1, \ldots, x_n), \mathbf{f}(y_1, \ldots, y_n)) \leftarrow \mathbf{noteq}(x_i, y_i)$
$(1 \leq i \leq n)$

(ii) $\mathbf{noteq}(\mathbf{f}(x_1, \ldots, x_n), \mathbf{g}(y_1, \ldots, y_m)) \leftarrow$
(**f**, **g** different).

Show: these rules define the inequality relation on $HU$ in **noteq**. Thus, the least Herbrand model of these rules satisfies the CET axioms of the *third* type.

*Hint.* To see that $\mathbf{noteq}(s, t)$ follows logically from these rules whenever $s, t \in HU$ are different, first apply induction with respect to $s$ (keeping $t$ variable), next, apply induction again, but now with respect to $t$.

**\*4.38** Suppose that the $k$-place relation symbol **r** occurs in a program $P$. Show that, for every $n$, the $k$-ary relation on $HU$ defined by: $\mathbf{r}(t_1, \ldots, t_k) \in T_P \!\uparrow\! n$, is *first-order definable* on the Herbrand algebra $HA$. That is, show that for every $n$, a first-order formula $\phi_{\mathbf{r}}^n$ with free variables $x_1, \ldots, x_k$ may be constructed (involving identity, constant and function symbols, but of course *no* relation symbol) such that for all $t_1, \ldots, t_k \in HU$:

$$HA \models \phi_{\mathbf{r}}^n \{x_1/t_1, \ldots, x_k/t_k\} \iff \mathbf{r}(t_1, \ldots, t_k) \in T_P \!\uparrow\! n.$$

N.B.: Usually, the condition $\mathbf{r}(t_1, \ldots, t_k) \in T_P \!\uparrow$ will *not* be first-order definable. For instance, a simple example of this phenomenon is the program of Exercise 4.10, which defines the ordering $<$ of $\mathbb{N}$ in terms of $0$ and $S$. No first-order formula can accomplish this.

Same question for the finite stages in the downward hierarchy of $T_P$.

## 4.6 Representing Domains as Herbrand Universes

When we seek to define a relation by means of a program, we need to *represent* the domain of the relation as a suitable Herbrand universe. Usually, several representations will be possible; the choice will be dictated by circumstances.

Contrasting with the case of "ordinary" logical settings, logic programming has an asymmetry in the roles of constant and function symbols on the one hand, and relation symbols on the other. Here, constant and function symbols generate the Herbrand universe (simulating a domain we're interested in), over which our programs *define* relations relevant for this domain.

In the following, we present a couple of representations of domains-as-Herbrand universes that are often encountered: the domain of natural numbers, domains of expressions over a finite alphabet (of course, the natural numbers form the special case where the alphabet consists of one symbol only) and domains with lists.

Finally, these representations are the source of an almost endless series of exercises. The readers may digest as many of these as they find suitable. (Some of the programs can be experimented with on the computer, using Prolog; to do this, we need the material in the next chapter.)

### 4.6.1 Natural Numbers

Time and again, we have used the fact that we can consider the set of natural numbers $\mathbb{N}$ as a Herbrand universe, generated by means of one individual constant $\mathbf{o}$ (for the natural number 0) and one unary function symbol $\mathbf{s}$ (for the successor-operation $S$). See Notation 3.20. Chapter 7 on computability deals extensively with this representation. Some of the following programs have been used already for illustration.

**Exercises**

**4.39** $P$ consists of the rules
$$\mathbf{N}(\mathbf{o}) \leftarrow$$
$$\mathbf{N}(\mathbf{s}x) \leftarrow \mathbf{N}(x).$$
Determine, for each $n$, $T_P \uparrow n$. Determine $M_P = T_P \uparrow$. Same questions for $T_P \downarrow$.

**4.40** $P$ consists of
$$\mathbf{r}(0, 2) \leftarrow$$
$$\mathbf{r}(\mathbf{s}x, \mathbf{s}y) \leftarrow \mathbf{r}(x, y)$$
$$\mathbf{r}(x, \mathbf{ss}y) \leftarrow \mathbf{r}(x, y).$$
Determine $M_P$. Note that the interpretation of $\mathbf{r}$ in $M_P$ is transitive. Find Herbrand models for $P$ in which the interpretation of $\mathbf{r}$ is not transitive.

**4.41** Consider the program SUM of Example 4.3. Is it true that $M_P = T_P \downarrow \omega$?

**4.42** Construct a program that defines the function $max$ ($max(n, m)$ is the maximum of $n$ and $m$) in some symbol.

**4.43** Consider the following program.

$$\mathbf{p}(x, \mathbf{o}, x) \leftarrow$$
$$\mathbf{p}(x, \mathbf{s}y, z) \leftarrow \mathbf{p}(\mathbf{s}x, y, z)$$
$$\mathbf{q}(x, y, \mathbf{o}, y) \leftarrow$$
$$\mathbf{q}(x, y, \mathbf{s}z, w) \leftarrow \mathbf{p}(x, y, u), \mathbf{q}(x, u, z, w)$$
$$\mathbf{r}(x, y, z) \leftarrow \mathbf{q}(x, \mathbf{o}, y, z).$$

What does it define in resp. **p**, **q** and **r**?

### 4.6.2 Binary Notation

To the language considered in the previous subsection we add one unary function symbol, but we change the notation. The individual constant is now denoted by $\mathbf{\Lambda}$, the two unary function symbols by $\mathbf{s}_0$ and $\mathbf{s}_1$. A ground term here can be thought of as representing a finite sequence of zeros and ones, $\mathbf{\Lambda}$ representing the empty sequence, and, e.g., $\mathbf{s}_0\mathbf{s}_0\mathbf{s}_1\mathbf{s}_0\mathbf{\Lambda}$ representing the sequence 0010. We use the notations $0t := \mathbf{s}_0(t)$ and $1t := \mathbf{s}_1(t)$ for an arbitrary term $t$.

### Exercises

**4.44** For $t \in HU$, the ground term $t1$ is recursively defined by the following equations: $\mathbf{\Lambda}1 = \mathbf{s}_1\mathbf{\Lambda}$, $(\mathbf{s}_1 t)1 = \mathbf{s}_1(t1)$ and $(\mathbf{s}_0 t)1 = \mathbf{s}_0(t1)$. I.e., $t1$ is obtained from $t$ by the replacement of $\mathbf{\Lambda}$ by 1. (Note that $t1$ is defined only for $t$ *ground*.) Consider the following program:

$$\mathbf{ap}_1(\mathbf{\Lambda}, 1) \leftarrow$$
$$\mathbf{ap}_1(1x, 1y) \leftarrow \mathbf{ap}_1(x, y)$$
$$\mathbf{ap}_1(0x, 0y) \leftarrow \mathbf{ap}_1(x, y).$$

Give a detailed proof that this program defines the relation $\{(t, t1) \mid t \in HU\}$ in the relation symbol $\mathbf{ap}_1$.

**4.45** Extend the program of the previous exercise with three rules involving a relation symbol $\mathbf{ap}_0$ defining the relation of appending 0 at the end of a sequence. For $s \in HU$, $\breve{s}$ denotes the *reverse version* of $s$; e.g., for $s = 10111$, $\breve{s} = 11101$. Add the following rules involving the relation symbol **rev**.

$$\mathbf{rev}(\mathbf{\Lambda}, \mathbf{\Lambda}) \leftarrow$$
$$\mathbf{rev}(1x, z) \leftarrow \mathbf{rev}(x, y), \mathbf{ap}_1(y, z)$$
$$\mathbf{rev}(0x, z) \leftarrow \mathbf{rev}(x, y), \mathbf{ap}_0(y, z).$$

Show that the resulting program (which has nine rules) defines the relation $\{(s,t) \mid t = \breve{s}\}$ on $HU$ in the relation symbol **rev**.

**4.46** Consider the following program:
$$\mathbf{r}(\Lambda, x, x) \leftarrow$$
$$\mathbf{r}(0x, y, z) \leftarrow \mathbf{r}(x, 0y, z)$$
$$\mathbf{r}(1x, y, z) \leftarrow \mathbf{r}(x, 1y, z)$$
$$\mathbf{q}(x, z) \leftarrow \mathbf{r}(x, \Lambda, z).$$
What does this program define?

**4.47** Construct a program defining the set of palindromes in some unary relation symbol. (A *palindrome* is a sequence $s$ for which $s = \breve{s}$.)

**4.48** Find out what the following program defines.
$$\mathbf{r}(\Lambda, x, x) \leftarrow$$
$$\mathbf{r}(0x, y, 0z) \leftarrow \mathbf{r}(x, y, z)$$
$$\mathbf{r}(1x, y, 1z) \leftarrow \mathbf{r}(x, y, z).$$

**4.49** Give a program that defines the set $\{\overbrace{1 \ldots 1}^{n} \mid n \geq 0\}$.

**4.50** Every ground term that does not begin with 0 and is different from $\Lambda$ can be conceived of as denoting a natural number written in binary notation. For the following, it is slightly easier (though not essential) to work with binary notations written from right to left. Produce a program defining the relation $\{(s,t) \mid s \in HU \text{ does not contain } \mathbf{s}_0 \text{ and } t \text{ is the number of occurrences of } \mathbf{s}_1 \text{ in } s \text{ in } \textit{binary notation}\}$ in a binary relation symbol $bin$.

(i) Try to find a solution of your own. Don't make it too complicated; you're supposed to prove that it works!

(ii) Here is a program that accomplishes this. It involves an extra relation symbol $\mathbf{q}$.
$$\mathbf{q}(x, x, \Lambda) \leftarrow$$
$$\mathbf{q}(x, y, 1i) \leftarrow \mathbf{q}(x, 11y, i)$$
$$bin(x, 0j) \leftarrow \mathbf{q}(x, \Lambda, i), bin(i, j)$$
$$bin(x, 1j) \leftarrow \mathbf{q}(x, 1, i), bin(i, j)$$
$$bin(1, 1) \leftarrow$$
$$bin(\Lambda, 0) \leftarrow.$$
Prove that this program accomplishes what it is supposed to.
*Hint.* First, show that $\mathbf{q}(n, m, p) \in M_P$ iff $n - m = 2p$.

**4.51** Again considering ground terms as binary notations for natural numbers, show that relations as *smaller than* and *addition* (conceived of as a ternary relation) can be defined by suitable programs.

**4.52** Construct a program that defines the relation $EQ := \{(s,t) \in HU^2 \mid s = t\}$ in a relation symbol **eq**. Construct a program that defines the relation $NOTEQ := \{(s,t) \in HU^2 \mid s \neq t\}$ in a relation symbol **noteq**. (See Exercise 4.37.)

### 4.6.3    Lists

Fix a constant symbol $[\,]$. Suppose that a *binary* function symbol $[.\,|\,.]$ is present. Denote the set of finite sequences $(t_1, \ldots, t_n)$ of elements of $HU$ by $HU^{<\omega}$. Using $[\,]$ and $[.\,|\,.]$, we can construct an injection $i : HU^{<\omega} \to HU$ using a recursion with respect to the length of the sequence involved:

   (i) $i$ maps the *empty* sequence to $[\;]$;

   (ii) $i(t, t_1, \ldots, t_n) = [t|i(t_1, \ldots, t_n)]$.

Thus, $i(t_1, \ldots, t_n) = [t_1|[t_2|\ldots|[t_n|[\;]]\ldots]])$.

Usually, $i(t_1, \ldots, t_n)$ is denoted by $[t_1, \ldots, t_n]$. We often shall confuse sequences of terms (usually called *lists*) with their $i$-image.

### Exercises

**4.53** Define the set of sequences of natural numbers.
Solution:
$$\mathbf{r}([\;]) \leftarrow$$
$$\mathbf{r}([x|y]) \leftarrow \mathbf{N}(x), \mathbf{r}(y).$$
(**N** defining $\mathbb{N}$, using the rules of Exercise 4.39.)

**4.54** $[t_1, \ldots, t_n, s_1, \ldots, s_m]$ is called the *concatenation* of $[t_1, \ldots, t_n]$ and $[s_1, \ldots, s_m]$. The *concatenation* of the lists $\alpha$ and $\beta$ is denoted by $\alpha {}^\frown \beta$. Construct a program defining concatenation as a 3-ary relation $(Conc(\alpha, \beta, \gamma) :\equiv \gamma = \alpha {}^\frown \beta)$ in a 3-ary relation symbol *append*.

**4.55** $B$ is the smallest set $\subset HU$ such that

   (i) $0, 1 \in B$, and

   (ii) every (finite) list of elements of $B$ is again in $B$.

(E.g., $[\;], [0], [1, [\;]]$ are all in $B$.) Construct a program defining $B$ as a unary relation. (N.B.: You cannot translate (ii) into *one* rule since lengths of lists vary. Next to the $B$-defining relation symbol, you'll need another one!)

**4.56** Construct a program defining the *length* of a list, that is, the function defined on lists that, when applied to a list, produces its length.

**4.57** Construct a program defining the function that produces the least element of a list of natural numbers.

**4.58** Find out what the following rules define.

$member(x, [x|v]) \leftarrow$
$member(x, [y|v]) \leftarrow member(x, v).$

**4.59** Same question for the following rules:

$\mathbf{last}([z], [\ ], z) \leftarrow$
$\mathbf{last}([z|u], [z|x], y) \leftarrow \mathbf{last}(u, x, y)$
$\mathbf{reverse}([\ ], [\ ]) \leftarrow$
$\mathbf{reverse}(u, [y|z]) \leftarrow \mathbf{last}(u, x, y), \mathbf{reverse}(x, z).$

**4.60** The *sorted version* of a list of numbers has the same elements as this list, but sorted in increasing order. Construct a program defining the binary relation *sort* (in a binary relation symbol **qs**), where $sort(s, t)$ iff $s$ is a list of numbers and $t$ is its sorted version.

*Solution.* The so-called *quicksort*-program consists of the following rules:

$\mathbf{qs}([\ ], [\ ]) \leftarrow$
$\mathbf{qs}(x, y, z) \leftarrow \mathbf{f}(x, y, y_1, y_2), \mathbf{qs}(y_1, z_1), \mathbf{qs}(y_2, z_2), append(z_1, [x|z_2], z)$
$\mathbf{f}(x, [\ ], [\ ], [\ ]) \leftarrow$
$\mathbf{f}(x, [y|z], [y|y_1], y_2) \leftarrow x > y, \mathbf{f}(x, z, y_1, y_2)$
$\mathbf{f}(x, [y|z], y_1, [y|y_2]) \leftarrow x \leq y, \mathbf{f}(x, z, y_1, y_2)$

plus the rules of the *append*-program asked for by Exercise 4.54.

Determine the relation defined in **f**.

## 4.7 Notes

The notion of implication tree, Definition 4.9, is from [Stärk 89], in which Lemma 4.10 is implicit.

The notions of immediate consequence operator, least Herbrand model and their elementary properties are due to [van Emden/Kowalski 76].

Yet another interesting domain over which to define relations by means of programs is that of finite trees (of, say, numbers, suitably represented).

# 5 Linear Resolution

## 5.1  Preliminaries

This chapter is devoted to the special case of first-order resolution where one of the two clauses to be resolved (the *goal clause*) consists of *negative* literals only, and the other one is a rule. Then, since the positive literal of the rule must be active in the resolution step, this results in a new goal clause of negative literals, preparing for a new step involving some rule.

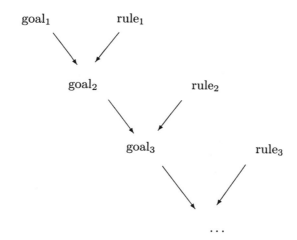

Thus, a derivation here contains a unique sequence of goal clauses. This accounts for the *linear character* of this version of resolution.

In Chapters 2 and 3, clauses are defined as *sets* of literals. From now on, a *clause* will be a *disjunction* of literals and we shall not use the set representation of disjunctions any longer.

Suppose that $K$ is a clause consisting of positive literals $A_1, \ldots, A_k$ and negative literals $\neg B_1, \ldots, \neg B_m$. Separating the positive from the negative literals, $K$ is usually written as

$$A_1, \ldots, A_k \leftarrow B_1, \ldots, B_m.$$

When $k = 1$, this is a rule.

**Definition 5.1** A *goal* is a clause with an empty positive part.  ∎

A goal that is the disjunction of the negative literals $\neg B_1, \ldots, \neg B_m$ can thus be written as:

$$\leftarrow B_1, \ldots, B_m.$$

Logically, this represents the universal closure $\forall(\neg B_1 \vee \cdots \vee \neg B_m)$ of the goal. Of course, other logical equivalents of this are $\forall \neg(B_1 \wedge \cdots \wedge B_m)$ and $\neg \exists(B_1 \wedge \cdots \wedge B_m)$.

If $C$ is the sequence $(B_1, \ldots, B_m)$, the goal $\leftarrow B_1, \ldots, B_m$ is also denoted by $\leftarrow C$. A particular case is the *empty* goal/disjunction $\perp$, which we keep referring to by $\square$.

**Definition 5.2** A *Horn sentence* is a universally quantified disjunction of literals of which at most *one* is positive.                                                                    ∎

Thus, goals and rules are Horn.

Rules are often called *definite* clauses (this notion of definiteness will be expanded in Chapter 8). Ultimately, we come to explain the notion of *SLD resolution*, which stands for *Selection rule driven Linear resolution for Definite clauses*. We have already indicated why this new version of resolution will have a linear character; and it is clear now what the 'D' stands for. The notion of a selection rule will be explained much later; see Definition 5.42.

Suppose that $P$ is a program and $\leftarrow C$ is a goal, where $C = (B_1, \ldots, B_m)$. As in the first-order case, linear resolution attempts to establish unsatisfiability of $P \cup \{\leftarrow C\}$ by *refuting* $\leftarrow C$ on the basis of $P$, that is, by *deriving* the goal $\square$ from $P$ and $\leftarrow C$.

Since the method is sound, deriving $\square$ implies that $\square$ logically follows from $P$ together with $\leftarrow C$, and hence (since $\square$ is the unsatisfiable clause par excellence) that $\leftarrow C$ cannot be satisfied in a model of $P$. As $\leftarrow C$ represents $\forall(\neg B_1 \vee \cdots \vee \neg B_m)$, this amounts to saying that the negation $\neg \forall(\neg B_1 \vee \cdots \vee \neg B_m)$, equivalently, that $\exists(B_1 \wedge \cdots \wedge B_m)$ logically follows from the rules of $P$. Therefore, the procedure can be conceived as a method for proving statements of the form $P \models \exists(B_1 \wedge \cdots \wedge B_m)$.

Thinking of linear resolution as a method to establish unsatisfiability of a goal $\leftarrow C$ relative to some program $P$ is more tiresome than thinking of it as trying to ascertain that $P \models \exists \bigwedge C$. Therefore, in what follows, we prefer to use *queries* instead of *goals*:

**Definition 5.3** A *query* is a finite sequence of atoms. The notation $\square$ is also used to denote the empty query.                                                                    ∎

In view of the aforementioned remarks, logically speaking, a query should be thought of as the conjunction of its elements.

Linear resolution now can be conceived as a (backward) search method for proofs of $\exists \bigwedge C$ from a program $P$, where $C$ is a query. Such a search succeeds if the empty query $\square$ has been derived, which, in this conception, should now be thought of as an empty *conjunction*, hence as $\top$ instead of as $\perp$.

At this point, the reader of Chapter 3 might ask (since linear resolution is just a special case of resolution in first-order logic): what more can be said here? The answer is that, by its linear character, this version of resolution, next to being a refutation method, is able to *compute* as well. To give a glance ahead: a proof that $P \models \exists \bigwedge C$ using linear resolution will actually produce values for the variables in $C$ witnessing this fact. That is, the linear resolution proof will produce a substition $\theta$ for which $P \models \bigwedge C\theta$. We shall see that $\theta$ can be looked at as the result of a computation process carried out by the linear resolution machinery.

## 5.2   Unrestricted Linear Resolution

It is time to get down to business. The proper notion of linear resolution will be introduced in Section 5.4. First, we define a more general version: *unrestricted* linear resolution. This notion is not of much importance; however, it has two special cases that are. The situation is similar to the one encountered in Chapter 3 (though a little more complex). Firstly, linear resolution is the special case of unrestricted linear resolution producing "maximal generality". Secondly, the opposite case regarding generality is that of *ground* linear resolution. Again, similar to the situation in Chapter 3, it is the first one we're really interested in. However, what this version actually establishes is seen by "lifting" the ground version, which is more closely related to the (Herbrand) models involved. Finally, the unrestricted notion offers the opportunity for the uninitiated to become familiar with linear resolution in a step-by-step fashion.

In the sequel, we use juxtaposition to denote concatenation of sequences. E.g., if $K = (A_1, \ldots, A_n)$ and $M = (B_1, \ldots, B_m)$ are (possibly empty) queries and $A$ is an atom, then $K, M$ or $(K, M)$ denotes the query $(A_1, \ldots, A_n, B_1, \ldots, B_m)$ and $K, A$ or $(K, A)$ denotes $(A_1, \ldots, A_n, A)$, etc.

**Definition 5.4** An *unrestricted resolvent* of the query $C = (K, A, L)$ *with respect to* the atom $A$ and the rule $R$ is a pair $(\alpha, D)$ such that

- $\alpha$ is a substitution such that $Dom(\alpha) \subset Var(C)$,
- $D = (K\alpha, M, L\alpha)$, where $A\alpha \leftarrow M$ is an instance of $R$.

In this context, $A$ is called the *selected* atom and $\alpha$ the *specialization*.

Instead of $(\alpha, D)$ we shall usually write $\xrightarrow{\alpha}_u D$.

The notation $C \xrightarrow{\alpha}_u D$ $(A, R)$ expresses that $\xrightarrow{\alpha}_u D$ is an unrestricted resolvent of $C$ with respect to the atom $A$ and the rule $R$; by $C \xrightarrow{\alpha}_u D$ we mean that $\xrightarrow{\alpha}_u D$ is an unrestricted resolvent with respect to some atom of $C$ and some rule that, in the case that some program is given, is understood to belong to that program.

A configuration $C \xrightarrow{\alpha}_u D$ will be referred to as an unrestricted *transition* or resolution *step*.

Finally, $D$ is called an *unrestricted resolvent* of $C$ in case some $\xrightarrow{\alpha}_u D$ is. ∎

Thus: if $C = (K, A, L) \xrightarrow{\alpha}_u D$ $(A, R)$, then $D$ is obtained from the query $C$ by two successive transformations:

(i) *instantiating* $C$ using $\alpha$, which yields $C\alpha = (K\alpha, A\alpha, L\alpha)$, and

(ii) *replacing* $A\alpha$ by $M$, obtaining $D = C\alpha\{A\alpha/M\} = (K\alpha, M, L\alpha)$[1]

where $A\alpha \leftarrow M$ is some instance of $R$.

The restriction on the domain of $\alpha$ avoids consideration of irrelevant variables and the reference to $\alpha$ in the unrestricted resolvent $\xrightarrow{\alpha}_u D$ allows us to retrieve $\alpha$.

While $A\alpha \leftarrow M$ is an instance of $R$, it does not need to be $R\alpha$. In fact, in general this instance of $R$ will be obtained by applying to $R$ a different substitution $\beta$. Then $A\alpha = B\beta$, where $B$ is the head of $R$. If $R$ and $C$ do not have common variables, the domains of $\alpha$ and $\beta$ may be assumed disjoint. Then $\alpha \cup \beta$ is well-defined, and we get $A(\alpha \cup \beta) = B(\alpha \cup \beta)$, $\alpha$ being part of the unification $\alpha \cup \beta$ of $A$ and $B$.

A query may contain several occurrences of the same atom. To have a completely unambiguous notation, we therefore should mention not the *atom* with respect to which the resolution step is carried out, but its selected *occurrence*.

Note that forming an unrestricted resolvent is in fact almost the same as for the case of first-order logic; the only difference being that resolvents are always formed here with respect to *singleton* (one-element) subclauses. For the rule, this is no restriction, since exactly one literal in it is positive, but for the query, it is.

## Example 5.5

(i) Consider the program SUM from Example 4.3.

We have that $\mathbf{sum}(x, y, \mathbf{s}z) \xrightarrow{\{y/\mathbf{s}y\}}_u \mathbf{sum}(x, y, z)$, using the second rule.

Also, we have $\mathbf{sum}(x, y, \mathbf{s}z) \xrightarrow{\{x/\mathbf{s}z, y/\mathbf{O}\}}_u \square$, using the first rule.

(ii) For any terms $s$ and $t$, the construct $\xrightarrow{\{x/t\}}_u \mathbf{q}(s)$ is an unrestricted resolvent of $\mathbf{r}(x)$ with respect to the atom $\mathbf{r}(x)$ and the rule $\mathbf{r}(x) \leftarrow \mathbf{q}(y)$. ∎

**Definition 5.6** Suppose that $C \xrightarrow{\alpha}_u D$. The implication $D \rightarrow C\alpha$ is called the *resultant* associated with this transition. In case $D$ is empty, we identify the resultant with $C\alpha$. ∎

---

[1] $E\{A/C\}$ denotes the expression obtained from $E$ replacing the sub-expression $A$ by $C$.

**Remark 5.7** From now on, sequences $C$ of atoms often will be identified with the conjunction $\bigwedge C$ of their elements. So, for instance, a resultant $D{\to}C\alpha$ is to be identified with $\bigwedge D{\to}\bigwedge C\alpha$ and a statement that, e.g., $P{\models}C$ is to be interpreted as $P{\models}\bigwedge C$. ∎
Logically speaking, the resultant of a transition is what is being established by the transition.

**Lemma 5.8** *If $Q$ is the resultant associated with an unrestricted resolution step produced by means of the rule $R$, then $R \models Q$.*

**Proof.** Suppose that $K, A, L \xrightarrow{\quad\alpha\quad}_u K\alpha, M, L\alpha$ $(A, R)$. The resultant associated with this step is the implication $K\alpha, M, L\alpha{\to}K\alpha, A\alpha, L\alpha$, which logically follows from the instance $M{\to}A\alpha$ of $R$, and of course, that $R{\models}(M{\to}A\alpha)$ is a consequence of Corollary 3.38(i). ∎

Unrestricted derivations are defined as sequences of successive unrestricted resolution transitions.

**Definition 5.9**

(i) A (finite or infinite) sequence

$$C_0 \xrightarrow{\quad\alpha_1\quad}_u C_1 \cdots C_i \xrightarrow{\quad\alpha_{i+1}\quad}_u C_{i+1} \cdots$$

is called an *unrestricted derivation relative to* a program $P$ if, for all (relevant) $i$, $\xrightarrow{\;\alpha_{i+1}\;}_u C_{i+1}$ is an unrestricted resolvent of $C_i$ with respect to some atom of $C_i$ and some rule of $P$.

If the derivation is finite and ends with $C_n$, it is called a derivation *of $C_n$ from $C_0$.*

(ii) The *resultant* of the finite unrestricted derivation

$$\Gamma := C_0 \xrightarrow{\quad\alpha_1\quad}_u \cdots \xrightarrow{\quad\alpha_{n'}\quad}_u C_n$$

is the implication

$$res(\Gamma) := C_n \to C_0\alpha_1 \cdots \alpha_n.$$

In case $C_n$ is empty we identify the resultant with $C_0\alpha_1 \cdots \alpha_n$. ∎

Thus, forming an unrestricted resolvent is making an unrestricted derivation of length 1. Note that the resultants of an unrestricted resolvent (Definition 5.6) and the corresponding 1-step unrestricted derivation (Definition 5.9(ii)) coincide.

Compare this definition of (unrestricted) *derivation* with that for the case of first-order resolution, Definition 3.46. Here, we do not include the rules (for a given context, they constitute a fixed program), but we *do* include the specializations used on the queries (which, back in Chapter 3, we did not).

The specializations involved in a finite derivation make up its resultant, about which we have the following lemma, generalizing Lemma 5.8 to derivations of length $> 1$.

**Lemma 5.10** *If $\Gamma$ is a finite unrestricted derivation relative to the program $P$, then* $P \models res(\Gamma)$.

**Proof.** Induction on the length $n$ of $\Gamma$.

*Basis $n = 1$.* This is Lemma 5.8.

*Induction step.* Suppose that

$$C_0 \xrightarrow{\alpha_1}_u \cdots \xrightarrow{\alpha_{n+1}}_u C_{n+1}$$

is an unrestricted derivation from the program $P$.

By Lemma 5.8 we have that $P \models (C_{n+1} \rightarrow C_n \alpha_{n+1})$. By induction hypothesis applied to the derivation $C_0 \xrightarrow{\alpha_1}_u \cdots \xrightarrow{\alpha_n}_u C_n$, we have that $P \models (C_n \rightarrow C_0 \alpha_1 \cdots \alpha_n)$. Thus, by Corollary 3.38(i), $P \models (C_n \rightarrow C_0 \alpha_1 \cdots \alpha_n) \alpha_{n+1}$; that is, $P \models (C_n \alpha_{n+1} \rightarrow C_0 \alpha_1 \cdots \alpha_{n+1})$. Combining these, we obtain $P \models (C_{n+1} \rightarrow C_0 \alpha_1 \cdots \alpha_{n+1})$, as desired. ∎

Recall (Definition 3.53) that for a substitution $\alpha$ and a set of variables $V$, the restriction $\alpha | V$ of $\alpha$ to $V$ is the substitution $\{x/x\alpha \mid x \in V \cap Dom(\alpha)\}$.

**Definition 5.11** A finite unrestricted derivation

$$\Gamma : C_0 \xrightarrow{\alpha_1}_u \cdots \xrightarrow{\alpha_n}_u C_n$$

is called *successful* or simply an unrestricted *success* (*for $C_0$*), if $C_n = \square$.

In that case ($C_n = \square$), the restriction $\alpha := (\alpha_1 \cdots \alpha_n) | Var(C_0)$ of the composition $\alpha_1 \cdots \alpha_n$ of the successive specializations to the variables of the initial query $C_0$ is called an (unrestrictedly) *computed answer substitution* (*c.a.s.*) for $C_0$. ∎

Note that an unrestricted computed answer substitution need not be ground; see the next example.

**Example 5.12** Consider the program SUM from Example 4.3. The following is a successful derivation (we use the convention of Notation 3.20):

$\mathbf{sum}(x, 3, y)$

$\qquad \xrightarrow{\{y/\mathsf{S}y\}}_u \mathbf{sum}(x, 2, y)$

$\qquad \xrightarrow{\{y/\mathsf{S}y\}}_u \mathbf{sum}(x, 1, y)$

$\qquad \xrightarrow{\{y/\mathsf{S}y\}}_u \mathbf{sum}(x, 0, y)$

$\qquad \xrightarrow{\{y/x\}}_u \square.$

Its resultant is $\mathbf{sum}(x, 3, \mathsf{sss}x)$ and its computed answer substitution is $\{y/\mathsf{sss}x\}$. ∎

**Definition 5.13** A substitution $\alpha$ is called a *correct answer* for the query $C$ with respect to the program $P$ if $P \models C\alpha$. ∎

Computed answer substitutions are obtained by means of unrestricted resolution and correct answer substitutions are obtained by referring to the logical content of the program. They are related to each other by the following *Soundness Theorem.*

**Theorem 5.14 (Soundness of Unrestricted Resolution)** *The computed answer substitution of a successful unrestricted derivation is correct.*

**Proof.** This is the special case of Lemma 5.10 where $\Gamma$ is a success.                    ∎

Conversely, every correct answer also is unrestrictedly computed; see Exercises 5.3 and 5.21.

**Exercises**

**5.1** Consider the program SUM of Example 4.3.

(i) Show that the substitution $\{x/1, y/2\}$ is a computed answer substitution for $\mathbf{sum}(x, y, 3)$.

(ii) Extend the program SUM to MULT by adding the rules
$$\mathbf{mult}(x, \mathbf{o}, \mathbf{o}) \leftarrow$$
$$\mathbf{mult}(x, \mathbf{s}y, z) \leftarrow \mathbf{mult}(x, y, z'), \mathbf{sum}(z', x, z).$$
What is the least Herbrand model of MULT?

(iii) Find a c.a.s. for $\mathbf{mult}(3, 2, z)$.

(iv) If $n$ and $m$ are natural numbers, then an unrestricted success for $\mathbf{mult}(n, m, z)$ ($z$ a variable) exists using this program. What is its length? What is its c.a.s.?

(v) Same question when the last rule of the program is changed to
$$\mathbf{mult}(x, \mathbf{s}y, z) \leftarrow \mathbf{mult}(x, y, z'), \mathbf{sum}(x, z', z).$$

**5.2** Assume that $P$ defines the (unary) function $f : HU \rightarrow HU$ in the (binary) relation symbol $\mathbf{f}$, cf. Definition 4.29. Let $y$ be a variable. Show: for all $s \in HU$: every unrestricted success for $\mathbf{f}(s, y)$ has the computed answer substitution $\{y/f(s)\}$.

## 5.3   Ground Completeness

In the *procedural* interpretation of a program, we conceive of its rules as a series of computing instructions. On the other hand, a *declarative* interpretation of the program refers to its logical content. The Soundness Theorem 5.14 provides one half of the match between the procedural interpretation given by unrestricted resolution and the declarative interpretation of programs. Completeness theorems provide the (more difficult) other half. This section proves ground completeness, a result that can be compared to the propositional Completeness Theorem 2.18 of Chapter 2. However, the proof here is rather different from its propositional companion. A parallel with the situation in the chapters on propositional and first-order logic is that ground completeness, as treated here, will allow us to establish stronger completeness results in later sections via a lifting procedure similar to the one from Chapter 3.

**Definition 5.15** An unrestricted derivation is called a *ground derivation* iff all its queries are ground.                                                                                             ∎

Of course, the specializations of a ground derivation all equal $\epsilon$, the identity substitution. Therefore, the resultant of a ground derivation $C_0 \xrightarrow{\epsilon}_u \cdots \xrightarrow{\epsilon}_u C_n$ is $C_n \rightarrow C_0$; and when this is a success ($C_n = \square$), the resultant is $C_0$.

The following ground completeness result states that ground queries logically following from the program start a successful ground derivation. The proof transforms a set of ground implication trees (see Definition 4.9) for the atoms of the query, which are obtained from Lemma 4.10, into the required derivation.

**Theorem 5.16 (Ground Completeness)** *Let $P$ be a program. If $C$ is a ground query such that $P \models C$, then there is a successful ground derivation for $C$ with respect to $P$.*

**Proof.** Suppose that $C = (A_1, \ldots, A_m)$ is ground. Since $P \models C$, by Lemma 4.10, there is a is a ground implication tree $\mathcal{T}_i$ for $A_i$ ($i = 1, \ldots, m$). Let $n$ be the total number of nodes in the trees $\mathcal{T}_1, \ldots, \mathcal{T}_m$.

*Claim.* For every $k \leq n$, there exist a ground derivation $C_0 = C \xrightarrow{\epsilon}_u \cdots \xrightarrow{\epsilon}_u C_k$ and a set of ground implication trees for the atoms of $C_k$ such that the total number of nodes in these trees is $n - k$.

Note that the theorem is just the special case of the claim where $k = n$. The claim itself is proved using induction on $k$. For $k = 0$, the claim holds by definition of $n$. Now suppose that we have constructed $C_0 = C \xrightarrow{\epsilon}_u \cdots \xrightarrow{\epsilon}_u C_k$ and a set of ground implication trees for the atoms of $C_k$ such that the total number of nodes in these trees is $n - k$. Choose any atom $A$ from $C_k$. Replace $A$ in $C_k$ by its children in the implication tree for $A$ to obtain $C_{k+1}$. To obtain a new set of implication trees, replace the implication tree for $A$ in the old one by its subtrees, the roots of which are the children of $A$. (So the one node $A$ vanishes.)                                                                     ∎

Eventually, we shall establish a completeness result for linear resolution by lifting the Ground Completeness Theorem once we have proved the lifting property for linear resolution.

**Corollary 5.17** *Let $P$ be a program and $C$ a ground query. The following are equivalent:*

*(i) $P \models C$,*

*(ii) $C \subset M_P$,*

*(iii) there is a successful ground derivation for $C$ relative to $P$,*

*(iv) there is an unrestricted successful derivation for $C$ with respect to $P$.*

**Proof.** By Definition 4.7, $(i) \Leftrightarrow (ii)$. By the Ground Completeness Theorem 5.16, $(i) \Rightarrow (iii)$. As to $(iii) \Rightarrow (iv)$, obviously, every successful ground derivation also is an unrestricted successful derivation. Finally, that $(iv) \Rightarrow (i)$ is due to the Soundness Theorem 5.14. ∎

### Exercises

**5.3** Prove the following partial converse of Theorem 5.14: every ground correct answer substitution is an unrestricted computed answer substitution.

**5.4** Prove, or give a counter-example to, the following statement: every ground derivation relative to $P$ for a query $C$ such that $C \subset M_P$ is finite.

**Definition 5.18** The *rank* $rk(A)$ of a ground atom $A \in M_P$ (relative to $P$) is the least $n$ for which $A \in T_P \uparrow n$.

For a ground query $D = (A_1, \ldots, A_k)$ of atoms $A_1, \ldots, A_k \in M_P$, the multiset $rk(D)$ associated with it is defined by $rk(D) := \{\!\{rk(A_1), \ldots, rk(A_k)\}\!\}$; it is called the *rank* of the query. ∎

Together with Theorem 1.13, the following exercise can be used to produce another proof of Theorem 5.16. However, the proof given is much more explicit about the resulting derivation.

**5.5** Assume that $C \subset M_P$. Show: $C$ has a ground unrestricted resolvent $D$ such that $rk(D)$ immediately precedes $rk(C)$ in the multiset ordering.

**5.6** The following is a sketch for a proof of Theorem 5.16, which resembles the one from Chapter 2 more, but here is much less informative.

Assume that no ground derivation using the $P$-rules and starting with the ground query $C$ ends with $\square$. The following argument shows $ground(P) \cup \{\neg C\}$ to be propositionally satisfiable.

Let $\Sigma$ be the set of all queries $D$ that end some $P$-ground derivation starting from $C$. We conceive of $\Sigma$ as a collection of finite, non-empty sets. By Lemma 2.21, $\Sigma$ has a minimal meet $S$. We identify $S$ with the truth assignment that assigns a ground atom $\mathbf{t}$ iff it is *not* in $S$.

*Claim.* $S$ satisfies $P \cup \{\neg C\}$.

*Proof.* Assume that $A \in S \cap C$. Then $S \models \neg A$, and a fortiori $S \models \neg C$. Next, suppose that $(A \leftarrow B_1, \ldots, B_n) \in ground(P)$ is *not* satisfied by $S$. Then $A \in S$, but $B_1, \ldots, B_n \notin S$. Since $S$ is a minimal meet for $\Sigma$, by Lemma 2.20, $D \in \Sigma$ exists such that $D \cap S = \{A\}$. Then $D\{A/(B_1, \ldots, B_n)\}$ is a ground unrestricted resolvent of $D$, hence, belongs to $\Sigma$, but does not contain an atom in $S$, contrary to the choice of $S$.

## 5.4  Linear Resolution

### 5.4.1  Motivation

First, we explain what is being gained by the notion of linear resolution compared to the unrestricted version treated before. Suppose that a program $P$ and a query $C$ are given. There are three or four things by which an unrestricted resolvent of $C$ relative to $P$ is determined.

(i) The *atom* selected from $C$,

(ii) the *rule* of $P$ involved in the unrestricted resolution step,

(iii) finally, the *specialization* for the variables in $C$ and the *instance* of the rule which together produce the unrestricted resolvent.

It follows that if we intend to implement the refutation procedure, then we have to supply strategies that produce these selections.

It can be shown that the selection of the atom in (i) is not critical (that is, if our interest only concerns *successes*). We do not stop to prove this for unrestricted resolution (but see the proof of Theorem 5.16), since eventually proofs will be given for linear resolution; see Corollary 5.48 and Theorem 5.49.

The choice of the rule in (ii) is critical for unrestricted resolution and will remain critical for linear resolution also.

What we shall see is that linear resolution completely eliminates the problem in (iii) of choosing specialization and rule-instance. The situation is similar to the one encountered for first-order resolution in Chapter 3. The solution adopted here also aims at maximal generality. However, a resolvent here consists not only of a query, but of a specialization as well; and so the situation is more complex. The solution consists in making resultants maximal.

### 5.4.2  Resolvents

Recall that an expression is *most general* in the class $K$ iff (Definition 3.73) every expression in $K$ is an instance of it.

**Definition 5.19** A *resolvent* of a query (with respect to some atom and rule) is an unrestricted resolvent (with respect to these same things) whose associated resultant is most general.

The notation $\xrightarrow{\alpha} D$ (now dropping the subscript 'u' from the arrow) is used for resolvents.  ∎

Other notations similar to the ones used in the unrestricted context will be used.

The definition states that $\xrightarrow{\alpha} D$ is a resolvent of the query $C$ with respect to the atom $A$ and the rule $R$ if it is an unrestricted resolvent with the additional property that, for every unrestricted resolvent $\xrightarrow{\alpha'} D'$ of $C$ (again, with respect to $A$ and $R$), there exists a substitution $\tau$ such that $(D{\to}C\alpha)\tau = D'{\to}C\alpha'$; that is:

- $C\alpha\tau \doteq C\alpha'$,
- $D\tau = D'$.

The following diagram depicts the situation.

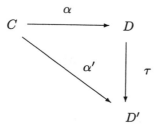

We shall often employ diagrams to illustrate situations like this one. In such a diagram, vertically downward pointing arrows indicate instantiations, and the other arrows stand for (possibly unrestricted) resolution steps.

The condition $C\alpha\tau = C\alpha'$ expresses commutativity of the diagram of substitutions on variables from $C$.

**Example 5.20**

(i) Reconsider Example 5.5 and the program SUM of Example 4.3. We noticed there that

$$\mathbf{sum}(x, y, sz) \xrightarrow[u]{\{y/Sy\}} \mathbf{sum}(x, y, z),$$

using the second rule. In fact, it is seen that

$$\mathbf{sum}(x, y, sz) \xrightarrow{\{y/Sy\}} \mathbf{sum}(x, y, z).$$

Similarly, we have that $\mathbf{sum}(x, y, sz) \xrightarrow{\{x/Sz, y/O\}} \square$, using the first rule.

(ii) Of course, $\xrightarrow{\epsilon} \mathbf{q}(y)$ is a resolvent of $\mathbf{r}(x)$ with respect to the rule $\mathbf{r}(x) \leftarrow \mathbf{q}(y)$. (Its resultant is $\mathbf{q}(y){\to}\mathbf{r}(x)$.)

$\xrightarrow{\epsilon} \mathbf{q}(x)$ is an *unrestricted* resolvent of $\mathbf{r}(x)$ (use the rule-instance $\mathbf{r}(x) \leftarrow \mathbf{q}(x)$), but it is not a *resolvent*. (Its resultant is $\mathbf{q}(x) \to \mathbf{r}(x)$.) However, the query $\mathbf{q}(x)$ *is* a resolvent; just use the specialization $\{x/y\}$ instead. The resultant obtained: $\mathbf{q}(x) \to \mathbf{r}(y)$, is a variant of $\mathbf{q}(y) \to \mathbf{r}(x)$.                                                                                ∎

The following lemma conditionally ensures existence of resolvents.

**Lemma 5.21 (Resolvent Existence)** *If a query has an unrestricted resolvent with respect to an atom and a rule, then it also has a resolvent with respect to these.*

**Proof.** The proof is analogous to the case for first-order resolution, handled in Lemma 3.76, and proceeds via separation of variables and most general unification, as follows.

Suppose that the following presents the details of an unrestricted resolution step $C \xrightarrow{\alpha}_u D'$ $(A, R)$:

$$C = (K, A, L)$$
$$R = (B \leftarrow M),\ A\alpha = B\beta,\ \text{specialization } \alpha,$$
$$D' = (K\alpha, M\beta, L\alpha).$$

We may assume that $Dom(\beta) \subset Var(R)$.

Note that, if rules $R$ and $R'$ are variants of each other, they have the same instances; and hence we have $C \xrightarrow{\theta}_u D$ $(A, R)$ iff $C \xrightarrow{\theta}_u D$ $(A, R')$. In particular, we have $C \xrightarrow{\theta} D$ $(A, R)$ iff $C \xrightarrow{\theta} D$ $(A, R')$. It follows that we may assume that $R$ and $C$ have no variables in common (otherwise, change to a variant of $R$). Under this condition, $\gamma := \alpha \cup \beta$ is well-defined, and unifies $A$ and $B$, since $A\gamma = A\alpha = B\beta = B\gamma$.

Let $\theta$ be an mgu of $A$ and $B$. We claim that the following unrestricted resolution transition:

$$C = (K, A, L)$$
$$\text{specialization } \theta|Var(C)$$
$$D = (K, M, L)\theta$$

is, in fact, a resolution step.

To see this, let $\tau$ be such that $\theta\tau = \gamma$. Then, e.g., the resultant associated with the former unrestricted resolvent: $K\alpha, M\beta, L\alpha \to (K, A, L)\alpha$, is the $\tau$-instance of the resultant associated with the latter one: $(K, M, L)\theta \to (K, A, L)\theta$.                                                                                ∎

The previous proof shows that we have the following recipe for obtaining resolvents.

**Corollary 5.22 (on Resolvents)** *If the query $C$ has a resolvent with respect to $A$ and $R = (B \leftarrow M)$, then a particular one can be obtained by*

   *(i) applying a renaming $\xi$ to $R$, separating its variables from $C$; and*

*(ii) constructing an mgu $\theta$ for $A$ and $B\xi$.*

*Then* $\xrightarrow{\theta|Var(C)}$ $C\theta\{A\theta/M\xi\theta\}$ *is a resolvent.* ∎

**Lemma 5.23 (Invariance for Renaming)** *If $C \xrightarrow{\alpha} D\ (A,\ R)$ and $\xi$ is a renaming for the associated resultant, then $C \xrightarrow{(\alpha\xi)|Var(C)} D\xi\ (A,\ R)$.*

**Proof.** That $C \xrightarrow{(\alpha\xi)|Var(C)}_u D\xi\ (A,\ R)$ follows by inspection. That this is, in fact, a resolution step is clear also, since its resultant is a variant of the resultant of the resolution step given. ∎

**Lemma 5.24** *Suppose that $R$ is a rule, $C$ and $D$ queries, $A$ an atom of $C$ and $\sigma$, $\beta$ substitutions. If $C\sigma \xrightarrow{\beta}_u D\ (A\sigma,\ R)$, then $C \xrightarrow{(\sigma\beta)|Var(C)}_u D\ (A,\ R)$.*

The situation is depicted by the following diagram.

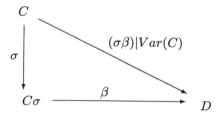

**Proof.** By a simple inspection of the definition. ∎

The Resolvent Existence Lemma 5.21 and Lemma 5.24 are now combined into the following.

**Lemma 5.25 (One Step Lifting)** *Assume that $C\sigma \xrightarrow{\beta}_u D\ (A\sigma,\ R)$.*

*(i) There exist a substitution $\alpha$ and a query $D^+$ such that $C \xrightarrow{\alpha} D^+\ (A,\ R)$,*

*(ii) for every $\alpha$ and $D^+$ such that $C \xrightarrow{\alpha} D^+\ (A,\ R)$, there exists a substitution $\tau$ for which*

    *(a) $(\sigma\beta)|Var(C) = (\alpha\tau)|Var(C)$ ("commutation"),*

    *(b) $D^+\tau = D$ ("instantiation").*

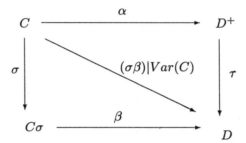

**Proof.** Suppose that $C\sigma \xrightarrow{\ \beta\ }_u D$ $(A\sigma, R)$. By Lemma 5.24, $C \xrightarrow{\ (\sigma\beta)|Var(C)\ }_u D$ $(A, R)$. See the diagram. Applying the Existence Lemma 5.21, part (i) follows; and part (ii) now is an immediate consequence of Definition 5.19. $\blacksquare$

The One Step Lifting Lemma states that (i) every unrestricted resolution step from $C\sigma$ can be "lifted" to a similar resolution step from $C$; and (ii) every such lift is related to the unrestricted step by a substitution $\tau$. The main purpose of the next subsection will be to generalize the One Step Lifting Lemma to the case of derivations (defined in the proper way).

**Exercises**

**5.7** Show that $\mathbf{p}(x), \mathbf{q}(y) \xrightarrow{\ \{y/\mathbf{f}y\}\ }_u \mathbf{p}(x), \mathbf{r}(z)$ and $\mathbf{p}(x), \mathbf{q}(y) \xrightarrow{\ \{y/x\}\ }_u \mathbf{p}(x), \mathbf{r}(z)$ are unrestricted resolution steps with respect to the atom $\mathbf{q}(y)$ and the rule $\mathbf{q}(y) \leftarrow \mathbf{r}(z)$ that are not resolution steps.

*Hint.* Show they don't lift the transition $\mathbf{p}(x), \mathbf{q}(y) \xrightarrow{\ \epsilon\ }_u \mathbf{p}(x), \mathbf{r}(z)$ (which, in fact, is a resolution step) in the sense of the One Step Lifting Lemma. (Compare Exercise 5.10.)

**5.8** Look through the unrestricted derivations you have produced up till now, and check which of the steps were, in fact, resolution steps.

Thanks to the use of the variables-separating renaming, the recipe described by the Resolvent Corollary 5.22 often introduces more variables than are necessary. Of course, we can always rename variables back to reduce their number, if only we take care that the two resultants are variants of each other.

**5.9** Show that the following problems are decidable.

(i) Whether a given unrestricted resolvent is, in fact, a resolvent.

(ii) Whether a given resolvent introduces a minimal number of new variables.

(iii) Whether a given resolvent uses a minimal specialization.

**5.10** (Compare Exercise 3.40.) Assume that $C \xrightarrow{\alpha}_u D$ $(A, R)$ is an unrestricted resolution step, that $R = (B \leftarrow M)$ and that $\beta$ is the unique substitution such that $Dom(\beta) \subset Var(R)$, $A\alpha = B\beta$, and $D = C\alpha\{A\alpha/M\beta\}$.

Show: this is a *resolution* step iff the following conditions are met:

(i) $A\alpha$ is a most general common instance of $A$ and $B$,

(ii) $\alpha|[Var(C) - Var(A)]$ and $\beta|[Var(R) - Var(B)]$ injectively map variables to variables,

(iii) the sets of variables $Var(A\alpha)$, $\{x\alpha \mid x \in Var(C) - Var(A)\}$ and $\{x\beta \mid x \in Var(R) - Var(B)\}$ are pairwise disjoint.

**5.11** Explain the reason for putting a restriction in the specialization in the claim of Lemma 5.24.

Is it true that $Dom(\sigma) \subset Var(C)$ and $Dom(\beta) \subset Var(C\sigma)$ imply $Dom(\sigma\beta) \subset Var(C)$?

**5.12** Suppose that $C \xrightarrow{\epsilon}_u D$ $(A, R)$. Show that for some $D$, $C \xrightarrow{\epsilon} D$ $(A, R)$.

### 5.4.3 Derivations

A *derivation* is simply defined as a sequence of resolution steps — except for *one* nasty detail. To explain this, we introduce a notion and present a couple of examples.

**Definition 5.26** A transition $C \xrightarrow{\alpha}_u D$ *releases* the variable $x$ if $x \in Var(C\alpha) - Var(D)$.

A variable is *released* by an unrestricted derivation if it is released by one of the steps of the unrestricted derivation. ∎

For instance, consider the program SUM of Example 4.3. The resolution step

$$\mathbf{sum}(x, y, \mathbf{s}z) \xrightarrow{\{x/\mathbf{s}z, y/\mathbf{0}\}} \square$$

(using the first rule $\mathbf{sum}(x, \mathbf{0}, x)\!\leftarrow$) releases the variable $z$.

**Example 5.27**

(i) Given the rules $\mathbf{r}(x) \leftarrow \mathbf{p}(y)$ and $\mathbf{p}(y) \leftarrow \mathbf{q}(x)$, the following is an unrestricted derivation every step of which is a resolution step:

$$\mathbf{r}(x) \xrightarrow{\epsilon} \mathbf{p}(y) \xrightarrow{\epsilon} \mathbf{q}(x).$$

Its resultant is $\mathbf{q}(x) \to \mathbf{r}(x)$. However, by just changing the first specialization $\epsilon$ to $\{x/z\}$ or using the rule-instance $\mathbf{p}(y) \leftarrow \mathbf{q}(z)$, we can obtain strictly more general resultants, namely (the variants) $\mathbf{q}(x)\rightarrow\mathbf{r}(z)$ resp. $\mathbf{q}(z)\rightarrow\mathbf{r}(x)$. The reason for not obtaining maximal generality here is re-introduction of the variable $x$ (released at the first step) in the last query of the unrestricted derivation.

(ii) Given the rules $\mathbf{r}(x,y)\leftarrow\mathbf{p}(y)$ and $\mathbf{p}(y)\leftarrow$, the following sequence is an unrestricted successful derivation using resolvents:

$$\mathbf{r}(x,y) \xrightarrow{\;\epsilon\;} \mathbf{p}(y) \xrightarrow{\;\{y/x\}\;} \square.$$

Its resultant is $\mathbf{r}(x,x)$. A more general resultant can be obtained by changing the second specialization to $\epsilon$ or the first one to $\{x/z\}$.

Here, the re-introduction of $x$ (released at the first step) by the second specialization is the culprit.                                                                                                   ∎

Note that in both examples non-maximality of the resultant of a two-step unrestricted derivation is due to the re-introduction of a variable released at the first step in the resultant of the second step. It turns out that this is the only cause that can endanger maximal generality of resultants. Therefore, we have the following definition.

**Definition 5.28** An unrestricted derivation is called a *derivation* if it consists of resolution steps and satisfies the following condition:

[ † ] no variable released at some step occurs in the resultant associated with a later one.                                                                                                                     ∎

In other words, a derivation is an unrestricted derivation made up of *resolvents* in which a variable, once released, is never re-introduced, either in a query or by a specialization.

The seemingly ad-hoc condition [ † ] can be motivated further, both from a syntactic and from a semantic viewpoint. Syntactically, it is clear that re-introduction of a variable released at the first step will account for a resultant not being most general. Semantically, re-introduction of a released variable allows for further instantiation at later steps; if the derivation culminates in a success, this is not what is intended. Of course, it remains to be seen that [ † ] not only is a necessary condition, but also a condition sufficient for our aims.

Note that, in the step-by-step construction of a derivation, it is never a problem to satisfy [ † ].

**Lemma 5.29** *Suppose that $\Delta$ is a derivation with last query $C$. If $C$ has a resolvent with respect to an atom and a rule, then there also is a resolvent $\xrightarrow{\;\alpha\;} D$ with respect to these things with the additional property that appending it at the end of $\Delta$ again results in a derivation.*

**Proof.** Use a variant of the rule that neither contains a variable from $Var(C)$ nor one that has been released previously. Let $\alpha$ be the restriction to $Var(C)$ of a *relevant* mgu (cf. Lemma 3.65) of the atom selected and the head of this variant. Apply the Resolvent Corollary 5.22. ∎

For some examples of how to regain [ † ], see Example 5.27.

**Definition 5.30** An unrestricted success that is a derivation is a *success*. ∎

From now on, it is understood (unless the contrary is indicated) that computed answer substitutions always are obtained by derivations (and not by unrestricted ones).

**Theorem 5.31 (Soundness of Resolution)** *Every computed answer substitution is correct.*

**Proof.** This is a special case of Theorem 5.14. ∎

**Example 5.32** Here is a successful derivation based on the program of Exercise 4.59. Each step resolves the left-most atom of the query at hand.
$\mathbf{reverse}([x_1, x_2], z)$

$$\xrightarrow{\{z/[y|z]\}} \mathbf{last}([x_1, x_2], x, y), \mathbf{reverse}(x, z)$$
$$\xrightarrow{\{x/[x_1|x]\}} \mathbf{last}([x_2], x, y), \mathbf{reverse}([x_1|x], z)$$
$$\xrightarrow{\{x/[\ ], y/x_2\}} \mathbf{reverse}([x_1], z)$$
$$\xrightarrow{\{z/[y|z]\}} \mathbf{last}([x_1], x, y), \mathbf{reverse}(x, z)$$
$$\xrightarrow{\{x/[\ ], y/x_1\}} \mathbf{reverse}([\ ], z)$$
$$\xrightarrow{\{z/[\ ]\}} \square.$$

This derivation releases $x_2$ at its third step and $x_1$ at its fifth. Its c.a.s. is $\{z/[x_2, x_1]\}$, which is in agreement with Theorem 5.31 and the result of Exercise 4.59. ∎

The following technicality is needed later on.

**Lemma 5.33** *If* $\Gamma : C_0 \xrightarrow{\alpha_1}_u \cdots \xrightarrow{\alpha_n}_u C_n$ *is an unrestricted derivation and* $x \in Var(C_0\alpha_1 \cdots \alpha_n) - Var(C_n)$, *then* $x$ *is released by* $\Gamma$.

**Proof.** Induction with respect to $n$.
*Basis.* For $n = 1$, this holds by definition.
*Induction step.* Assume the result for unrestricted derivations of length $n$. Suppose that $\Gamma : C_0 \xrightarrow{\alpha_1}_u \cdots \xrightarrow{\alpha_{n+1}}_u C_{n+1}$ now is an unrestricted derivation of length $n + 1$ and $x \in Var(C_0\alpha_1 \cdots \alpha_{n+1}) - Var(C_{n+1})$. By Lemma 3.52, $y \in Var(C_0\alpha_1 \cdots \alpha_n)$ exists such that $x \in Var(y\alpha_{n+1})$.

(a) $y \notin Var(C_n)$. By induction hypothesis, $y$ is released at one of the first $n$ steps of $\Gamma$. Also, since $Dom(\alpha_{n+1}) \subset Var(C_n)$, we have $y\alpha_{n+1} = y$ and hence, $x = y$. Thus, $x$ is released by $\Gamma$.

(b) $y \in Var(C_n)$. Thus, $x \in Var(C_n\alpha_{n+1})$. So, $x \in Var(C_n\alpha_{n+1}) - Var(C_{n+1})$, i.e.: $x$ is released at the last step of $\Gamma$.                                                                ∎

It is the *lifting property* of derivations which shows that our derivation concept is the right one, in the sense that it produces most general resultants. To explain what this is about, we introduce a notion of *similarity* for queries and unrestricted derivations.

**Definition 5.34** Queries $(A_1, \ldots, A_n)$ and $(B_1, \ldots, B_n)$ of the same length $n$ are called *similar* if, for $1 \leq i \leq n$, the atoms $A_i$ and $B_i$ carry the same relation symbol.            ∎

Suppose that $C$ and $D$ are similar in this sense. Form unrestricted resolvents of $C$ resp. $D$ by selecting atoms $A_i$ resp. $B_i$ in the same $i$-th position and applying the same rule. Then obviously, these unrestricted resolvents will be similar again. Thus, similarity of queries is propagated through unrestricted derivations as long as we keep selecting atoms in the same position and applying the same rule at corresponding stages of the two derivations.

**Definition 5.35**

(i) Unrestricted derivations $\Gamma$ and $\Delta$ are *similar* if they start from similar queries, have the same length and, at corresponding places, apply the same rule to selected (occurrences of) atoms in the same position.

(ii) The derivation $\Delta$ is a *lift* of the unrestricted derivation $\Gamma$ if $\Delta$ is similar to $\Gamma$ and the initial query of $\Gamma$ is an instance of the initial query of $\Delta$.            ∎

The following key-result shows that (i) lifts always exist and (ii) lifts are related to the unrestricted derivation they lift by means of a sequence of substitutions satisfying instantiation and commutation properties; compare the One Step Lifting Lemma 5.25. The following piece of notation is used.

**Notation 5.36** If $\Gamma : C_0 \xrightarrow{\alpha_1}_u C_1 \xrightarrow{\alpha_2}_u C_2 \cdots$ is a (possibly, unrestricted) derivation and $i < j$, then $\Gamma_{i,j}$ denotes the subderivation $C_i \xrightarrow{\alpha_{i+1}}_u \cdots \xrightarrow{\alpha_j}_u C_j$ which derives $C_j$ from $C_i$, and $\alpha_{i,j}$ ($i < j$) stands for the composition $(\alpha_{i+1} \cdots \alpha_j)$ of the specializations of $\Gamma_{i,j}$.            ∎

**Theorem 5.37 (Lifting)** *Suppose that $D_0 = C_0\sigma$, where $Dom(\sigma) \subset Var(C_0)$.*

(i) *Every (finite or infinite) unrestricted derivation starting from $D_0$ has a lift starting from $C_0$.*

(ii) *If $\Delta : C_0 \xrightarrow{\beta_1} \cdots$ lifts the unrestricted derivation $\Gamma : D_0 \xrightarrow{\alpha_1}_u \cdots$, then there exists a sequence $\boldsymbol{\sigma} : \sigma^0, \sigma^1, \sigma^2, \ldots$ of substitutions such that, for $i < j$:*

*(a)* $\sigma^0 = \sigma$,

*(b)* $D_j = C_j \sigma^j$ *("instantiation")*,

*(c)* $(\sigma^i \alpha_{i,j}) | Var(C_i) = (\beta_{i,j} \sigma^j) | Var(C_i)$ *("commutation")*,

*(d)* $res(\Gamma_{i,j}) = res(\Delta_{i,j}) \sigma^j$.

The following diagram illustrates part (ii)(b,c) of the theorem.

$$
\begin{array}{ccccccccc}
\Delta: & C_0 & \xrightarrow{\beta_1} & \cdots & \xrightarrow{\beta_n} & C_n & \xrightarrow{\beta_{n+1}} & C_{n+1} & \xrightarrow{\beta_{n+2}} & \cdots \\
 & \Big\downarrow & & & & \Big\downarrow & & \Big\downarrow & & \\
\sigma: & \sigma = \sigma^0 & & \cdots & & \sigma^n & & \sigma^{n+1} & & \cdots \\
 & \Big\downarrow & & & & \Big\downarrow & & \Big\downarrow & & \\
\Gamma: & D_0 & \xrightarrow{\alpha_1} & \cdots & \xrightarrow{\alpha_n} & D_n & \xrightarrow{\alpha_{n+1}} & D_{n+1} & \xrightarrow{\alpha_{n+2}} & \cdots
\end{array}
$$

## Proof.

(i) Repeatedly, apply the One Step Lifting Lemma 5.25 and Lemma 5.29.

Let $\Gamma : D_0 \xrightarrow{\alpha_1}_u \cdots$ be the given unrestricted derivation from $D_0$. By 5.25(i), we can lift the first step $D_0 \xrightarrow{\alpha_1}_u D_1$ of $\Gamma$ to a resolution step $C_0 \xrightarrow{\beta_1} C_1$. By 5.25(ii), there exists a substitution $\tau^1$ such that $D_1 = C_1 \tau^1$.

Therefore, again by 5.25(i), we can lift the second step $D_1 \xrightarrow{\alpha_2}_u D_2$ of $\Gamma$ to a resolution step $C_1 \xrightarrow{\beta_2} C_2$. By 5.29, we can satisfy [ † ] for the resulting two-step derivation. By 5.25(ii), $\tau^2$ exists such that $D_2 = C_2 \tau^2$.

Obviously, this construction can be repeated until we have lifted *all* of $\Gamma$, obtaining the required lift.

(ii) First note that (d) is nothing but (b) and (c) put together. We show how to obtain the sequence $\sigma$.

Suppose that $\sigma^0, \ldots, \sigma^n$ have been found, satisfying conditions (a–d) for $i < j \le n$.

Since $\Delta$ is made up of resolvents, by Lemma 5.25(ii) we obtain a substitution $\tau$ such that both $D_{n+1} = C_{n+1} \tau$ and $(\sigma^n \alpha_{n+1}) | Var(C_n) = (\beta_{n+1} \tau) | Var(C_n)$.

Since $\Delta$ satisfies [ † ], no variable released somewhere along $\Delta_{0,n}$ is in $Var(C_n \beta_{n+1}, C_{n+1})$. This is exactly what is needed to be able to extend $\tau$ to a substitution $\sigma^{n+1}$ by defining

$$
x\sigma^{n+1} := \begin{cases} x\tau & \text{if } x \in Var(C_n \beta_{n+1}, C_{n+1}), \\ x\sigma^n \alpha_{n+1} & \text{if } x \text{ has been released along } \Delta_{0,n}. \end{cases}
$$

It now follows that, for $m < n$, $C_m \alpha_{m,n+1} \sigma^{n+1} = C_m \sigma^m \beta_{m,n+1}$. Note first that (1) if $x \in Var(C_n)$, then $x\beta_{n+1}\sigma^{n+1} = x\beta_{n+1}\tau = x\sigma^n \alpha_{n+1}$; (2) if $x$ has been released along

$\Delta_{0,n}$, then $x\beta_{n+1} = x$, hence again: $x\beta_{n+1}\sigma^{n+1} = x\sigma^{n+1} = x\sigma^n\alpha_{n+1}$. Now assume that $y \in Var(C_m)$ and $y\beta_{m,n} = t$. Since by Lemma 5.33 any variable in $t$ either occurs in $C_n$ or is released along $\Delta_{0,n}$, we have: $y\beta_{m,n+1}\sigma^{n+1} = t\beta_{n+1}\sigma^{n+1} = t\sigma^n\alpha_{n+1} = y\beta_{n,m}\sigma^n\alpha_{n+1} = y\sigma^m\alpha_{m,n}\alpha_{n+1} = y\sigma^m\alpha_{m,n+1}$. ∎

**Corollary 5.38** *If $P$ successfully unrestrictedly resolves $C\sigma$ in $n$ steps via the specializations $\alpha_1, \ldots, \alpha_n$, then $P$ successfully resolves $C$ in $n$ steps via specializations $\beta_1, \ldots, \beta_n$ such that for some $\tau$: $C\sigma\alpha_1 \cdots \alpha_n = C\beta_1 \cdots \beta_n\tau$.*

**Proof.** By Theorem 5.37, a suitable lift of the unrestricted derivation of $C\sigma$ will do. Note that a lift of a *success* is a success again, since □ can be only an instance of □. ∎

The following completeness result is weak in two respects: it is about ground instances of queries only, and it does not take into account selection rules. A completeness result that remedies both defects is in the next section.

**Corollary 5.39 (Weak Completeness)** *If $C\gamma$ is ground and $P \models C\gamma$, then a computed answer substitution $\theta$ exists for $C$ such that $C\gamma$ is an instance of $C\theta$.*

**Proof.** By the Ground Completeness Theorem 5.16, $P$ has a successful unrestricted derivation for $C\gamma$. Apply Corollary 5.38. ∎

### Exercises

**5.13** Show: a resolution step can release variables only if it is performed by means of a rule $B \leftarrow M$ for which $Var(B) - Var(M) \neq \emptyset$.

**5.14** The following is a succesful unrestricted derivation based on the program of Exercise 4.59.

**reverse**$([u, u], [u, u])$

$\xrightarrow{\quad\epsilon\quad}_u$ **last**$([u, u], [u], u),$ **reverse**$([u], [u])$

$\xrightarrow{\quad\epsilon\quad}_u$ **last**$([u], [\ ], u),$ **reverse**$([u], [u])$

$\xrightarrow{\quad\epsilon\quad}_u$ **reverse**$([u], [u])$

$\xrightarrow{\quad\epsilon\quad}_u$ **last**$([u], [\ ], u),$ **reverse**$([\ ], [\ ])$

$\xrightarrow{\quad\epsilon\quad}_u$ **reverse**$([\ ], [\ ])$

$\xrightarrow{\quad\epsilon\quad}_u$ □.

Check that the derivation of Example 5.32 lifts this unrestricted derivation. Construct the sequence of substitutions $\sigma^0 = \{x_1/u, x_2/u, z/[u, u]\}, \ldots, \sigma^6$ that relates the two derivations in the sense of the Lifting Theorem 5.37 part (ii). Note that, though the empty query □ ends both derivations, $\sigma^6 \neq \epsilon$. Thus, the instantiation property does not suffice to construct the sequence.

**5.15** Show: if $C \xrightarrow{\beta} D$ $(A, R)$, $\sigma$, $\alpha$ and $\tau$ are substitutions such that $C\sigma\alpha = C\beta\tau$ and $Dom(\alpha) \subset Var(C\sigma)$, then $C\sigma \xrightarrow{\alpha}_u D\tau$ $(A\sigma, R)$. (Hence, the first step lifts the second one.)

In particular, $C\beta\tau \xrightarrow{\epsilon}_u D\tau$ $(A\beta\tau, R)$.

Show by means of a simple example that these transitions are not necessarily resolution steps.

**5.16** (Compare Lemma 5.29.) Suppose that $\Delta$ is a derivation with last query $C$, and that $C$ has an unrestricted resolvent $\xrightarrow{\epsilon}_u D$ with respect to an atom and a rule. Show: $C$ also has a resolvent $\xrightarrow{\epsilon} D$ with respect to these things with the additional property that appending it at the end of $\Delta$ again results in a derivation.

**5.17** Assume that the query $C$ has an unrestricted success (relative to some program) with computed answer substitution $\theta$. Show: $\theta$ has a successful derivation with computed answer substitution $\epsilon$.

**5.18** Show that the converse of Lemma 5.33 is false, even if we require $\Gamma$ to be a derivation.

Show: $C_0 \xrightarrow{\alpha_1} \cdots \xrightarrow{\alpha_n} C_n$ releases $x$ iff for some $i < n$: $x \in Var(C_i\alpha_{i+1} \cdots \alpha_n) - Var(C_n)$.

**5.19** Give an example of an *infinite* derivation that does *not* lift a ground derivation. (Chapter 6 contains information about derivations like these.)

**5.20** Show: every *finite* derivation lifts a ground derivation.
*Hint.* Use Exercise 5.15, or cf. Lemma 6.11.

**5.21** Compare Exercise 5.3. Prove the full converse of Theorem 5.14: every correct answer for a query (with respect to some program) is the computed answer substitution of an *unrestricted* derivation for that query (with respect to that program).

Show — by means of a simple example — that the adjective *unrestricted* cannot be dropped here.

**Definition 5.40** Let some program be fixed. Suppose that $C$ and $D$ are queries and $\alpha$ is a substitution. By the notation $C \xrightarrow{\alpha} D$ we mean that $Dom(\alpha) \subset Var(C)$ and for some derivation $C_0 = C \xrightarrow{\alpha_1} \cdots \xrightarrow{\alpha_n} C_n = D$ $(n \geq 1)$ using rules of the program, we have $\alpha = (\alpha_1 \cdots \alpha_n)|Var(C)$. ∎

**Lemma 5.41** If $C \xrightarrow{\alpha} D$, $D \xrightarrow{\beta} E$ and $Var(C\alpha) \cap Var(D\beta) \subset Var(D)$, then $C \xrightarrow{(\alpha\beta)|Var(C)} E$.

**5.22** Prove Lemma 5.41.

**5.23** (Cf. also Chapter 8, Definition 8.12.) Fix some program $P$. Let $\mathbf{R}$ be the smallest relation between queries and substitutions such that

(i) $\Box\mathbf{R}\epsilon$,

(ii) if $D\mathbf{R}\beta$, $C \xrightarrow{\alpha} D$ (using some rule of $P$) and $Var(C\alpha) \cap Var(D\beta) \subset Var(D)$, then $C\mathbf{R}(\alpha\beta)|Var(C)$.

Show: $C\mathbf{R}\alpha$ iff $\alpha$ is c.a.s. of some successful $P$-derivation starting from $C$.

**5.24** (Cf. also Chapter 8, Definition 8.47.) Fix some program $P$. Let $\mathcal{YES}$ be the least set of queries such that

(Y1) $\Box \in \mathcal{YES}$,

(Y2) if $C \xrightarrow{\epsilon} D$ (using some $P$-rule) and $D \in \mathcal{YES}$, then $C \in \mathcal{YES}$.

Show:

(i) if $C\sigma \in \mathcal{YES}$, then there is a computed answer substitution $\theta$ for $C$ such that $C\sigma$ is an instance of $C\theta$,

(ii) if $\theta$ is a computed answer substitution for $C$, then $C\theta \in \mathcal{YES}$.

## 5.5 SLD-Resolution

At the beginning of the previous section, it was noted that an unrestricted resolvent is determined by three choices: (i) selection of an atom from the query, (ii) choice of an (applicable) rule, (iii) determination of specialization and rule instance. Only the last problem in this list is eliminated by the concept of resolution.

One of the topics of the present section is to eliminate — in some sense — the first one. Also, the completeness result of Corollary 5.39 is generalized.

Intuitively, a selection rule is a function that handles choice (i) in the construction of a derivation. In order to obtain a simpler formulation of the next definition, we consider a query as a derivation of length 0.

**Definition 5.42** A *selection rule* is a function defined on finite (possibly, unrestricted) derivations that do not end with the empty query. When applied to such a derivation, it outputs (an occurrence of) one of the atoms of the last query.                                   ∎

Note that a selection rule is not at all required to pick atoms that unify with the head of some (variant of a) program rule. Even if there are such atoms in the query under consideration, it may select one to which no rule is applicable (and so the derivation comes to an unsuccessful end).

*SLD-resolution*, in full: Selection-rule driven Linear Resolution for Definite clauses, is constructing derivations where the atoms are selected by means of some selection rule.

A very simple example of a selection rule is to always pick the leftmost atom in a query. This is the *leftmost* rule; it is the selection rule Prolog uses. This rule does not take into account the "history" of the query in which it selects—the derivation by which it has been obtained. The selection rule that alternates between left- and rightmost atom selection is a simple example of a rule that is not completely history-independent.

Here are two simple properties a selection rule may possess.

**Definition 5.43** A selection rule is *lifting invariant* if, whenever applied to a derivation $\Gamma$ and its lift $\Delta$, it always selects atoms in the same position.

A selection rule is *fair* if, for every *infinite* derivation produced by it, every atom occurring in a query of the derivation is eventually selected. ∎

In other words, if the infinite derivation $\Gamma$ is produced by a *fair* rule, has specializations $\theta_1$, $\theta_2$, $\theta_3$, ..., and if an atom $A$ occurs in the $i$-th query of $\Gamma$, then either the rule immediately selects $A$ in this query, or for some (first) $j > i$, it selects the descendant $A\theta_{i,j}$ of $A$ in the $j$-th query of $\Gamma$.

Note that the leftmost rule is lifting invariant. However, it is not fair. For instance, let the program $P$ consist of the one rule $p \leftarrow p$. Then the query $(p, q)$, with the leftmost rule, starts an infinite derivation in which the atom $q$ is never selected.

Derivations from a fixed query, conceived of as sequences of successive resolvents, can be organized into trees. If we consider only derivations produced using a fixed selection rule, then we obtain an SLD-tree.

Let us call a rule *applicable* to the atom $A$ if its head and $A$ have a common instance.

**Definition 5.44** Let $P$ be a program, $C$ a query and $\rho$ a selection rule. A $\rho$-*SLD-tree* for $C$ with respect to $P$ is a tree $\mathcal{T}$ with root $C$ in which all other nodes are of the form $\xrightarrow{\alpha} D$, and such that

- for every such node, the unique path $\Gamma = C \longrightarrow \cdots \xrightarrow{\alpha} D$ through $\mathcal{T}$ is a derivation, and
- for every such node $D$ and path $\Gamma = C \longrightarrow \cdots \xrightarrow{\alpha} D$, if $D \neq \square$ and $\rho(\Gamma) = A \in D$, then for every rule $R \in P$ applicable to $A$, the node $\xrightarrow{\alpha} D$ has exactly one child $\xrightarrow{\beta} E$ in $\mathcal{T}$ for which $D \xrightarrow{\beta} E \ (A, R)$.

  Of course, this stipulation is also required of the root $C$, that is, if $C \neq \square$ and $\rho(C) = A \in C$, then for every rule $R \in P$ applicable to $A$, the root $C$ has exactly one child $\xrightarrow{\beta} E$ in $\mathcal{T}$ for which $C \xrightarrow{\beta} E \ (A, R)$.

Finally, an empty node is a leaf of $\mathcal{T}$. ∎

The actual construction of SLD-trees presupposes some way of picking, for each applicable rule, exactly one resolvent among infinitely many variants.

Let $\mathcal{T}$ be the SLD-tree determined by $P$, $C_0$ and $\rho$, and suppose that $\Gamma := C_0 \xrightarrow{\theta_1} \cdots$ $\xrightarrow{\theta_n} C_n$ is a path through $\mathcal{T}$, where $C_n \neq \square$. Let $A := \rho(\Gamma)$ be the $\rho$-selected atom of $C_n$. Then the node $C_n$ (actually, the node $\xrightarrow{\theta_n} C_n$) has as many children in $\mathcal{T}$ as there are $A$-applicable rules in $P$. Since there are only *finitely* many rules in a program, it follows that SLD-trees are finitely branching.

Three things may happen in climbing an SLD-tree.

(i) The climb follows a successful derivation, after finitely many steps ending at a success leaf $\square$. A tree containing a success is called *successful,* otherwise it *fails.*

(ii) After finitely many steps the climb ends at a leaf different from $\square$ (the selection rule selects an atom here for which no applicable rule exists in the program). Such a leaf is called a *failure.*

(iii) The climb goes on forever, along an infinite branch. This can happen if the tree is not well-founded.

**Example 5.45** Consider the following three rules:
$$path(x, z) \leftarrow arc(x, y), path(y, z)$$
$$path(x, x) \leftarrow$$
$$arc(\mathbf{d}, \mathbf{c}) \leftarrow.$$
The SLD-tree for the query $path(x, \mathbf{c})$ generated using the leftmost selection rule is finite. It has three leaves: two successes and one failure; there are no infinite branches. The rightmost selection rule (which always picks the rightmost atom in a query) generates an infinite, non well-founded SLD-tree for the same query.                    ∎

Here follows a completeness result incorporating the selection rule independence phenomenon.

**Theorem 5.46 (Completeness)** *Let $P$ be a program, $C$ a query and $\sigma$ a substitution ground for $C$ such that $P \models C\sigma$. Then every SLD-tree for $C$ contains a success with a computed answer substitution $\theta$ such that $C\sigma$ is an instance of $C\theta$.*

**Proof.** We mix the proof of the Ground Completeness Theorem 5.16 with a lifting construction.

Assume that $P \models C\sigma$, where $C\sigma$ is ground. By Lemma 4.10, every atom in $C\sigma$ has a ground implication tree. Let $n$ be the total number of nodes in these trees. We show that for $k \leq n$, a $\rho$-derivation $\Gamma_{0,k} : C_0 = C \xrightarrow{\theta_1} \cdots \xrightarrow{\theta_k} C_k$, a ground substitution $\sigma^k$ and a set of ground implication trees for the atoms in $C_k\sigma^k$ exist such that $C\sigma = C\theta_1 \cdots \theta_k \sigma^k$ and the total number of nodes in these trees is $n - k$.

The required result follows by putting $k = n$.

For $k = 0$, these conditions are satisfied by hypothesis. As an induction hypothesis, assume they are satisfied for the derivation $\Gamma_{0,k}$ and a set of ground implication trees for the atoms in $C_k\sigma^k$, where $k < n$. Suppose that $A \in C_k$ is the atom selected by $\rho$. Let $A\sigma^k \leftarrow E$ be the ground instance of the rule $R$ of $P$ such that the children of $A$ in the implication tree for $A$ are precisely the elements of $E$. Now, $C_k\sigma^k \longrightarrow_u D = C_k\sigma^k\{A\sigma^k/E\}$ is a ground resolution step. Lift this to a step $C_k \xrightarrow{\theta_{k+1}} C_{k+1}$, not re-introducing variables from $\Gamma_{0,k}$, and suppose that $\tau$ is such that $C_{k+1}\tau = D$ and $C_k\sigma^k = C_k\theta_{k+1}\tau$. Extend $\tau$ to $\sigma^{k+1}$ as required, putting $x\sigma^{k+1} = x\sigma^k$ for variables $x$ released along $\Gamma_{0,k}$. (Compare the proof of Theorem 5.37.) The set of ground implication trees for the atoms in $D$ is obtained from the set for the atoms of $C_k\sigma^k$ replacing the tree for $A\sigma^k$ by its subtrees for the children of $A\sigma^k$. ∎

The following result strengthens Theorem 5.46 by admitting $\sigma$ to be non-ground.

**Corollary 5.47 (Strong Completeness)** *Let $\gamma$ be a substitution such that $P \models C\gamma$. Then every SLD-tree for $C$ contains a success with a computed answer substitution $\theta$ such that $C\gamma$ is an instance of $C\theta$.*

**Proof.** The trick is to consider the variables of $C\gamma$ as new constant symbols. Let $\mathcal{T}$ be an SLD-tree for $C$. Let $\sigma$ be a substitution mapping $Var(C\gamma)$ 1–1 onto a set of new constant symbols. Since $P \models C\gamma$, we have that $P \models C\gamma\sigma$, as well.

Note that the addition of the new constant symbols to the language does not stop $\mathcal{T}$ from being an SLD-tree for $C$.

By the Completeness Theorem 5.46, $\mathcal{T}$ contains a success $\Delta$ with a computed answer substitution $\theta$ such that $C\gamma\sigma$ is an instance of $C\theta$. Clearly then, since $C\theta$ does not contain any of the new constant symbols, $C\gamma$ also is an instance of $C\theta$. ∎

Note that this theorem eliminates the problem of selecting atoms — at least if it is a success we're after.

For a nice alternative to the proof of Corollary 5.47, see Exercises 6.4 and 6.5.

**Corollary 5.48 (Irrelevance of Selection Rule)** *If a query has a success using some selection rule, then it has a success using any selection rule.* ∎

A stronger, more informative version of this result can be obtained by switching steps in a derivation. This shows that the use of a different selection rule cannot result in a computed answer substitution that is more general, nor in a success that is shorter.

**Theorem 5.49 (Strong Independence of Selection Rule)** *Let $\rho$ be a selection rule and $C$ a query. For every success for $C$ there exists a $\rho$-success for $C$ of the same length and with the same computed answer substitution.*

**Proof.** Since we are only interested in $\rho$ as far as derivations from $C$ are concerned, we may as well assume that $\rho$ is lifting-invariant.

Let $\Delta$ be a success for $C$ with c.a.s. $\delta$. Then $\Delta$ lifts an unrestricted success $\Gamma$ for $C\delta$ that has all its specializations equal to $\epsilon$.

Construct a $\rho$-unrestricted success $\Sigma$ of $C\delta$ stepwise by moving steps from $\Gamma$ to the front, if this is required in order to satisfy $\rho$. Note that this is possible, since every $\rho$-selected atom — or a descendant — must be selected somewhere along $\Gamma$ as $\Gamma$ is a success. All specializations remain unchanged equal to $\epsilon$; we need modify only in queries.

Lift $\Sigma$ to a $\rho$-success $\Sigma^+$ for $C$. Let $\sigma$ be the c.a.s. of $\Sigma^+$. By the Lifting Theorem, $C\sigma$ is more general than $C\delta$.

Of course, $\Sigma^+$ can be projected-switched-and-lifted again, using the same procedure. I.e.: project $\Sigma^+$ to an unrestricted similar success for $C\sigma$ with all specializations $= \epsilon$, subsequently, modify this to an unrestricted success similar to $\Delta$ with all specializations $= \epsilon$.

By the Lifting Theorem, $C\sigma$ is an instance of $C\delta$. Therefore, $C\delta$ and $C\sigma$ are variants of each other.

By invariance for renamings, there is a $\rho$-success for $C$ with the same c.a.s. $\delta$, as well. $\blacksquare$

### Exercises

**5.25** Check the details of Example 5.45. Note that the rightmost tree also contains two successes, corresponding to the two of the leftmost tree. This illustrates the phenomenon of irrelevance of the selection rule.

**5.26** Assume that the query $C$ has an SLD-tree relative to the program $P$ (and some selection rule) that does not contain a success. Let $C'$ be an instance of $C$. Show that $C'$ has such a tree as well (possibly using a different selection rule). Describe it.

**5.27** Let $\rho$ be an arbitrary selection rule and $C$ a query. Show, using Corollary 5.47 alone: for every successful derivation of $C$ with computed answer substitution $\gamma$ there exists a successful $\rho$-derivation of $C$ with computed answer substitution $\theta$ such that $C\gamma$ is an instance of $C\theta$.

**5.28** Suppose that a given two-step derivation $C_0 \xrightarrow{\alpha_1} C_1 \xrightarrow{\alpha_2} C_2$ first applies the rule $R$ and next the rule $Q$.

Show that a two-step derivation $C_0 \xrightarrow{\beta_1} D_1 \xrightarrow{\beta_2} C_2$ exists that first performs $Q$ and then $R$, such that $C_0\beta_1\beta_2 = C_0\alpha_1\alpha_2$.

**5.29** Prove: if $\gamma$ is a correct answer substitution for $C$ with respect to the program $P$ and $\mathcal{T}$ is an SLD-tree for $C\gamma$, then $\mathcal{T}$ contains a success of which the computed answer substitution is a renaming for $C\gamma$.

Instead of computing, logic programming can also be used to find solutions to a problem in a large search space. The following two exercises illustrate this possibility. See Exercise 5.32 for a general observation concerning programs accomplishing such searches.

**\*5.30** Construct a program and a query with the following property. The leftmost SLD-tree for the query is finite, and the computed answer substitutions along its successes coincide with all solutions to the game of Solitaire (coded appropriately).

**\*5.31** Construct a program that "finds" (in the sense of Exercise 5.30) all sequences of length 27 in which each of the numbers $1,\ldots,9$ occurs exactly three times, and which have the property that, between two successive occurrences of a number $n$, there are exactly $n$ occurrences of other numbers $(n = 1,\ldots,9)$. (There are six pairwise-symmetric solutions; one of them is $[7,5,3,8,6,9,3,5,7,4,3,6,8,5,4,9,7,2,6,4,2,8,1,2,1,9,1]$.)

*Solution.* Consider the rules:

$find(x) \leftarrow$

$\qquad twentyseven(x),$

$\qquad sublist([1, x_{11}, 1, x_{12}, 1], x),$

$\qquad sublist([2, x_{21}, x_{22}, 2, x_{23}, x_{24}, 2], x),$

$\qquad sublist([3, x_{31}, x_{32}, x_{33}, 3, x_{34}, x_{35}, x_{36}, 3], x),$

$$\cdots$$

$\qquad sublist([9, x_{91}, x_{92}, \ldots, x_{99}, 9, x_{100}, \ldots, x_{108}, 9], x)$

$twentyseven([x_1, \ldots, x_{27}]) \leftarrow$

$sublist(x, y) \leftarrow append(u, x, v), append(v, w, y)$

plus rules for *append*. Note that the declarative interpretation of these rules leaps into the eye: they straightforwardly formulate, in logical terms, the conditions a solution must satisfy.

**5.32** Assume that $HU$ is infinite. Suppose that the query $C$ has only finitely many correct answer substitutions (w.r.t. some program). Show: its correct answer substitutions and its computed answer substitutions coincide.

## 5.6   Notes

One of the oldest references in the subject is [Kowalski 74]. At about the same time, Colmerauer was developing Prolog.

In the literature and in Prolog, the inverted implication symbol also is written as $:-$.

For the name Horn, see: A. Horn, On sentences true of direct unions of algebras, *J. Symbolic Logic* 16 (1951) pp 1–14.

The unrestricted version of resolution occurs in [Lloyd 87].

The way to define resolvents in Definition 5.19 is similar to the one used in Chapter 3, and different from the traditional, ad-hoc set-up that defines resolvents using the explicit recipe of Corollary 5.22. Similarly, the notion of derivation, Definition 5.28, is different from the traditional one, which avoids confusion of previously released variables with new ones using so-called *standardization-apart* conditions, of which there are many competing ones occurring in the literature. About a quarter of a century ago, *Curry's Principle* ("every paper dealing with substitutions contains at least one mistake") still held. This logical tradition seems to have been taken over by workers in the field of logic programming for some time (be it that the type of mistake has changed). We hope the present chapter contributes to putting an end to this remarkable phenomenon.

The arrow notation as in $C \xrightarrow{\alpha} D$ does not correspond properly to the direction in which the rules point (it is the resultant $D{\to}C\alpha$ that logically follows from the rule employed for this step); however, it does correspond both with the direction in which a derivation is constructed and with the commutation property of diagrams.

Shepherdson's notion of *resultant* (Definitions 5.6 and 5.9) is in [Lloyd/Shepherdson 91].

Much of the material from this chapter is taken from [Doets b] (that paper uses a more abstract notion of *derivation*, proved to be equivalent with the simpler one used here), which also discusses the precise relationship with the traditional approach.

Example 5.45 is from [Apt 90].

Theorem 5.49 appears to be new.

The note [Stärk 89] contains a short and beautiful proof of Corollary 5.47 (indicated in Exercises 6.4 and 6.5) of which the proof for Theorem 5.46 is a special case. The proof of Theorem 5.16 is implicit in [Stärk 89].

The observation contained in Exercise 5.32 is due to Apt.

# 6 Infinite Derivations

## 6.1 Negative Information

Linear resolution only deduces *positive* information from programs. What it proves are statements of the form $\exists \bigwedge C$, where $C$ is a sequence of atoms. In many practical situations, however, it makes perfectly good sense to deduce negative information as well. E.g., from the fact that the time table does not list a train leaving at 12.08, I should be able to rightly and correctly make the inference that no train will leave at that time. Thus arises the need to construct inference systems that make up for this deficiency. Now for every program $P$ and every ground atom $A$, $P \cup \{A\}$ is satisfiable (the Herbrand base HB is a Herbrand model for it); and so we never have that $P \models \neg A$. Therefore, if such an inference system permits the derivation of $\neg A$ from $P$, it necessarily is *unsound*. Secondly, the train example shows that whatever our approach to this problem, an inference system that is able to deduce negative facts probably will be *non-monotone*. The edition of the time table in our possession may have been incomplete and its latest revision may show us that a train does leave at 12.08 after all. Thus, although $\neg A$ "follows" from $P$, $\neg A$ need no longer be corroborated by an updating $P' \supset P$ of $P$ that, in fact, possibly might entail that $A$.

Now, let us have a look at some possible ways of drawing negative conclusions from programs. Naively, at least three possible answers come to mind.

Recall, that $M_P = T_P \uparrow \subset T_P \downarrow \subset T_P \downarrow \omega$. Let $A$ be a ground atom.

(i) If we consider the least Herbrand model $M_P$ of $P$ to be its "real" meaning, then one can consider $\neg A$ to be inferred in case $A \notin M_P$.

This rule is known as the *Closed World Assumption*.

(ii) Somewhat less liberal, one can consider $\neg A$ to be inferred in case $A \notin T_P \downarrow$.

This is called *Herbrand's rule*.

(iii) Even less liberal, one may consider $\neg A$ inferred in case $A \notin T_P \downarrow \omega$.

This is known as *negation as (finite) failure*; this terminology will be explained shortly.

Of these three, the Closed World Assumption may well be the most sensible one. Note that, for ground atoms $A$, $A \notin M_P$ amounts to $P \not\models A$; hence, the Closed World Assumption considers a ground atom to be false just in case it does not follow from $P$. However, computationally, it often is not a feasible rule, even in the widest possible sense of this term. Chapter 7 shows that $M_P$ is positively decidable but possibly not decidable.

Therefore, its complement $HB - M_P$ may not be positively decidable; and it follows that no effective deduction method exists that will allow us to conclude that $A \notin M_P$ in all cases where this is true.

Herbrand's rule is even more problematic in this respect: Chapter 7 shows that $T_P \downarrow$ can be even more complex.

From the Completeness Theorem 5.46 we know that, for a program $P$ and a ground atom $A$, $A \notin M_P$ iff $A$ has an unsuccessful SLD-tree.

The reason this condition may not be positively decidable is that an SLD-tree can be infinite; hence, generating it, we can never be sure that it will indeed turn out to eventually fail.

It is clear that one possible (but rather ad-hoc) way to restore positive decidability consists in requiring $A$ not to have an *arbitrary* failing SLD-tree, but a *finite* failing tree. For, since we can systematically search through all finite SLD-trees, this obviously is a positively decidable condition.

One of the results in this chapter is the equivalence of this condition with that of negation as failure. Another equivalent uses the notion of *completion* of a program, cf. Definition 6.19. It has been argued that the "real" meaning of a program is given by its completion. And it turns out that $A \in HB - T_P \downarrow \omega$ iff $\neg A$ follows from the completion of $P$, cf. Corollary 6.20.

Other upcoming results are related to the question of when these ways of inferring negative information are different and when not; that is, under what conditions the sets $M_P = T_P \uparrow$, $T_P \downarrow$ and $T_P \downarrow \omega$ differ and under which circumstances they coincide.

For a discussion of negative information in the proper context of general queries and programs (which fully allow negations), see Chapter 8.

## 6.2   Non-standard Algebras

Given a non-empty set of constant and function symbols, the *standard Herbrand algebra* $HA$ (Definition 3.19) consists of the ground terms constructed using these symbols, together with the *canonical* interpretation for them. We are going to consider seriously other algebras as well. Note that $HA$ satisfies the set CET of *free equality axioms* introduced by Definition 3.68, which are repeated here.

(i) $\mathbf{f}(x_1, \ldots, x_n) = \mathbf{f}(y_1, \ldots, y_n) \to (x_1 = y_1 \wedge \cdots \wedge x_n = y_n)$,

(ii) $\mathbf{f}(x_1, \ldots, x_n) \neq \mathbf{g}(y_1, \ldots, y_m)$ ($\mathbf{f}, \mathbf{g}$ *different*),

(iii) $x \neq t$ (for $x$ a proper subterm of $t$).

Axioms of type (iii) are called *occur check axioms*. To see these axioms spelled out for the simplest non-trivial language $\{\mathbf{o}, \mathbf{s}\}$, see Exercise 3.7(i)–(iii). An application of the first two axioms (a program defining non-equality on $HU$) is contained in Exercise 4.37.

The theory of SLD-resolution from Chapter 5 is based on the Herbrand algebra $HA$. As we shall see, the theory CET derives its importance from the fact that we can generalize SLD-resolution, replacing $HA$ by just *any* model of CET. I.e.: the free equality axioms exactly express the properties of $HA$ that make SLD-resolution possible.

Recall the notion of an algebra from Definition 3.19 and the discussion following it.

**Definition 6.1** A *CET-algebra* is an algebra that satisfies CET. ∎

Of course, the primary example of a CET-algebra is the standard Herbrand algebra $HA$. See the following examples. Next to the CET-axioms, $HA$ satisfies yet another sentence, the *Domain Closure Axiom* DCA (as in the CET-axioms, we conceive of a constant symbol as a 0-argument function symbol):

$$\forall x \bigvee \{\exists y_1 \ldots \exists y_n [x = \mathbf{f}(y_1, \ldots, y_n)] \mid \mathbf{f} \text{ an arbitrary function symbol }\}$$

that says every element is the value of a function.

From now on, let a CET-algebra $J$ be fixed.

**Lemma 6.2** *The function $t \mapsto t^J$, mapping a ground term $t \in HU$ to its value $t^J$ in $J$, is injective.*

**Proof.** By induction on $t$, we verify the following

*Claim.* If $t \in HU$, then $\forall s \in HU[t^J = s^J \Rightarrow t = s]$.

For $t$ a constant symbol, this immediately follows from the second CET-axiom. Next, suppose that $t = \mathbf{f}(t_1, \ldots, t_n)$. Assume that $t^J = s^J$. Again by the second axiom, $s$ cannot be a constant symbol. Suppose that $s = \mathbf{g}(s_1, \ldots, s_m)$. Now by the second axiom $\mathbf{f} = \mathbf{g}$ and $n = m$; hence, by the first axiom, $t_1^J = s_1^J, \ldots, t_n^J = s_m^J$. Therefore, by induction hypothesis, $t_1 = s_1, \ldots, t_n = s_m$. (The argument does not involve the occur check axiom.) ∎

It follows that (up to isomorphism) $J$ extends $HA$; i.e., $HA$ is a submodel (Definition 3.42) of $J$. Compare Remark 3.21. Without loss of generality, we can thus make the following simplifying assumption comfortably.

**Assumption.** Every CET-algebra extends $HA$.

CET-algebras properly extending $HA$ are called *non-standard*. There are two ways of non-standardness, which may coexist. The simpler one looks as follows.

**Definition 6.3** Let $V$ be any set of variables. $HU(V)$ is the set of all terms $t$ with $Var(t) \subset V$. Just as is the case with $HU$, $HU(V)$ can be turned into an algebra $HA(V)$ (in fact, a *CET*-algebra) by interpreting constants and function symbols canonically. ∎

Note that $HA(\emptyset) = HA$. If $V$ is the set of all variables, then $HA(V) = TM$, the algebra of all terms. If $V \neq \emptyset$, then $HA(V)$ does not satisfy the domain-closure axiom DCA.

The more complicated form of non-standardness is the presence of elements with an infinite parsing tree. The simplest example of this is the following.

**Example 6.4** The language consists of one individual constant: $\mathbf{o}$, and one function symbol that is unary: $\mathbf{s}$. That is, $HU = \mathbb{N}$. We now describe the non-standard CET-algebra $\mathbb{N} + \mathbb{Z}$ relative to this language. The universe of this algebra is the union of the set of natural numbers and a copy $\{\ldots, -1', 0', 1', 2', \ldots\}$ of the set of integers $\mathbb{Z}$ disjoint from $\mathbb{N}$. $\mathbf{o}$ is interpreted as the natural number 0. $\mathbf{s}$ is interpreted as the ordinary successor operation $S$ on the natural numbers, as well as on the copy of the integers. Now every element of the $\mathbb{Z}$-copy of $\mathbb{N} + \mathbb{Z}$ has an infinite parsing tree. For instance, $0' = S(-1') = SS(-2') = SSS(-3') = \ldots$. ∎

If $t$ is a term and $\sigma$ is an assignment of elements of $J$ to the variables in $t$, then we have the notation $(t\sigma)^J$ for the *value* of the $J$-term $t\sigma$ in $J$, see Definitions 3.10(ii) and 3.8. In the sequel we drop the superscript $^J$ and use the notation $t\sigma$ for $(t\sigma)^J$ if $J$ is clear from the context. Of course, by Definition 3.10(ii), the notation $t\sigma$ previously stood for the $J$-term obtained from $t$ by replacing its variables by their $\sigma$-image. Thus from now on, to avoid possible confusion, (complex) $J$-terms can not be discussed any longer.

The notation $t\sigma$, with $\sigma$ now a substitution, is subsumed by the one in which $\sigma$ is an assignment; letting $J := TM$ be the algebra of all terms, the two notions collapse into one.

By our basic assumption, $HU \subset J$. Extend the language of $J$ by adding every element of $J - HU$ as a new constant symbol.

**Definition 6.5**

(i) An atom $\mathbf{r}(a_1, \ldots, a_n)$ with $a_1, \ldots, a_n \in J$ is called $J$-*ground*. Variable-free expressions which contain only terms from $J$ are called $J$-ground as well.

(ii) Let $A := \mathbf{r}(t_1, \ldots, t_n)$ be an atomic formula. A $J$-*instance* of the atom $A$ is a $J$-ground instance $A\sigma = \mathbf{r}(t_1\sigma, \ldots, t_n\sigma)$ of $A$ where $\sigma$ is a $J$-assignment for the variables in $A$.

(iii) If $\varphi$ is a quantifier-free formula and $\sigma$ a $J$-assignment for its variables, then $\varphi\sigma$ is obtained from $\varphi$ by replacing every atomic subformula $A$ by $A\sigma$. If $C = (A_1, \ldots, A_k)$ is a query, then $C\sigma = (A_1\sigma, \ldots, A_k\sigma)$.

(iv) The *Herbrand base over $J$* (relative to a set of relation symbols), notation: $HB^J$, is the set of all $J$-ground atoms. ∎

Note that $HB^J$ extends the ordinary Herbrand base $HB$.

**Definition 6.6** Let $J$ be an algebra the (algebraic) language of which is $L$. Suppose that $L' \supset L$ is obtained by adding a finite number of relation symbols to $L$. The $L'$-model **M** is a model *over* $J$ if it has the same universe and interprets symbols from $L$ in the same way. ∎

Thus, a model *over* $J$ simply is obtained by adding to $J$ some relations over its universe. Adding structure to a model without changing its universe or previously existing structure is called *expanding* it; the new model obtained is an *expansion* of the old one, while the old one is a *reduct* of its expansion.

Recall that a model over $HA$ — a Herbrand model — is identified with the set of atomic sentences in $HB$ true in it. Similarly, a model over the CET-algebra $J$ can be identified with the set of $J$-ground atoms from $HB^J$ true in it.

We can now generalize the definition of the immediate consequence operator relative to a program to this extended context.

**Definition 6.7** Let $P$ be a program. $T_P^J$ is the operator mapping subsets of $HB^J$ to subsets of $HB^J$ that is defined by:

- $T_P^J(X) := \{A \in HB^J \mid$ for some $C \subset X$, $A \leftarrow C$ is $J$-instance of a $P$-rule $\}$. ∎

Note that $T_P^J$ still is a finitary (Definition 4.23), monotone operator. Therefore (cf. Chapter 4), it has a least fixed point $T_P^J \uparrow$ and a greatest fixed point $T_P^J \downarrow$, which both are models of $P$; there are upward and downward hierarchies with their stages $T_P^J \uparrow \xi$ and $T_P^J \downarrow \xi$ of which these are the limits, and the upward hierarchy stabilizes after $\omega$ steps: $T_P^J \uparrow = T_P^J \uparrow \omega$.

## Exercises

A function $h : I \rightarrow J$ from the algebra $I$ into the algebra $J$ is a *homomorphism* if

(i) $h(\mathbf{c}^I) = \mathbf{c}^J$ for every constant symbol **c** ($\mathbf{c}^I$ and $\mathbf{c}^J$ the interpretations of **c** in $I$ resp. $J$)

(ii) $h(\mathbf{f}^I(a_1, \ldots, a_n)) = \mathbf{f}^J(h(a_1), \ldots, h(a_n))$ for every function symbol **f** and elements $a_1, \ldots, a_n \in I$ ($\mathbf{f}^I$ and $\mathbf{f}^J$ interpreting **f** in $I$ resp. $J$).

**6.1** Show:

(i) $\mathbb{N} + \mathbb{Z}$ is a CET-algebra,

(ii) $\mathbb{N} + \mathbb{Z}$ is a model of DCA,

(iii) every CET-algebra for the language $\{\mathbf{o}, \mathbf{s}\}$ can be homomorphically mapped into $\mathbb{N} + \mathbb{Z}$.

**6.2** Consider the algebra $J = \mathbb{N} + \mathbb{Z}$. Let $P$ consist of the two rules $\mathbf{N}(\mathbf{o}) \leftarrow$ and $\mathbf{N}(\mathbf{s}x) \leftarrow \mathbf{N}(x)$. Determine $T_P^J \uparrow$ and $T_P^J \downarrow$.

Add the rule $\mathbf{q}(\mathbf{o}) \leftarrow \mathbf{N}(x)$. Determine the resulting fixed points and their approximations.

Determine least and greatest fixed points for some other programs relevant to this algebra.

**6.3** Again, consider the case of one individual constant and one unary function symbol. Show that there are only countably many non-isomorphic CET-algebras corresponding to this language.

What about the case that has one constant and *two* unary function symbols? And what if there is a binary function symbol?

Exercise 4.5 contains the simplest of examples, showing that a (necessarily non-ground) atom true in $M_P$ does not need to follow from $P$. The following exercise shows that extending the Herbrand universe may remedy this defect. A ground version of (part of) it occurs in Exercise 4.10.

**6.4** Let $V$ be the set of all variables and put $J := HA(V)$ (Definition 6.3). Show that for every program $P$ and atom $A$ (which may contain variables) the following are equivalent:

(i) $P \models A$,

(ii) $T_P^J \uparrow \models A$,

(iii) $A$ has an implication tree (see Definition 4.9).

*Hint.* Warning for the different roles variables play in this context.

The next exercise (together with the previous one) provides an alternative proof for Corollary 5.47.

**6.5** Suppose $T_i$ is an implication tree for $A_i\sigma$ $(i = 1, \ldots, m)$, where $C = (A_1, \ldots, A_m)$ is a query ($C\sigma$ is allowed to contain variables). Let $n$ be the total number of nodes in $T_1, \ldots, T_m$. Let $\rho$ be any selection rule. Show that a successful $\rho$-derivation for $C$ exists of length $n$, which has a computed answer substitution $\theta$ such that for some $\gamma$, $C\sigma = C\theta\gamma$.

*Hint.* Show by induction on $k \leq n$ that a derivation $C_0 = C \xrightarrow{\theta_1} \cdots \xrightarrow{\theta_k} C_k$, a substitution $\sigma^k$ and implication trees for the atoms in $C_k\sigma^k$ exist such that the total number of nodes in these trees is $n - k$ and $C\sigma = C\theta_1 \cdots \theta_k \sigma^k$.

## 6.3 Resolution over Non-standard Algebras

Let a program $P$ and a CET-algebra $J$ be fixed. We are going to relativize the notions of resolvent and derivation to $J$. Next, we shall consider the lifting of such derivations.

**Definition 6.8**

(i) The $J$-ground query $D$ is called a $J$-*ground resolvent* of the $J$-ground query $C$ with respect to the atom $A$ of $C$ and the rule $R$, if for some $M$, $A \leftarrow M$ is a $J$-ground instance of $R$, and $D = C\{A/M\}$ is obtained from $C$ replacing $A$ by $M$.

(ii) A $J$-*ground derivation* with respect to the program $P$ is a sequence of successive $J$-ground resolvents with respect to the rules of $P$.  ∎

We employ the, by now familiar, arrow notation for $J$-ground resolvents and derivations. If from the context it is clear that by $C \xrightarrow{\ \epsilon\ }_u D$ a $J$-ground unrestricted resolution step is meant, we omit $\epsilon$ and the subscript '$u$' and just write $C \longrightarrow D$.

The $J$-assignment $\sigma$ is said to *unify* the expressions (terms or atoms) $s$ and $t$ *over* $J$ if $s\sigma = t\sigma$. Note that unification *tout court* is nothing but unification over the term algebra $TM$.

Recall Lemma 3.69, according to which every two terms that unify over some CET-algebra $J$ unify (over $TM$). (In fact, if $\sigma : Var(s,t) \rightarrow J$ unifies the terms $s$ and $t$, then an idempotent mgu $\theta$ of $s$ and $t$ exists such that $\sigma = \theta\sigma$ on $Var(s,t)$.) This observation allows us to extend the resolution-machinery, that is, ordinary resolution ("over $TM$"), to resolution over an arbitrary CET-algebra. As a result of this, $J$-ground resolution steps can be lifted.

**Lemma 6.9 (One Step Ground Lifting)** *Suppose that $C\sigma$ is a $J$-ground instance of the query $C$. Let $D$ be a $J$-ground resolvent of $C\sigma$ with respect to the atom $A\sigma$ and the rule $R$. Then:*

(i) *$C$ has a resolvent $\xrightarrow{\ \theta\ } D^+$ with respect to $A$ and $R$; and*

(ii) *for every resolvent $\xrightarrow{\ \theta\ } D^+$ of $C$ with respect to $A$ and $R$ there is a $J$-assignment $\tau$ for which*

    (a) *$\sigma = \theta\tau$ on variables from $Var(C)$ (commutation),*

    (b) *$D = D^+\tau$ (instantiation).*

**Proof.** (i) Suppose that $C = (A, K)$; $R = B \leftarrow M$ and $A\sigma = B\sigma'$, $\sigma'$ is a $J$-assignment for the variables in $R$. Let $\xi$ be a renaming for $B$ such that $Var(A) \cap Var(B\xi) = \emptyset$. Let $\delta$ undo this, i.e., let $B\xi\delta = B$. Now, $A\sigma = B\sigma' = B\xi\delta\sigma'$, and it follows that $A$ and $B\xi$ unify over $J$ by the assignment $\gamma$ for which $\gamma|Var(A) = \delta|Var(A)$ and $\gamma|Var(B\xi) = (\delta\sigma')|Var(B\xi)$. By Lemma 3.69, $A$ and $B\xi$ unify (over $TM$). For the rest of the proof, see the proof of Lemma 5.21.

(ii) The proof of (i) produces a resolvent $\xrightarrow{\ \theta'\ } D'$ of $C$ and a $J$-assignment $\tau'$ such that $\sigma = \theta'\tau'$ on $Var(C)$ and $D = D'\tau'$. However, the two resultants $D'\rightarrow C\theta'$ and $D^+\rightarrow C\theta$

are variants of each other; in particular, $\alpha$ exists such that $(D^+{\rightarrow}C\theta)\alpha = D'{\rightarrow}C\theta'$. Now, define $\tau := \alpha\tau'$.                                                                 ∎

There are two ways of looking at lifting $J$-ground derivations: one syntactical and one more model-theoretic. It is useful to have them both. The model-theoretic approach uses the notion of *realization*.

**Definition 6.10** Suppose that $\Delta : C_0 \xrightarrow{\alpha_1} C_1 \xrightarrow{\alpha_2} C_2 \cdots$ is a derivation. Recall Notation 5.36 according to which $\alpha_{i,j} = \alpha_{i+1} \cdots \alpha_j$ $(i < j)$. The sequence of $J$-assignments $\boldsymbol{\sigma}$: $\sigma^0$, $\sigma^1$, $\sigma^2$, ... (of the same length as $\Delta$) *realizes* $\Delta$ in $J$ if for all relevant $i < j$ we have that $\sigma^i | Var(C_i) = (\alpha_{i,j}\sigma^j) | Var(C_i)$.                                                                 ∎

Thus, realization of $\Delta$ by $\boldsymbol{\sigma}$ just means that a suitable commutation property is satisfied.

**Example.** Language: $\{\mathbf{o}, \mathbf{s}, \mathbf{r}\}$. Consider the rule $\mathbf{r}(\mathbf{s}x) \leftarrow \mathbf{r}(x)$. If $\boldsymbol{\sigma}$: $\sigma^0$, $\sigma^1$, $\sigma^2$, ... realizes the infinite derivation $\mathbf{r}(x) \xrightarrow{\{x/\mathbf{S}x\}} \mathbf{r}(x) \xrightarrow{\{x/\mathbf{S}x\}} \mathbf{r}(x) \cdots$ in $J$, then we must have $\sigma^0(x) = S\sigma^1(x) = SS\sigma^2(x) = \ldots = SSS\ldots$ in $J$ ($S = \mathbf{s}^J$); in particular, $J$ must (up to isomorphism) contain $\mathbb{N} + \mathbb{Z}$.                                                                 ∎

Note that the notion of lift makes sense for $J$-ground derivations. The following theorem collects all we need about lifting such derivations and realizability. In particular, parts (ii) and (iii) show the close relationship between $J$-realizability and lifting a $J$-ground derivation.

### Lemma 6.11 (Lifting Ground Derivations)

(i) Let $\sigma$ be a $J$-assignment for the variables of the query $C$. Every (finite or infinite) $J$-ground derivation starting from $C\sigma$ has a lift starting from $C$.

(ii) If the derivation $\Delta$ : $C_0 \xrightarrow{\theta_1} C_1 \cdots$ lifts the $J$-ground derivation $\Gamma$ : $D_0 = C_0\sigma \longrightarrow D_1 \longrightarrow D_2 \cdots$, then a sequence $\boldsymbol{\sigma}$: $\sigma^0 = \sigma$, $\sigma^1$, $\sigma^2$, ... of $J$-ground substitutions exists such that

- $\boldsymbol{\sigma}$ realizes $\Delta$ in $J$ (commutation)

- for all (relevant) $i$: $D_i = C_i\sigma^i$ (instantiation).

(iii) If the sequence of $J$-assignments $\boldsymbol{\sigma}$: $\sigma^0$, $\sigma^1$, $\sigma^2$, ... realizes the derivation $\Delta$ : $C_0 \xrightarrow{\theta_1} C_1 \cdots$, then $\Delta\boldsymbol{\sigma}$: $C_0\sigma^0 \longrightarrow C_1\sigma^1 \longrightarrow C_2\sigma^2 \cdots$ is a $J$-ground derivation of which $\Delta$ is a lift.

(iv) Every finite derivation lifts a $HU$-ground derivation.

(v) Every infinite derivation is realized in some $CET$-algebra.

**Proof.** (iii). By inspection.

(i)/(ii). These are the $J$-modifications of the Lifting Theorem. Compare the one-step case Lemma 6.9.

(iv). Let $\Delta : C_0 \xrightarrow{\theta_1} \cdots \xrightarrow{\theta_n} C_n$ be a finite derivation. Choose an arbitrary substitution $\sigma^n$ ground for all variables in $Var(C_n)$ and all variables released somewhere along $\Delta$. Define, for $j < n$, the substitution $\sigma^j$ by $\sigma^j := \theta_{j,n}\sigma^n$. Clearly then, for $i < j < n$: $\sigma^i = \theta_{i,n}\sigma^n = \theta_{i,j}\theta_{j,n}\sigma^n = \theta_{i,j}\sigma^j$. I.e., the sequence $\sigma^0, \ldots, \sigma^n$ realizes $\Delta$ in HU. The ground derivation lifted is $C_0\sigma^0 \longrightarrow \cdots \longrightarrow C_n\sigma^n$.

(v). Let $\Delta : C_0 \xrightarrow{\theta_1} C_1 \cdots$ be an infinite derivation. Assume that $Var(C_0) = \{x_1, \ldots, x_k\}$. Choose new constant symbols $\mathbf{c}_1, \ldots, \mathbf{c}_k$. For every $n \in \mathbb{N}$, we can construct a sentence $\varphi_n$ (involving the new constant symbols but no relation symbol) that is true in the expansion $(J, a_1, \ldots, a_k)$ of an algebra $J$ ($a_i$ interpreting $\mathbf{c}_i$ for $i = 1, \ldots k$) iff the initial $\Delta_{0,n}$ of $\Delta$ is realized in $J$ by a sequence of assignments starting with $\{x_1/a_1, \ldots, x_k/a_k\}$. By (iv), for every $n$ there is an expansion of $HU$ satisfying ($\varphi_1, \ldots, \varphi_{n-1}$ and) $\varphi_n$. By the Compactness Theorem 3.41, we can satisfy all of $\{\varphi_1, \varphi_2, \varphi_3, \ldots\}$ in a model of the CET-axioms. ∎

There is an algebraic construction (a *direct limit* of algebras $HA(V_i)$ *induced by* the specializations of the given derivation) for an algebra $I$ satisfying Lemma 6.11(v), avoiding first-order compactness. See Exercise 6.6.

**Exercise**

**6.6** Let $\Delta : C_0 \xrightarrow{\theta_1} C_1 \cdots$ be an infinite derivation.
Make disjunct copies $TERM_i$ of the sets $TERM(V_i)$ ($i \in \mathbb{N}$, $TERM(V_i) = \{t \mid Var(t) \subset V_i\}$, $V_i$ being the set of variables occurring up to the $i$-th stage of the derivation) by defining $TERM_i := \{(t, i) \mid t \in TERM(V_i)\}$. $Tm$ is the union of all those copies. Define the relation $\sim$ on $Tm$ by

$$(t, i) \sim (s, j) :\equiv \exists k \geq i, j : t\theta_{i,k} = s\theta_{j,k}.$$

Check that this is an equivalence. $Tm/\sim$ is the quotient of $Tm$ modulo $\sim$ consisting of all equivalence classes $|(t, i)| := \{(s, j) \mid (s, j) \sim (t, i)\}$.
$Tm/\sim$ is turned into an algebra $J$ by defining interpretations for constant and function symbols as follows:

- $\mathbf{c}^J := |(\mathbf{c}, 0)|$,
- $\mathbf{f}^J(|(t_1, i_1)|, \ldots, |(t_n, i_n)|) := |(\mathbf{f}(t_1\theta_{i_1,k}, \ldots, t_n\theta_{i_n,k}), k)|$,
  where $k := max\{i_1, \ldots, i_n\}$.

(i) Show that this definition does not depend on the representatives chosen.

(ii) Show that $\mathbf{f}^J(|(t_1, i)|, \ldots, |(t_n, i)|) = |(\mathbf{f}(t_1, \ldots, t_n), i)|$.

(iii) Show that $J$ is a CET-algebra.

(iv) Define $\sigma^i : V_i \rightarrow J$ by: $\sigma^i(x) := |(x, i)|$.

    (a) Show that for every term $t \in TERM(V_i)$: $t\sigma^i = |(t, i)|$.
       *Hint.* Induction with respect to $t$.

    (b) Show that the sequence $\sigma^0, \sigma^1, \sigma^2, \ldots$ realizes $\Delta$ in $J$.

## 6.4   Realization Trees

Let a program $P$ be fixed. Suppose that $T$ is the SLD-tree of all $P$-derivations from a query $C$ relative to some selection rule. Let $\sigma$ be a $J$-assignment for the variables of $C$.

**Definition 6.12** $GRD(T, J, \sigma)$, the *realization tree* over $J$ relative to $T$ and $\sigma$, is the tree the paths through which are all sequences $\boldsymbol{\sigma}$: $\sigma^0 = \sigma, \sigma^1, \sigma^2, \ldots$ of $J$-assignments starting with $\sigma$ and realizing a derivation from $T$.      ■

Note that, by Lemma 6.11(ii/iii), we can define $GRD(T, J, \sigma)$ equivalently as the tree of $J$-ground derivations $\Gamma : C\sigma \longrightarrow \cdots$ that possess a lift in $T$. In the sequel, we shall take the viewpoint that is best suited for the situation at hand.

    If $T$ is infinite, then, by König's lemma, it must have a branch. Nevertheless, $J$ need not realize any of the branches through $T$, and hence, $GRD(T, J, \sigma)$ need not have branches; i.e.: $GRD(T, J, \sigma)$ may very well be well-founded.

    The theorems following give a complete picture of the situation. Let us give an example first.

**Example.** $HU = \mathbb{N}$. $P$ has two rules: $\mathbf{r}(\mathbf{s}x) \leftarrow \mathbf{r}(x)$ and $\mathbf{q}(\mathbf{o}) \leftarrow \mathbf{r}(x)$. The initial query is $\mathbf{q}(\mathbf{o})$. There is no selection-rule problem for this situation: $T$ has one branch

$$\mathbf{q}(\mathbf{o}) \xrightarrow{\epsilon} \mathbf{r}(x) \xrightarrow{\{x/\mathbf{s}x\}} \mathbf{r}(x) \xrightarrow{\{x/\mathbf{s}x\}} \mathbf{r}(x) \longrightarrow \cdots$$

(i) $GRD(T, \mathbb{N}, \epsilon)$ has branches of every finite length, corresponding to the ground resolvents $\mathbf{r}(0)$, $\mathbf{r}(1)$, $\mathbf{r}(2), \ldots$ of $\mathbf{q}(0)$. E.g., $\mathbf{q}(0) \longrightarrow \mathbf{r}(1) \longrightarrow \mathbf{r}(0)$ is the $\mathbb{N}$-ground derivation of length 2. However, there is *no* infinite branch; the realization tree is well-founded.

(ii) On the other hand, $GRD(T, \mathbb{N} + \mathbb{Z}, \epsilon)$ *does* have infinite branches as well; just lift the infinite $\mathbb{N} + \mathbb{Z}$-ground derivation

$$\mathbf{q}(0) \longrightarrow \mathbf{r}(0') \longrightarrow \mathbf{r}(-1') \longrightarrow \mathbf{r}(-2') \cdots$$

Therefore, it is non-well-founded.  ∎

The following is a symmetric form of soundness and completeness for this extended context.

**Theorem 6.13 (Success)**
*Let $T$ be an SLD-tree for the query $C_0$ and let $\sigma : Var(C_0) \to J$ be an assignment. The following are equivalent:*

*(i) $C_0\sigma \subset T_P^J \uparrow$ ;*
*(ii) $GRD(T, J, \sigma)$ contains a $J$-ground success.*

**Proof.** For the implication (i) $\Rightarrow$ (ii), see Exercise 6.5.  ∎

The *height* of a well-founded tree is measured by an ordinal; see Definition 1.18. To have *infinite height* means to be either well-founded of height $\geq \omega$ or to be non-well-founded.

A (finite or infinite) derivation $\Delta : C_0 \xrightarrow{\theta_1} C_1 \xrightarrow{\theta_2} C_2 \longrightarrow \cdots$ is *fair* if, for every $i$ and every atom $A$ occurring in $C_i$, there exists $j \geq i$ such that $A\theta_{i+1} \cdots \theta_j$ is the selected atom of $C_j$. Thus, every success is fair, but a finite failing derivation isn't. A selection rule is *fair* (Definition 5.43) if every infinite derivation produced by it is fair. An SLD-tree is *fair* if it is produced using a fair selection rule.

The following theorems constitute symmetric results on failing queries.

**Theorem 6.14 (Finite Failure)**
*Let $T$ be an SLD-tree for the query $C_0$ and $\sigma : Var(C_0) \to J$.*

*(i) Suppose that $C_0\sigma \not\subset T_P^J \uparrow$. If $C_0\sigma \subset T_P^J \downarrow \omega$, then $GRD(T, J, \sigma)$ has infinite height.*
*(ii) Suppose that $T$ is fair. Then, conversely:*
    *if $GRD(T, J, \sigma)$ has infinite height, then $C_0\sigma \subset T_P^J \downarrow \omega$.*

**Theorem 6.15 (Infinite Failure)**
*Let $T$ be an SLD-tree for the query $C_0$ and $\sigma : Var(C_0) \to J$.*

*(i) Suppose that $C_0\sigma \not\subset T_P^J \uparrow$. If $C_0\sigma \subset T_P^J \downarrow$, then $GRD(T, J, \sigma)$ is not well-founded.*
*(ii) Suppose that $T$ is fair. Then, conversely:*
    *if $GRD(T, J, \sigma)$ is not well-founded, then $C_0\sigma \subset T_P^J \downarrow$.*

The proofs of these results are similar. However, we begin with the last one since it is slightly easier.

**Proof** of 6.15.
(i) Assume that $D_0 := C_0\sigma \subset T_P^J \downarrow$. We have to produce an infinite branch through $GRD(T, \sigma)$.

We employ the definition of $GRD(\mathcal{T}, J, \sigma)$ in terms of $J$-ground-derivations. Simultaneously, produce an infinite derivation

$$\Delta: C_0 \xrightarrow{\theta_1} C_1 \xrightarrow{\theta_2} C_2 \xrightarrow{\theta_3} \cdots$$

through $\mathcal{T}$ and a $J$-ground derivation

$$\Gamma: D_0 \longrightarrow D_1 \longrightarrow D_2 \longrightarrow \cdots$$

of which $\Delta$ is a lift, such that, for all $i$, we have $D_i \subset T_P^J \downarrow$ and $D_i \not\subset T_P^J \uparrow$.

To start with, we have $D_0 = C_0\sigma \subset T_P^J \downarrow$ and $D_0 \not\subset T_P^J \uparrow$ by hypothesis.

Suppose now that $\Gamma_{0,i}: D_0 \longrightarrow \cdots \longrightarrow D_i$ and its lift $\Delta_{0,i}: C_0 \xrightarrow{\theta_1} \cdots \xrightarrow{\theta_i} C_i$ have been constructed up to and including stage $i$ such that $D_i \subset T_P^J \downarrow$ and $D_i \not\subset T_P^J \uparrow$.

Note that $C_i$ cannot be empty, otherwise, $D_i$ would be empty as well and we would have that $D_i \subset T_P^J \uparrow$.

$\mathcal{T}$ selects an atom in $C_i$. Let $A$ be the atom of $D_i$ corresponding to it. Since $A \in D_i \subset T_P^J \downarrow = T_P^J(T_P^J \downarrow)$, $D_i$ has a $J$-ground resolvent $D_{i+1}$ with respect to $A$ such that $D_{i+1} \subset T_P^J \downarrow$. And if $A \leftarrow L$ is the rule-instance employed and $A \notin T_P^J \uparrow$, then $L \not\subset T_P^J \uparrow$. So, $D_{i+1} \not\subset T_P^J \uparrow$. By Lemma 6.9, this $J$-ground resolution transition can be lifted to a resolvent $\xrightarrow{\theta_{i+1}} C_{i+1}$ of $C_i$ in $\mathcal{T}$.

(ii) Now we employ the definition of the realization tree in terms of realizing sequences. Suppose that

$$\Delta: C_0 \xrightarrow{\theta_1} C_1 \xrightarrow{\theta_2} C_2 \xrightarrow{\theta_3} \cdots$$

is an infinite derivation through $\mathcal{T}$, realized in $J$ by the sequence $\sigma$: $\sigma^0 = \sigma$, $\sigma^1$, $\sigma^2$, ....

Define the model $X$ over $J$ by: $X := \{A\sigma^i | A \in C_i\}$. It suffices to prove the

*Claim.* $X \subset T_P^J(X)$.

For then, since $T_P^J \downarrow$ is the greatest post-fixed point, we have that $X \subset T_P^J \downarrow$, and the required result follows.

To prove the claim, suppose that $A\sigma^i \in X$, i.e., $A \in C_i$. We have to show that $A\sigma^i \in T_P^J(X)$. Since $\mathcal{T}$ is fair, at some stage $C_j$ ( $j \geq i$) the descendant of $A$ at that stage, which is $A\theta_{i,j}$, must be selected. Then for some instance $B \leftarrow K$ of a $P$-rule, $A\theta_{i,j+1} = A\theta_{i,j}\theta_{j+1} = B$ and $K$ is part of $C_{j+1}$. By definition of $X$ we have $K\sigma^{j+1} \subset X$. Therefore, $B\sigma^{j+1} \in T_P^J(X)$. However, $A\sigma^i = A\theta_{i,j+1}\sigma^{j+1} = B\sigma^{j+1}$. ∎

**Proof** of Theorem 6.14.

(i) Assume that not $C_0\sigma \subset T_P^J \uparrow$ and $D_0 := C_0\sigma \subset T_P^J \downarrow \omega$. Fix a natural number $n$. We show that $GRD(\mathcal{T}, J, \sigma)$ has a path of length at least $n$.

Simultaneously, produce a derivation

$$\Delta: C_0 \xrightarrow{\theta_1} \cdots \xrightarrow{\theta_n} C_n$$

through $\mathcal{T}$ and a $J$-ground derivation $\Gamma: D_0 \longrightarrow \cdots \longrightarrow D_n$ of which $\Delta$ is a lift such that for all $j \le n$, the condition

$$[\,j\,]: \qquad\qquad D_j \subset T_P \downarrow (n-j)$$

is satisfied.

By assumption, $D_0 = C_0\sigma \subset T_P \downarrow \omega \subset T_P \downarrow n$; which means that we do satisfy the initial requirement $[\,0\,]$.

Suppose that $\Delta$ and $\Gamma$ have been constructed up to and including stage $i < n$, satisfying $[\,j\,]$ for every $j \le i$. If $C_i$ is empty, then $D_i$ is empty as well and we have a $J$-ground refutation of $\leftarrow C_0\sigma$. That would entail $C_0\sigma \subset T_P^J\uparrow$, contrary to hypothesis. Therefore, $C_i$ is non-empty. $\mathcal{T}$ selects some atom in $C_i$. Let $A$ be the atom in $D_i$ that corresponds to it. Since by $[\,i\,]$ we have $A \in D_i \subset T_P^J\downarrow(n-i)$ and $n-i > 0$, $D_i$ has a $J$-ground resolvent $D_{i+1}$ with respect to $A$ such that $D_{i+1} \subset T_P^J\downarrow(n-i-1)$. By Lemma 6.9, $C_i$ has a resolvent $\xrightarrow{\theta_{i+1}} C_{i+1}$ in $\mathcal{T}$ lifting this $J$-ground step, as required.

(ii) Let $\mathcal{T}'$ be the subtree of $\mathcal{T}$ consisting of all derivations $\Delta$ that possess a realization in $GRD(\mathcal{T}, J, \sigma)$. By assumption, $\mathcal{T}'$ has infinite height. Since $\mathcal{T}'$ is finitely splitting, by König's lemma it must have an infinite branch $\Delta: C_0 \xrightarrow{\theta_1} C_1 \ldots$.

Fix $n$. We show that $C_0\sigma \subset T_P^J\downarrow n$.

By fairness, choose indices $m_0 = 0 < m_1 < \ldots < m_n$ (in *that* order) such that (a descendant of) every atom in $C_{m_i}$ has been selected in $\Delta$ before stage $m_{i+1}$ $(i < n)$. Choose $\boldsymbol{\sigma}: \sigma^0 = \sigma, \ldots, \sigma^{m_n}$ realizing $\theta_1, \ldots, \theta_{m_n}$.

*Claim.* If $i \le n$ and $j \le m_i$, then $C_j\sigma^j \subset T_P^J\downarrow(n-i)$.

Induction with respect to $n - i$.

For $n - i = 0$, this is trivial.

For the induction step, assume that $j \le m_i$ and $A \in C_j$. We have to show that $A\sigma^j \in T_P^J\downarrow(n-i)$. By fairness, assume that $A\theta_{j,k}$ is selected in $C_k$. By construction, $k < m_{i+1}$. There is an instance $A\theta_{j,k+1} \leftarrow L$ of a rule such that $L$ is part of $C_{k+1}$. Since $k+1 \le m_{i+1}$, we can apply the inductive hypothesis, obtaining $L\sigma^{k+1} \subset T_P^J\downarrow(n-i-1)$. But then, $A\sigma^j = A\theta_{j,k+1}\sigma^{k+1} \in T_P^J\downarrow(n-i)$.    ∎

## Exercises

**6.7** Let $J$ be a CET-algebra. A model $\mathbf{M} \subset HB^J$ over $J$ is called *good* if for every query $C$ the following holds: if $C\sigma \subset \mathbf{M}$ for some $J$-assignment $\sigma$, then for some substitution $\theta$ we have $C\theta \subset \mathbf{M}$. Prove the following.

(i) If $\mathbf{M}$ is good, then $T_P^J(\mathbf{M})$ is good.

(ii) If $\mathbf{M}$ is good, then $HB \cap T_P^J(\mathbf{M}) = T_P(HB \cap \mathbf{M})$.

(iii) For all $n$, $T_P^J \uparrow n$ and $T_P^J \downarrow n$ are good.

(iv) For all $n$, $HB \cap T_P^J \uparrow n = T_P \uparrow n$ and $HB \cap T_P^J \downarrow n = T_P \downarrow n$.

(v) $HB \cap T_P^J \uparrow \omega = T_P \uparrow \omega$ and $HB \cap T_P^J \downarrow \omega = T_P \downarrow \omega$.

*Hint.* Here is a proof for part (i). Assume that the model $\mathbf{M}$ over the algebra $J$ is good, and that for $C = (A_0, \ldots, A_{k-1})$ and $\sigma : Var(C) \to J$ we have $C\sigma \subset T_P^J(\mathbf{M})$. By extending $\sigma$, we may assume that, for $i < k$, $B_i \leftarrow L_i$ is a rule of the underlying program $P$ such that $A_i\sigma = B_i\sigma$ and $L_i\sigma \subset \mathbf{M}$. By Lemma 3.69, for some substitution $\theta$ we have, for $i < k$, $A_i\theta = B_i\theta$ and $\sigma = \theta\sigma$ on all variables under consideration. Hence, $L_i\theta\sigma = L_i\sigma \subset \mathbf{M}$. Since $\mathbf{M}$ is good, a ground substitution $\gamma$ exists such that, for $i < k$, we have that $L_i\theta\gamma \subset \mathbf{M}$. Therefore, $A_i\theta\gamma = B_i\theta\gamma \in T_P^J(\mathbf{M})$.

**\*6.8** Assume that $P$ is a program and $A \in HB - T_P \downarrow$. Relate the height of the realization tree corresponding to a (fair) SLD-tree for the query $A$ to the least ordinal $\alpha$ for which $A \notin T_P \downarrow \alpha$.

## 6.5   The Interplay of SLD-trees and Realization Trees

As in the previous section, we fix a program $P$ and a CET-algebra $J$.

The following is a compactness phenomenon for the present context.

**Lemma 6.16 (Adding a Branch)** *Let $\mathcal{T}$ be an SLD-tree for the query $C_0$ and suppose that $\sigma : Var(C_0) \to J$. If $GRD(\mathcal{T}, J, \sigma)$ has infinite height, then for some CET-algebra $I \supset J$, $GRD(\mathcal{T}, I, \sigma)$ is not well-founded.*

**Proof.** Assume that $GRD(\mathcal{T}, J, \sigma)$ has infinite height. Argue as in the proof of Theorem 6.14. Let $\mathcal{T}'$ be the subtree of $\mathcal{T}$ consisting of all derivations $\Delta$ that possess a realization in $J$ starting with $\sigma$. By assumption, $\mathcal{T}'$ has infinite height. Since it is finitely splitting, it has an infinite branch $\Delta: C_0 \xrightarrow{\theta_1} C_1 \cdots$. By definition of $\mathcal{T}'$, every initial sequence $\theta_1, \ldots, \theta_n$ of the sequence of specializations of $\Delta$ is realized in $J$ by a sequence of assignments starting with $\sigma$. By the Compactness Theorem 3.41, the infinite sequence $\theta_1, \theta_2, \theta_3, \ldots$ is realized in some elementary extension $I$ of $J$ (Definition 3.42) by a sequence starting with $\sigma$. But then, $GRD(\mathcal{T}, I, \sigma)$ is not well-founded. ∎

**Corollary 6.17 (Pushing Up a Goal)** *Let $C$ be a query and $\sigma$ a $J$-assignment for its variables. If $C\sigma \subset T_P^J \downarrow \omega$ then, for some CET-algebra $I \supset J$, $C\sigma \subset T_P^I \downarrow$.*

**Proof.** Assume that $C\sigma \subset T_P^J \downarrow \omega$. If $C\sigma \subset T_P^J \uparrow$, then we may take $I = J$. Therefore, assume that $C\sigma \not\subset T_P^J \uparrow$. Let $\mathcal{T}$ be a fair SLD-tree for $C$. By the Finite Failure Theorem

6.14(i), $GRD(\mathcal{T}, J, \sigma)$ has infinite height. By Lemma 6.16, for some $I \supset J$, $GRD(\mathcal{T}, I, \sigma)$ is not well-founded. By the Infinite Failure Theorem 6.15(ii), $C\sigma \subset T_P^I\downarrow$.                      ∎

For $X \subset HB^J$ a model over $J$, $X \models P$ amounts to $X$ being a pre-fixed point of $T_P^J$. (This is the $J$-relativized version of Lemma 4.16.) Similarly, we can characterize post-fixed points and fixed points using suitable sets of first-order sentences obtained from $P$.

**Lemma 6.18** *There is a first-order sentence $IFF(P)$ (not depending on $J$) such that, for $X \subset HB^J$: $X \models IFF(P)$ iff $T_P^J(X) = X$.*

**Proof.** A first-order sentence $IFF(P)$ satisfying the equivalence from the lemma may be explicitly constructed by the procedure from Definition 6.19.                      ∎

The following definition introduces the completion of a program.

**Definition 6.19** $IF(P)$ is the set of sentences obtained from the program $P$ by the following procedure consisting of steps 1–5. First, fix a sequence of new variables $x_1, x_2, x_3, \ldots$

*Step 1: Remove terms from rule heads.*
Replace every rule $\mathbf{r}(t_1, \ldots t_n) \leftarrow B_1, \ldots, B_m$ by $\mathbf{r}(x_1, \ldots, x_n) \leftarrow x_1 \approx t_1 \wedge \cdots \wedge x_n \approx t_n \wedge B_1 \wedge \cdots \wedge B_m$.

*Step 2: Introduce existential quantifiers.*
Transform each formula $\mathbf{r}(x_1, \ldots, x_n) \leftarrow F$ obtained in the previous step into

$$\mathbf{r}(x_1, \ldots x_n) \leftarrow \exists y_1 \cdots \exists y_k F,$$

where $y_1, \ldots, y_k$ are all variables of $Var(F) - \{x_1, \ldots, x_n\}$.

*Step 3: Group formulas with the same head.*
If $\mathbf{r}(\vec{x}) \leftarrow F_1; \ldots ; \mathbf{r}(\vec{x}) \leftarrow F_l$ are all formulas obtained with $\mathbf{r}$ in their head, replace them by $\mathbf{r}(\vec{x}) \leftarrow F_1 \vee \cdots \vee F_l$.

The formula $F_1 \vee \cdots \vee F_l$ is called the *defining formula* for $\mathbf{r}$.

*Step 4: Handle "undefined" relation symbols.*
For every $n$-ary relation symbol $\mathbf{r}$ that does not occur in a rule head, add the formula $\mathbf{r}(\vec{x}) \leftarrow \perp$. (Indeed, this is the special case of 3 where $l = 0$; of course, $\perp$ here is the defining formula for $\mathbf{r}$.)

*Step 5: Introduce universal quantifiers.*
Replace each formula obtained by its universal closure.

Replacing the left-pointed arrows by right-pointing implication-signs everywhere in $IF(P)$, we obtain the set $ONLY - IF(P)$.

Next, replacing them by equivalences, we obtain the set $IFF(P)$.

Finally, the *completion comp(P)* of $P$ is the set of first-order sentences consisting of (i) the sentences of $IFF(P)$ and (ii) all free equality axioms of CET.                                    ∎

Note that $IF(P)$ and $P$ are logically equivalent sets, since transformations 1–5 preserve logical equivalence.

The completion of a program will play an important role in Chapter 8. It could well be that, for "sensible" programs $P$, $comp(P)$ is what we have in mind when writing down the rules of $P$. Therefore, it is not unreasonable to use $comp(P)$ instead of $P$ when formulating soundness and completeness results.

Note that, by Lemma 6.18, a model $M$ satisfies $comp(P)$ iff for some CET-algebra $J$, $M$ is a model over $J$ that is a fixed point of $T_P^J$.

**Corollary 6.20** *Let $P$ be a program and $C$ a query. The following are equivalent.*

*(i) There is a finite failing SLD-tree for $C$,*
*(ii) every fair SLD-tree for $C$ fails finitely,*
*(iii) for every CET-algebra $I$: $T_P^I \downarrow \models \neg \exists \bigwedge C$,*
*(iv) $comp(P) \models \neg \exists \bigwedge C$.*

*Furthermore, these conditions imply*

*(v) $T_P \downarrow \omega \models \neg \exists \bigwedge C$;*

*and in the case that $C$ is HU-ground, (v) implies the other conditions.*

The rule $\mathbf{r}(\mathbf{s}x) \leftarrow \mathbf{r}(x)$ and the query $\mathbf{r}(x)$ illustrate that we can have $T_P \downarrow \omega \models \neg \exists \bigwedge C$ without there being a finite failing SLD-tree for $\mathbf{r}(x)$.

**Proof.**

(ii)⇒(i) Trivial.

(i)⇒(iii) Let $\mathcal{T}$ be a finite failing tree for $C$. Suppose that $I$ and $\sigma$ are such that $C\sigma \subset T_P^I \downarrow$. By the Success Theorem, $C\sigma \not\subset T_P^I \uparrow$. By the Infinite Failure Theorem part 1, $GRD(\mathcal{T}, I, \sigma)$ is not well-founded. But then $\mathcal{T}$ cannot be finite.

(iii)⇒(ii) Suppose that $\mathcal{T}$ is a fair tree for $C$. If $\mathcal{T}$ contains a success with computed answer $\theta$, then every HU-ground instance of $C\theta$ is satisfied in $T_P \uparrow \subset T_P \downarrow$, contradicting (iii). If $\mathcal{T}$ is infinite, it has an infinite branch by König's Lemma. By Lemma 6.11(v), this branch is realized in some algebra $I$. Since $\mathcal{T}$ is fair, by the Infinite Failure Theorem part 2, $C\sigma \subset T_P^I \downarrow$, where $\sigma$ is the first assignment of the realization, again contradicting (iii).

(iii)⇒(iv) Every model $M$ of $comp(P)$ over some algebra $I$ must be included in $T_P^I \downarrow$.

(iv)⇒(iii) This is immediate.

Corollary 6.17 shows (iii) to imply (v).

Finally, we show that (v) implies (ii) when $C$ is ground.

Let $\mathcal{T}$ be a fair SLD-tree for the ground query $C$ that is not finitely failing. Distinguish two cases. (a) $\mathcal{T}$ contains a success. Then $C \subset T_P \uparrow \subset T_P \downarrow \omega$. (b) $\mathcal{T}$ contains an infinite derivation. By Lemma 6.11(iv), $GRD(\mathcal{T}, HU, \epsilon)$ has infinite height. ($\epsilon$ is the empty assignment.) By the Finite Failure Theorem we have, once more, $C \subset T_P \downarrow \omega$. ∎

**Remark.** In Corollary 6.20, the implication (i) $\Rightarrow$ (iv)—if $C$ has a finitely failing tree, then $comp(P) \models \neg \exists \bigwedge C$— is known as *Soundness of Negation as Failure* (also, see Exercise 6.17); its converse is known as *Completeness of Negation as Failure*. This terminology refers to the viewpoint that a better declarative interpretation of programs is obtained by referring to the completion of a program and not to the program itself. In particular, negative queries often logically follow from completions, whereas they never follow from programs. However, see Exercise 6.10. The proper context for these notions is Chapter 8. There, the soundness-half will be generalized in Corollary 8.29. ∎

**Lemma 6.21** *If* $J \subset I$, *then* $T_P^J \downarrow \subset T_P^I \downarrow$.

**Proof.** It suffices to show that $T_P^J \downarrow \subset T_P^I(T_P^J \downarrow)$, since $T_P^I \downarrow$ is the largest post-fixed point of the operator $T_P^I$. Now if $X \subset HB^J$, then obviously $T_P^J(X) \subset T_P^I(X)$. Hence in particular $T_P^J \downarrow = T_P^J(T_P^J \downarrow) \subset T_P^I(T_P^J \downarrow)$. ∎

A more direct proof of the following theorem is given in Chapter 8 by Theorem 8.36.

**Theorem 6.22** *For every CET-algebra $J$ there exists a CET-algebra $I \supset J$ such that for every program $P$: $T_P^I \downarrow = T_P^I \downarrow \omega$.*

**Proof.** Construct a countable sequence of CET-algebras $J_0 = J \subset J_1 \subset J_2 \subset \ldots$ such that for all programs $P$, atoms $A$, and $\sigma : Var(A) \to J_n$, we have: if for some $I \supset J_n$ we have $A\sigma \in T_P^I \downarrow \omega$, then $A\sigma \in T_P^{J_{n+1}} \downarrow$.
$J_n$ constructed, $J_{n+1}$ is taken to be the union of a sequence of algebras of length $|J_n|$ produced by Lemma 6.16. By Lemma 6.21, once an instance $A\sigma$ has been maneuvered into a greatest fixed point, it remains there upon extending the algebra any further. Now, just let $I$ be the union of the $J_n$.
To see that $T_P^I \downarrow \omega \subset T_P^I \downarrow$, assume that $A\sigma \in T_P^I \downarrow \omega$. For some $n$, we have $\sigma : Var(A) \to J_n$. By construction, $A\sigma \in T_P^{J_{n+1}} \downarrow$. Therefore, $A\sigma \in T_P^I \downarrow$. ∎

### Exercises

**6.9** Let $P$ be a program and $C$ a clause. Show: if $comp(P) \models \exists \bigwedge C$, then $P \models \exists \bigwedge C$. Also, show: if $comp(P) \models \forall \bigwedge C$, then $P \models \forall \bigwedge C$.

**6.10** Consider the following rules.

$\mathbf{p(o)} \leftarrow$
$\mathbf{p}(x) \leftarrow \mathbf{p}(\mathbf{ss}x).$

Characterize the fixed points of the consequence operator associated with this program. Construct the completion of it. Show that neither $\mathbf{p}(\mathbf{so})$ nor $\neg\mathbf{p}(\mathbf{so})$ logically follows from the completion.

**6.11** Motivated by the previous exercise, let us call $comp(P)$ *weakly complete* if for every ground atom $A$, either $comp(P){\models}A$ or $comp(P){\models}\neg A$.
Show: if $T_P{\uparrow} = T_P{\downarrow}\omega$, then $comp(P)$ is weakly complete.
Prove, or give a counter-example to the implication: if $T_P{\uparrow} = T_P{\downarrow}$, then $comp(P)$ is weakly complete.

**6.12** $HU = \mathbb{N}$. $P$ consists of the following rules.

$\mathbf{r}(\mathbf{o}, \mathbf{sso}) \leftarrow$
$\mathbf{r}(\mathbf{s}x, \mathbf{s}y) \leftarrow \mathbf{r}(x,y)$
$\mathbf{r}(x, \mathbf{ss}y) \leftarrow \mathbf{r}(x,y).$

(i) Construct $comp(P)$.
(ii) Show that $comp(P) \models \neg\mathbf{r}(\mathbf{sso}, \mathbf{ssso})$.
(iii) The interpretation $r$ of $\mathbf{r}$ in the model $M_P$ is transitive. Show that the sentence $\forall x\forall y\forall z[\mathbf{r}(x,y) \wedge \mathbf{r}(y,z) \rightarrow \mathbf{r}(x,z)]$ that expresses transitivity does *not* logically follow from $comp(P)$. (Cf. Exercise 4.40.)

**Definition 6.23** Let $J$ be a CET-algebra for a language containing $\mathbf{o}$, $\mathbf{s}$ and $[\,.\,|\,.\,]$. Suppose that $f : \mathbb{N}{\rightarrow}HU$ (e.g., $f$ might be a number theoretic function). The element $a \in J$ *represents* $f$ if for some (by the CET-axioms, unique) sequence $a_0 = a, a_1, a_2, \ldots \in J$ we have, for all $i$: $a_i = [f(i)|a_{i+1}]$. ∎

If $a$ represents $f$, then, in some sense, we thus have: $a = [f(0), f(1), f(2), \ldots]$.

**6.13** Show that every number theoretic function is represented in some CET-algebra in the sense of Definition 6.23.

**6.14** Assume that the program $P$ defines the function $f : \mathbb{N}{\rightarrow}HU$ in the 2-ary relation symbol $\mathbf{f}$. Show that $P$ can be extended to a program (using a new unary relation symbol $\mathbf{q}$) that, confronted with the query $\mathbf{q}(z)$, produces an infinite derivation $\Delta$ with the property that, for every algebra $J$ and every sequence of assignments $\sigma^0, \ldots$ realizing the specializations of $\Delta$ in $J$, $z\sigma^0$ represents $f$ in $J$.
*Hint.* Consider the rules

$\mathbf{r}(x, [y|z]) \leftarrow \mathbf{f}(x,y), \mathbf{r}(\mathbf{s}x, z)$
$\mathbf{q}(z) \leftarrow \mathbf{r}(\mathbf{o}, z).$

**6.15** Concoct a notion of representation for number theoretic functions using only the constant $\Lambda$ and the two successor functions $\mathbf{s}_0$ and $\mathbf{s}_1$. Modify the previous exercises for this setting.

**6.16** Let $J := \mathbb{N} + \mathbb{Z}$. Show: for every program $P$, we have that $T_P^J \downarrow = T_P^J \downarrow \omega$.

**6.17** Give a direct, simple proof that $comp(P) \models \neg \exists \bigwedge C$ for every query $C$ with a finitely failing tree.

*Hint.* Use induction with respect to the height of a finitely failing tree. (This proof does not use at all the fact that the derivations of the tree satisfy [ † ].)

## 6.6 Notes

The closed world assumption was introduced by [Reiter 78]. In [Clark 78] it is argued that it is $comp(P)$, not the program $P$ itself, that provides the real meaning of $P$ and that, for "sensible" programs $P$, $comp(P)$ is what we have in mind when writing down the rules of $P$. If "sensible" here means that $T_P \uparrow = T_P \downarrow$, i.e.: $T_P$ has exactly one fixed point, this sounds reasonable. But if $T_P$ has several fixed points, then $comp(P)$ (which "axiomatizes" fixed points by Lemma 6.18) cannot fix the meaning of $P$. In particular, $comp(P)$ does not axiomatize $M_P$-truth. If we want to axiomatize the notion of least Herbrand model, there are rather obvious induction schemas to be added to $comp(P)$.

The material from this chapter is mainly from [Doets b].

Exercises 6.4 and 6.5, which together constitute a proof of strong SLD-completeness, are from [Stärk 89].

Exercise 6.7 is from [Apt 90].

Theorem 6.22 is due to [Blair/Brown 90], and so are the representability notion from Definition 6.23 and the result of Exercise 6.14.

# 7 Computability

## 7.1 Preliminaries

In this chapter it is shown, among other things, how to compute an arbitrary recursive function by means of a logic program. As a corollary, recursive complexity of least Herbrand models for logic programs is identified. Contrasting to this, it is shown that greatest fixed points $T_P \downarrow$ can be very complex.

For the basics of recursion theory, the reader is referred to the literature. The fundamental notions run as follows. In standard recursion theory, the basic domain of objects is $\mathbb{N}$, but we take a more general stand. In the following, $D$ is any domain of concrete objects. Usually, $D = HU$, with $D = \mathbb{N}$ as special case. Sometimes, $D = HB$.

In this chapter, it is always assumed that the language $\mathcal{L}$ is finite and that there is a function symbol present.

**Definition 7.1**

(i) An $n$-ary relation $R \subset D^n$ is *decidable* if there is a decision method for membership in $R$ that, when applied to an arbitrary $n$-tuple $\vec{s}$ from $D^n$, after a finite number of steps terminates with output 'yes' if $R(\vec{s})$ is true, and with 'no' if $R(\vec{s})$ is false.

(ii) An $n$-ary relation $R \subset D^n$ is *positively decidable* if there is a decision method for membership in $R$ that, when applied to an $n$-tuple $\vec{s}$ from $D^n$, after a finite number of steps terminates with output 'yes' iff $R(\vec{s})$ is true. (It may or may not terminate and output 'no' when $R(\vec{s})$ is false, but of course it will not output 'yes' in that case.)

(iii) An $n$-ary function $F : Dom(F) \to D$ such that $Dom(F) \subset D^n$ is called *calculable* or *computable* if there is an algorithm such that for every sequence $\vec{s} \in D^n$

    (a) the algorithm terminates on input $\vec{s}$ iff $\vec{s} \in Dom(F)$;

    (b) if $\vec{s} \in Dom(F)$ then, on input $\vec{s}$, the algorithm outputs the value $F(\vec{s})$.   ■

We sometimes also admit relations and functions of mixed types and extend the definitions to these contexts. E.g., we might have that $R \subset \mathbb{N} \times HU$, $F : \mathbb{N} \to HU$, etc.

It trivially follows from the definitions that every decidable relation is positively decidable.

As we shall see (cf. Exercise 7.8), partiality is an essential ingredient of the theory of calculability. Therefore, the notation $F : D^n \to D$ henceforth allows for the possibility that $Dom(F) \neq D^n$. In the case that $Dom(F) = D^n$, we shall leave no doubt about this circumstance and call $F$ *total*.

By the assumption that at least one function symbol is present, there is a representation of $\mathbb{N}$ in $HU$. For, let $\mathbf{c}$ be an individual constant and $\mathbf{f}$ a function symbol. Then the equations

$$
\begin{aligned}
rep(0) &= \mathbf{c} \\
rep(n+1) &= \mathbf{f}(rep(n), \ldots, rep(n))
\end{aligned}
$$

recursively define an injective map $rep : \mathbb{N} \to HU$ representing $\mathbb{N}$. In the following, $\mathbb{N}$ may refer to the set of natural numbers, or to a Herbrand universe generated from one constant and one unary function symbol, or to a representation of the natural numbers of the type indicated in any Herbrand universe.

An important coding ingredient is given by the following lemma.

**Lemma 7.2** *There exists a computable bijection $j : \mathbb{N}^2 \to \mathbb{N}$ with computable left- and right-inverses $j_1$ and $j_2$, i.e., such that for all $p \in \mathbb{N}$ we have $j(j_1(p), j_2(p)) = p$.*

**Proof.** Let $p \in \mathbb{N}$, $p \neq 0$. There are $p$ pairs $(n, m) \in \mathbb{N}^2$ such that $n + m = p - 1$. It follows that the number of pairs $(n, m)$ such that $n+m \leq p-1$ is $1+2+\cdots+p = \frac{1}{2}p(p+1)$.

Define the linear ordering $\prec$ on $\mathbb{N}^2$ by

$$(n', m') \prec (n, m) :\equiv n' + m' < n + m, \text{ or: } [n' + m' = n + m \wedge m' < m].$$

Then $(n, m)$ has $\frac{1}{2}(n + m)(m + m + 1) + m$ predecessors in this ordering. Therefore, the map $j$ defined by $j(n, m) := \frac{1}{2}(n + m)(n + m + 1) + m$ is a bijection as desired. It is left to the reader to check that $j_1$ and $j_2$ are computable. ∎

Next, the computable pairing can be used to computably enumerate the domains we're interested in.

**Lemma 7.3** *There are computable bijections $gnr : HU \to \mathbb{N}$ and $gnr' : HB \to \mathbb{N}$ with computable inverses $tm$ and $at$.*

**Proof.** N.B.: '$gnr$' stands for 'Gödel number'. Gödel (in his proof of the incompleteness theorems) was one of the first to employ an enumeration of syntactic objects.

We consider one example only. Cf. also Exercise 7.4. Let $HU$ be generated by the constants $\mathbf{o}$, $\mathbf{\Lambda}$, the unary function symbol $\mathbf{s}$ and the binary one $[\,.\,|\,.\,]$.

We let $gnr(\mathbf{o}) = 0$ and $gnr(\mathbf{\Lambda}) = 1$. From the remaining numbers $> 1$, we reserve the even ones as values of terms $\mathbf{s}(t) \in HU$, the odd ones we reserve as values of terms $[s|t] \in HU$.

It is now clear that the following equations recursively establish the desired bijection:

(i) $gnr(\mathbf{o}) = 0$, $gnr(\mathbf{\Lambda}) = 1$

(ii) $gnr(\mathbf{s}(t)) = 2gnr(t) + 2$

(iii) $gnr([s|t]) = 2j(gnr(s), gnr(t)) + 3.$

Since $j$ has computable inverses, it is easy to see that the inverse of $gnr$ is computable as well.  ∎

Recall the notion of the graph of a (partial) function (which is the relational representation of the function) from Definition 4.29.

Here is a simple relationship between calculability and positive decidability.

**Lemma 7.4** *The $k$-ary partial function $F : D^k \to D$ is calculable iff its graph is positively decidable.*

**Proof.** Assume that $D = HU$.

Only if: assume that $F$ is calculable. To positively decide the relation $F(\vec{s}) = t$, first calculate the value of $F(\vec{s})$. If the calculation terminates, it produces the value $F(\vec{s})$. Now, compare this value with $t$.

If: assume that $F$ has a graph that is positively decidable by means of a method $\mathcal{M}$. Given a sequence of arguments $\vec{s}$, let $\mathcal{M}$ work for some time on the problem of whether $F(\vec{s}) = tm(0)$. If it terminates with **yes**, we know that $F(\vec{s}) = tm(0)$. If not, give it some time to figure out whether $F(\vec{s}) = tm(1)$. If it terminates with **yes** this time, we know that $F(\vec{s}) = tm(1)$. If not, we give it some *more* time to figure out whether $F(\vec{s}) = tm(0)$, and, if need be, whether $F(\vec{s}) = tm(1)$ or maybe $F(\vec{s}) = tm(2)$. If a positive decision is not reached yet, give it yet more time for working on the questions of whether $F(\vec{s}) = tm(0)$, $F(\vec{s}) = tm(1)$, $F(\vec{s}) = tm(2)$ or $F(\vec{s}) = tm(3)$. If we go on this way (letting $\mathcal{M}$ work longer and longer on more and more possible answers), eventually the function value (if there is one) must turn up.  ∎

The following theorem establishes positive decidability of two subsets of the Herbrand base related to a program: its least Herbrand model and its finite failure set.

**Theorem 7.5** *For every program $P$, $M_P$ and $HB - T_P \downarrow \omega$ are positively decidable.*

**Proof.** A decision method ascertaining positive decidability of $M_P$ is (ground) resolution. That $HB - T_P \downarrow \omega$ is positively decidable follows immediately from the characterization of finite failure, cf., e.g., Corollary 6.20 of Chapter 6.  ∎

Recall the notions of program definability for relations and functions, Definition 4.29. As an easy consequence of the previous result, we have the following lemma.

**Lemma 7.6**

(i) *Every program definable relation is positively decidable.*

(ii) *Every program definable function is calculable.*

**Proof.** See Exercise 7.5.                                                                                          ∎

The next section is devoted to proofs of converses of this lemma.

**Lemma 7.7** *A relation $R \subset D^n$ is decidable iff both $R$ and its complement $D^n - R$ are positively decidable.*

**Proof.** If: combine the two decision methods into one.                                              ∎

**Definition 7.8** The program $P$ is called *determinate* if $M_P = T_P \downarrow \omega$.                    ∎

**Corollary 7.9** *If $P$ is determinate, then $M_P$ and $T_P \downarrow \omega$ are decidable.*

**Proof.** Immediate from Lemma 7.7 and Theorem 7.5.                                              ∎

The following presents some standard characterizations of positive decidability.

**Lemma 7.10** *For $R \subset HU$ (resp., $R \subset HB$), the following are equivalent:*

*(i) $R$ is positively decidable (as a unary relation),*
*(ii) $R$ is the domain of a calculable function,*
*(iii) either $R = \emptyset$ or $R$ is the range of a calculable function $F$ for which $Dom(F) = \mathbb{N}$,*
*(iv) for some decidable relation $S \subset \mathbb{N} \times HU$ (resp. $S \subset \mathbb{N} \times HB$) we have the equivalence $s \in R \Longleftrightarrow \exists n : S(n, s)$.*

**Proof.** Assume that $R \subset HU$.

(i)⇒(ii). Let $t \in HU$ be arbitrary. A function satisfying (ii) is $\{(s,t)|R(s)\}$.

(ii)⇒(i). Assume that $R = Dom(F)$ for some calculable function $F$. To decide whether $R(s)$, calculate $F(s)$. Now, $R(s)$ holds iff a function value is found.

(i)⇒(iii). Suppose that $R$ is a non-empty set with a positive decision method $\mathcal{M}$. Fix an arbitrary $t$ such that $R(t)$. The required function $F$ is defined by

$$F(n) = \begin{cases} tm(j_2(n)) & \text{if } \mathcal{M} \text{ ascertains } R(tm(j_2(n))) \text{ within } j_1(n) \text{ steps} \\ t & \text{if not.} \end{cases}$$

(iii)⇒(i). Suppose that $F$ enumerates $R$. In order to positively decide $R(s)$ for a given $s$, just start generating $F(0), F(1), F(2), \ldots$. Clearly, $R(s)$ holds iff $s$ turns up in this sequence.

(iii)⇒(iv). Let $R = Ran(F)$, $Dom(F) = \mathbb{N}$. Note that $\mathbb{N}$, and hence the graph of $F$, is decidable. We have that $s \in R \Leftrightarrow \exists n[n \in Dom(F) \wedge F(n) = s]$, and the right-hand side of this equivalence has the required form.

(iv)⇒(ii). Assume the equivalence $s \in R \Leftrightarrow \exists n S(n, s)$. Just define the required function $F$ by letting $F(s)$ be the least number $n$ such that $S(n, s)$.

Obvious modifications prove this lemma for $R \subset HB$.                                              ∎

The following simple existence result is one of the cornerstones of the theory.

**Theorem 7.11 (Turing)** *There exists a relation that is positively decidable but not decidable.*

**Proof.** Note that there is a problem here of a methodological nature. Experience shows that we can always recognize a decision method as such. We have just seen some instances of this phenomenon. However, in order to be able to give a precise proof that for a certain set no decision method exists, we need a precise definition of *decision method*. Turing was the first to provide such a (well-motivated) definition (in terms of his Turing machines) and prove the present theorem. The following sketch makes clear what the basic ingredients for such a definition should be.

We may assume that a decision method can be described in a formal way. In fact, we shall assume that one Herbrand universe $HU$ exists such that every method is described by a term in $HU$. By effectively enumerating all possible descriptions, this is seen to be true in fact for $HU = \mathbb{N}$, although a little more structure can make life more pleasant.

Consider the following binary relation $R$ (the *halting problem*) on $HU$.

$R(p, e) :\equiv$ the method described by $p$ (if any) terminates on the input $e$.

Note that this relation is in fact positively decidable: given $p$ and $e$, just put the method described by $p$ at work on the input $e$ and see what happens.

We proceed to show that $R$ cannot be decidable. We argue by contradiction. Suppose that $R$ *is* decidable. Consider its modification $U$ defined by

$U(p, e) :\equiv$ the method described by $p$ (if any) terminates on the input $e$ with output **yes**.

Clearly, if $R$ is decidable, then so is $U$. Also, if $S$ is any positively decidable unary relation, then for some description $s$ of a decision method for $S$, we have $\forall e[S(e) \iff U(s, e)]$. (A relation $U$ with this property is called *universal* for the class of unary positively decidable relations.) Now, since we have argued that $U$ is decidable, $\neg U(e, e)$ is decidable as well. Therefore, we can choose $u$ such that $\forall e[\neg U(e, e) \iff U(u, e)]$. Then, in particular for $e := u$, we obtain $\neg U(u, u) \iff U(u, u)$, a contradiction. ∎

The notions of (positive) decidability and calculability as introduced here have an intuitive content. However, for $HU = \mathbb{N}$, there exist mathematically precise definitions of *recursive* and *recursively enumerable* for relations $R \subset \mathbb{N}^n$ and of *(partially) recursive* for functions $F : \mathbb{N}^n \to \mathbb{N}$. There is overwhelming evidence for the following

**Extended Church's Thesis.**

(i) A relation $R \subset \mathbb{N}^n$ is decidable iff it is recursive,

(ii) a relation $R \subset \mathbb{N}^n$ is positively decidable iff it is recursively enumerable,

(iii) a number theoretic (partial) function is calculable iff it is (partially) recursive. ∎

(The usual formulation of Church's thesis consists of part (iii) only.)

There are many equivalent definitions of *recursive* (using machines and formal systems of several kinds). In the next section, such a definition is obtained in the context of the logic programming paradigm. The following definition is the direct number theoretic one. In it we use the $\lambda$-*notation* for functions, which works as follows. If $T(\vec{x})$ ($\vec{x} = (x_1, \ldots, x_n)$ a sequence of $n$ variables) is an expression every instance $T(\vec{s})$ of which denotes an object, then the expression $\lambda\vec{x}.T(\vec{x})$ denotes the $n$-ary function that sends a sequence $\vec{s}$ to the object denoted by $T(\vec{s})$. Example: $(\lambda xy.x^2 + y)(2,3) = 7$, since $\lambda xy.x^2 + y$ is the function that sends a pair of numbers $x$, $y$ to $x^2 + y$.

Finally, let $T(n)$ be a statement involving a natural number $n$ that may be either true or false or have no definite truth value at all. Then $\mu m.T(m)$ (the *least* number satisfying $T$) denotes the number $m$ such that (i) for all $m' < m$, $T(m')$ is false, and (ii) $T(m)$ holds. There may be no such numbers, in which case the expression has no denotation at all.

**Definition 7.12** A number theoretic (partial) function $F$ is *partially recursive* if it has a *recursive definition*, that is, a finite list $F_0, \ldots, F_q = F$ such that for every $k \leq q$ one of the following six possibilities obtains:

R1. $F_k = \lambda n.n + 1$
   (the *successor* function),

R2. $F_k = \lambda n_1 \cdots n_l.n_j$, where $1 \leq j \leq l$
   (the $j$-th *projection function* of $l$ variables),

R3. $F_k = \lambda n.0$
   (the *constant* $= 0$ function),

R4. for some $j, j_1, \ldots, j_p < k$:

$$F_k = \lambda n_1 \cdots n_l.F_j(F_{j_1}(n_1, \ldots, n_l), \ldots, F_{j_p}(n_1, \ldots, n_l))$$

   (the *composition* of $F_j, F_{j_1}, \ldots, F_{j_p}$),

R5. For some $j, i < k$, $F_k$ is the unique function satisfying

   (a) $F_k(n_1, \ldots, n_l, 0) = F_j(n_1, \ldots, n_l)$

   (b) $F_k(n_1, \ldots, n_l, p + 1) = F_i(n_1, \ldots, n_l, p, F_k(n_1, \ldots, n_l, p))$

   (*primitive recursion*),

R6. For some $j < k$, $F_k = \lambda n_1 \cdots n_l.\mu m[F_j(n_1, \ldots, n_l, m) = 0]$
   (*minimalization*).                                                                      ∎

If part (6) of the definition is left out, the class of so-called *primitive recursive* functions is obtained. These are all total functions. But note that the minimalization (6) is responsible for the fact that a lot of recursive functions are *partial*, i.e., have a domain that is properly included in some $\mathbb{N}^n$.

To obtain the class of *total* recursive functions, i.e., partially recursive functions defined on *all* tuples from $\mathbb{N}$, the definition should be augmented with the *existence condition* in part (6) that for all $n_1, \ldots, n_l \in \mathbb{N}$ an $m$ exists such that $F_j(n_1, \ldots, n_l, m) = 0$.

Once we have the notion of *recursive* for functions, definitions for the other notions are motivated by Lemma 7.10 and Lemma 7.7.

## Definition 7.13

(i) $R \subset \mathbb{N}^k$ is *recursively enumerable* if it is the domain of a partial recursive function.
(ii) $R \subset \mathbb{N}^k$ is *recursive* if both $R$ and its complement $\mathbb{N}^k - R$ are recursively enumerable.

∎

In the sequel, we feel free to use the Extended Church's Thesis whenever needed. For instance, there are results parallel to those for (positively) decidable relations and calculable functions, obtained by exchanging these notions by *recursively enumerable* resp. *recursive*.

## Exercises

**7.1** Let $\mathbb{N}$ be a representation of the natural numbers in some Herbrand universe $HU$ of the type indicated. Show that $\mathbb{N}$ is decidable by describing a decision method for it.

**7.2** Give a (simple) program defining the relation $\{(n, m, p) | j(n, m) = p\}$ on $\mathbb{N}$, where $j$ is defined in the proof of Lemma 7.2.
*Hint.* Consider the following rules.

$$\mathbf{j}(\mathbf{o}, \mathbf{o}, \mathbf{o}) \leftarrow$$
$$\mathbf{j}(x, \mathbf{s}y, \mathbf{s}z) \leftarrow \mathbf{j}(\mathbf{s}x, y, z)$$
$$\mathbf{j}(\mathbf{s}y, \mathbf{o}, \mathbf{s}z) \leftarrow \mathbf{j}(\mathbf{o}, y, z).$$

**7.3** Produce programs defining the functions *gnr* and *tm* from the proof of Lemma 7.3.

**7.4** Suppose that $HU$ is generated by constants $\mathbf{a}, \mathbf{b}, \mathbf{c}$, a unary function symbol $\mathbf{f}$, a binary one $\mathbf{g}$ and a ternary $\mathbf{h}$. Establish a bijection between $HU$ and $\mathbb{N}$.
*Hint.* The map $(n, m, p) \mapsto j(j(n, m), p)$ is a bijection: $\mathbb{N}^3 \to \mathbb{N}$. Assign numbers $0, 1, 2$ to resp. $\mathbf{a}, \mathbf{b}, \mathbf{c}$; assign numbers $3n+3$ to $\mathbf{f}$-terms, numbers $3n+4$ to $\mathbf{g}$-terms and numbers $3n + 5$ to $\mathbf{h}$-terms.

**7.5** Prove Lemma 7.6.
*Hint.* Use Theorems 7.5 and Lemma 7.4.

**7.6** Let $P$ be a program. Show: $M_P$ is decidable iff every relation defined by $P$ is decidable.

**7.7** Let $F$ be calculable. Show: if $Dom(F)$ is decidable, then the graph of $F$ is decidable. Show that the converse of this is false.
*Hint.* Try $F(n) = m :\equiv$ the method described by $j_1(n)$ terminates on input $j_2(n)$ in exactly $m$ steps.

**7.8** Show that a calculable partial function $F : HU \to HU$ exists that cannot be extended to a *calculable* function $G$ such that $Dom(G) = HU$.
*Hint.* Use Turing's theorem.

**7.9** Show that addition, multiplication and exponentiation are (primitive) recursive.

**7.10** Show: $R \subset \mathbb{N}$ is recursive iff it has a characteristic function that is recursive.

## 7.2 Computability of Recursive Functions

In this section it is shown that recursive functions can be computed by logic programs.

By Definition 4.7, it is seen that the first and second parts of the following definition are equivalent with the corresponding parts of Definition 4.29.

**Definition 7.14** Let $P$ be a program.

(i) $P$ *defines* the relation $R \subset HU^n$ in the $n$-ary relation symbol $\mathbf{r}$ if

$$R(t_1, \ldots, t_n) \Longleftrightarrow \mathbf{r}(t_1, \ldots, t_n) \in M_P.$$

(ii) $P$ *defines* the partial $n$-ary function $F : HU^n \to HU$ in the $(n+1)$-ary relation symbol $\mathbf{f}$ if it defines the graph of $F$ in $\mathbf{f}$.

(iii) $P$ *computes* the partial $n$-ary function $F : HU^n \to HU$ in the $(n+1)$-ary relation symbol $\mathbf{f}$ if, for all ground terms $t_1, \ldots, t_n$ and all terms $s$ (possibly containing variables), $\{y/s\}$ is a computed answer substitution for $\mathbf{f}(t_1, \ldots, t_n, y)$ iff $F(t_1, \ldots, t_n) = s$. ∎

**Lemma 7.15** $P$ *defines the function $F$ in $\mathbf{f}$ iff it computes $F$ in $\mathbf{f}$.*

**Proof.** See Exercise 7.11. ∎

**Theorem 7.16** *Every partially recursive function is computable over $HU = \mathbb{N}$ by some logic program.*

**Proof.** Let $F_0, \ldots, F_q = F$ be a recursive definition for $F$ in the sense of Definition 7.12. We construct a program for every function $F_k$ ($k \le q$) in the definition, as follows. The construction distinguishes cases R1–6 from Definition 7.12.
R1. $F_k = \lambda n.n + 1$.

This function is computed in $\mathbf{f}_k$ by the single rule

$$\mathbf{f}_k(x, \mathbf{s}x) \leftarrow .$$

R2. We have $1 \leq j \leq l$ and $F_k = \lambda n_1, \cdots, n_l.n_j$.
This function is computed in $\mathbf{f}_k$ by the rule

$$\mathbf{f}_k(x_1, \ldots, x_l, x_j) \leftarrow .$$

R3. $F_k = \lambda n.0$.
This function is computed in $\mathbf{f}_k$ by the rule

$$\mathbf{f}_k(x, \mathbf{o}) \leftarrow .$$

R4. $j, j_1, \ldots, j_p < k$, and $F_k = \lambda n_1, \cdots, n_l.F_j(F_{j_1}(n_1, \ldots, n_l), \ldots, F_{j_p}(n_1, \ldots, n_l))$.
By induction hypothesis, assume that we have programs (which we may assume to be without common relation symbols) computing $F_j$ and $F_{j_1}, \ldots, F_{j_p}$ in the symbols $\mathbf{f}_j$ and $\mathbf{f}_{j_1}, \ldots, \mathbf{f}_{j_p}$. Add the following rule to the rules of these programs:

$$\mathbf{f}_k(x_1, \ldots, x_l, z) \leftarrow \mathbf{f}_{j_1}(x_1, \ldots, x_l, y_1), \ldots, \mathbf{f}_{j_p}(x_1, \ldots, x_l, y_p), \mathbf{f}_j(y_1, \ldots, y_p, z).$$

The resulting program computes $F_k$ in $\mathbf{f}_k$.
R5. Suppose that $j, i < k$, and $F_k$ (which for simplicity we take to have 2 arguments) satisfies

(a) $F_k(n, 0) = F_j(n)$

(b) $F_k(n, p+1) = F_i(n, p, F_k(n, p))$.

To the rules that compute $F_j$ and $F_i$ in $\mathbf{f}_j$ resp. $\mathbf{f}_i$ (without common relation symbols), add the following two:

1. $f_k(x, \mathbf{o}, z) \leftarrow f_j(x, z)$

2. $f_k(x, \mathbf{s}y, z) \leftarrow f_k(x, y, z'), f_i(x, y, z', z).$

This computes $F_k$ in $\mathbf{f}_k$.
R6. Finally, suppose that $F = F_k$, $j < k$, $G = F_j$ and $F = \lambda n.\mu m[G(n, m) = 0]$ (for simplicity assuming that $G$ has two arguments).
Suppose we have rules computing $G$ in $\mathbf{g}$. Define the relation $H$ by:

$$H(n, m) :\equiv \forall m' < m[G(n, m') \neq 0].$$

Adding the two rules

1. $\mathbf{h}(x, \mathbf{o}) \leftarrow$

2. $\mathbf{h}(x, \mathbf{s}y) \leftarrow \mathbf{g}(x, y, \mathbf{s}z), \mathbf{h}(x, y)$

produces a program that defines $H$ in $\mathbf{h}$.

Now, add one more rule

$$\mathbf{f}(x, y) \leftarrow \mathbf{g}(x, y, \mathbf{o}), \mathbf{h}(x, y).$$

This computes $F$ in $\mathbf{f}$. ∎

The following theorem shows that the present theory of programs forms an adequate approach to computability theory.

### Theorem 7.17

(i) $R \subset HU^k$ is positively decidable iff $R$ is program definable.

(ii) $F : HU^k \rightarrow HU$ is calculable iff $F$ is program definable.

**Proof.** (ii) Let $F : HU \rightarrow HU$ be calculable. By Church's Thesis, the number theoretic function $F'$ defined by: $F'(n) := gnr(F(tm(n)))$, is recursive. Construct a program that computes $F'$. Note that $F(s) = tm(F'(gnr(s)))$. ($tmF'gnr = tm\ gnrF tm\ gnr = F$.) Construct rules computing $tm$ and $gnr$ (Exercise 7.3). Since $F$ is the composition of $tm$, $F'$ and $gnr$, it is program computable as well. Conversely, every program computable function is calculable (modulo Lemma 7.15), which is the content of Lemma 7.6(ii).

(i) Let $R \subset HU$ be positively decidable. Say, $R = Dom(F)$, with $F$ calculable. Let $P$ compute $F$ in the symbol $\mathbf{f}$. Adding the rule $\mathbf{r}(x) \leftarrow \mathbf{f}(x, y)$ produces a program defining $R$ in $\mathbf{r}$. Conversely, every program definable relation is positively decidable, which is the content of Lemma 7.6(i). ∎

**Theorem 7.18** *There exists a program $P$ such that $M_P$ is undecidable.*

**Proof.** Let $P$ define an undecidable relation. ∎

The following is the basic undecidability result in first-order logic. It is straightforwardly derivable from what we have so far.

**Theorem 7.19 (Church)** *There is no decision method for logical validity and unsatisfiability in first-order logic.*

**Proof.** By Theorem 7.18, let $P$ be a program such that $M_P$ is undecidable. For a ground atom $A$, we have: $\models (P \rightarrow A)$ iff $P \models A$ iff $A \in M_P$. Hence, logical validity of sentences $P \rightarrow A$ is undecidable. ∎

The rules R6 that compute a minimalization are not very satisfactory. Though it is true that if $\mu m[G(n, m) = 0]$ exists and has value $p$, then the rules produce a success for $\mathbf{f}(n, y)$ with a computed answer substitution $\{y/p\}$, the actual *finding* of this success

seems to require knowledge of the value $p$ of $\mu m[G(n,m) = 0]$. Indeed, using the second
**h**-rule over and over again will result in an infinite derivation; and we can only avoid this
by starting to resolve the **g**-atoms at exactly the right time, determined by this value.

Example: assume that $2 = \mu m[G(0,m) = 0]$. We get the following derivation starting
with the initial query $\mathbf{f}(\mathbf{o}, y)$:

$$\mathbf{f}(\mathbf{o}, y) \xrightarrow{\ \epsilon\ } \mathbf{g}(\mathbf{o}, y, \mathbf{o}), \mathbf{h}(\mathbf{o}, y)$$
$$\xrightarrow{\ \{y/\mathbf{S}y\}\ } \mathbf{g}(\mathbf{o}, \mathbf{s}y, \mathbf{o}), \mathbf{g}(\mathbf{o}, y, \mathbf{s}z), \mathbf{h}(\mathbf{o}, y)$$
$$\xrightarrow{\ \{y/\mathbf{S}y\}\ } \mathbf{g}(\mathbf{o}, \mathbf{s}\mathbf{s}y, \mathbf{o}), \mathbf{g}(\mathbf{o}, \mathbf{s}y, \mathbf{s}z), \mathbf{g}(\mathbf{o}, y, \mathbf{s}z'), \mathbf{h}(\mathbf{o}, y).$$

At exactly this spot, we use our knowledge that $2 = \mu m[G(0,m) = 0]$, which implies that
the $\{y/\mathbf{o}\}$-instance of the last query can be successfully resolved; and hence, by lifting,
that the query itself can be successfully resolved.

Trying to resolve the **g**-atoms before or after this stage will fail. And finally, there does
not seem to be a good way to find a success for the query other than the one obtained
by lifting a success for the proper instance.

Because of this, the following alternative R6′ to the rules R6 is offered. To motivate
this alternative, consider the relation $ZERO$, defined as follows.

$$ZERO(n,i,j) :\equiv \forall j' < j[G(n,i+j') \neq 0] \wedge G(n,i+j) = 0.$$

The following rules are valid for this relation:

R6′.

  1. $\mathbf{zero}(x, y, \mathbf{o}) \leftarrow \mathbf{g}(x, y, \mathbf{o})$

  2. $\mathbf{zero}(x, y, \mathbf{s}z) \leftarrow \mathbf{g}(x, y, \mathbf{s}u), \mathbf{zero}(x, \mathbf{s}y, z)$

  3. $\mathbf{f}(x, z) \leftarrow \mathbf{zero}(x, \mathbf{o}, z)$.

*Claim:* these rules (together with appropriate ones for **g**) define $ZERO$ in **zero** and $F$
in **f**.

Again consider the example where $2 = \mu m[G(0,m) = 0]$. We now get the following
derivation:

$$\mathbf{f}(\mathbf{o}, z) \xrightarrow{\ \epsilon\ } \mathbf{zero}(\mathbf{o}, \mathbf{o}, z)$$

Now, two **zero**-rules are applicable, producing the resolvents:

  a. $\xrightarrow{\ \{z/\mathbf{o}\}\ } \mathbf{g}(\mathbf{o}, \mathbf{o}, \mathbf{o})$, which fails eventually;

  b. $\xrightarrow{\ \{z/\mathbf{s}z\}\ } \mathbf{g}(\mathbf{o}, \mathbf{o}, \mathbf{s}u), \mathbf{zero}(\mathbf{o}, 1, z)$, which, since the **g**-atom here eventually succeeds,
resolves to $\mathbf{zero}(\mathbf{o}, 1, z)$.

Again, there are two resolvents:

  a. the failing $\xrightarrow{\ \{z/\mathbf{o}\}\ } \mathbf{g}(\mathbf{o}, 1, \mathbf{o})$, and

b. $\xrightarrow{\{z/\mathbf{S}z\}}$ $\mathbf{g}(\mathbf{o}, 1, \mathbf{s}u), \mathbf{zero}(\mathbf{o}, 2, z)$, which, after resolving the $\mathbf{g}$-atom, reduces to $\mathbf{zero}(\mathbf{o}, 2, z)$.

The first resolvent of the following two

a. $\xrightarrow{\{z/\mathbf{O}\}}$ $\mathbf{g}(\mathbf{o}, 2, \mathbf{o})$ now succeeds, producing the c.a.s. $\{z/2\}$.

b. The other one $\xrightarrow{\{z/\mathbf{S}z\}}$ $\mathbf{g}(\mathbf{o}, 2, \mathbf{s}u), \mathbf{zero}(\mathbf{o}, 3, z)$ must fail because of the presence of the $\mathbf{g}$-atom.

The upshot of this example is that the implementation R6′ of the $\mu$-operator almost automatically generates the desired success. A precise formulation of this is the content of the following theorem.

**Theorem 7.20** *Suppose that $F$ is a $k$-ary total recursive function and $P$ is a program computing $F$ in $\mathbf{f}$ constructed using R1–5 and R6′. For every $(n_1, \ldots, n_k)$ the SLD-tree for $\mathbf{f}(n_1, \ldots, n_k, y)$ constructed using the leftmost selection rule is finite, has exactly one successful leaf, and the computed answer substitution corresponding to this leaf is $\{y/F(n_1, \ldots, n_k)\}$.*

**Proof.** The theorem is an immediate consequence of the observation that for every $(k + 1)$-ary relation symbol $\mathbf{r}$ and every $n_1, \ldots, n_k \in \mathbb{N}$ and term $t$, the leftmost SLD-tree for $\mathbf{r}(n_1, \ldots, n_k, t)$ is finite, has at most one success, and, if present, this derivation has a computed answer substitution $\theta$ such that $t\theta \in \mathbb{N}$. ∎

**Lemma 7.21** *Let $P$ be a program. If there exists a selection rule such that every SLD-tree for a ground atomic goal produced by it is finite, then $P$ is determinate.*

**Proof.** Immediate from the finite failure-characterization, Corollary 6.20.(i) ⇒ (v), from Chapter 6. ∎

**Example.** The converse of this fails badly. E.g., let $P$ consist of the rules $\mathbf{r}(x) \leftarrow \mathbf{r}(x)$ and $\mathbf{r}(x) \leftarrow$. Then $T_P\uparrow = T_P\downarrow = T_P\downarrow\omega = HB$, but no selection rule can prevent the infinite derivation $\mathbf{r}(\mathbf{c}) \xrightarrow{\epsilon} \mathbf{r}(\mathbf{c}) \xrightarrow{\epsilon} \mathbf{r}(\mathbf{c}) \cdots$ ∎

**Corollary 7.22** *Every total recursive function can be computed by a determinate program.*

**Proof.** Programs constructed by means of R1–5 and R6′ for *total* recursive functions are determinate. If the leftmost selection rule produces an infinite derivation starting from a ground atom $\mathbf{r}(n, m)$, this can be lifted to an infinite derivation from $\mathbf{r}(n, y)$. Apply Theorem 7.20 and Lemma 7.21. ∎

## Exercises

**7.11** Give a detailed proof for Lemma 7.15.

**7.12** Verify the necessary details of the proof of Theorem 7.16.

**Definition 7.23** A program $P$ is called *weakly recurrent* with respect to the "level function" $l : HB \to \mathbb{N}$ if for every ground instance $A \leftarrow C$ of a rule of $P$ such that $A \notin T_P \uparrow$, there exists a $B \in C$ with $l(B) < l(A)$ such that $B \notin T_P \uparrow$. ∎

**7.13** Show that every program constructed by means of R1–5 is weakly recurrent with respect to some function $l$. Extend this result to programs constructed using R1–5 and R6′.

**7.14** Show that a program is determinate iff it is weakly recurrent with respect to some function.

*Hint.* Only if: use the downward hierarchy to construct the required function $l$. If: show that a fair SLD-tree for a ground atom $A \notin M_P$ must be finite. Use Corollary 6.20.

**Definition 7.24**

(i) A program $P$ is called *recurrent* with respect to the function $l : HB \to \mathbb{N}$ if for every ground instance $A \leftarrow C$ of a rule of $P$ and for all $B \in C$ we have $l(B) < l(A)$.

(ii) An atom $A$ is *bounded* with respect to $l : HB \to \mathbb{N}$ if $\{l(A') \mid A'$ a ground instance of $A\}$ has a maximum. This maximum is denoted by $l(A)$.

(iii) A query $C$ is *bounded* if all its elements are. When $C = (A_1, \ldots, A_k)$ is bounded, then $l(C)$ is the multiset of numbers $\{\{l(A_1), \ldots, l(A_k)\}\}$. ∎

**7.15** Show that every recurrent program is weakly recurrent.
Are the programs constructed using R1–5, R6′ recurrent?

**7.16** Let $P$ be recurrent with respect to $l$. Show that if $D$ is a resolvent of a bounded query $C$, then (i) $D$ is bounded, and (ii) $l(D) < l(C)$ in the multiset ordering over $\mathbb{N}$.

*Hint.* Assume that $C \xrightarrow{\alpha} D$. (i) Let $D\tau$ be a ground instance of $D$. Let $C'$ be $C\alpha\tau$ if this is ground, or a ground instance of $C\alpha\tau$ otherwise. Then $C' \xrightarrow{\epsilon}_u D\tau$ and $l(D\tau) < l(C') \le l(C)$. (ii) Let $D\tau$ be a ground instance of $D$ such that $l(D\tau) = l(D)$. If $C'$ is as before, then $l(D) = l(D\tau) < l(C') \le l(C)$.

Note that, by Exercise 7.16 and Theorem 1.13, no derivation starting from a bounded goal can be infinite.

**Definition 7.25** A program is *terminating* if it cannot produce infinite derivations for ground atomic queries (under *any* selection rule). ∎

**7.17** Show: a program is terminating iff it is recurrent with respect to some function $l : HB \to \mathbb{N}$.

*Hint.* For the only-if-part: define $l : HB \to \mathbb{N}$ by putting $l(A)$ equal to the maximum length a derivation from $A$ can have. Use König's lemma to see that this maximum always exists.

**7.18** Reconsider previously given programs and determine whether they are recurrent, resp. weakly recurrent.

**7.19** Consider the quicksort program of Exercise 4.60. Show that it does not produce infinite derivations starting with a query $\mathbf{qs}([t_1, \ldots, t_n], t)$ where $t_1, \ldots, t_n$ and $t$ are arbitrary terms, and using the leftmost selection rule.

**7.20** Exercise 4.22 offers a condition on programs $P$ that suffices for $T_P$ to have exactly one fixed point: the relation $\prec$, defined by

> $B \prec A$ iff $B$ occurs in the body of a ground instance of a $P$-rule of which $A$ is the head

should be well-founded. What do you need to know about $\prec$ in order that $P$ is determinate?

By Theorem 7.5, $HB - T_P \downarrow \omega$ is positively decidable. The following exercise shows that $T_P \downarrow \omega$ can be undecidable.

**7.21** For the following, assume that $HU = \mathbb{N}$.

(i) The program $P_1$ involves the binary $\mathbf{r}$. Choose a new binary relation symbol $\mathbf{q}$. $P_2$ is formed by adding the rule

$$\mathbf{q}(x, y) \leftarrow \mathbf{r}(x, y), \mathbf{q}(x, \mathbf{s}y).$$

$T_1$ and $T_2$ are the operators of $P_1$ resp. $P_2$. Show that the following are equivalent:

(a) $\mathbf{q}(n, \mathbf{o}) \in T_2 \downarrow \omega$,

(b) $\forall m : \mathbf{q}(n, m) \in T_2 \downarrow \omega$,

(c) $\forall m : \mathbf{r}(n, m) \in T_1 \downarrow \omega$.

(ii) Assume that $P_1$ is determinate and defines the complement $\neg R$ of the relation $R$ in $\mathbf{r}$. Form $P_3$ by adding to $P_2$ the rule

$$\mathbf{p}(x) \leftarrow \mathbf{q}(x, \mathbf{o}).$$

Let $T_3$ be the operator of $P_3$. Show that
$\mathbf{p}(n) \in T_3 \downarrow \omega \iff \neg \exists m : R(n, m)$.

(iii) Show: for every recursively enumerable relation $S$ there exists a program $P$ using a relation symbol $\mathbf{p}$ such that $S(n) \iff \mathbf{p}(n) \notin T_P \downarrow \omega$.

(iv) Show that $T_P \downarrow \omega$ can be undecidable.

**7.22** Reconsider the implementation of primitive recursion, R5. Assume that $F : \mathbb{N}^2 \to \mathbb{N}$ is recursively defined from the functions $G$ and $H$ by the equations

$F(n, 0) = G(n)$

$F(n, m + 1) = H(n, m, F(n, m))$.

Assume that the program $P$ computes $G$ and $H$ in the symbols **g** resp **h**. Extend $P$ by the following rules.

$\mathbf{f}(x, y, z) \leftarrow \mathbf{g}(x, v), \mathbf{up}(x, y, \mathbf{o}, v, z)$

$\mathbf{up}(x, y, u, v, z) \leftarrow \mathbf{h}(x, u, v, w), \mathbf{up}(x, y, \mathbf{s}u, w, z)$

$\mathbf{up}(x, y, y, z, z) \leftarrow$.

Show that this computes $F$ in **f**. What exactly is defined by **up**? What is the advantage of this implementation over the one given before? (Note that the computational or procedural content of these rules is much clearer than their logical or declarative content.)

**7.23** Compare the previous exercise. We can save one argument-place from **up**. Consider the following rules.

$\mathbf{f}(x, y, z) \leftarrow \mathbf{g}(x, v), \mathbf{down}(x, y, v, z)$

$\mathbf{down}(x, \mathbf{s}u, v, z) \leftarrow \mathbf{h}(x, u, v, w), \mathbf{down}(x, u, w, z)$

$\mathbf{down}(x, \mathbf{o}, z, z) \leftarrow$.

Answer the same questions with respect to these rules.

## 7.3  Complexity of $T_P \downarrow$

### 7.3.1  Analytical Hierarchy

The classes of recursive and recursively enumerable relations form the lowest levels of the infinite arithmetical hierarchy of number theoretic relations. The other levels of this hierarchy are defined as follows.

Let $K$ be a class of number theoretic relations. Then $\Sigma(K)$ is the class of relations $R$ that can be written as an existential quantification of some $S \in K$:

$$R(n_1, \ldots, n_k) \iff \exists m_1 \ldots \exists m_l \, S(n_1, \ldots, n_k, m_1, \ldots, m_l).$$

$\Sigma_1^0$ is the class of recursively enumerable sets and relations. The *arithmetical hierarchy* now proceeds from this, by

(i)  $\Pi_n^0 := \{\neg R \mid R \in \Sigma_n^0\}$

(ii)  $\Sigma_{n+1}^0 := \Sigma(\Pi_n^0)$

(iii)  $\Delta_n^0 := \Sigma_n^0 \cap \Delta_n^0$.

A relation is *arithmetical* iff it belongs to some level $(\Sigma_n^0, \Pi_n^0)$ of the arithmetical hierarchy. By Lemma 7.7, $\Delta_1^0$ is the class of recursive relations and sets. By Theorem 7.11, $\Sigma_1^0 - \Pi_1^0$ is non-empty since it contains the halting problem. In fact, there is a *Hierarchy Theorem* stating that $\Pi_n^0 - \Sigma_n^0$ and $\Sigma_n^0 - \Pi_n^0$ are non-empty for all $n$.

Obviously, we can generalize these notions to refer to sets and relations over an arbitrary Herbrand universe or Herbrand base using our computable enumerations of these classes. We use the same notations for the hierarchies so generalized.

Next we introduce relation arguments in program definable relations, as follows.

**Definition 7.26**

(i) Let $R \subset HU^k$ be an arbitrary relation. Let $P$ be a program and $\mathbf{r}$ a $k$-ary relation symbol not occurring in the head of a rule of $P$. $P(R)$ is the program consisting of (1) all rules of $P$ and (2) all rules $\mathbf{r}(t_1, \ldots, t_k) \leftarrow$ such that $R(t_1, \ldots, t_k)$ holds $(t_1, \ldots, t_k \in HU)$.

(ii) Extend the class $\Sigma_1^0$ by allowing relations of relations as follows. $Rel(HU, k)$ is the class of all $k$-ary relations on $HU$. A relation $Q \subset Rel(HU, k) \times HU^m$ is in $\Sigma_1^0$ if for some program $P$ involving an $m$-ary relation symbol $\mathbf{q}$, we have $Q(R, t_1, \ldots, t_m) \Longleftrightarrow \mathbf{q}(t_1, \ldots, t_m) \in T_{P(R)} \uparrow$. ∎

The previous definitions may be generalized, allowing for a finite *sequence* of relations instead of just one; we can extend all classes $\Sigma_n^0$, $\Pi_n^0$ and $\Delta_n^0$ admitting relations as arguments; and, finally, we can generalize these notions to relations on $HB$ as well.

Note that a program $P(R)$ — if $R$ is infinite — has infinitely many rules. We deviate here thus expressly from our convention, that programs shall be finite. Nevertheless, consequence operators remain monotone and fixed points exist and can be finitely approximated.

Also, note that the relation $Q$ of part (ii) of the definition is *monotone* in its relation argument.

**Lemma 7.27** *If $Q \in \Sigma_1^0$, $R \subset R'$ and $Q(R, t_1, \ldots, t_m)$ holds, then $Q(R', t_1, \ldots, t_m)$ holds as well.* ∎

Admitting relation arguments in relations, we can now quantify with respect to relations and obtain a more extensive classification:

**Definition 7.28**

(i) $Q \subset HU$ is in $\Pi_1^1$ if, for some arithmetical $S$, we have that $Q(t) \Longleftrightarrow \forall R : S(R, t)$.

(ii) $\Sigma_1^1$ is the class of complements of relations in $\Pi_1^1$.

(iii) $\Delta_1^1 = \Pi_1^1 \cap \Sigma_1^1$ is the class of so-called *hyperarithmetical* relations. ∎

The previous definition gives the lowest levels of the *Analytical Hierarchy*, the building of which parallels the arithmetical hierarchy, but now uses quantification over relations instead of numbers. Of course, these classes also contain relations of more than one argument, and arguments may be relations themselves; but we have no need for these generalizations.

A simple example of a hyperarithmetical set that is not arithmetical is the set of sentences true in the standard model of arithmetic. It is hyperarithmetical basically because the recursion equations $E$ for satisfaction in this model are arithmetical conditions with exactly one solution: the satisfaction relation relative to this model. Therefore, the truth set $T$ for this model can be defined both by $\varphi \in T \Longleftrightarrow \exists S[E(S) \wedge \varphi \in S]$, making it $\Sigma_1^1$, and by $\varphi \in T \Longleftrightarrow \forall S[E(S) \Rightarrow \varphi \in S]$, making it $\Pi_1^1$. Finally, $T$ is not arithmetical by Tarski's theorem on undefinability of truth, see Exercise 7.25.

The a priori complexity of greatest fixed points is $\Sigma_1^1$:

**Theorem 7.29** *For every logic program $P$: $T_P \downarrow \in \Sigma_1^1$.*

**Proof.** We have: $A \in T_P \downarrow$ iff $A \in X$ for some $X \subset HB$ such that $X \subset T_P(X)$; the condition $X \subset T_P(X)$ is arithmetical (in fact, it is $\Pi_2^0$). ∎

As a consequence of this, greatest fixed points define relations that are $\Sigma_1^1$.

**Corollary 7.30** *If $P$ is a logic program involving the $k$-ary relation symbol $\mathbf{r}$, then the relation $R \subset HU^k$ defined by $R(t_1, \ldots, t_k) \Leftrightarrow \mathbf{r}(t_1, \ldots, t_k) \in T_P \downarrow$ is in $\Sigma_1^1$.* ∎

The purpose of this section is to prove the following converse. In view of the coming definition, we formulate it in the dual form:

**Theorem 7.31** *If $R \subset HU^k$ is in $\Pi_1^1$, then for some program $P$ involving a $k$-ary relation symbol $\mathbf{r}$, we have $R(t_1, \ldots, t_k) \Leftrightarrow \mathbf{r}(t_1, \ldots, t_k) \notin T_P \downarrow$.*

**Definition 7.32** *$P$ co-defines the relation $R$ in the symbol $\mathbf{r}$ if*
$$R(t_1, \ldots, t_k) \Longleftrightarrow \mathbf{r}(t_1, \ldots, t_k) \notin T_P \downarrow.$$ ∎

Thus, Theorem 7.31 states that every $\Pi_1^1$-relation can be co-defined. To prove it, we employ Kleene's Normal Form Theorem for $\Pi_1^1$-relations, which is the subject of the next section.

### Exercises

Identify $\mathbb{N}$ with the ("standard") model of arithmetic that has universe $\mathbb{N}$ and the structure of which comprises addition, multiplication, and whatever is convenient (ordering, constants $0, 1, 2, \ldots$).

**7.24** Show that a number theoretic relation $R$ is arithmetical iff it is definable on $\mathbb{N}$; that is, for some formula $\psi$ in the arithmetical language, we have the equivalence $R(n_1, \ldots, n_k)$ iff $\mathbb{N} \models \psi[n_1, \ldots, n_k]$.

**7.25** (*Tarski's theorem.*) Let $gnr$ be a computable function injectively mapping formulas from the arithmetical language to integers. Show that the set $TRUE := \{gnr(\varphi) \mid \varphi$ an $L$-sentence true in $\mathbb{N}\}$ is not arithmetical.

*Hint.* Otherwise, the relation $\{(n, gnr(\psi)) \mid \psi$ a formula satisfied by $n$ in $\mathbb{N}\}$ would be definable on $\mathbb{N}$ by some formula $\eta = \eta(x, y)$. Thus, for all $n$ and $\psi$, $\mathbb{N} \models \psi[n]$ iff $\mathbb{N} \models \eta[n, gnr(\psi)]$. Apply this to $\psi$ set to $\neg \eta(x, x)$ and $n := gnr(\neg \eta(x, x))$.

**7.26** Show that every arithmetical relation is in $\Delta_1^1$.

### 7.3.2  Kleene Normal Form

To make life a little easier, we will always assume the presence of a binary function symbol in the language under consideration, and so have lists in $HU$. In agreement with what is usual, the relations we quantify over will be functions defined on all of $\mathbb{N}$ always. This does not change the concepts previously introduced: every total function $\sigma : \mathbb{N} \to HU$ can be considered to code the $k$-ary relation $\{(t_1, \ldots, t_k) \mid \sigma(nr([t_1, \ldots, t_k])) = [\,]\}$; hence, every definition involving quantification over relations can be turned into one involving quantification over (unary, total) functions.

In the sequel $HU^{\mathbb{N}}$ is the set of all total functions $\sigma : \mathbb{N} \to HU$ and $HU^{<\omega}$ is the set of all finite functions $\alpha$ such that for some $p \in \mathbb{N}$, we have $\alpha : \{i \mid i < p\} \to HU$. When $\alpha : \{i \mid i < p\} \to HU$, we shall identify $\alpha$ with the finite sequence $(\alpha(0), \ldots, \alpha(p-1))$ of length $p$.

For $p \in \mathbb{N}$ and $\sigma : \mathbb{N} \to HU$, $\overline{\sigma}(p)$ denotes the function defined on $\{i \mid i < p\}$ by $\overline{\sigma}(p)(i) := \sigma(i)$. In other words, $\overline{\sigma}(p)$ is $\sigma | \{i \mid i < p\}$, the finite approximation of $\sigma$ on $\{i \mid i < p\}$.

The following lemma states that $\Sigma_1^0$ involving relation-arguments can be reduced to $\Sigma_1^0$ without such arguments.

**Lemma 7.33** *For every $\Sigma_1^0$-relation $Q \subset HU^{\mathbb{N}} \times HU$ there exists a decidable relation $R \subset HU \times HU$ such that $Q(\sigma, t) \Leftrightarrow \exists p\, R(\overline{\sigma}(p), t)$.*

**Proof.** By Definition 7.26(ii) of $\Sigma_1^0$, there exists a program $P$ involving a relation symbol $\mathbf{q}$, such that $Q(\sigma, t)$ holds iff the program $P(\sigma)$ (Definition 7.26(i)) successfully resolves the query $\mathbf{q}(t)$. In some computable way, injectively assign numbers to finite derivations. Now, note that, since a success can only use finitely many rules: $P(\sigma)$ successfully resolves $\mathbf{q}(t)$ iff for some $p$, we have: $P(\overline{\sigma}(p))$ has a success for $\mathbf{q}(t)$ that has a number $< p$. The relation $S \subset HU^{<\omega} \times HU$ defined by

$R(\alpha, t) :\equiv P(\alpha)$ has a success for $\mathbf{q}(t)$ with a number $<$ the length of $\alpha$ is the required decidable relation. ∎

Next, we blow this up to deal with $\Pi_1^1$.

**Lemma 7.34** *For every $\Pi_1^1$-relation $Q \subset HU$ there exists a decidable relation $R$ such that $Q(t) \Leftrightarrow \forall \sigma \in HU^{\mathbb{N}} \, \exists p \in \mathbb{N} \, R(\overline{\sigma}(p), t)$.*

**Proof.** By a Skolemization-procedure, eliminate all universal quantifiers over terms in the prefix of the $\Pi_1^1$-definition of $Q$ in favor of universal quantifiers over functions. E.g., replace $\exists s \forall t \, S(s, t)$ by: $\forall \tau \exists s \, S(s, \tau(nr(s)))$. If it is not clear that these expressions are equivalent, replace them by their negations and note that $\forall s \exists t \, \neg S(s, t)$ is equivalent to: $\exists \tau \forall s \, \neg S(s, \tau(nr(s)))$.

Next, contract similar quantifiers. E.g., replace $\exists s \exists t \, S(s, t)$ by $\exists p \, S(tm(j_1(p)), tm(j_2(n))$; and replace $\exists \sigma \exists \tau \, S(\sigma, \tau)$ by $\exists v \, S(\lambda n.v(2n), \lambda n.v(2n + 1))$.

Eventually, find that $Q$ can be defined by one universal function quantification applied to a (by Church's Thesis) $\Sigma_1^0$-relation. Now, apply the previous lemma. ∎

A *prefix tree* is a tree $T$ the nodes of which are finite sequences with the empty sequence as root, where $\alpha = (a_1, \ldots, a_n)$ is by definition a child of $\beta = (b_1, \ldots, b_m)$ if $n = m + 1$ and for $i = 1, \ldots, m$, $a_i = b_i$; that is, $\alpha$ extends $\beta$ by one element. In order that such a set $T$ satisfies the defining condition of trees, it is necessary that any sequence extended by an element of $T$ is in $T$ too.

Assume that $Q \subset HU$ is a $\Pi_1^1$ relation. By the previous lemma, it can be rendered thus:

$$Q(t) \Longleftrightarrow \forall \sigma \exists p \, R(\overline{\sigma}(p), t)$$

with a decidable $R$, ultimately obtained by the proof of Lemma 7.33, and hence monotone in its relation argument (Lemma 7.27). Define the relation $\prec$ on finite sequences by $\alpha \prec \beta :\equiv \beta = \alpha | Dom(\beta)$, i.e.: $\alpha$ extends $\beta$. Note that, by monotonicity,

$$\alpha \prec \beta \wedge R(\beta, t) \Longrightarrow R(\alpha, t).$$

Define $T_t := \{\alpha | \neg R(\alpha, t)\}$. Then by contraposition

$$\alpha \prec \beta \wedge \alpha \in T_t \Longrightarrow \beta \in T_t.$$

Hence, $T_t$ is a prefix tree for every $t \in HU$.

The following is the required normal form result.

**Theorem 7.35 (Kleene)** *For every $\Pi_1^1$-relation $Q \subset HU$ there exists a decidable relation $R \subset HU^{<\omega} \times HU$ such that* *(i)* $\mathcal{T}_t := \{\alpha | \neg R(\alpha, t)\}$ *is a prefix tree for every* $t \in HU$,

*(ii)* $Q(t)$ *holds iff* $\mathcal{T}_t$ *is well-founded.*

**Proof.** Let $R$ be given by the previous discussion. Then (i) is clear.

(ii) $\Rightarrow$. If $\prec$ is not well-founded on $\mathcal{T}_t$, choose $\alpha_0 \succ \alpha_1 \succ \alpha_2 \succ \ldots$ through $\mathcal{T}_t$. Let $\sigma := \bigcup_n \alpha_n$. Then $\forall p \neg R(\overline{\sigma}(p), t)$, hence $\neg Q(t)$.

(ii) $\Leftarrow$. If $\neg Q(t)$, then for some $\sigma$ we have $\forall p \neg R(\overline{\sigma}(p), t)$. Then $\overline{\sigma}(0) \succ \overline{\sigma}(1) \succ \overline{\sigma}(2) \succ \ldots$ constitutes an infinite branch through $\mathcal{T}_t$, and so $\mathcal{T}_t$ is not well-founded. ∎

### 7.3.3   Well-founded Part

Next, the normal form result 7.35 is transformed into one involving inductive definability, so as to connect it with (complements of) greatest fixed points.

Let $\prec$ be a binary relation on a set $\mathcal{T}$.

$V \subset \mathcal{T}$ is a $(\prec\text{-})initial$ of $\mathcal{T}$ iff $\forall \alpha \in V \,\forall \beta \prec \alpha \,[\beta \in V]$.

**Definition 7.36** $Wf(\mathcal{T}, \prec)$, the *well-founded part* of $\mathcal{T}$ (relative to $\prec$), is the union of all initials of $\mathcal{T}$ on which $\prec$ is well-founded. ∎

**Lemma 7.37** $Wf(\mathcal{T}, \prec)$ *is the largest well-founded initial of* $\mathcal{T}$.

**Proof.** Immediate from Exercise 7.27. ∎

**Lemma 7.38** *Define the monotone operator* $\Phi : \mathcal{P}(\mathcal{T}) \to \mathcal{P}(\mathcal{T})$ *by* $\Phi(X) := \{\alpha \in \mathcal{T} \mid \forall \beta \prec \alpha [\beta \in X]\}$. *Then* $\Phi{\uparrow} = Wf(\mathcal{T}, \prec)$. 

**Proof.** Exercise 7.28. ∎

Recall the notion of co-definability from Definition 7.32. The connection with well-founded parts and co-definability is made in the next result.

**Theorem 7.39** *Assume that* $\mathcal{T} \subset HU$ *and* $\prec \; \subset HU^2$. *Suppose that the program* $P$ *co-defines* $\mathcal{T}$ *and the complement of* $\prec$ *in the symbols* $nt$ *and* $pr$, *respectively. Then addition of the following two rules*

*(i)* $wf(\alpha) \leftarrow pr(\beta, \alpha), wf(\beta)$

*(ii)* $wf(\alpha) \leftarrow nt(\alpha)$

*produces a program* $Q$ *that co-defines* $Wf(\mathcal{T}, \prec)$ *in* $wf$.

**Proof.** Let $T$ and $S$ be the immediate consequence operators associated with $P$ resp. $Q$. Defining $\Phi(X) := \{\alpha \in \mathcal{T} \mid \forall \beta \prec \alpha \,[\beta \in X]\}$, by 7.38 we have that $Wf(\mathcal{T}, \prec) = \Phi{\uparrow}$. Therefore, we have to establish the equivalence

$$\alpha \in \Phi{\uparrow} \Longleftrightarrow wf(\alpha) \notin S{\downarrow}.$$

$\Longrightarrow$ Put $\Gamma := \{\alpha \mid wf(\alpha) \notin S\downarrow\}$. We show that $\Phi\uparrow \subset \Gamma$. We have the following equivalences.

$\alpha \in \Gamma$

$\qquad \Longleftrightarrow wf(\alpha) \notin S\downarrow$

$\qquad \Longleftrightarrow \neg\exists\beta\,[pr(\beta,\alpha), wf(\beta) \in S\downarrow] \wedge nt(\alpha) \notin S\downarrow$

$\qquad\qquad$ (by the $wf$-rules, since $S\downarrow$ is a fixed point)

$\qquad \Longleftrightarrow \neg\exists\beta\,[pr(\beta,\alpha) \in T\downarrow \wedge wf(\beta) \in S\downarrow] \wedge nt(\alpha) \notin T\downarrow$

$\qquad\qquad$ (on the $P$-language, $Q$ and $P$ behave similarly)

$\qquad \Longleftrightarrow \neg\exists\beta\,[\beta \prec \alpha \wedge wf(\beta) \in S\downarrow] \wedge \alpha \in T$

$\qquad\qquad$ (by assumption on $P$)

$\qquad \Longleftrightarrow \forall\beta \prec \alpha\,[wf(\beta) \notin S\downarrow] \wedge \alpha \in T$

$\qquad\qquad$ (by logic)

$\qquad \Longleftrightarrow \alpha \in \Phi(\Gamma)$

$\qquad\qquad$ (by definition of $\Phi$ and $\Gamma$).

So, $\Gamma$ is a fixed point of $\Phi$, and it follows that $\Phi\uparrow \subset \Gamma$.

$\Longleftarrow$ This part uses ordinals and the downward fixed point hierarchy. It clearly suffices to show that, for every ordinal $\xi$, we have

$$wf(\alpha) \notin S\downarrow\xi \Rightarrow \alpha \in \Phi\uparrow.$$

This is accomplished by induction with respect to $\xi$. The cases $\xi = 0$ and $\xi$ a limit are unproblematic. For the successor-step, note the following equivalences and implications.

$wf(\alpha) \notin S\downarrow(\xi+1)$

$\qquad \Longleftrightarrow wf(\alpha) \notin S(S\downarrow\xi)$

$\qquad\qquad$ (by definition of the fixed point hierarchy)

$\qquad \Longleftrightarrow \neg\exists\beta\,[pr(\beta,\alpha), wf(\beta) \in S\downarrow\xi] \wedge nt(\alpha) \notin S\downarrow\xi$

$\qquad\qquad$ (by the $wf$-rules)

$\qquad \Longleftrightarrow \neg\exists\beta\,[pr(\beta,\alpha) \in T\downarrow\xi \wedge wf(\beta) \in S\downarrow\xi] \wedge nt(\alpha) \notin T\downarrow\xi$

$\qquad\qquad$ (since $pr$ and $nt$ belong to the $P$-language)

$\qquad \Longleftrightarrow \forall\beta\,[pr(\beta,\alpha) \in T\downarrow\xi \Rightarrow wf(\beta) \notin S\downarrow\xi] \wedge nt(\alpha) \notin T\downarrow\xi$

$\qquad\qquad$ (by logic)

$\qquad \Longrightarrow \forall\beta\,[\beta \prec \alpha \Rightarrow wf(\beta) \notin S\downarrow\xi] \wedge \alpha \in T$

$\qquad\qquad$ (we have $\beta \prec \alpha \Leftrightarrow pr(\beta,\alpha) \in T\downarrow \Rightarrow pr(\beta,\alpha) \in T\downarrow\xi$;

$\qquad\qquad$ and $nt(\alpha) \notin T\downarrow\xi \Rightarrow nt(\alpha) \notin T\downarrow \Leftrightarrow \alpha \in T$)

$\qquad \Longrightarrow \forall\beta\,[\beta \prec \alpha \Rightarrow \beta \in \Phi\uparrow] \wedge \alpha \in T$

$\qquad\qquad$ (by inductive hypothesis on $\xi$)

$\qquad \Longleftrightarrow \alpha \in \Phi(\Phi\uparrow) = \Phi\uparrow$

$\qquad\qquad$ (by definition of $\Phi$).

## Exercises

**7.27** Show: a union of well-founded initials of $T$ is well-founded. Give a simple example showing that a union of well-founded subsets of $T$ need not be well-founded.

**7.28** Prove Lemma 7.38.

**7.29** With reference to Lemma 7.38, show that the closure ordinal of $\Phi$ (the least $\xi$ such that $\Phi \uparrow \xi = \Phi \uparrow (\xi + 1)$) is equal to the height of $Wf(T, \prec)$.

### 7.3.4   Co-defining $\Pi_1^1$-Relations

**Theorem 7.40** *Suppose that $A \subset HU$ and $P$ are such that*

*(i)  $t \in A$ iff $\prec$ is well-founded on $T_t := \{\alpha \mid R(\alpha, t)\}$,*
*(ii)  $P$ co-defines $R$ and the complement of $\prec$ in nr resp. pr,*
*(iii)  $P$ co-defines the complement of $R$ in $r$.*

*Then addition of the following rules*

*(i)  $wf(\alpha, t) \leftarrow pr(\beta, \alpha), wf(\beta, t)$*
*(ii)  $wf(\alpha, t) \leftarrow nr(\alpha, t)$*
*(iii)  $a(t) \leftarrow r(\alpha, t), wf(\alpha, t)$*

*produces a program $Q$ that co-defines $A$ in $a$.*

**Proof.** For every $t$, define $\Phi_t : \mathcal{P}(T_t) \to \mathcal{P}(T_t)$ by $\Phi_t(X) := \{\alpha \in T_t \mid \forall \beta \prec \alpha \, [\beta \in X]\}$. Then $\Phi_t \uparrow = Wf(T_t, \prec)$. Therefore, $T_t$ is well-founded iff $T_t \subset \Phi_t \uparrow$. It follows that $t \in A \Leftrightarrow T_t \subset \Phi_t \uparrow$. By Theorem 7.39 (adding the parameter $t$), the $wf$-rules co-define the relation $\alpha \in \Phi_t \uparrow$ in $wf$.

Let $U$ be the operator associated with $Q$. We have the following equivalences:
$a(t) \notin U \downarrow$

$\quad \Longleftrightarrow \neg \exists \alpha \, [r(\alpha, t), wf(\alpha, t) \in U \downarrow]$
$\qquad$ (by the third rule, since $U \downarrow$ is a fixed point)
$\quad \Longleftrightarrow \forall \alpha \, [r(\alpha, t) \in U \downarrow \Rightarrow wf(\alpha, t) \notin U \downarrow]$
$\qquad$ (by logic)
$\quad \Longleftrightarrow \forall \alpha \, [R(\alpha, t) \Rightarrow \alpha \in \Phi_t \uparrow]$
$\qquad$ (since $Q$ co-defines $\alpha \in \Phi_t \uparrow$ in $wf$)
$\quad \Longleftrightarrow T_t \subset \Phi_t \uparrow$
$\qquad$ (by definition of $T$)
$\quad \Longleftrightarrow t \in A$
$\qquad$ (as was indicated at the beginning of the proof).  ∎

**Corollary 7.41** *Every $\Pi_1^1$-relation is co-defined by some program.*

**Proof.** By Corollary 7.22, decidable relations can be defined by determinate programs. Therefore, decidable relations are co-definable. Now use the Kleene normal form and the previous theorem. ∎

An ordinal is *recursive* if it is the height of a well-founded decidable prefix tree $(\mathcal{T}, \prec)$.

**Exercise**

**7.30** Show: every recursive ordinal is the height of a downward fixed point hierarchy. *Hint.* Use Exercise 7.29.

The least non-recursive ordinal is denoted by $\omega_1^{CK}$ (Church-Kleene-$\omega_1$). This is a countable ordinal since there are only countably many recursive ordinals. It is known that the height of the downward fixed point hierarchy of a program $P$ is a recursive ordinal iff $T_P \downarrow$ is hyperarithmetical. Since there are non-hyperarithmetical $\Pi_1^1$-sets, it follows that some downward fixed point hierarchies have height equal to $\omega_1^{CK}$.

## 7.4 Notes

A beautiful recent reference on recursion theory is [Odifreddi 89].

The notion of determinateness, Corollary 7.22 and the result from Exercise 7.21 are from [Blair 82]. The proof of 7.22 given, involving the R6'-implementation of the $\mu$-operator, is from [Doets a].

The notions of (weak) recurrency and boundedness and the related exercises are from [Bezem 93], which also contains the strengthening of Corollary 7.22 that total recursive functions can be computed by recurrent programs. For work that extends Bezem's to termination of Prolog programs, the reader is referred to [Apt/Pedreschi 91], which also contains an elaborated solution for Exercise 7.19.

Corollary 7.41 and Exercise 7.30 are from [Blair 82]; another reference for the first result is [Kunen 87]. The details of the proof given here are taken from [Doets 92].

# 8 Negation

## 8.1 Introduction

According to a well-known slogan, *Algorithm* equals *Logic* plus *Control*. The ideal of logic programming is to write programs directly in logic so as to have a clear-cut declarative interpretation, immediately available to the practical programmer, and to leave the control to the implementation of the interpreter. This ideal is satisfactorily realized for the case of positive programs and queries dealt with in Chapter 5. The way in which logic programming makes use of negation destroys this simple picture. This chapter discusses only one of the many approaches to the semantics of negation in logic programming. Unfortunately, this is a semantics that departs from the classical, 2-valued one. Consequently, it can be doubted whether it is of much use to the practical programmer. And even then, it is far from adequate in a lot of cases. However, the recent result covered in Section 8.7 indicates that maybe things might not be as bad as they look.

We start with some motivating remarks. Recall the introductory discussion in Section 6.1. The set-up of logic programming with positive programs and queries from Chapter 5 is rather weak in some respects. In particular, there are cases where one would like to be able to infer negative information from a program. There are two a priori solutions to overcome this deficiency. The first solution is to use all of first-order logic. This still has the clear-cut declarative interpretation given by the Tarski-semantics from Chapter 3. Unfortunately, first-order theorem-proving procedures (such as the notion of resolution as treated in that chapter) are not very well-behaved and "combinatorial explosions" are common. At the other end of the scale of possibilities is using positive programs in combination with queries in which negative literals are allowed. Chapter 6 contains an overview of some of the semantical issues raised in that context. If one is not prepared to add some essential derivation rule next to the one of resolution, then a somewhat naive but practical way to treat negative literals is to use negation as (finite) failure. This is what happens in Prolog, and what this chapter is about.

The allowance of negative literals in queries calls for a redefinition of this notion.

**Definition 8.1** A (*general*) *query* is a finite sequence of literals. ∎

From the procedural standpoint, the following generalization now seems only a minor one, since resolving a general query using a general rule will produce a general query again.

**Definition 8.2** A (*general*) *rule* is an expression $A \leftarrow M$, where $A$ is an atom (the *head*) and $M$ is a (general) query (the *body*); a (*general*) *program* is a finite set of such rules. ∎

Conceived of as a clause, that is, a disjunction of literals, a general rule is thus a clause with one designated positive literal, its head. Extending the terminology from Chapter 5, we go on calling such rules *definite*. Programs and queries in the old sense from now on will be called *positive*. Note that a clause with more than one positive literal can be written as a rule in more than one way; we shall consider these as *different* rules.

It seems now rather straightforward to extend linear resolution to the new context with general queries and positive rules, to resolve positive literals using resolution, and to handle the negative ones using negation as finite failure. This is the "procedural" side of the coin. However, it is sensible to ask what is being established exactly by following this recipe; that is, what about the "declarative" aspects of negation as finite failure?

It turns out that this question has no straightforward answer. Compare the situation for SLD discussed in Chapter 5. For positive programs $P$ and queries $C$, if $\alpha$ is a computed answer substitution for $C$, then (soundness) $P \models C\alpha$, equivalently: $C\alpha \subset M_P$. However, negative literals never follow from a program (the largest Herbrand model $HB$ always is a model), and a general program does not need to have a least Herbrand model.

To see exactly what can be generalized, assume that $P$ is a general program. With it, we still can associate the immediate consequence operator $T_P$ over the space of Herbrand models, defined by $T_P(X) := \{A \in HB \mid \text{for some } C \subset X, A \leftarrow C \text{ is ground instance of a } P\text{-rule}\}$. We still have that the Herbrand models of $P$ coincide with the pre-fixed points of $T_P$. However, existence of a *least* pre-fixed point needs monotonicity of the operator, and operators corresponding to *general* programs usually will not be monotone.

**Examples.** Consider the program consisting of the rule $A \leftarrow \neg A$. Now, $\emptyset \subset \{A\}$. However, if $T$ is the operator of the program, then $T(\emptyset) = \{A\} \not\subset \emptyset = T(\{A\})$. $T$ has no fixed point; the completion of the program has no model. (It does have a least Herbrand model though.)

Another example: consider the program consisting of the rule $A \leftarrow \neg B$. There are *two* minimal Herbrand models, $\{A\}$ and $\{B\}$, but there is no *least* one.                                     ∎

A more promising idea is the one from Chapter 6, to use $comp(P)$ as the "meaning" of $P$ ($comp(P)$ still defined by the procedure from Definition 6.19), and try to establish that if $\alpha$ is a computed answer substitution for $C$, then $comp(P) \models C\alpha$. This soundness result indeed will hold (Corollary 8.29). However, there is a more faithful, 3-valued, semantics for general logic programs, which preserves the least fixed point-idea as well.

The rest of this chapter is planned as follows. Section 8.2 defines SLDNF-resolution, which extends SLD-resolution by implementing the negation of finite failure rule. Section 8.3 explains the 3-valued semantics for general programs and queries (and, indeed, for all of first-order logic); Section 8.4 discusses the consequence operator and its fixed point hierarchy in the 3-valued setting. Soundness of SLDNF-resolution with respect to this semantics is proved in Section 8.5; this result extends the soundness of negation-as-failure theorem (in Corollary 6.20 and Exercise 6.17). Finally, Section 8.6 contains technical material preparing for Section 8.7, which contains what is probably the strongest known completeness result on SLDNF.

## 8.2  Negation Implemented: SLDNF

We start with four preliminary definitions, introducing a number of auxiliary notions and simultaneously expanding a couple of old ones to the present context.

**Definition 8.3**

(i) The query $C$ *resolves to $D$ via $\alpha$ with respect to* $\Sigma$, or: $\xrightarrow{\alpha} D$ is a *resolvent of $C$* with respect to $\Sigma$, notation: $C \xrightarrow{\alpha} D$ $(\Sigma)$, if

  *either*: $\Sigma = (A, R)$, and $C \xrightarrow{\alpha} D$ $(A, R)$ in the sense of Definition 5.19 (the presence of negative literals here is no obstacle),

  *or*: $\Sigma$ is (an occurrence of) a negative literal in $C$, $\alpha = \epsilon$, and $D = C - \{\Sigma\}$ is obtained from $C$ by removing $\Sigma$.

(ii) As before (Definition 5.26), the transition $C \xrightarrow{\alpha} D$ $(\Sigma)$ *releases* the variables from $Var(C\alpha) - Var(D)$. ∎

**Definition 8.4** A (finite or infinite) sequence $C_0 \xrightarrow{\alpha_1} \cdots \xrightarrow{\alpha_n} C_n \xrightarrow{\alpha_{n+1}} \cdots$ of resolution steps in the previous sense is a *pseudo-derivation* if condition [ † ] of Definition 5.28 is obeyed, that is, no variable released at some step occurs in the resultant of a later one. ∎

Intuitively, an SLDNF-derivation is a pseudo-derivation in which the deletion of negative literals $\neg A$ (8.3(i)) is justified by means of a subsidiary (finitely failed SLDNF-) tree for $A$. Success or failure of a tree derives from markers on its leaves, as follows.

**Definition 8.5** A tree is called

- *successful* if it has a leaf marked as *success*,
- *finitely failed* if it is finite and all its leaves are marked as *failed*. ∎

In the sequel we consider *systems* of trees, which are naturally called *forests*.

**Definition 8.6** A *forest* is a system $\mathcal{T} = (\mathcal{T}, T, subs)$ where

- $\mathcal{T}$ is a set of trees,
- $T$ is an element of $\mathcal{T}$ called the *main* tree,
- *subs* is a function that, to some nodes of trees in $\mathcal{T}$, assigns a ("subsidiary") tree from $\mathcal{T}$.

Viewing *subs* as contributing a special type of edge, a *path* in $\mathcal{T}$ is a (finite or infinite) sequence of nodes $C_0, \ldots, C_i, \ldots$ such that for all $i$, $C_{i+1}$ either is a child of $C_i$ in some tree in $\mathcal{T}$ or it is the root of the tree $subs(C_i)$. ∎

Thus a forest is a special directed graph with two types of edges: the "usual" ones stemming from the tree structures, and the ones connecting a node with the root of a subsidiary tree. We shall consider only forests that are outgrowths of their main tree, and the directed graph of which is a tree as well.

After these preliminaries, we now come to the main definition. An SLDNF-tree is a special type of forest built as a limit of certain finite forests: *pre-SLDNF-trees*.

**Definition 8.7** A *pre-SLDNF-tree* (relative to some program) is a forest, the nodes of which are (possibly marked) queries (or pairs $\xrightarrow{\alpha} D$) of (possibly marked) literals. For queries, there are markers *failed* and *success*; for literals, the marker *selected*. The function *subs* assigns to nodes containing a *selected* negative literal $\neg A$ a tree in $\mathcal{T}$ with root $A$. The class of pre-SLDNF-trees is defined inductively:

- For every query $C$, the forest consisting of the main tree with the single node $C$ is an (*initial*) pre-SLDNF-tree,
- If $\mathcal{T}$ is a pre-SLDNF-tree, then any *extension* of $\mathcal{T}$ is a pre-SLDNF-tree.

Here, an *extension* of a pre-SLDNF-tree $\mathcal{T}$ is obtained by (simultaneously) performing the following actions for every non-empty query $C$ that is an unmarked leaf in some tree $T \in \mathcal{T}$.

First, if no literal in $C$ is marked yet as *selected*, then mark one as *selected*. Let $L$ be the (now or at some earlier stage) selected literal of $C$.

- $L$ is positive.

  - No rule of the program is applicable to $L$.

    Then $C$ is marked as *failed*.

  - Otherwise.

    Then for every rule $R$ of the program which is applicable to $L$, choose one resolvent $\xrightarrow{\alpha} D$ of $C$ with respect to $L$ and $R$ and add this resolvent as child of $C$ in $T$. These resolvents are to be chosen in such a way that branches through $T$ remain pseudo-derivations. (This is possible by a straightforward extension of Lemma 5.29.)

- $L = \neg A$ is negative.

  - $subs(C)$ is undefined.

    Then a new tree $T'$ with the single node $A$ is added to $\mathcal{T}$ and $subs(C)$ is set to $T'$.

– $subs(C)$ is defined and successful, and the successive specializations towards at least one success of $subs(C)$ compose to a substitution $\alpha$ such that $A\alpha$ is a variant of $A$.

Then $C$ is marked as *failed*.

– $subs(C)$ is defined and finitely failed.

Then the resolvent $\xrightarrow{\epsilon} (C - \{L\})$ of $C$ is added as the only child of $C$ in $T$. Additionally, all empty queries are marked as *success*. ∎

Note that if no tree in $T$ has unmarked leaves, then trivially $T$ is an extension of itself, and the extension process becomes stationary.

One detail in the previous definition may be puzzling: the condition, in the case of a negative literal $L = \neg A$ being selected in $C$, that $C$ is marked failed when $subs(C)$ contributes a computed answer substitution $\alpha$ such that $A\alpha$ is a *variant* of $A$. Without the latter condition, the resolution notion becomes unsound in the sense that negations of finitely failing queries no longer follow from the completion of the program. Remarkably, most implementations of Prolog use the unsound version!

**Example.** Consider the rule $p(a) \leftarrow$ and the query $\neg p(x)$. The subsidiary tree for $p(x)$ succeeds with computed answer substitution $\{x/a\}$. If we would not mind $p(a)$ not being a variant of $p(x)$, then we consequently should consider $\neg p(x)$ as failing. However, $\neg\neg p(x)$ does not follow logically from the completion of this rule. (Consider the model over $\{a, b\}$ in which $p$ is interpreted as $\{a\}$.) ∎

Examples such as these can also be avoided by requiring that negative literals may be selected *only* if they are *ground*. This restriction is usually taken to be part of the definition of SLDNF, and what we are defining via Definition 8.7 is called SLDNF$E$ (SLDNF *extended*). However, it may happen that, somewhere in the resolution process, a query arises containing only negative literals that are non-ground. This is called *floundering*. One problem with floundering is that the question whether it will occur for a given initial query is (in general) undecidable. The condition of *allowedness* on programs and queries (Definition 8.46) is a severe one, avoiding floundering.

Since every pre-SLDNF-tree is a tree with two types of edges between possibly marked nodes, the concepts of *inclusion* between such trees and of *limit* of a growing sequence of such trees have a clear meaning.

**Definition 8.8**

- An *SLDNF-tree* for $C$ is the limit of a sequence $T_0, \ldots, T_i, \ldots$ such that $T_0$ is the initial pre-SLDNF-tree, the main tree of which consists of $C$ only, and for all $i$, $T_{i+1}$ is an extension of $T_i$.

- A (pre-)SLDNF-tree is called *successful* (resp. *finitely failed*) if its main tree is successful (resp. *finitely failed*).
- An SLDNF-tree is called *finite* if it has no infinite path.                                        ∎

Finally, we define the concept of SLDNF-derivation.

**Definition 8.9** A *(pre-) SLDNF-derivation for* $C$ is a pseudo-derivation through the main tree of a (pre-) SLDNF-tree $\mathcal{T}$ for $C$ together with the set of all trees in $\mathcal{T}$ whose roots are path-connected with the nodes of this pseudo-derivation.
An SLDNF-derivation is called *finite* if all paths through it are finite.                              ∎

It is clear now how to define the notion of a computed answer substitution.

**Definition 8.10** Consider a pseudo-derivation through the main tree of a (pre-) SLDNF-tree for $C$ that ends with the empty query. Let $\alpha_1, \ldots, \alpha_n$ be the consecutive specializations along this pseudo-derivation. Then $(\alpha_1 \cdots \alpha_n)|C$ is called a *computed answer substitution (c.a.s.)* of $C$.                                                                                              ∎

**Examples.** We illustrate the definitions by depicting some SLDNF-trees. In them, horizontal arrows are used for the edges contributed by *subs*.
(i) $P = \{A \leftarrow A\}$. The only SLDNF-tree for $\neg A$ has then the following form.

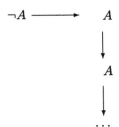

(ii) $P = \{A \leftarrow \neg A\}$. There is only one SLDNF-tree for $A$:

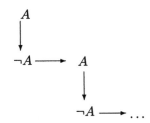

(iii) According to our definition, the construction of a subsidiary tree can go on forever even if the information about its "status" has already been passed to the main tree. The following general program illustrates this point.

$P = \{A \leftarrow \neg B,\ B \leftarrow,\ B \leftarrow B\}$. The only SLDNF-tree for $A$ looks as follows:

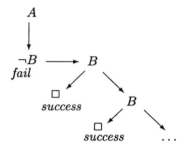

Here the subsidiary tree with the root $B$ grows forever. However, once an extension of this subsidiary tree becomes successful, then in the next extension the node $\neg B$ of the main tree is marked as *failed*. Consequently, the SLDNF-tree for $A$ is finitely failed even though it is not finite.  ∎

Pre-SLDNF-trees may keep growing forever. However, when the resulting SLDNF-tree is successful or finitely failed, this fact becomes apparent after a finite number of steps. More precisely, we have the following result.

**Theorem 8.11**

 (i) *Every pre-SLDNF-tree is finite.*

 (ii) *Every SLDNF-tree is the limit of a unique sequence of pre-SLDNF-trees.*

 (iii) *If the SLDNF-tree $\mathcal{T}$ is the limit of the sequence $\mathcal{T}_0, \ldots, \mathcal{T}_i, \ldots$, then:*

> (a) *$\mathcal{T}$ is successful and yields $\tau$ as c.a.s. iff some $\mathcal{T}_i$ is successful and yields $\tau$ as c.a.s.,*
>
> (b) *$\mathcal{T}$ is finitely failed iff some $\mathcal{T}_i$ is finitely failed.*

**Proof.**

(i) Obvious.

(ii) The only way in which two extensions of the same pre-SLDNF tree can become different is by the selection of different literals in a non-empty node. But this selection is prescribed by the SLDNF-tree that is the limit of the pre-SLDNF trees.

(iii) ($\Rightarrow$) A pseudo-derivation of the main tree of $\mathcal{T}$ ending in □, resp. a finitely failed main tree of $\mathcal{T}$, consists of finitely many, possibly marked, nodes. Each of these nodes (markings included) belongs to some $\mathcal{T}_i$ and the $\mathcal{T}_i$ with the largest $i$ is the desired pre-SLDNF-tree.

($\Leftarrow$) Each $\mathcal{T}_i$ is contained (markings included) in $\mathcal{T}$. ∎

Part (iii) of this theorem allows us to apply induction on the height of a successful resp. finitely failed pre-SLDNF-tree witnessing success resp. finite failure of a given SLDNF-tree.

In our definition of an SLDNF-tree, the selection rule is "incorporated" into the construction of an extension through the selection of literals in the last generated nodes. Clearly, this selection process can be separated from the construction of an extension. Let us drop the selection of literals in the last generated nodes from the definition of the pre-SLDNF tree. Thus, a *selection rule* is a function defined on pre-SLDNF-trees selecting a literal in every non-empty, non-marked leaf. In this set-up an SLDNF-tree is obtained by alternating the process of applying the selection rule with the process of extending the pre-SLDNF-tree.

There is a remarkably simple, direct way to inductively define the notions of success and finite failure. See the following definition. For the general principle behind a simultaneous inductive definition of this type, see Exercise 4.32.

**Definition 8.12** Let $P$ be a general program. The set $\mathbf{F} = \mathbf{F}_P$ of queries and the set $\mathbf{R} = \mathbf{R}_P$ of pairs $(C, \sigma)$ — $C$ a query and $\sigma$ a substitution for which $Dom(\sigma) \subset Var(C)$ — are defined by a simultaneous inductive definition as the least sets satisfying the following closure principles.

0) $\Box \mathbf{R}\epsilon$,

R+) if $C \xrightarrow{\alpha} D$ $(A, R)$, $R \in P$, $D\mathbf{R}\sigma$, and $Var(C\alpha) \cap Var(D\sigma) \subset Var(D)$, then $C\mathbf{R}(\alpha\sigma)|C$,

R−) if $A$ is an atom in $\mathbf{F}$ and $(C, C')\mathbf{R}\sigma$, then $(C, \neg A, C')\mathbf{R}\sigma$,

F+) if $A \in C$ and for every $R \in P$ that is applicable to $A$ there exist $\alpha$ and $D \in \mathbf{F}$ such that $C \xrightarrow{\alpha} D$ $(A, R)$, then $C \in \mathbf{F}$,

F−) if $A$ is an atom and $A\alpha$ is a variant of $A$ such that $A\mathbf{R}\alpha$, then $(C, \neg A, C') \in \mathbf{F}$. ∎

The intention here is of course that $\mathbf{R}$ is the set of pairs $(C, \sigma)$ such that $\sigma$ is a c.a.s. for $C$ and $\mathbf{F}$ is the set of queries $C$ that have a finitely failed SLDNF-tree. Note that *only* 0) and R+) already define the corresponding notions relative to SLD.

**Lemma 8.13** *If $C \in \mathbf{F}$ and $C \subset D$, then $D \in \mathbf{F}$.*

**Proof.** See Exercise 8.2. ∎

**Theorem 8.14** *If $C$ is a query, then*

- $CR\tau$ *iff $\tau$ is a c.a.s. for $C$,*
- $C \in \mathbf{F}$ *iff $C$ has a finitely failed SLDNF-tree.*

**Proof.** See Exercise 8.3. ∎

**Exercises**

**8.1** Extend Lemma 5.41 to the present context; that is, show: if $C \xrightarrow{\alpha} D$ $(A, R)$ and $\sigma$ is a c.a.s. for $D$ such that $Var(C\alpha) \cap Var(D\sigma) \subset Var(C)$, then $(\alpha\sigma)|Var(C)$ is a c.a.s. for $C$.

**8.2** Prove Lemma 8.13.

*Hint.* Straightforward induction using only clauses F+) and F−) of Definition 8.12.

**8.3** Prove Theorem 8.14.

**8.4** Show: if $C \in \mathbf{F}$, then $C\sigma \in \mathbf{F}$.

The following exercise illustrates a use of negation that most elegantly forces termination in a situation that does not directly seems to call for negative information.

**8.5** Let $R$ be a finite set of rules of the form $\mathbf{r}(s,t) \leftarrow$ with $s$ and $t$ being ground. $R$ defines the finite relation $r := \{(s,t) \mid \mathbf{r}(s,t) \leftarrow \, \in R\}$ on $HU$. To $R$, add the following rules.

$\quad \mathbf{q}(x,y) \leftarrow \mathbf{r}(x,y),$
$\quad \mathbf{q}(x,z) \leftarrow \mathbf{r}(x,y), \mathbf{q}(y,z).$

According to Exercise 4.34, these rules define the *transitive closure* $r^{tr}$ of $r$ in $\mathbf{q}$ (cf. Definition 1.9).

Assuming that $r$ contains a loop, give an example of an infinite derivation using these rules and the leftmost selection rule.

Computation of $r^{tr}$ avoiding infinite search can be done by the following trick. Define the ternary relation $S$ by

$S(s,t,l) :\equiv$ there is a sequence $s_0 = s, \ldots, s_{n+1} = t$ such that for $0 \le i \le n$, $r(s_i, s_{i+1})$, and $l$ is a finite sequence of elements of $HU$ not containing an element of $s_1, \ldots, s_n$. That is, there exists an $r$-path connecting $s$ with $t$ avoiding the elements of the list $l$. In particular then, $S(s,t,[\,])$ iff $r^{tr}(s,t)$.

Check that $S(s,u,l)$ holds iff: $r(s,u)$, or for some $t$ outside $l$: $r(s,t)$ and $S(t,u,[t|l])$.

This motivates the following rules defining $S$ (for the last two rules, see Exercise 4.58):

$\quad \mathbf{s}(x,z,v) \leftarrow \mathbf{r}(x,z)$
$\quad \mathbf{s}(x,z,v) \leftarrow \mathbf{r}(x,y), \neg member(y,v), \mathbf{s}(y,z,[y|v])$
$\quad member(x,[x|v]) \leftarrow$

$member(x, [y|v]) \leftarrow member(x, v)$.

Show that these rules do in fact define $S$ and that, moreover, no query $\mathbf{s}(x, y, [z_1, \ldots, z_n])$ starts an infinite derivation using the leftmost rule.

**8.6** Discuss the workings of the program EVEN2, made up of the following rules.

**even(o)** $\leftarrow$
**even(s$x$)** $\leftarrow \neg$**even($x$)** .

## 8.3   3-Valued Models

In the introduction to this chapter, we hinted at the problem of giving a satisfying semantics corresponding to the notion of SLDNF-resolution. The least Herbrand model-approach does not work in the context with negation. Consideration of 3-valued logic arises as follows. When given a query, the SLDNF-interpreter (on the basis of a given program) may return a computed answer substitution, it may halt with the answer NO, or it may return no answer at all, going on forever. The third truth value $\mathbf{u}$ for *undefined* allows for this third possibility. We shall see that this simple device is able to provide a rather natural semantics for SLDNF resolution.

**Definition 8.15** Let $J$ be an algebra. A *3-valued model over* $J$ is a function $\mathbf{M}$ : $HB^J \rightarrow \{\mathbf{t}, \mathbf{f}, \mathbf{u}\}$, mapping each $J$-ground atom to one of the three truth values $\mathbf{t}$, $\mathbf{f}$ and $\mathbf{u}$. ∎

An ordinary 2-valued model will be considered as a 3-valued model that never assumes the value $\mathbf{u}$.

The notion of 3-valued truth for sentences is defined using truth tables. These can be explained (not very accurately) as follows: the truth value of a complex expression is $\mathbf{t}$ (resp., $\mathbf{f}$) if, replacing the values $\mathbf{u}$ of atomic subexpressions by either $\mathbf{t}$ or $\mathbf{f}$ arbitrarily, always yields the classical truth value $\mathbf{t}$ (resp., $\mathbf{f}$) for the complex expression. Here is the formal definition that, in fact, doesn't mention $\mathbf{u}$ at all.

**Definition 8.16** Let $\mathbf{M}$ be a 3-valued model over the algebra $J$. We extend $\mathbf{M}$ to a function that maps $J$-sentences to truth values by the following "3-valued truth definition".

($\neg$)  $\mathbf{M}(\neg\varphi) = \mathbf{t}$ iff $\mathbf{M}(\varphi) = \mathbf{f}$
      $\mathbf{M}(\neg\varphi) = \mathbf{f}$ iff $\mathbf{M}(\varphi) = \mathbf{t}$,
($\wedge$)  $\mathbf{M}(\bigwedge \Phi) = \mathbf{t}$ iff for all $\varphi \in \Phi$, $\mathbf{M}(\varphi) = \mathbf{t}$
      $\mathbf{M}(\bigwedge \Phi) = \mathbf{f}$ iff for some $\varphi \in \Phi$, $\mathbf{M}(\varphi) = \mathbf{f}$,
($\vee$)  $\mathbf{M}(\bigvee \Phi) = \mathbf{t}$ iff for some $\varphi \in \Phi$, $\mathbf{M}(\varphi) = \mathbf{t}$
      $\mathbf{M}(\bigvee \Phi) = \mathbf{f}$ iff for all $\varphi \in \Phi$, $\mathbf{M}(\varphi) = \mathbf{f}$,

$(\forall)$ $\mathbf{M}(\forall x\varphi) = \mathbf{t}$ iff for all $a \in J$, $\mathbf{M}(\varphi\{x/a\}) = \mathbf{t}$
$\quad\quad$ $\mathbf{M}(\forall x\varphi) = \mathbf{f}$ iff for some $a \in J$, $\mathbf{M}(\varphi\{x/a\}) = \mathbf{f}$,
$(\exists)$ $\mathbf{M}(\exists x\varphi) = \mathbf{t}$ iff for some $a \in J$, $\mathbf{M}(\varphi\{x/a\}) = \mathbf{t}$
$\quad\quad$ $\mathbf{M}(\exists x\varphi) = \mathbf{f}$ iff for all $a \in J$, $\mathbf{M}(\varphi\{x/a\}) = \mathbf{f}$.

We shall not need $\rightarrow$. We *do* need $\leftrightarrow$ (but only to form completions of programs) and define 2-valued-style

$(\leftrightarrow)$ $\mathbf{M}(\varphi\leftrightarrow\psi) = \mathbf{t}$ iff $\mathbf{M}(\varphi) = \mathbf{M}(\psi)$
$\quad\quad$ $\mathbf{M}(\varphi\leftrightarrow\psi) = \mathbf{f}$ iff $\mathbf{M}(\varphi) \neq \mathbf{M}(\psi)$. $\quad\quad\quad\quad\quad\quad\quad\quad\quad\quad\quad\quad$ ∎

Thus, an equivalence never obtains the value $\mathbf{u}$.

For convenience, the propositional truth tables are summarized in the following table, which only contains the *binary* $\wedge$ and $\vee$:

| $\varphi$ | $\psi$ | $\neg\varphi$ | $\varphi \wedge \psi$ | $\varphi \vee \psi$ | $\varphi\leftrightarrow\psi$ |
|---|---|---|---|---|---|
| $\mathbf{t}$ | $\mathbf{t}$ | $\mathbf{f}$ | $\mathbf{t}$ | $\mathbf{t}$ | $\mathbf{t}$ |
| $\mathbf{t}$ | $\mathbf{f}$ | | $\mathbf{f}$ | $\mathbf{t}$ | $\mathbf{f}$ |
| $\mathbf{t}$ | $\mathbf{u}$ | | $\mathbf{u}$ | $\mathbf{t}$ | $\mathbf{f}$ |
| $\mathbf{f}$ | $\mathbf{t}$ | $\mathbf{t}$ | $\mathbf{f}$ | $\mathbf{t}$ | $\mathbf{f}$ |
| $\mathbf{f}$ | $\mathbf{f}$ | | $\mathbf{f}$ | $\mathbf{f}$ | $\mathbf{t}$ |
| $\mathbf{f}$ | $\mathbf{u}$ | | $\mathbf{f}$ | $\mathbf{u}$ | $\mathbf{f}$ |
| $\mathbf{u}$ | $\mathbf{t}$ | $\mathbf{u}$ | $\mathbf{u}$ | $\mathbf{t}$ | $\mathbf{f}$ |
| $\mathbf{u}$ | $\mathbf{f}$ | | $\mathbf{f}$ | $\mathbf{u}$ | $\mathbf{f}$ |
| $\mathbf{u}$ | $\mathbf{u}$ | | $\mathbf{u}$ | $\mathbf{u}$ | $\mathbf{t}$ |

**Definition 8.17** For $\mathbf{v} \in \{\mathbf{t}, \mathbf{f}, \mathbf{u}\}$, we say that $\varphi$ is $\mathbf{v}$ in $\mathbf{M}$ in case $\mathbf{M}(\varphi) = \mathbf{v}$. For $\mathbf{v} = \mathbf{t}$, we also use the shorthand $\mathbf{M}\models_3\varphi$ and say that $\mathbf{M}$ is a *3-valued model* of $\varphi$. By $\Sigma\models_3\varphi$ we understand that $\varphi$ is $\mathbf{t}$ in every 3-valued model of (all sentences in) $\Sigma$. $\quad$ ∎

Note that Definition 8.16 extends the clauses of the 2-valued case. Therefore, the following lemma holds.

**Lemma 8.18**

(i) If $\mathbf{M}$ is a 2-valued model and $\varphi$ a sentence, then $\mathbf{M}\models_3\varphi$ iff $\mathbf{M}\models\varphi$;

(ii) if $\Sigma\models_3\varphi$, then $\Sigma\models\varphi$. $\quad\quad\quad\quad\quad\quad\quad\quad\quad\quad\quad\quad\quad\quad\quad\quad\quad$ ∎

The following definition introduces a partial ordering $\leq$ between 3-valued models over the same algebra. $\mathbf{M} \leq \mathbf{N}$ means that $\mathbf{N}$ is obtained from $\mathbf{M}$ by changing some undefined values to either true or false.

**Definition 8.19** For 3-valued models $\mathbf{M}$, $\mathbf{N}$ over an algebra $J$, define $\mathbf{M} \leq \mathbf{N} :\equiv$ for all $J$-ground atoms $A$, if $\mathbf{M}(A) \neq \mathbf{u}$, then $\mathbf{N}(A) = \mathbf{M}(A)$. $\quad\quad\quad\quad\quad$ ∎

Earlier, we identified the 2-valued models over $J$ with their set of true $J$-ground atoms in $HB^J$. We now can identify a 3-valued model $\mathbf{M}$ over $J$ with the pair $(T_{\mathbf{M}}, F_{\mathbf{M}})$ of *disjunct* sets $T_{\mathbf{M}} := \{A \in HB^J \mid \mathbf{M}(A) = \mathbf{t}\}$ and $F_{\mathbf{M}} := \{A \in HB^J \mid \mathbf{M}(A) = \mathbf{f}\}$. Then we have that $\mathbf{M} \leq \mathbf{N}$ iff both $T_{\mathbf{M}} \subset T_{\mathbf{N}}$ and $F_{\mathbf{M}} \subset F_{\mathbf{N}}$.

The intuition behind the 3-valued semantics is brought out by the following lemma.

**Lemma 8.20** *If $\mathbf{M}$ and $\mathbf{N}$ are 3-valued models over the algebra $J$ such that $\mathbf{M} \leq \mathbf{N}$ and $\varphi$ is a $J$-sentence (not containing $\leftrightarrow$) that is $\mathbf{t}$ in $\mathbf{M}$, then $\varphi$ is also $\mathbf{t}$ in $\mathbf{N}$.*

**Proof.** See Exercise 8.9. ∎

### Exercises

**8.7** Produce a 3-valued truth table for $\rightarrow$ such that $(\varphi \rightarrow \psi) \leftrightarrow (\neg \varphi \vee \psi)$ is a 3-valued tautology.

Produce a 3-valued truth table for $\rightarrow$ such that $(\varphi \rightarrow \psi) \wedge (\psi \rightarrow \varphi)$ has the same truth table as $\varphi \leftrightarrow \psi$.

**8.8** Show that 3-valued logic has no *logical truths*; that is, there are no sentences $\varphi$ (not containing $\leftrightarrow$) such that $\models_3 \varphi$.
*Hint.* Consider a model that has all its relations identical $\mathbf{u}$.

**8.9** Prove Lemma 8.20.
*Hint.* Induction with respect to $\varphi$. Simultaneously, show that if a sentence is $\mathbf{f}$ in $\mathbf{M}$, then it is $\mathbf{f}$ in $\mathbf{N}$.

## 8.4  3-Valued Consequence Operator

The following definition generalizes the notion of immediate consequence operator to the 3-valued context.

**Definition 8.21** Let $J$ be an algebra and $P$ a program. The *3-valued consequence operator* $T3_P^J$ associated with $P$ maps 3-valued models over $J$ to 3-valued models over $J$, and is defined as follows. If $\mathbf{M}$ is a 3-valued model over $J$ and $A \in HB^J$, then

(i)  $T3_P^J(\mathbf{M})(A) = \mathbf{t}$ iff for some $J$-ground instance $A \leftarrow C$ of a $P$-rule, $\mathbf{M}(C) = \mathbf{t}$,
(ii) $T3_P^J(\mathbf{M})(A) = \mathbf{f}$ iff for all $J$-ground instances $A \leftarrow C$ of $P$-rules, $\mathbf{M}(C) = \mathbf{f}$

(as usual identifying a sequence $C$ with the conjunction of its elements).
We use the shorthand $T3_P$ for $T3_P^{HU}$. ∎

Note that, by this definition, no $A \in HB^J$ can receive *both* values $\mathbf{t}$ and $\mathbf{f}$ in $T3_P^J(\mathbf{M})$. So, $T3_P^J(\mathbf{M})$ is a well-defined 3-valued model over $J$ whenever $\mathbf{M}$ is one.

The following lemma says that the completion of a program still characterizes fixed points. (Compare Lemma 6.18.) It is this characterization that dictates the 2-valued truth table for equivalence.

**Lemma 8.22** *Let* $\mathbf{M}$ *be a 3-valued model over the algebra* $J$. *Then* $\mathbf{M}\models_3 comp(P)$ *iff* $T3_P^J(\mathbf{M}) = \mathbf{M}$.

**Proof.** Note that we have given $\leftrightarrow$ the *classical*, 2-valued semantics. ∎

The 3-valued consequence operator is monotone, but now in the sense of $\leq$:

**Lemma 8.23** *If* $\mathbf{M} \leq \mathbf{N}$, *then* $T3_P^J(\mathbf{M}) \leq T3_P^J(\mathbf{N})$.

**Proof.** See Exercise 8.10. ∎

The ordering of 3-valued models provides a natural notion of *limit* of an increasing sequence of models. If $(\mathbf{M}_\xi \mid \xi < \gamma)$ is a $\leq$-increasing sequence of 3-valued models over $J$ (i.e., if $\xi < \delta < \gamma$ implies $\mathbf{M}_\xi \leq \mathbf{M}_\delta$), then $\mathrm{Lim}_{\xi<\gamma}\mathbf{M}_\xi$ is the 3-valued model over $J$ that assigns a $J$-ground atom the value $\mathbf{t}$ (resp., $\mathbf{f}$) iff for some $\xi < \gamma$, $\mathbf{M}_\xi(A) = \mathbf{t}$ (resp., $\mathbf{f}$). Conceiving of models as pairs of sets, we clearly have that $\mathrm{Lim}_{\xi<\gamma}\mathbf{M}_\xi = (\bigcup_{\xi<\gamma} T_{\mathbf{M}_\xi}, \bigcup_{\xi<\gamma} F_{\mathbf{M}_\xi})$.

Now we can define the simultaneous analogue of both upward and downward fixed-point hierarchy for this setting.

**Definition 8.24** Let $J$ be an algebra and $P$ a general program. For every ordinal $\xi$, $T3_P^J\!\restriction\!\xi$ is the 3-valued model over $J$ recursively defined by

  (i) $T3_P^J\!\restriction\!0$ is identically $= \mathbf{u}$,
  (ii) $T3_P^J\!\restriction\!(\xi + 1) = T3_P^J(T3_P^J\!\restriction\!\xi)$,
  (iii) $T3_P^J\!\restriction\!\gamma = \mathrm{Lim}_{\xi<\gamma}T3_P^J\!\restriction\!\xi$ for limits $\gamma$.

We abbreviate: $T3_P\!\restriction\!\alpha := T3_P^{HU}\!\restriction\!\alpha$. ∎

By Lemma 8.23, the hierarchy of $T3_P^J\!\restriction\!\xi$ increases in the sense of $\leq$, and hence it must become stationary at some closure ordinal. (Compare Exercise 4.16.)

**Definition 8.25** $T3_P^J\!\uparrow = T3_P^J\!\restriction\!\kappa$, where $\kappa$ is the *closure ordinal* of the $T3_P^J$-hierarchy, that is, the least ordinal such that $T3_P^J\!\restriction\!(\kappa + 1) = T3_P^J\!\restriction\!\kappa$.
Abbreviating again, $T3_P\!\uparrow := T3_P^{HU}\!\uparrow$. ∎

Thus:

**Theorem 8.26** *The completion of a program has a least 3-valued model over any algebra.* ∎

**Example.** Once more, let $P$ consist of the one rule $A \leftarrow \neg A$. Note that $T3_P{\uparrow} = T3_P{\uparrow}0$. Note also that this is a $\leq$-*maximal* 3-valued model of $comp(P)$. Therefore, the truth value $\mathbf{u}$ is unavoidable in this case, and $comp(P)$ does not have any 2-valued model at all.                                                                         ∎

The following lemma shows that the present hierarchy neatly subsumes both the upward and the (complements of the) downward hierarchy in the context of positive programs.

**Lemma 8.27** *If $P$ is positive, then for $J$-ground atoms $A \in HB^J$:*

(i) $T3_P^J{\upharpoonright}\xi(A) = \mathbf{t}$ *iff* $A \in T_P^J{\upharpoonright}\xi$,

(ii) $T3_P^J{\upharpoonright}\xi(A) = \mathbf{f}$ *iff* $A \notin T_P^J{\upharpoonright}\xi$.

**Proof.** See Exercise 8.11.                                                        ∎

Conceiving of models as pairs of sets, note that Lemma 8.27 can be succinctly stated as: $T3_P^J{\upharpoonright}\xi = (T_P^J{\upharpoonright}\xi, HB^J - T_P^J{\upharpoonright}\xi)$.

By this lemma and the results of Chapter 7 (see Exercise 7.30), it follows that 3-valued hierarchies may close arbitrarily high up to the least non-recursive ordinal $\omega_1^{CK}$.

**Exercises**

**8.10** Prove Lemma 8.23.

**8.11** Prove Lemma 8.27.

**8.12** Show: if $P$ consists of $n$ rules that are ground, then $T3_P{\uparrow} = T3_P{\uparrow}(n+1)$.

## 8.5   Soundness

Completions of programs plus 3-valued semantics offer a sound interpretation of what is going on.

**Theorem 8.28 (Soundness)** *Let $P$ be a program and $C$ a query.*

(i) *If $\alpha$ is a computed answer substitution for $C$, then $comp(P) \models_3 \forall \bigwedge C\alpha$,*

(ii) *if $C$ has a finitely failed SLDNF-tree, then $comp(P) \models_3 \neg \exists \bigwedge C$.*

**Proof.** Simultaneous induction on the height of a pre-SLDNF-tree witnessing success or failure. Thus, assume that $\mathcal{T}$ is a pre-SLDNF-tree for $C$ with a main tree $T$ that either is successful or finitely failed. We distinguish a number of cases.

1. The height of $\mathcal{T}$ is 1. Then $C = \Box$. So, $\alpha = \epsilon$, and $comp(P) \models_3 \Box \epsilon$ is trivial.

Thus, suppose that the height of $\mathcal{T}$ is $> 1$. Then $C \neq \Box$.

2. Suppose that $T$ selects a positive literal $A$ in $C$.

(i) $T$ has a success leaf $\square$.

Suppose that $\xrightarrow{\alpha} D$ is the child of $C$ towards this success. By induction hypothesis (applied to the subtree with root $D$), $comp(P)\models_3 \forall \bigwedge D\beta$, where $\beta$ is the composition of the remaining substitutions towards the success. We need to show that $comp(P)\models_3 \forall \bigwedge C\alpha\beta$. Assume that $\mathbf{M}\models_3 comp(P)$ and let $\tau$ be an $\mathbf{M}$-assignment. Then $C\alpha\beta\tau \xrightarrow{\epsilon}_u D\beta\tau$ is an $\mathbf{M}$-ground resolution step. By assumption, $\mathbf{M}\models_3 \bigwedge D\beta\tau$. Thus, $\mathbf{M}\models_3 \bigwedge C\alpha\beta\tau$.

(ii) $T$ is finitely failed.

By induction hypothesis (applied to the subtrees the roots of which are the children of $C$), for every child $\xrightarrow{\alpha} D$ of $C$ in $T$, we have that $comp(P)\models_3 \neg\exists \bigwedge D$. We need to show that $comp(P)\models_3 \neg\exists \bigwedge C$. Fix $\mathbf{M}\models_3 comp(P)$ and let $\tau$ be an $\mathbf{M}$-assignment; we have to verify that $\mathbf{M}(\bigwedge C\tau) = \mathbf{f}$. Now if $\mathbf{M}(\bigwedge C\tau) \neq \mathbf{f}$, then in particular $\mathbf{M}(A\tau) \neq \mathbf{f}$. Since $\mathbf{M}\models_3 comp(P)$, some $\mathbf{M}$-ground resolvent of $A\tau$ is not $\mathbf{f}$ in $\mathbf{M}$. Use this to form an $\mathbf{M}$-ground resolution step $C\tau \xrightarrow{\epsilon}_u E$ with $E$ not $\mathbf{f}$ in $\mathbf{M}$. Lift this to a step $C \xrightarrow{\alpha} D$ in $T$. Then $D$ has the non-$\mathbf{f}$ instance $E$, contradicting $comp(P)\models_3 \neg\exists \bigwedge D$.

3. $T$ selects a negative literal $\neg A$ in $C$.

Note that, since $T$ is either successful or finitely failed, $C$ cannot be an unmarked leaf of $T$, and so $subs(C)$ necessarily is successful (yielding a c.a.s. $\alpha$ for $A$ such that $A$ and $A\alpha$ are variants) or finitely failed.

(i) $subs(C)$ is finitely failed.

Then $\xrightarrow{\epsilon} (C - \{\neg A\})$ is the child of $C$ in $T$. Now if $T$ is finitely failed, then by induction hypothesis $comp(P)\models_3 \neg\exists \bigwedge(C-\{\neg A\})$ and a fortiori we have $comp(P)\models_3 \neg\exists \bigwedge C$ as well. Thus, suppose that $T$ has a success. By induction hypothesis, $comp(P)\models_3 \forall \bigwedge(C - \{\neg A\})\alpha$, where $\alpha$ is the computed answer substitution corresponding to this success. Since $subs(C)$ is finitely failed, again by induction hypothesis $comp(P)\models_3 \neg\exists A$, and therefore we have $comp(P)\models_3 \neg\exists A\alpha$ as well. It follows that $comp(P)\models_3 \forall \bigwedge C\alpha$.

(ii) $subs(C)$ yields a computed answer substitution $\alpha$ for $A$ such that $A$ and $A\alpha$ are variants.

By induction hypothesis, $comp(P)\models_3 \forall A\alpha$; hence, $comp(P)\models_3 \forall A$ holds as well. A fortiori, $comp(P)\models_3 \neg\exists \bigwedge C$. ∎

Note that if, in case 3(ii) of the proof, we did not possess the information that $A\alpha$ and $A$ were variants, then we could have only concluded that $comp(P)\models_3 \neg\exists \bigwedge C\alpha$ but not that $comp(P)\models_3 \neg\exists \bigwedge C$.

Part (ii) of the following corollary generalizes the soundness of negation as failure result from Chapter 6.

**Corollary 8.29 (2-Valued Soundness)**

(i) *If $\alpha$ is a computed answer substitution for $C$, then $comp(P) \models \forall \bigwedge C\alpha$,*

(ii) *if $C$ has a finitely failed SLDNF-tree, then $comp(P) \models \neg \exists \bigwedge C$.*

**Proof.** Immediate from Theorem 8.28 and Lemma 8.18.                                           ∎

## 8.6   Saturation

This section contains model theoretic preliminaries needed for the next section. The reader primarily interested in the completeness result may well take Corollary 8.37 for granted and skip to the next section.

**Definition 8.30** Let $\Phi = (\varphi^i \mid i \in \mathbb{N})$ be a sequence of formulas $\varphi^i$ in finitely many free variables $x_1, \ldots x_k, y_1, \ldots, y_m$ and let $J$ be a (ordinary, 2-valued) model.

$J$ is called $\Phi$-*saturated* if for all assignments $\tau : \{y_1, \ldots, y_m\} \rightarrow J$, either some $\sigma \supseteq \tau$ exists such that for all $i$, $J \models \varphi^i \sigma$ —; that is, $\{\varphi^i \tau \mid i \in \mathbb{N}\}$ is satisfiable in $J$ —, or there exists $N \in \mathbb{N}$ such that for no $\sigma \supseteq \tau$, $J \models \bigwedge_{i<N} \varphi^i \sigma$ —; that is, $\{\varphi^i \tau \mid i < N\}$ is not satisfiable in $J$.

$J$ is *saturated* if it is $\Phi$-saturated for every sequence $\Phi$. $J$ is *recursively saturated* if it is $\Phi$-saturated for every computable sequence $\Phi$.                                           ∎

For the notion of computable sequence of formulas (and hence, of recursive saturation) to make sense, we require that the underlying language $\mathcal{L}$ is effectively enumerated as $\mathcal{L} = \{\sigma_i \mid i \in \mathbb{N}\}$. Moreover, the number of arguments of a relation or function symbol should be computable from its index in the enumeration.

**Remark 8.31** Note that in the context of Definition 8.30, $J$ is $\Phi$-saturated iff the following implication holds for all $\tau : \{y_1, \ldots, y_m\} \rightarrow J$ (where $\psi^i$ replaces $\neg\varphi^i$):

if $\forall \sigma \supseteq \tau \exists i \, J \models \psi^i \sigma$, then for some $N \in \mathbb{N}$: $\forall \sigma \supseteq \tau \exists i < N \, J \models \psi^i \sigma$.                 ∎

Recall the notion of elementary extension from Definition 3.42.

**Lemma 8.32**

(i) *Every model has a saturated elementary extension,*

(ii) *every countable model has a countable recursively saturated elementary extension.*

**Proof.** (i) Here is a sketch. Let $J$ be a model.

Using first-order compactness (more precisely, Exercise 3.21), construct an elementary chain

$$J_0 = J \prec J_1 \prec J_2 \prec \cdots$$

of models such that for every $n$, $\Phi = (\varphi^i \mid i \in \mathbb{N})$ a sequence in free variables $x_1, \ldots, x_k, y_1, \ldots, y_m$ and all $\tau : \{y_1, \ldots, y_m\} \rightarrow J_n$:

either $\{\varphi^i \tau \mid i \in \mathbb{N}\}$ is satisfiable in $J_{n+1}$,

or there exists an $N \in \mathbb{N}$ such that $\{\varphi^i \tau \mid i < N\}$ is not satisfiable in $J_n$.

The required model is the union of the $J_n$ (see Exercise 3.22).

(ii) Essentially the same construction is used. Since there are only countably many computable sequences, it is possible to keep all $J_i$ countable. ∎

The presence of the variables $y_1, \ldots, y_m$ in the formulas of the sequences $\Phi$ (cf. Definition 8.30) is responsible for the fact that the previous proofs require the construction of a *limit* structure. In their absence, the required model is produced by just one application of compactness. This special case in fact suffices for the application to completeness in the next section.

**Lemma 8.33** *Let $P$ be a program. For every formula $\varphi$, $i \in \mathbb{N}$ and $\mathbf{v} \in \{\mathbf{t}, \mathbf{f}, \mathbf{u}\}$ there exists a first-order formula $\varphi^{i,\mathbf{v}}$ (computable in $i$) in the algebraic language with the same free variables as $\varphi$ such that for every algebra $J$ and every $\sigma : Var(\varphi) \to J$, we have that: $J \models \varphi^{i,\mathbf{v}} \sigma$ iff $(T3_P^J \hspace{-0.15em}\upharpoonright\hspace{-0.15em} i)(\varphi\sigma) = \mathbf{v}$.*

**Proof.** (Compare Exercise 4.38.)

Let $L$ be the language of $P$. Let $\mathbf{r}$ be some $n$-ary relation symbol of $L$. We indicate how to construct the required formulas $\mathbf{r}(x_1, \ldots, x_n)^{i,\mathbf{t}}$ and $\mathbf{r}(x_1, \ldots, x_n)^{i,\mathbf{f}}$. Once this is done, the rest is rather easy. For $\varphi^{i,\mathbf{v}}$, where $\varphi$ is non-atomic and $\mathbf{v} = \mathbf{t}$ or $\mathbf{v} = \mathbf{f}$, we follow the calculations given by the 3-valued truth definition (keeping $i$ fixed). And of course for $\varphi^{i,\mathbf{u}}$ we can take $\neg\varphi^{i,\mathbf{t}} \wedge \neg\varphi^{i,\mathbf{f}}$.

For $i = 0$, put $\mathbf{r}(x_1, \ldots, x_n)^{i,\mathbf{t}} = \mathbf{r}(x_1, \ldots, x_n)^{i,\mathbf{f}} := \bot$.

The following move may be helpful in constructing the remaining formulas ($i > 0$). For every relation symbol $\mathbf{q}$ of $L$, add a new relation symbol $\sim\mathbf{q}$. This extends $L$ to $L^\sim$. Let $T3_P^J \hspace{-0.15em}\upharpoonright\hspace{-0.15em} \alpha$ be the 3-valued $L$-model which is the $\alpha$-th stage of the 3-valued hierarchy over $J$ generated by $P$. We transform $T3_P^J \hspace{-0.15em}\upharpoonright\hspace{-0.15em} \alpha$ into a 2-valued $L^\sim$-model $T2_P^J \hspace{-0.15em}\upharpoonright\hspace{-0.15em} \alpha$ over $J$, by taking $\{(a_1, \ldots, a_k) \in J^k \mid \mathbf{q}(a_1, \ldots, a_k) \text{ is } \mathbf{t} \text{ in } T3_P^J \hspace{-0.15em}\upharpoonright\hspace{-0.15em} \alpha\}$ as the interpretation of $\mathbf{q} \in L$ and $\{(a_1, \ldots, a_k) \in J^k \mid \mathbf{q}(a_1, \ldots, a_k) \text{ is } \mathbf{f} \text{ in } T3_P^J \hspace{-0.15em}\upharpoonright\hspace{-0.15em} \alpha\}$ as the interpretation of $\sim\mathbf{q} \in L^\sim$. (Of course any 3-valued model can be so transformed.) Thus,

$$T2_P^J \hspace{-0.15em}\upharpoonright\hspace{-0.15em} \alpha \models \mathbf{q}(a_1, \ldots, a_k) \Leftrightarrow T3_P^J \hspace{-0.15em}\upharpoonright\hspace{-0.15em} \alpha \models_3 \mathbf{q}(a_1, \ldots, a_k),$$

$$T2_P^J \hspace{-0.15em}\upharpoonright\hspace{-0.15em} \alpha \models \sim\mathbf{q}(a_1, \ldots, a_k) \Leftrightarrow T3_P^J \hspace{-0.15em}\upharpoonright\hspace{-0.15em} \alpha \models_3 \neg\mathbf{q}(a_1, \ldots, a_k).$$

Let $\delta$ be any $L$-formula (not containing $\leftrightarrow$) in which negation symbols occur in front of atoms only. $\Delta$ is the $L^\sim$-formula obtained from $\delta$ by replacing every negated atom $\neg\mathbf{q}(t_1, \ldots, t_k)$ by the $L^\sim$-atom $\sim\mathbf{q}(t_1, \ldots, t_k)$. By induction on $\delta$, it follows that

$$T2_P^J \hspace{-0.15em}\upharpoonright\hspace{-0.15em} \alpha \models \Delta(a_1, \ldots, a_n) \Leftrightarrow T3_P^J \hspace{-0.15em}\upharpoonright\hspace{-0.15em} \alpha \models_3 \delta(a_1, \ldots, a_n).$$

In particular, we can apply this transformation to the the defining formula $\delta$ for $\mathbf{r}$ (see Definition 6.19). Thus, $\Delta$ does not contain any negation and its quantifiers are all existential. $\Delta^d$ is obtained from the negation $\neg\Delta$ by (i) moving the negation symbol inward and (ii) replacing negations $\neg\mathbf{q}(t_1,\ldots,t_k)$ and $\neg \sim\mathbf{q}(t_1,\ldots,t_k)$ by $\sim\mathbf{q}(t_1,\ldots,t_k)$ resp. $\mathbf{q}(t_1,\ldots,t_k)$. Note that in $\Delta^d$, negations occur only in front of identities and quantifiers are all universal. We now have that

$$T2_P^J{\upharpoonright}\alpha{\models}\Delta^d(a_1,\ldots,a_n) \;\Leftrightarrow\; T3_P^J{\upharpoonright}\alpha{\models}_3\neg\delta(a_1,\ldots,a_n).$$

The point of these transformations is contained in the following claim.

*Claim.* For all $J$, $a_1,\ldots,a_n \in J$ and $\alpha$,

(i) $T2_P^J{\upharpoonright}(\alpha+1){\models}\mathbf{r}(a_1,\ldots,a_n)$ iff $T2_P^J{\upharpoonright}\alpha{\models}\Delta(a_1,\ldots,a_n)$,

(ii) $T2_P^J{\upharpoonright}(\alpha+1){\models} \sim\mathbf{r}(a_1,\ldots,a_n)$ iff $T2_P^J{\upharpoonright}\alpha{\models}\Delta^d(a_1,\ldots,a_n)$.

These equivalences form an explicit description as to how the hierarchy of models $T3_P^J{\upharpoonright}\alpha$ $(T2_P^J{\upharpoonright}\alpha)$ is recursively defined. Restricting them to finite $\alpha$, they can be used to produce the desired formulas. For instance, $\mathbf{r}(x_1,\ldots,x_n)^{1,\mathbf{t}}$ is obtained from $\Delta$, replacing all atoms $\mathbf{q}(t_1,\ldots,t_k)$ and $\sim\mathbf{q}(t_1,\ldots,t_k)$ by $\bot$ (since both $\mathbf{q}(y_1,\ldots,y_k)^{0,\mathbf{t}}$ and $\mathbf{q}(y_1,\ldots,y_k)^{0,\mathbf{f}}$ are defined to be $\bot$). Similarly, $\mathbf{r}(x_1,\ldots,x_n)^{1,\mathbf{f}}$ is obtained from $\Delta^d$ by carrying out the same replacements. Next, $\mathbf{r}(x_1,\ldots,x_n)^{2,\mathbf{t}}$ is obtained from $\Delta$, replacing all atoms $\mathbf{q}(t_1,\ldots,t_k)$ and $\sim\mathbf{q}(t_1,\ldots,t_k)$ by the formulas $\mathbf{q}(t_1,\ldots,t_k)^{1,\mathbf{t}}$ resp. $\mathbf{q}(t_1,\ldots,t_k)^{1,\mathbf{f}}$. Similarly, $\mathbf{r}(x_1,\ldots,x_n)^{2,\mathbf{f}}$ is obtained from $\Delta^d$ by the same replacements, etc. See Exercise 8.14. ∎

**Corollary 8.34** *Suppose that $J$ elementarily extends $HA$. Then for every sentence $\varphi$ and $n \in \mathbb{N}$, $T3_P{\upharpoonright}n{\models}_3\varphi$ iff $T3_P^J{\upharpoonright}n{\models}_3\varphi$.*

**Proof.** Using the formulas of Lemma 8.33, $T3_P{\upharpoonright}n{\models}_3\varphi$ iff $HA{\models}\varphi^{n,\mathbf{t}}$ iff $J{\models}\varphi^{n,\mathbf{t}}$ iff $T3_P^J{\upharpoonright}n{\models}_3\varphi$. ∎

The following continuity property is crucial.

**Lemma 8.35** *If the CET-algebra $J$ is recursively saturated then, for every $J$-sentence $\varphi$ (not containing $\leftrightarrow$): if $\varphi$ is $\mathbf{t}$ (resp., $\mathbf{f}$) in $T3_P^J{\upharpoonright}\omega$, then for some $n \in \mathbb{N}$, $\varphi$ is $\mathbf{t}$ (resp., $\mathbf{f}$) in $T3_P^J{\upharpoonright}n$.*

**Proof.** (That $J$ satisfies the CET axioms has no role in the proof.) Induction with respect to $\varphi$. For atomic $\varphi$, this is trivial. The following case is the one that needs recursive saturation of $J$. Assume that $\forall x\psi$ is $\mathbf{t}$ in $T3_P^J{\upharpoonright}\omega$. Thus,

for all $a \in J$, $\psi\{x/a\}$ is $\mathbf{t}$ in $T3_P^J{\upharpoonright}\omega$.

By induction hypothesis,

for all $a \in J$ there exists $i \in \mathbb{N}$ such that $\psi\{x/a\}$ is **t** in $T3_P^J\uparrow i$.

By saturation (Lemma 8.33, Remark 8.31), $n \in \mathbb{N}$ exists such that

for all $a \in J$ there exists $i < n$ such that $\psi\{x/a\}$ is **t** in $T3_P^J\uparrow i$.

But then $\forall x\psi$ is **t** in $T3_P^J\uparrow n$. ∎

The closure ordinal of a 3-valued hierarchy can be anything $\leq \omega_1^{CK}$. The following result says that any 3-valued hierarchy over a recursively saturated algebra will close at or before $\omega$. Together with Lemma 8.32, this produces another proof for Theorem 6.22.

**Theorem 8.36** *If the CET-algebra $J$ is recursively saturated, then for every program $P$: $T3_P^J\uparrow = T3_P^J\uparrow\omega$.*

**Proof.** Assume the hypothesis. Let $A = \mathbf{r}(a_1, \ldots, a_n)$ be an arbitrary $J$-ground atom. We have to show that if $A$ is **t** (**f**) in $T3_P^J\uparrow(\omega + 1)$, then $A$ is **t** (resp., **f**) already in $T3_P^J\uparrow\omega$. This is an almost immediate result of Lemma 8.35 and the explanations given in the proof of Lemma 8.33.

For instance (letting $\Delta$ be the formula obtained from the defining formula $\delta$ for $\mathbf{r}$ in the way described there), $\mathbf{r}(a_1, \ldots, a_n)$ is **t** in $T3_P^J\uparrow(\omega + 1)$ iff $\mathbf{r}(a_1, \ldots, a_n)$ is true in the two-valued companyon model $T2_P^J\uparrow(\omega + 1)$, iff $\Delta(a_1, \ldots, a_n)$ is true in $T2_P^J\uparrow\omega$, iff $\delta(a_1, \ldots, a_n)$ is true in $T3_P^J\uparrow\omega$. By Lemma 8.35, this implies 3-valued truth of $\delta(a_1, \ldots, a_n)$ in some $T3_P^J\uparrow n$. But then, $\Delta(a_1, \ldots, a_n)$ is true in $T2_P^J\uparrow n$, $\mathbf{r}(a_1, \ldots, a_n)$ is true in $T2_P^J\uparrow(n + 1)$, and hence in $T3_P^J\uparrow(n + 1)$ and in $T3_P^J\uparrow\omega$.

Similarly, $\mathbf{r}(a_1, \ldots, a_n)$ is **f** in $T3_P^J\uparrow(\omega + 1)$ iff $\sim\mathbf{r}(a_1, \ldots, a_n)$ is true in $T2_P^J\uparrow(\omega + 1)$, iff $\Delta^d(a_1, \ldots, a_n)$ is true in $T2_P^J\uparrow\omega$, iff $\neg\delta(a_1, \ldots, a_n)$ is true in $T3_P^J\uparrow\omega$. By Lemma 8.35, this implies that $\neg\delta(a_1, \ldots, a_n)$ is **t** in some $T3_P^J\uparrow n$, whence $\Delta^d(a_1, \ldots, a_n)$ is true in $T2_P^J\uparrow n$, so $\sim\mathbf{r}(a_1, \ldots, a_n)$ is true in $T2_P^J\uparrow(n + 1)$, and hence $\mathbf{r}(a_1, \ldots, a_n)$ is false in $T3_P^J\uparrow(n + 1)$ and in $T3_P^J\uparrow\omega$. ∎

By Lemma 8.27(ii), the following result for ground atoms $A$ can be seen to generalize the implication $comp(P)\models\neg A \Rightarrow A \notin T_P\downarrow\omega$ (related to completeness of negation as finite failure) for $P$ positive and $A$ a ground atom (cf. Corollary 6.20). In it we may in fact replace the Herbrand algebra $HA$ by an arbitrary CET-algebra. It is this result that is instrumental in the completeness proof of the next section. For the converse implication, see Example 8.38.

**Corollary 8.37** *Let $\varphi$ be any sentence (not containing $\leftrightarrow$). If $comp(P)\models_3\varphi$, then for some $n$, $T3_P\uparrow n \models_3 \varphi$.*

**Proof.** Assume that $comp(P)\models_3\varphi$. By Lemma 8.32, choose an elementary extension $J$ of $HA$ that is recursively saturated. Since (by Theorem 8.36 and Lemma 8.22) $T3_P^J\uparrow\omega$ is a 3-valued model of $comp(P)$, $\varphi$ is $\mathbf{t}$ in $T3_P^J{\uparrow}\omega$. By Lemma 8.35, $\varphi$ is $\mathbf{t}$ in some $T3_P^J{\uparrow}n$. Now, use Corollary 8.34.  ∎

**Example 8.38** Here is a counter-example to the implication $T3_P{\uparrow}n\models_3\varphi \Rightarrow comp(P)\models_3\varphi$. $P$ consists of the following rules.

   $\mathbf{q(a)} \leftarrow$
   $\mathbf{r} \leftarrow \neg\mathbf{q}(x).$

In the following table we calculate the truth values produced by the 3-valued hierarchy over the universe $HU = \{\mathbf{a}\}$, indicating the level at which an atom becomes $\mathbf{t}$ or $\mathbf{f}$.

| level | t | f |
|-------|------|------|
| 1 | q(a) | |
| 2 | | r |

Therefore, $T3_P{\uparrow}2\models_3\neg\mathbf{r}$.

However, over the algebra $J := \{\mathbf{a}, \mathbf{b}\}$, we have the following calculation:

| level | t | f |
|-------|------|------|
| 1 | q(a) | q(b) |
| 2 | r | |

Therefore, $comp(P) \not\models_3 \neg\mathbf{r}$.  ∎

The lesson this example teaches is that, in the context with negation, what is true may change upon adding elements to the underlying algebra *without changing the program*. With a Herbrand universe that is sufficiently large, there is no such dependency, and the converse of Corollary 8.37 holds. See Exercise 8.16.

### Exercises

**8.13** Show: every finite model is saturated.

**8.14** Complete the proof of Lemma 8.33.

**8.15** Complete the remaining details of the proof of Lemma 8.35.

**8.16** *Fact:* if the algebraic language is infinite, then every CET-algebra elementarily extends $HA$.
Assume the algebraic language is infinite. Show that the converse of Corollary 8.37 holds.
*Hint.* If $\mathbf{M}$ is a 3-valued model of $comp(P)$ over the algebra $J$, then $T3_P^J{\uparrow} \leq \mathbf{M}$.

**8.17** Show that the algebra $\mathbb{N}+\mathbb{Z}$ (see Example 6.4) is not recursively saturated. Show that there is exactly one countable recursively saturated CET-algebra for the language $\{\mathbf{o}, \mathbf{s}\}$. Describe it. (See Exercise 6.16.)

## 8.7    Completeness for SLDNF

Until very recently, theorists failed to obtain completeness results of much importance. An abundance of examples provided evidence for the belief that such completeness results would remain an illusion. On the other hand, practice indicated that, for reasonable programs, SLDNF would accomplish what was intended, whereas the counter-examples often did not seem to be related to real life. And so the question arose: exactly what makes a program reasonable? The completeness result that is the topic of this section suggests that this is to be found in the well-moding of programs. At the same time, the proof itself uses very little of the information provided by having this property.

### 8.7.1    Modes

The notion of a mode arises from the following considerations. Consider a general rule

$$A \leftarrow A_0, \ldots, A_{m-1}, \neg B_0, \ldots, \neg B_{n-1}.$$

In a practical context, the use of a rule like this (according to leftmost selection) causes a "data flow". An instance of $A$ is resolved using this rule, containing some input values. Next, when a corresponding instance of $A_0$ with these values is resolved, certain output values are computed, serving as input values for a subsequential resolution of an instance of $A_1$, etc. Finally, (instances of) $B_0, \ldots, B_{n-1}$ are tested. If they finitely fail, the output finally produced by $A_{m-1}$ is assigned to some output variables of $A$ by way of computed answer substitution.

This dynamic way of looking at rules can be made explicit by a mode specification for relation symbols. Each of the $n$ argument places of an $n$-ary relation symbol can be assigned one of three *modes*: in (for input), out (for output) and neutral.

**Definition 8.39**

- (i) A *mode specification* for an $n$-ary relation symbol is an $n$-tuple of elements from the set $\{\text{in}, \text{out}, \text{neutral}\}$.
- (ii) If $\alpha = (\alpha_1, \ldots, \alpha_n)$ is a mode specification for the $n$-ary symbol $\mathbf{r}$ and $t_1, \ldots, t_n$ are terms, then $in(\mathbf{r}(t_1, \ldots, t_n), \alpha) := \bigcup_{\alpha_i = \text{in}} Var(t_i)$.
  Similarly, $out(\mathbf{r}(t_1, \ldots, t_n), \alpha) := \bigcup_{\alpha_i = \text{out}} Var(t_i)$.
- (iii) An *input/output specification* is a function $S$ assigning to every relation symbol $\mathbf{r}$ a set $S^+(\mathbf{r}) \subset \{\text{in}, \text{out}, \text{neutral}\}^n$ of *positive* mode specifications for $\mathbf{r}$ ($n$ the arity of $\mathbf{r}$) and a set $S^-(\mathbf{r}) \subset \{\text{in}, \text{neutral}\}^n$ of *negative* mode specifications for $\mathbf{r}$. ∎

The idea is that positive calls of $\mathbf{r}$ will be made according to some of its positive mode specifications, whereas a negative mode specification is used when $\mathbf{r}$ is called in a negated position. Negative mode specifications do not use the mode **out**, reflecting the idea that negative literals do not contribute to the computation of output. It is allowed that, in a mode specification $S$, one or both sets $S^+(\mathbf{r})$, $S^-(\mathbf{r})$ are empty.

The fact that an input/output specification can assign more than one mode specification to a single symbol reflects the different ways in which the symbol may be used by the program. For instance, the rules for *append* (Exercise 4.54) may be used to concatenate lists according to the mode specification (**in, in, out**), but it may be used also to decompose a list (according to (**out, out, in**)).

The following definitions are meant to capture the intuitive picture previously sketched. In it we use the notations $S^+(A)$ and $S^-(A)$ for $S^+(\mathbf{r})$ resp. $S^-(\mathbf{r})$ whenever $A = \mathbf{r}(t_1, \ldots, t_n)$ is an **r**-atom.

For the rest of this section, let some input/output specification $S$ be fixed.

**Definition 8.40** A general rule $A \leftarrow K$ is *S-correct* if

(R1) for all $\alpha \in S^+(A)$, the body $K$ can be permuted to a sequence $A_0, \ldots, A_{m-1}, \neg B_0, \ldots, \neg B_{n-1}$ such that for some $\alpha_i \in S^+(A_i)$ $(i < m)$:

    (a) if $k < m$, then $in(A_k, \alpha_k) \subset in(A, \alpha) \cup \bigcup_{i<k} out(A_i, \alpha_i)$,

    (b) $out(A, \alpha) \subset in(A, \alpha) \cup \bigcup_{i<m} out(A_i, \alpha_i)$,

    (c) if $j < n$, then $S^-(B_j) \neq \emptyset$, and $Var(B_j) \subset in(A, \alpha) \cup \bigcup_{i<m} out(A_i, \alpha_i)$,

(R2) for all $\alpha \in S^-(A)$:

    (a) for all positive literals $A_i \in K$, there exists $\alpha_i \in S^-(A_i)$ such that $in(A_i, \alpha_i) \subset in(A, \alpha)$, and

    (b) for all negative literals $\neg B_j \in K$, there exists $\beta_j \in S^+(B_j)$ such that $in(B_j, \beta_j) \subset in(A, \alpha)$.

A program is *S-correct* if all its rules are. ∎

**Lemma 8.41** *An instance of an S-correct rule is S-correct.*

**Proof.** Exercise 8.20. ∎

**Definition 8.42** A query is *S-correct* if it can be permuted to a sequence $A_0, \ldots, A_{m-1}$, $\neg B_0, \ldots, \neg B_{n-1}$ such that for some $\alpha_i \in S^+(A_i)$ $(i < m)$:

(Q1) if $k < m$, then $in(A_k, \alpha_k) \subset \bigcup_{i<k} out(A_i, \alpha_i)$,

(Q2) if $j < n$, then $S^-(B_j) \neq \emptyset$ and $Var(B_j) \subset \bigcup_{i<m} out(A_i, \alpha_i)$. ∎

**Definition 8.43** A query is *S-closed* if for every positive literal $A$ in it, there is an $\alpha \in S^-(A)$ such that $in(A, \alpha) = \emptyset$ and for every negative literal $\neg B$ in it, there is a $\beta \in S^+(B)$ for which $in(B, \beta) = \emptyset$. ∎

For some examples, see Exercises 8.22, 8.23 and 8.30.

Very few consequences of correctness are needed in the forthcoming completeness proof. The following lemma isolates the *Stärk conditions* actually used.

For the rest of this section fix a program $P$ that is correct with respect to the input/output specification $S$.

**Definition 8.44** $C^+ = C_S^+$ is the set of $S$-correct queries; $C^- = C_S^-$ is the set of $S$-closed queries. ∎

**Lemma 8.45 (Stärk conditions)**

*(A1)* if $C \in C^+$, then $C\sigma \in C^+$,

*(A2)* if $C \in C^+$ and $C \xrightarrow{\epsilon}_u D$ *(using a P-rule), then $D \in C^+$,*

*(A3)* if $(\neg A_1, \ldots, \neg A_k) \in C^+$, then, for $1 \le i \le k$, $A_i$ is ground and $A_i \in C^-$,

*(B1)* if $C \in C^-$, then $C\sigma \in C^-$,

*(B2)* if $C \in C^-$ and $C \xrightarrow{\epsilon}_u D$ *(using a P-rule), then $D \in C^-$,*

*(B3)* if $\neg A \in C \in C^-$, then $A \in C^+$.

**Proof.** For (A3), see 8.42(Q2). For (B2), use Lemma 8.41. For (B3), see Exercise 8.19. See Exercise 8.21. ∎

Note that (A1/2) imply that an unrestricted resolvent of a query in $C^+$ is in $C^+$; similarly, (B1/2) imply that an unrestricted resolvent of a query in $C^-$ is in $C^-$.

Note that the Completeness Theorem 8.52 holds with respect to any two classes $C^+$ and $C^-$ satisfying the Stärk conditions (A1–B3). Except for (A3), these are closure principles that can easily be satisfied. It is (A3) which makes this more problematic. Well-moding provides a practical way to obtain non-trivial classes satisfying (A1–B3). See Exercise 8.26 for another way to realize the Stärk conditions.

**Exercises**

**8.18** Show: a fact $A \leftarrow$ is $S$-correct iff for all $\alpha \in S^+(A)$, $out(A, \alpha) \subset in(A, \alpha)$.

**8.19** Show: a query is $S$-closed iff for everyone of its negative literals $\neg A$, the query $A$ is $S$-correct.

**8.20** Prove Lemma 8.41.

**8.21** Complete the proof of Lemma 8.45.

**8.22** Consider the input/output specification $S$ that assigns one positive resp. negative mode specification (**neutral**, ..., **neutral**) to every relation symbol. Show: every positive program is $S$-correct; a general query is $S$-correct iff all its negative literals are ground and every query is $S$-closed.

**8.23** Verify that the s-program of Exercise 8.5 is correct with respect to the following mode specification $S$.

$S^+(\mathbf{s}) = \{(\text{out}, \text{out}, \text{in})\}$,
$S^-(\mathbf{s}) = \{(\text{neutral}, \text{neutral}, \text{neutral})\}$,
$S^+(member) = \{(\text{neutral}, \text{neutral}), (\text{out}, \text{in})\}$,
$S^-(member) = \{(\text{neutral}, \text{neutral})\}$.

Check that every query $\mathbf{s}(x, y, [\,])$ is correct.

**8.24** Add the usual rules for *member* to the following rules, involving binary relation symbols $\not\subset$, $\subset$, and $=$, that determine whether two lists contain the same elements.

$\not\subset (y, z) \leftarrow member(x, y), \neg member(x, z)$,
$\subset (y, z) \leftarrow \neg \not\subset (y, z)$,
$= (y, z) \leftarrow \subset (y, z), \subset (z, y)$.

Find a mode specification with respect to which this program and ground queries $= (s, t)$ are correct.

**8.25** Partially order the input/output specifications for a set $\mathcal{R}$ of relation symbols by $S_1 \leq S_2 :\equiv$ for all $\mathbf{r} \in \mathcal{R}$, $S_1^+(\mathbf{r}) \subset S_2^+(\mathbf{r})$ and $S_1^-(\mathbf{r}) \subset S_2^-(\mathbf{r})$. Show: if a program is $S$-correct for some $S$, then there is a greatest $S$ for which it is correct.
*Hint.* If $P$ is $S_i$-correct ($i = 1, 2$), then $P$ is $(S_1 \cup S_2)$-correct. ($S_1 \cup S_2$ defined by $(S_1 \cup S_2)^{+/-}(\mathbf{r}) = S_1^{+/-}(\mathbf{r}) \cup S_2^{+/-}(\mathbf{r})$.)

**8.26** Assume that $\mathcal{D}^+$ and $\mathcal{D}^-$ are classes of queries satisfying the following conditions.

(i) If $C \in \mathcal{D}^+$ (resp. $C \in \mathcal{D}^-$) and $C \xrightarrow{\alpha} D$ $(A, R)$, where $R$ is a $P$-rule, then $D \in \mathcal{D}^+$ (resp. $D \in \mathcal{D}^-$),

(ii) if $(\neg A_1, \ldots, \neg A_k) \in \mathcal{D}^+$, then, for $1 \leq i \leq k$, $A_i$ is ground and $A_i \in \mathcal{D}^-$,

(iii) if $\neg A \in C \in \mathcal{D}^-$, then $A \in \mathcal{D}^+$.

Show that the classes $\mathcal{C}^+ := \{C\sigma \mid C \in \mathcal{D}^+\}$ and $\mathcal{C}^- := \{C\sigma \mid C \in \mathcal{D}^-\}$ satisfy (A1–B3).

The following notion of allowedness was concocted to avoid floundering.

**Definition 8.46** A general rule is *allowed* if every variable that occurs in it has an occurrence in a positive literal in the body of the rule. A general program is *allowed* if all its rules are.
A general query is *allowed* if every variable that occurs in it has an occurrence in a positive literal of the query. ∎

Allowedness is a severe restriction on programs. E.g., every allowed fact is ground. This excludes many useful rules. For instance the following one, defining equality over $HU$, is not allowed:

$\mathbf{eq}(x, x) \leftarrow$.

The first addition-defining rule is not allowed:

**sum**$(x, \mathbf{o}, x) \leftarrow$.

The usual rules defining membership in a list (Exercise 4.58) are not allowed:

$member(x, [x|z]) \leftarrow$

$member(x, [y|z]) \leftarrow member(x, z)$.

**8.27** Suppose that $C$ and $R$ are allowed and that $C \xrightarrow{\alpha} D(A, R)$. Show that $D$ is allowed.

*Hint.* An instance of an allowed query (resp. rule) is allowed.

It follows that floundering cannot occur when dealing with allowed queries and programs.

**8.28** Show that every computed answer substitution for an allowed query relative to an allowed program is ground.

*Solution.* The following proof uses an amusing trick. Suppose that $\lambda$ is the computed answer substitution of the successful SLDNF-tree $\mathcal{T}$ for the allowed query $C$ relative to an allowed program. Let $L$ be a negative literal such that $Var(L) = Var(C)$. (E.g., $L$ might be of the form $\neg\mathbf{r}(x_1, \ldots, x_n)$ or $\neg\mathbf{r}(\mathbf{f}(x_1, \ldots, x_n))$.) Modify $\mathcal{T}$ by replacing its initial query $C$ by $(C, L)$ and making the obvious change in derived queries, adding instances of $L$. The resulting SLDNF-tree then will have a leaf $L\lambda$. Since $(C, L)$ is allowed, it follows (mainly by Exercise 8.27) that $L\lambda$ is allowed also. Therefore, $L\lambda$ cannot contain a variable. Therefore, $\lambda$ is ground.

**8.29** Suppose that $P$ and $C$ are allowed. Show that, for every $n$, there are only finitely many $\sigma : Var(C) \rightarrow HU$ such that $T3_P{\uparrow}n \models_3 C\sigma$.

*Solution.* Induction with respect to $n$. Fix an allowed query $C$. The case $Var(C) = \emptyset$ is trivial. Choose $x \in Var(C)$. We have to show that the set $\{x\sigma \mid \sigma : Var(C) \rightarrow HU$ and $T3_P{\uparrow}n \models_3 C\sigma\}$ is finite. Assume that $\sigma : Var(C) \rightarrow HU$ and $T3_P{\uparrow}n \models_3 C\sigma$. Since $C$ is allowed, $x$ occurs in a positive literal $A \in C$. Take any ground instance $A\sigma \leftarrow D$ of a $P$-rule such that $T3_P{\uparrow}(n-1) \models_3 D$.

Lift the ground resolution step $A\sigma \xrightarrow{\epsilon}_u D$ to a resolution step $A \xrightarrow{\alpha} E$. There exists $\pi$ such that $Dom(\pi) \subset Var(A\alpha, E)$, $D = E\pi$ and $A\sigma = A\alpha\pi$; in particular, $x\sigma = x\alpha\pi$. Since $P$ is allowed, $Var(A\alpha) \subset Var(E)$. Thus, $Dom(\pi) \subset Var(E)$. Since $D = E\pi$ is ground, $\pi : Var(E) \rightarrow HU$.

Now $T3_P{\uparrow}(n-1) \models_3 E\pi$. By Exercise 8.27, $E$ is allowed. By induction hypothesis, there are only finitely many $\pi : Var(E) \rightarrow HU$ such that $T3_P{\uparrow}(n-1) \models_3 E\pi$. Since $A$ (up to variants) has only finitely many resolvents, this proves the claim: $x\sigma = x\alpha\pi$; and there are but finitely many $\alpha$ and $\pi$ available.

**8.30** Consider the input/output specification $S$ that to every relation symbol assigns one positive mode specification of the form $\alpha^+ = (\mathbf{out}, \ldots, \mathbf{out})$ and one negative mode specification of the form $\alpha^- = (\mathbf{neutral}, \ldots, \mathbf{neutral})$. Thus for every atom $A$, $in(A, \alpha^+) = \emptyset$

and $out(A, \alpha^+) = Var(A)$. Show that rules and queries are $S$-correct iff they are allowed and that every query is $S$-closed.

### 8.7.2 Completeness

The following auxiliary definition introduces two sets of queries $\mathcal{YES} = \mathcal{YES}_P$ and $\mathcal{NO} = \mathcal{NO}_P$ (depending on the program $P$) that are closely related to the sets of provable and finitely failed ones. See Exercise 4.32 for the general principle on which definitions of this type are based.

**Definition 8.47** The sets of queries $\mathcal{YES}$ and $\mathcal{NO}$ are inductively defined as the least ones satisfying the following closure principles.

(Y1) $\square \in \mathcal{YES}$,

(Y2) if $C \xrightarrow{\epsilon}_u D$ (using some $P$-rule) and $D \in \mathcal{YES}$, then $C \in \mathcal{YES}$,

(Y3) if $A_1, \ldots, A_k \in \mathcal{NO}$, then $(\neg A_1, \ldots, \neg A_k) \in \mathcal{YES}$,

(N1) if $A \in C$ and, for all $R \in P$ that are applicable to $A$ and for all $\alpha$ and $D$:

$$\text{if } C \xrightarrow{\alpha}_u D \ (A, \ R), \text{ then } D \in \mathcal{NO};$$

then $C \in \mathcal{NO}$,

(N2) if $A \in \mathcal{YES}$ is an atom, then $(C, \neg A, C') \in \mathcal{NO}$.                      ∎

The following is a straightforward consequence of this definition.

**Lemma 8.48**

*(i) If $C \in \mathcal{YES}$, then $C\sigma \in \mathcal{YES}$,*

*(ii) if $C \in \mathcal{NO}$, then $C\sigma \in \mathcal{NO}$,*

**Proof.** (i) and (ii) are proved simultaneously, by induction, following the clauses of Definition 8.47.

(i)

(Y1). $C = \square$.

Then $C\sigma = \square \in \mathcal{YES}$, by (Y1).

(Y2). $C \xrightarrow{\epsilon}_u D \in \mathcal{YES}$.

Then $C\sigma \xrightarrow{\epsilon}_u D\sigma$. By induction hypothesis for (i), $D\sigma \in \mathcal{YES}$. By (Y2), $C\sigma \in \mathcal{YES}$.

(Y3). $C = (\neg A_1, \ldots, \neg A_k)$, $A_1, \ldots, A_k \in \mathcal{NO}$.

By induction hypothesis for (ii), $A_1\sigma, \ldots, A_k\sigma \in \mathcal{NO}$. By (Y3), $C\sigma \in \mathcal{YES}$.

(ii)

(N1). $A \in C$, and if $R \in P$ and $C \xrightarrow{\alpha}_u D \ (A, \ R)$, then $D \in \mathcal{NO}$.

Assume that $R \in P$ and $C\sigma \xrightarrow{\alpha}_u E \ (A\sigma, \ R)$. Lift this to $C \xrightarrow{\beta} D \ (A, \ R)$. For some $\tau$, $D\tau = E$. By hypothesis, $D \in \mathcal{NO}$. By induction hypothesis for (ii), $E = D\tau \in \mathcal{NO}$.

Therefore, it follows by (N1) that $C\sigma \in \mathcal{NO}$.

(N2). $C = (C', \neg A, C'')$, $A \in \mathcal{YES}$.

By induction hypothesis for (i), $A\sigma \in \mathcal{YES}$. Therefore by (N2), $C\sigma = (C'\sigma, \neg A\sigma, C''\sigma) \in \mathcal{NO}$. $\blacksquare$

The following lemma shows $\mathcal{YES}$ and $\mathcal{NO}$ to be closely related to the sets of (SLDNF) provable and finitely failed queries; also, see Exercise 8.33.

Note that the version of SLDNF employed here is the one that (a) let $\neg A$ succeed if $A$ is ground and finitely failed (this is according to the usual formulation of SLDNF); (b) let $\neg A$ fail if $A$ succeeds with a computed answer substitution that is a renaming for it (this is from what is called SLDNFE).

**Lemma 8.49**

(i) *If $C \in \mathcal{C}^+$ and $C\sigma \in \mathcal{YES}$, then there exists a computed answer substitution $\theta$ for $C$ such that $C\sigma$ is an instance of $C\theta$,*

(ii) *if $C \in \mathcal{C}^-$ and $C \in \mathcal{NO}$, then $C$ has a finitely failed SLDNF-tree.*

**Proof.** Induction via Definition 8.47.

(i)

(Y1). $C\sigma = \square$. Then $\sigma = \epsilon$. Take $\theta = \epsilon$.

(Y2). $C\sigma \overset{\epsilon}{\longrightarrow}_u D \in \mathcal{YES}$. By lifting, assume that $C \overset{\alpha}{\longrightarrow} E$. For some $\tau$, $C\sigma = C\alpha\tau$ and $E\tau = D$. By (A1/2), $E \in \mathcal{C}^+$. By induction hypothesis for $E$ and $\tau$, for some $\lambda$ we have that $E \overset{\lambda}{\longrightarrow} \square$ and $E\tau$ is an instance of $E\lambda$. We may assume this success is such that $(Var(C\alpha) - Var(E)) \cap Var(E\lambda) = \emptyset$. Then, however, $\theta := (\alpha\lambda)|Var(C)$ is a computed answer substitution for $C$ and $C\sigma$ is an instance of $C\alpha\lambda = C\theta$.

(Y3). Suppose that $C = (\neg A_1, \ldots, \neg A_k) \in \mathcal{C}^+$, $A_i\sigma \in \mathcal{NO}$ ($i = 1, \ldots, k$). By (A3), every $A_i$ is ground and in $\mathcal{C}^-$. In particular, $A_i\sigma = A_i$. By induction hypothesis for (ii), every $A_i$ has a finitely failed SLDNF-tree. Thus, we have that $C \overset{\theta := \epsilon}{\longrightarrow} \square$ in $k$ steps, using these trees.

(ii)

(N1). $A \in C \in \mathcal{C}^-$ and for every $R \in P$ applicable to $A$ and all $\alpha$: if $C \overset{\alpha}{\longrightarrow}_u D$ $(A, R)$, then $D \in \mathcal{NO}$. By induction hypothesis for (ii), if $C \overset{\alpha}{\longrightarrow} D$ $(A, R)$, then (since by (B1/2), $D \in \mathcal{C}^-$) $D$ has a finitely failed SLDNF-tree. But then $C$ has such a tree as well.

(N2). $C = (C', \neg A, C'')$, $A \in \mathcal{YES}$. By (B3), $A \in \mathcal{C}^+$. By induction hypothesis for (i), $A$ has a computed answer substitution $\theta$ such that $A = A\epsilon$ is an instance of $A\theta$. Thus, $\theta$ is a renaming for $A$. So, $C$ has a finitely failed SLDNF-tree. $\blacksquare$

Before coming to the main lemma, we have to dispose of a technicality.

**Lemma 8.50** *Suppose that $C \in \mathcal{C}^+$ and $\theta = \{x_1/c_1, \ldots, x_m/c_m\}$ is a substitution where $c_1, \ldots, c_m$ are pairwise different constant symbols not occurring in $P$ or $C$. If $C\theta \in \mathcal{YES}$, then $C \in \mathcal{YES}$.*

**Proof.** Induction via the definition of $\mathcal{YES}$ (keeping $\theta$ variable). (That (N1/2) do not enter the argument is due to (A3).)

(Y1). $C\theta = \Box$. Then $C = \Box \in \mathcal{YES}$ by (Y1).

(Y2). $C\theta \xrightarrow{\epsilon}_u D \in \mathcal{YES}$.

If $D$ does not contain any of the variables $x_1, \ldots, x_m$, obtain $D'$ from $D$ by changing the $c_i$ back to the $x_i$. Then $D = D'\theta$, $C \xrightarrow{\epsilon}_u D'$. By (A2), $D' \in \mathcal{C}^+$. By induction hypothesis, $D' \in \mathcal{YES}$. Thus, $C \in \mathcal{YES}$ by (Y2).

If $D$ does contain some of the $x_i$, then we argue as follows. Choose variables $y_1, \ldots, y_m$ not in $C$ or $D$. Put $\theta' := \{y_1/c_1, \ldots, y_m/c_m\}$. There is a variant $C'$ of $C$ and a query $D'$ such that $C\theta = C'\theta'$ and $D = D'\theta'$. (To obtain $C'$ from $C$, replace the $x_i$ by the $y_i$; to obtain $D'$ from $D$, replace the $c_i$ by the $y_i$.) Now, $C' \xrightarrow{\epsilon}_u D'$. By (A1), $C' \in \mathcal{C}^+$. By (A2), $D' \in \mathcal{C}^+$. Since $D'\theta' = D \in \mathcal{YES}$, by induction hypothesis for $D'$ and $\theta'$, $D' \in \mathcal{YES}$. By (Y2), $C' \in \mathcal{YES}$. Therefore, by Lemma 8.48(i), $C \in \mathcal{YES}$.

(Y3). $C = (\neg A_1, \ldots, \neg A_k)$, where $\neg A_1\theta, \ldots, \neg A_k\theta \in \mathcal{NO}$. By (A3), $C$ is ground. Thus, $\neg A_i\theta = \neg A_i \in \mathcal{NO}$ and, by (Y3), $C \in \mathcal{YES}$. ∎

Next comes the main lemma. It employs the following notions of rank with respect to the 3-valued hierarchy. (Compare Definition 5.18.)

Suppose that $C = (L_1, \ldots, L_k)$ is a query and $\eta = \{\{n_1, \ldots, n_k\}\}$ a multiset. $\eta$ is a *positive rank* of $C$ if $C$ is ground and for all $i$, $i = 1, \ldots, k$, $L_i$ is **t** in $T3_P{\uparrow}n_i$. $\eta$ is a *negative rank* of $C$ if for every assignment $\sigma$ of its variables in $HU$, some $L_i\sigma$ is **f** in $T3_P{\uparrow}n_i$.

If a ground query has a positive rank, then it also has a (in the multiset ordering) least one, which we might call *the* positive rank of the query. However, a least negative rank need not exist.

**Lemma 8.51** *Assume that the language has infinitely many constant symbols. Let $C = (L_1, \ldots, L_k)$ be a query and $\eta = \{\{n_1, \ldots, n_k\}\}$ a multiset.*

*(i) If $C \in \mathcal{C}^+$ and $\eta$ is a positive rank of $C$, then $C \in \mathcal{YES}$,*

*(ii) if $C \in \mathcal{C}^-$ and $\eta$ is a negative rank of $C$, then $C \in \mathcal{NO}$.*

**Proof.** We prove (i) and (ii) simultaneously, using multiset induction with respect to $\eta$; that is, Theorem 1.13. The proof splits into cases I–IV. Cases I and IV together make up part (i) of the lemma; cases II and III make up part (ii).

Case I. $C \in \mathcal{C}^+$ is ground, $\eta$ is a positive rank of $C$, and at least one literal $L_i$ is positive, $L_i = A$.

Since $A$ is $\mathbf{t}$ in $T3_P{\uparrow}n_i$, we have that $n_i > 0$, $T3_P{\uparrow}n_i = T3_P(T3_P{\uparrow}(n_i - 1))$ and so there is a ground unrestricted resolution step of the form $C \xrightarrow{\epsilon}_u D$ $(A, R)$, where $R$ is a $P$-rule. Let $R$ have $m$ body literals. Obtain $\eta'$ from $\eta$, replacing $n_i$ by $m$ occurrences of $n_i - 1$. Then $\eta'$ precedes $\eta$ in the multiset ordering and $\eta'$ is a positive rank for $D$. By (A1/2), $D \in C^+$. By induction hypothesis for (i), $D \in \mathcal{YES}$. By (Y2), $C \in \mathcal{YES}$.

Case II. $C \in C^-$, $\eta$ is a negative rank of $C$, and for some $i$ $(1 \leq i \leq k)$, $L_i$ is positive, $L_i = A$, and $n_i > 0$.

Let $R$ be any $P$-rule applicable to $A$ and suppose that $C \xrightarrow{\alpha}_u D$ $(A, R)$. Obtain the multiset $\eta'$ from $\eta$, replacing $n_i$ by as many occurrences of $n_i - 1$ as $R$ has body literals. Then $\eta'$ precedes $\eta$ in the multiset ordering.

*Claim.* $\eta'$ is a negative rank for $D$.

Assuming the claim, since by (B1/2) we have that $D \in C^-$, it follows by induction hypothesis that $D \in \mathcal{NO}$. Since this holds for every $P$-rule applicable to $A$, by (N1) we have that $C \in \mathcal{NO}$.

*Proof of Claim.* Let $\tau$ be ground for $D$. We must find a literal in $D\tau$ $\mathbf{f}$ in $T3_P{\uparrow}n$ where $n$ is the element of $\eta'$ corresponding to this literal. Extend $\alpha\tau$ to a substitution $\sigma$ ground for $C$. Then $C \xrightarrow{\alpha}_u D$ lifts the ground resolution step $C\sigma \xrightarrow{\epsilon}_u D\tau$. Since $\eta = \{\{n_1, \ldots, n_k\}\}$ is a negative rank for $C$, there exists $j$ $(1 \leq j \leq k)$ such that the $j$-th literal of $C\sigma$ is $\mathbf{f}$ in $T3_P{\uparrow}n_j$.

(a) $j \neq i$. Then this literal occurs in $D\tau$ as well, and $n_j$ is the corresponding element of $\eta'$.

(b) $j = i$. Then this literal, $A\sigma$, has been replaced by instances of body literals of $R$ in $D\tau$, and, since $A\sigma$ is $\mathbf{f}$ in $T3_P{\uparrow}n_i = T3_P(T3_P{\uparrow}(n_i - 1))$, at least one of them is $\mathbf{f}$ in $T3_P{\uparrow}(n_i - 1)$, and $n_i - 1$ is the corresponding element of $\eta'$.

Case III. $C \in C^-$, $\eta$ is a negative rank of $C$, and for all $i$ $(1 \leq i \leq k)$, if $L_i$ is positive, then $n_i = 0$.

Suppose that $Var(C) = \{x_1, \ldots, x_m\}$. Choose distinct constant symbols $c_1, \ldots, c_m$ that do not occur in $P$ or $C$. Put $\theta := \{x_1/c_1, \ldots, x_m/c_m\}$. Since $\theta$ is ground for $C$, for some $i$ $(1 \leq i \leq k)$, $L_i\theta$ is $\mathbf{f}$ in $T3_P{\uparrow}n_i$. But then $n_i > 0$ and so $L_i$ must be negative, $L_i = \neg A$. Thus, $A\theta$ is $\mathbf{t}$ in $T3_P{\uparrow}n_i$. By (B3), since $\neg A \in C \in C^-$, we have that $A \in C^+$. By (A1), $A\theta \in C^+$.

Now if $\neg A$ is not the only literal of $C$ (that is, if $k > 1$), then the positive rank $\{\{n_i\}\}$ for $A\theta$ precedes $\eta$ in the multiset ordering. By induction hypothesis for (i), $A\theta \in \mathcal{YES}$. But also, if $C = \neg A$ (that is, $k = 1$ and $\{\{n_i\}\} = \eta$), then by the argument of Case I, it still follows that $A\theta \in \mathcal{YES}$. So we have that $A\theta \in \mathcal{YES}$ anyway.

Then by Lemma 8.50, $A \in \mathcal{YES}$. Finally, by (N2) (whatever $k$), $C \in \mathcal{NO}$.

Case IV. $C \in \mathcal{C}^+$ is ground, $\eta$ is a positive rank of $C$, and all literals $L_i$ are negative, $L_i = \neg A_i$.

By (A3), $A_i \in \mathcal{C}^-$ $(i = 1, \ldots, k)$.

Now if $C$ has more than one literal (that is, if $k > 1$), then the negative rank $\{\{n_i\}\}$ for $A_i$ $(i = 1, \ldots, k)$ precedes $\eta$ in the multiset ordering. By induction hypothesis for (ii), $A_i \in \mathcal{NO}$ $(i = 1, \ldots, k)$. Therefore, by (Y3), $C \in \mathcal{YES}$.

But also, if $C = \neg A_1$ consists of one literal only $(k = 1)$, then by the argument of Case II it still follows that $A_1 \in \mathcal{NO}$. And again by (Y3), $C \in \mathcal{YES}$. ∎

Combining these results with Corollary 8.37, the following completeness result now is easy.

### Theorem 8.52 (Completeness)

(i) *Suppose that* $C \in \mathcal{C}^+$. *If* $comp(P) \models_3 \forall \bigwedge C\sigma$, *then* $C$ *has a computed answer substitution* $\theta$ *such that* $C\sigma$ *is an instance of* $C\theta$.

(ii) *Suppose that* $C \in \mathcal{C}^-$. *If* $comp(P) \models_3 \neg \exists \bigwedge C$, *then there is a finitely failed SLDNF-tree for* $C$.

**Proof.** If necessary, extend the language with infinitely many new constant symbols. Then $P$ remains $S$-correct. This move extends the classes $\mathcal{C}^+$ and $\mathcal{C}^-$. We prove the theorem with respect to these extended classes.

(i). Assume that $C \in \mathcal{C}^+$ and $comp(P) \models_3 \forall \bigwedge C\sigma$. Let $Var(C\sigma) = \{x_1, \ldots, x_m\}$. Choose constant symbols $c_1, \ldots, c_m$ outside $C$ and $P$. Put $\theta := \{x_1/c_1, \ldots, x_m/c_m\}$. Then $comp(P) \models_3 \bigwedge C\sigma\theta$. By Corollary 8.37, $n$ exists such that $\bigwedge C\sigma\theta$ is $\mathbf{t}$ in $T3_P{\uparrow}n$. Thus, $\eta := \{\{n, \ldots, n\}\}$ is a positive rank of $C\sigma\theta$. By (A1), $C\sigma$ and $C\sigma\theta$ are in $\mathcal{C}^+$. By Lemma 8.51, $C\sigma\theta \in \mathcal{YES}$. By Lemma 8.50, $C\sigma \in \mathcal{YES}$. Now the claim follows from Lemma 8.49(i).

(ii). Suppose that $C \in \mathcal{C}^-$ and $comp(P) \models_3 \neg \exists \bigwedge C$. By Corollary 8.37, $n$ exists such that $\neg \exists \bigwedge C$ is $\mathbf{t}$ in $T3_P{\uparrow}n$. Thus, $\eta := \{\{n, \ldots, n\}\}$ is a negative rank for $C$. By Lemma 8.51, $C \in \mathcal{NO}$. The claim follows from Lemma 8.49(ii). ∎

### Exercises

**8.31** Show:

(i) every permutation of a query in $\mathcal{YES}$ (resp. $\mathcal{NO}$) is in $\mathcal{YES}$ (resp. $\mathcal{NO}$),

(ii) $(C, D)$ is in $\mathcal{YES}$ iff both $C$ and $D$ are in $\mathcal{YES}$.

**8.32** Show: if $A \in \mathcal{NO}$ and $C \in \mathcal{YES}$, then $(\neg A, C) \in \mathcal{YES}$.

*Hint.* Induction with respect to the hypothesis that $C \in \mathcal{YES}$.

**8.33** Show:

(i) if $\theta$ is a computed answer substitution for $C$, then $C\theta \in \mathcal{YES}$,

(ii) if $C$ has a finitely failed SLDNF-tree, then $C \in \mathcal{NO}$.

*Hint.* Use Exercise 8.32.

## 8.8 Notes

The slogan "Algorithm=Logic+Control" is from [Kowalski 79]. For the semantical issues raised by negation as finite failure, see [Kunen 91], [Shepherdson] and [Apt/Bol 93]. The problem that any semantics that is adequate with respect to negation as finite failure necessarily must be rather involved, entails what [Kunen 91] calls the *Ph.D. effect*, which means a Ph.D. in logic is needed to understand it. With deplorable consequences for the poor *programmer at work*. But note that [Kunen 89] shows that 3- and 2-valued semantics coincide for programs that are *strict*.

Negation as (finite) failure was suggested in [Clark 78]. At first glance, it appears that a formal definition of the resulting derivability notion will not present any difficulties. However, this impression seems to be mistaken. (The definitions in both editions of [Lloyd 87] do not always yield what is expected.) What is presented in Section 8.2 constitutes the proposal from [Apt/Doets]. The term *forest* was suggested by Roland Bol.

Undecidability of the problem whether floundering will occur is shown in [Apt 90].

For a proof of Theorem 8.14 (Exercise 8.3) in a somewhat different context, see [Apt/Doets].

The material from Exercise 8.5 is elaborated upon in [Apt/Pedreschi 91].

The idea to use a 3-valued semantics with respect to SLDNF is from [Fitting 85], following the example of [Kripke 75]. The 3-valued truth tables are due to Kleene.

Exercise 8.12 occurs in [Kunen 87] as Lemma 6.1.

The almost purely model theoretic material of Section 8.6 replaces the exotic limit of 3-valued ultrapowers of the models $T3_P{\uparrow}n$ from [Kunen 87] by recursive saturation. For more on this notion, see [Chang/Keisler 90] section 2.4. Lemma 8.32 occurs there as Corollary 2.4.2. Or see [Hodges 93].

The final results of Section 8.6 can be generalized — with the same proofs — to the more general context where $J$ is an arbitrary model (in the sense of first-order logic, that is, with relations) and where the bodies of the rules of $P$ may refer to the relations of $J$. In particular, they can be generalized to the context of *constraint logic programming*. Theorem 8.36 is a special case of the general phenomenon that first-order definable monotone operators over a recursively saturated model have their hierarchy close at $\omega$. For consequence operators, the proof of this fact happens to be particularly simple.

Lemma 8.35 is from [Kunen 87], but transposed to the context of recursive saturation.

Section 8.7 is entirely based on [Stärk 93], which dramatically strengthens [Kunen 89]. Using proof-theoretic methods, completeness results stronger than Kunen's were already obtained in [Stärk 91]. The Ph.D. effect is felt here. Except for the use of three-valuedness, the present completeness result appears to close the gap between theory and practice quite satisfactorily; in any case, it connects a positive solution to the completeness problem of the theory with the way in which programs are used in practice. Also, the solution given does not depend on the terminating behavior of programs. Of course, to actually find the SLDNF proofs the existence of which is claimed, a breadth-first search is needed. For SLDNF, there is no selection rule independence result. As a first approximation, it is worthwhile to delay selection of negative literals as far as possible until they have become ground. Also, the completeness result still is a far cry from what would be needed for Prolog, with its meta-level facilities.

For work pursuing that of [Stärk 93], see [Stärk 93a].

The amusing solution to Exercise 8.28 is Apt's; the result is in [Lloyd/Topor 86].

Exercise 8.29 is from [Kunen 89].

The proof of Lemma 8.51 goes back to an induction in [Kunen 89]. Exercise 8.30 shows Kunen's result, which is about allowed programs and queries, to be subsumed by Stärk's. Stärk gives credit to Buchholz for the use of $\mathcal{YES}$ and $\mathcal{NO}$. His notion of SLDNF is that of Definition 8.12, which is from [Kunen 89]. Since completeness only is about success and finite failure, this simple "bottom-up" inductive definition forms an elegant way to avoid considering SLDNF-trees and SLDNF-derivations altogether. Though Definition 8.12 suffices when dealing with completeness of SLDNF-resolution, it cannot be used to reason about properties that inherently refer to SLDNF-trees, such as termination. Note that [Kunen 89] and [Stärk 93] do not put the restriction $Var(C\alpha) \cap Var(D\sigma) \subset Var(D)$ in R+), thereby allowing answers that are not maximally general.

On the topic of termination, largely left untouched here, the reader should consult [Apt/Pedreschi 91].

To get better 2-valued semantics, theorists have concentrated on special programs, e.g., (locally) stratified ones, and programs permitting natural, e.g., stable, well-founded models. This line of research has not been considered here.

# Bibliography

[Apt 90]  K.R. Apt: Logic programming. In: *Handbook of Theoretical Computer Science.* (J. van Leeuwen, ed.) Elsevier 1990, pp 493-574.

[Apt/Bezem 91]  K.R. Apt and M.A. Bezem: Acyclic programs. *New Generation Computing* 29 (1991) pp 335–363.

[Apt/Bol 93]  K.R. Apt and R. Bol: Logic programming and negation. Manuscipt 1993. Submitted for publication.

[Apt/Doets]  K.R. Apt and K. Doets: A new definition of SLDNF. *J. Logic Programming*, forthcoming.

[Apt/Pedreschi 91]  K.R. Apt and D. Pedreschi: Proving termination of general Prolog programs. In *Proceedings of the International Conference on Theoretical Aspects of Computer Software* (T. Ito and A. Meyer, editors), Lecture Notes in Computer Science 526, pp 265–289, Springer, Berlin 1991.

[Apt/Pellegrini 92]  K.R. Apt and A. Pellegrini: On occur-check free Prolog programs. Report CS-R9238, CWI Amsterdam 1992. Also *ACM Toplas,* forthcoming.

[Barwise 75]  J. Barwise: *Admissible sets and structures.* Springer, Berlin etc. 1975.

[Bezem 90]  M.A. Bezem: Completeness of resolution revisited. *Th. Computer Science* 74 (1990) pp 227–237.

[Bezem 93]  M.A. Bezem: Strong termination of logic programs. *J. Logic Programming* 15 (1993) pp 79–97.

[Bezem/Hurkens 92]  M.A. Bezem and A.J.C. Hurkens: Yet another equivalent of the Axiom of Choice. Problem 10245, *Am. Math. Monthly* 99 (1992) p 675.

[Blair 82]  H. A. Blair: The recursion-theoretic complexity of predicate logic as a programming language. *Information and Control* 54 (1982) pp 25–47.

[Blair/Brown 90]  H.A. Blair and A.L. Brown: Definite clause programs are canonical over a suitable domain. *Annals of Mathematics and Artificial Intelligence* 1 (1990) pp 1–19.

[Chang/Keisler 90]  C.C. Chang and H.J. Keisler: *Model theory,* Amsterdam 1990.

[Church 36]  A. Church: A note on the Entscheidingsproblem. *J. Symbolic Logic* 1 (1936) pp 40–41 and 101–102. Reprinted in *The Undecidable*, M. Davis editor, pp 110–115, Raven Press 1965.

[Clark 78]  K.L. Clark: Negation as failure. In: *Logic and Data Bases,* (H. Gallaire and J. Minker, eds.) Plenum, New York 1978, pp 293–322.

[Davis/Putnam 60]  M. Davis, H. Putnam: A computing procedure for quantification theory. *J. ACM* 7 (1960) pp 201–215.

[Dershowitz/Manna 79]  N. Dershowitz and Z. Manna: Proving termination with multiset orderings. *Comm. ACM* 22 (1979) pp 465–476.

[Doets 92]  K. Doets: A slight strengthening of a theorem of Blair and Kunen. *Th. Computer Science* 97 (1992) pp 175–181.

[Doets a]  K. Doets: Left termination turned into termination. *Th. Computer Science*, forthcoming.

[Doets b]  K. Doets: Levationis laus. *Logic and Computation*, forthcoming.

[Fitting 85]  M. Fitting: A Kripke-Kleene semantics for logic programs. *J. Logic Programming* 2 (1985) pp 295–312.

[Herbrand 30]                    J. Herbrand: *Recherches sur la théorie de la démonstration*, The-
                                 sis, Paris 1930. In: *Écrits logiques de Jacques Herbrand*, Paris PUF
                                 1968. English translation *Investigations in Proof Theory* in: *Jacques
                                 Herbrand, Logical Writings*, W. Goldfarb editor, Harvard University
                                 Press 1971.

[Hodges 93]                      W. Hodges: *Model theory*, Cambridge University Press 1993. (Vol.42,
                                 Encycl. of Math. and its Applications.)

[Kowalski 74]                    R.A. Kowalski: Predicate logic as a programming language. *Proceed-
                                 ings IFIP'74* North-Holland 1974, pp 569–574.

[Kowalski 79]                    R.A. Kowalski: Algorithm=logic+control. *Comm. ACM* 22 (1979) pp
                                 424–435.

[Kripke 75]                      S. Kripke: Outline of a theory of truth. *J. Philosophy* 72 (1975) pp
                                 690–715.

[Kunen 87]                       K. Kunen: Negation in logic programming. *J. Logic Programming* 4
                                 (1987) pp 289–308.

[Kunen 89]                       K. Kunen: Signed data dependencies in logic programs. *J. Logic Pro-
                                 gramming* 7 (1989) pp 231–245.

[Kunen 91]                       K. Kunen: Declarative semantics of logic programming. *Bulletin of
                                 the European Ass. for Theoretical Computer Science* 44 (1991) pp
                                 147–167.

[Lassez/Maher/Marriott 88]       J.L. Lassez, M.J. Maher and K. Marriott: Unification revisited.
                                 In: *Foundations of Deductive Databases and Logic Programming*
                                 (J. Minker ed.) Morgan Kaufmann, Los Altos 1988.

[Lloyd 87]                       J.W. Lloyd: *Foundations of Logic Programming*. 2nd, extended edi-
                                 tion, Springer 1987.

[Lloyd/Shepherdson 91]           J.W. Lloyd, J.C. Shepherdson: Partial evaluation in logic program-
                                 ming. *J.Logic Programming* 11 (1991), pp 217–242.

[Lloyd/Topor 86]                 J.W. Lloyd and R. Topor: A basis for deductive databases II. *J. Logic
                                 programming* 3 (1986) pp 55–67.

[Martelli/Montanari 82]          A. Martelli and U. Montanari: An efficient unification algorithm.
                                 *ACM Trans. on Programming Languages and Systems* 4 (1982) pp
                                 258–282.

[Odifreddi 89]                   P. Odifreddi: *Classical recursion theory*. Studies in logic and the foun-
                                 dations of mathematics Vol. 125, North-Holland, Amsterdam 1989.

[Paterson-Wegman 78]             M.S. Paterson and M.N. Wegman: Linear unification. *J. Comput.
                                 Systems Sci.* 16 (1978) pp 158–167.

[Reiter 78]                      R. Reiter: On closed world data bases. In: *Logic and Databases*, (eds.
                                 Gallaire and Minker), Plenum 1978, pp 55–76.

[Robinson 65]                    J.A. Robinson: A machine-oriented logic based on the resolution prin-
                                 ciple. *J. ACM* 12 (1965) pp 23–41.

[Shepherdson]                    J. Shepherdson: Negation as failure, completion and stratification.
                                 Draft; to appear in *Handbook of logic in artificial intelligence and
                                 logic programming* Vol. IV, Chapter 4.5.

[Smullyan 79]                    R. M. Smullyan: Trees and ball games. *Annals of the New York
                                 Academy of Sciences* 321 (1979) pp 86–90.

[Stärk 89]          R.F. Stärk: A direct proof for the completeness of SLD-resolution. In:
                    E. Börger, H. Kleine Büning, M.M. Richter (Eds.): *CSL '89*. Springer
                    Lecture Notes in Computer Science 440, Springer-Verlag 1990, pp
                    382–383.

[Stärk 91]          R.F. Stärk: A complete axiomatization of the three-valued completion
                    of logic programs. *J.Logic and Computation* 1 (1991) pp 811–834.

[Stärk 93]          R.F. Stärk: Input/output dependencies of normal logic programs.
                    Report 93–66, Universität München, Centrum für Informations- und
                    Sprachverarbeitung. *J. Logic and Computation*, forthcoming.

[Stärk 93a]         R.F. Stärk: From logic programs to inductive definitions. Manuscript,
                    submitted to Logic Colloquium '93.

[Sterling/Shapiro 86]    L. Sterling and E. Shapiro: *The Art of Prolog*. MIT Press 1986.

[van Emden/Kowalski 76]  M.H. van Emden and R.A. Kowalski: The semantics of predicate logic
                    as a programming language. *J. ACM* 23 (1976) pp 733–742.

# Rules and Programs

# Notation

$:\equiv$, definitionally equivalent with, 1
$:=$, definitionally equal to, 1

*sets:*
$a \in A$, $a$ element of $A$
$\{a, b, c, \ldots\}$, set of $a, b, c, \ldots$
$\{a \in A \mid E(a)\}$, set of $a \in A$ satisfying $E$
$\cap$, $\bigcap$, $\cup$, $\bigcup$, intersection, union
$-$, difference
$A \subset B$, $A$ (not necessarily proper) subset of $B$
$\mathcal{P}(K)$, powerset of $K$, 76
$0, 1, 2, \ldots$, natural numbers
$\mathbb{N}$, set of natural numbers, 1
$\mathbb{Z}$, set of integers, 40
$\{\{a_1, \ldots, a_n\}\}$, multiset of $a_1, \ldots, a_n$, 6
$\omega$, first infinite ordinal, 10
$sup A$, supremum of set of ordinals $A$, 10

*relations:*
$(a, b)$, $(a_1, \ldots, a_n)$, ordered pair, $n$-tuple
$A \times B$, (Cartesian) product
$A^2$, $A^n$, sets of pairs, $n$-tuples from $A$
$aRb$, $a$ $R$-related to $b$
$R^{tr}$, transitive closure of $R$, 6

*functions:*
$f : A \rightarrow B$, $f$ function from $A$ to $B$, 3
$f : a \mapsto b$, $f(a) = b$, $f$ sends $a$ to $b$
$Dom(f)$, domain of $f$

*logic, informally used:*
$\Rightarrow$, $\Leftrightarrow$, if$\cdots$then, iff (if and only if)
$\wedge$, $\vee$, $\neg$, and, or, not
$\forall$, $\exists$, for all, there exists

*formal logic:*
$\neg$, $\wedge$, $\bigwedge$, $\vee$, $\bigvee$, $\rightarrow$, $\leftrightarrow$, connectives, 13

# Index